T0321855

Human Factors in Global Software Engineering

Mobashar Rehman
Universiti Tunku Abdul Rahman, Malaysia

Aamir Amin
Universiti Tunku Abdul Rahman, Malaysia

Abdul Rehman Gilal
Sukkur IBA University, Pakistan

Manzoor Ahmed Hashmani
University Technology PETRONAS, Malaysia

A volume in the Advances in
Systems Analysis, Software
Engineering, and High Performance
Computing (ASASEHPC) Book Series

Published in the United States of America by
    IGI Global
    Engineering Science Reference (an imprint of IGI Global)
    701 E. Chocolate Avenue
    Hershey PA, USA 17033
    Tel: 717-533-8845
    Fax: 717-533-8661
    E-mail: cust@igi-global.com
    Web site: http://www.igi-global.com

Library of Congress Cataloging-in-Publication Data

Names: Rehman, Mobashar, 1982- editor.
Title: Human factors in global software engineering / Mobashar Rehman, Aamir
  Amin, Abdul Rehman Gilal, and Manzoor Ahmed Hashmani, editors.
Description: Hershey, PA : Engineering Science Reference, [2020] | Includes
  bibliographical references.
Identifiers: LCCN 2019001910| ISBN 9781522594482 (h/c) | ISBN 9781522594505
  (eISBN) | ISBN 9781522594499 (s/c)
Subjects: LCSH: Human-computer interaction.
Classification: LCC QA76.9.H85 H8657 2020 | DDC 004.01/9--dc23 LC record available at https://
lccn.loc.gov/2019001910

This book is published in the IGI Global book series Advances in Systems Analysis, Software Engineering, and High Performance Computing (ASASEHPC) (ISSN: 2327-3453; eISSN: 2327-3461)

British Cataloguing in Publication Data
A Cataloguing in Publication record for this book is available from the British Library.

All work contributed to this book is new, previously-unpublished material.
The views expressed in this book are those of the authors, but not necessarily of the publisher.

For electronic access to this publication, please contact: eresources@igi-global.com.

Advances in Systems Analysis, Software Engineering, and High Performance Computing (ASASEHPC) Book Series

ISSN:2327-3453
EISSN:2327-3461

Editor-in-Chief: Vijayan Sugumaran, Oakland University, USA

MISSION

The theory and practice of computing applications and distributed systems has emerged as one of the key areas of research driving innovations in business, engineering, and science. The fields of software engineering, systems analysis, and high performance computing offer a wide range of applications and solutions in solving computational problems for any modern organization.

The **Advances in Systems Analysis, Software Engineering, and High Performance Computing (ASASEHPC) Book Series** brings together research in the areas of distributed computing, systems and software engineering, high performance computing, and service science. This collection of publications is useful for academics, researchers, and practitioners seeking the latest practices and knowledge in this field.

COVERAGE

- Metadata and Semantic Web
- Performance Modelling
- Computer System Analysis
- Storage Systems
- Parallel Architectures
- Virtual Data Systems
- Software Engineering
- Distributed Cloud Computing
- Computer Graphics
- Enterprise Information Systems

IGI Global is currently accepting manuscripts for publication within this series. To submit a proposal for a volume in this series, please contact our Acquisition Editors at Acquisitions@igi-global.com or visit: http://www.igi-global.com/publish/.

Titles in this Series

For a list of additional titles in this series, please visit:
https://www.igi-global.com/book-series/advances-systems-analysis-software-engineering/73689

Interdisciplinary Approaches to Information Systems and Software Egineering
Alok Bhushan Mukherjee (North-Eastern Hill University Shillong, India) and Akhouri Pramod Krishna (Birla Institute of Technology Mesra, India)
Engineering Science Reference • ©2019 • 299pp • H/C (ISBN: 9781522577843) • US $215.00

Cyber-Physical Systems for Social Applications
Maya Dimitrova (Bulgarian Academy of Sciences, Bulgaria) and Hiroaki Wagatsuma (Kyushu Institute of Technology, Japan)
Engineering Science Reference • ©2019 • 440pp • H/C (ISBN: 9781522578796) • US $265.00

Integrating the Internet of Things Into Software Engineering Practices
D. Jeya Mala (Thiagarajar College of Engineering, India)
Engineering Science Reference • ©2019 • 293pp • H/C (ISBN: 9781522577904) • US $215.00

Analyzing the Role of Risk Mitigation and Monitoring in Software Development
Rohit Kumar (Chandigarh University, India) Anjali Tayal (Infosys Technologies, India) and Sargam Kapil (C-DAC, India)
Engineering Science Reference • ©2018 • 308pp • H/C (ISBN: 9781522560296) • US $225.00

Handbook of Research on Pattern Engineering System Development for Big Data Analytics
Vivek Tiwari (International Institute of Information Technology, India) Ramjeevan Singh Thakur (Maulana Azad National Institute of Technology, India) Basant Tiwari (Hawassa University, Ethiopia) and Shailendra Gupta (AISECT University, India)
Engineering Science Reference • ©2018 • 396pp • H/C (ISBN: 9781522538707) • US $320.00

Incorporating Nature-Inspired Paradigms in Computational Applications
Mehdi Khosrow-Pour, D.B.A. (Information Resources Management Association, USA)
Engineering Science Reference • ©2018 • 385pp • H/C (ISBN: 9781522550204) • US $195.00

For an entire list of titles in this series, please visit:
https://www.igi-global.com/book-series/advances-systems-analysis-software-engineering/73689

701 East Chocolate Avenue, Hershey, PA 17033, USA
Tel: 717-533-8845 x100 • Fax: 717-533-8661
E-Mail: cust@igi-global.com • www.igi-global.com

Editorial Advisory Board

Table of Contents

Detailed Table of Contents

    Abdul Rehman Gilal, Sukkur IBA University, Pakistan
    Muhammad Zahid Tunio, Beijing University of Posts and
        Telecommunication, China
    Ahmad Waqas, Sukkur IBA University, Pakistan
    Malek Ahmad Almomani, University Technology PETRONAS, Malaysia
    Sajid Khan, Sukkur IBA University, Pakistan
    Ruqaya Gilal, Universiti Utara Malaysia, Malaysia

An open call format of crowdsourcing software development (CSD) is harnessing potential, diverse, and unlimited people. But, several thousand solutions are being submitted at platform against each call. To select and match the submitted task with the appropriate worker and vice versa is still a complicated problem. Focusing the issue, this study proposes a task assignment algorithm (TAA) that will behave as an intermediate facilitator (at platform) between task (from requester) and solution (from worker). The algorithm will divide the tasks' list based on the developer's personality. In this way, we can save the time of both developers and platform by reducing the searching time.

    Antoine Trad, IBISTM, France

The KMGSE offers a real-life case for detecting and processing an enterprise knowledge management model for global business transformation, knowledge management systems, global software engineering, global business engineering and enterprise architecture recurrent problems solving. This global software engineering (GSE) subsystem is a driven development model that offers a set of possible solutions in the form of architecture, method, patterns, managerial and technical recommendations, coupled with an applicable framework. The proposed executive and technical recommendations are to be applied by the business environment's knowledge officers, architects, analysts and engineers to enable solutions to knowledge-based, global software engineering paradigms' development and maintenance.

Chapter 3

Ergonomic assessment of advanced manufacturing technology (AMT) involves several attributes. Most of these attributes can be assessed only subjectively. Several models have been developed to assess AMT from an ergonomic approach. However, these models have several deficiencies, such as 1) assessment for all alternatives in all their ergonomic attributes should be done in a single period. It lacks time pauses when decision-makings include several decisors and alternatives, 2) every person can access the information and change it, and 3) they lack the propriety of correcting mistakes once users (or decisors) have entered an unwished data. Then, the objective of this research is to develop a software for the ergonomic assessment of AMT that deletes these deficiencies. As method, axiomatic design (AD) was applied jointly with the TRIZ methodology. Software was validated with results of a previous case study. Finally, authors developed a software that removed the deficiencies of previous models.

This mapping study aims to investigate knowledge sharing initiatives in software companies based on existing studies from 2005 to 2017. Initially, search string was applied in seven digital repositories. Snowballing and direct search on publications were conducted to reduce the limitation of accessing specific databases. Regarding 15 selected studies, a variety of aspects; publication year and source, research type, purpose, and types of knowledge been used; were concerned. According to findings, a majority of studies have been focused on factors affecting knowledge sharing and point out organizational commitment as the most undergoing influencer on knowledge sharing. Findings further prove criticality of knowledge sharing for sustainability of software companies. Contrary to that, findings provide convincing evidence on improper knowledge sharing systems as the highly referred problem associated with knowledge sharing in software companies and provide new directions to future research.

Chapter 5
Shanmuganathan Vasanthapriyan, Sabaragamuwa University of Sri Lanka, Sri Lanka

Agile software development (ASD) is a knowledge-intensive and collaborative activity and thus Knowledge Management (KM) principals should be applied to improve the productivity of the whole ASD process from the beginning to the end of the phase. The goal is to map the evidence available on existing researches on KM initiatives in ASD in order to identify the state of the art in the area as well as the future research. Therefore, investigation of various aspects such as purposes, types of knowledge, technologies and research type are essential. The authors conducted a systematic review of literature published between 2010 and December 2017 and identified 12 studies that discuss agile requirements engineering. They formulated and applied specific inclusion and exclusion criteria in two distinct rounds to determine the most relevant studies for their research goal. Reuse of knowledge of the team is the perspective that has received more attention.

Chapter 6
Ramgopal Kashyap, Amity University Chhattisgarh, India

A large vault of terabytes of information created every day from present-day data frameworks and digital innovations, for example, the internet of things and distributed computing. Investigation of this enormous information requires a ton of endeavors at different dimensions to separate learning for central leadership. An examination is an ebb-and-flow territory of innovative work. The fundamental goal of this paper is to investigate the potential effect of enormous information challenges, open research issues, and different instruments related to it. Subsequently, this article gives a stage to study big data at various stages. It opens another skyline for analysts to build up the arrangement in light of the difficulties, and open research issues. The article comprehended that each large information stage has its core interest. Some of this is intended for bunch handling while some are great at constant scientific. Each large information stage likewise has explicit usefulness. Unique procedures were utilized for the investigation.

Software engineering has been an active working area for many decades. It evolved in a bi-folded manner. First research and subsequently development. Since the day of its inception, the massive number of variants and methods of software engineering were proposed. Primarily, these methods are designed to cater the time-varying need of modern approach. In this connection, the Global Software Engineering (GSE) is one of the growing trends in the modern software industry. At the same time, the employment of Agile development methodologies has also gained the significant attention in the literature. This has created a rationale to explore and adopt agile development methodology in GSE. It gained rigorous attention as an alternative to traditional software development methodologies. This paper has presented a comprehensive review on the adaptation of modern agile practices in GSE. In addition, the strength and limitation of each approach have been highlighted. Finally, the open area in the said domain is submitted as one of the deliverables of this work.

Along with the advancement of the technology, software companies have to face a huge competition in the global market. To face this competition, innovations can be used as a strategic weapon. As employees are the main driving forces of innovation, their behavior can be a crucial factor in boosting innovation. Innovative behavior is referred as the introduction and application of new ideas, products, processes, and procedures to a person's work role or an organization. This behavior directly affects innovation performance of an organization. The main aim of this study is to identify the factors that affect employee innovative behavior and their effect in Sri Lankan software companies using a quantitative methodology. Apart from that, this study provides a conclusive summary of the current status of innovative behavior of employees. The initial step mapping study was done to find the past literature related to the research topic. From that study, 17 papers were identified as primary studies.

Chapter 9

Muhammad Sulleman Memon, QUEST, Pakistan

With the growth of software vulnerabilities, the demand for security integration is increasingly necessary to more effectively achieve the goal of secure software development globally. Different practices are used to keep the software intact. These practices should also be examined to obtain better results depending on the level of security. The security of a software program device is a characteristic that permeates the whole system. To resolve safety issues in a software program security solutions have to be implemented continually throughout each web page. The motive of this study is to offer a complete analysis of safety, wherein protection testing strategies and equipment can be categorized into: technical evaluation strategies and non-technical assessment strategies. This study presents high-level ideas in an easy form that would help professionals and researchers solve software security testing problems around the world. One way to achieve these goals is to separate security issues from other enforcement issues so that they can be resolved independently and applied globally.

Chapter 10

Ali Akber, Institute of Business Management, Pakistan
Syed Sajjad Hussain Rizvi, Hamdard University, Pakistan
Muhammad Waqar Khan, Institute of Business Management, Pakistan
Vali Uddin, Hamdard University, Pakistan
Manzoor Ahmed Hashmani, University Technology PETRONAS,
*   Malaysia*
Jawwad Ahmad, Usman Institute of Technology, Pakistan

Over the last few decades, software security has become significant in parallel to general software testing. Previously, the scope of software security was relatively limited as compared to the software functionality. But now, in global software engineering, the scope and budget of software security are far more than its basic functionality. This has created a pressing need to devise the separate set of working boundaries between software quality testing, and software security testing in global software engineering. In the past literature, a massive number of software security testing methods has been devised. In this paper, a comprehensive literature review is presented on the recent global software security testing methods. In addition, the strength and limitation of each framework are discussed and analyzed. Finally, this work submits the open areas in the domain of global software security testing methods as one of the deliverables of this research work.

    Ayub Muhammad Latif, PAF Karachi Institute of Economics and
        Technology, Pakistan
    Khalid Muhammad Khan, PAF Karachi Institute of Economics and
        Technology, Pakistan
    Anh Nguyen Duc, University of South-Eastern Norway, Norway

Software cost estimation is the process of forecasting the effort needed to develop the software system. Global software engineering (GSE) highlights that software development knows no boundaries and majority of the software products and services are developed today by globally-distributed teams, projects, and companies. The problem of cost estimation gets more complex if the discussion is carried out in the context of GSE, which has its own issues. Temporal, cultural, and geographical distance creates communication and software process implementation issues. Traditional software process models such as capability maturity model (CMM) lacks the dynamism to accommodate the recent trends in GSE. The chapter introduces GSE and discusses various cost estimation techniques and different levels of CMM. A couple of GSE-based case studies having CMM-level projects from multiple organizations are studied to analyze the impacts of highly mature processes on effort, quality, and cycle time.

    Manzoor Ahmed Hashmani, University Technology PETRONAS,
        Malaysia
    Maryam Zaffar, University Technology PETRONAS, Malaysia
    Reham Ejaz, NUST College of Electrical and Mechanical Engineering,
        Pakistan

Scenario is an account of description of user interaction with the system, presented in a sequence. They can be represented using unified modeling language (UML) diagrams such as use case diagram, state charts, activity diagrams etc. Scenario-based testing can be performed at higher abstraction level using the design diagrams. In this work activity diagrams are used which are annotated with action semantics to test scenario dependencies. The action semantics make activity diagram executable and the dependencies between multiple scenarios can be seen at execution level. The authors intend to propose an approach for scenario dependency testing. Dependency graphs will be then generated against all the dependencies present on activity diagram under test. The test paths extracted from these dependency graphs help in testing.

Chapter 13

Mazni Omar, Universiti Utara Malaysia, Malaysia
Mawarny Md Rejab, Universiti Utara Malaysia, Malaysia
Mazida Ahmad, Universiti Utara Malaysia, Malaysia

Global software engineering (SE) has increased in popularity and is now commonplace in most software organizations. This is due to the fact that business and technology have evolved, which has had an impact on the borderless world. As a consequence, software teams are often geographically dispersed, though they all have the same goal—to produce high-quality software. In order to achieve that goal, quality teamwork is important to build a high-performance team. This study aims to get an in-depth understanding of what quality teamwork is, as well as investigate how communication and socialization can have an impact on team performance. This study took a qualitative approach to the data collection process by carrying out interviews with three experts of agile distributed teams. The results of this study demonstrate that active communication stimulates socialization, and thus increases and maintains morale and motivation among team members. Future studies could focus on the impact of other quality teamwork, such as the influence of trust on team performance among global SE teams.

Foreword

Issues related to human factor are essential for every software development and engineering process in maintaining the quality of the software product. Furthermore, nowadays, there is hardly any software product or service, which concentrate their activities in one place or by only specific internal team. Hence, the phenomenon of Global Software Development (GSD), which has been in practice for the last decade, has significantly impacted the software industry.

We are currently living in the world of Fourth Industrial Revolution (IR 4.0), where globalization and rapid changes in technology has become a challenge for software industry. These rapid changes not only impact the technology sphere of software engineering but also the social or human sphere. Human factors are an integral part of software process and organizational and office culture and ambiance, teamwork, team dynamics and knowledge management play an important role in the success of a software organization. Hence, these human factors need to be clearly and carefully addressed in order to assist many software companies which are struggling with the successful implementation of global software engineering.

This book provides a valuable window on global software engineering and covers the necessary components related to Global Software engineering especially the issues related to the influence of human factor on the success of global software engineering. These include the aspects related to the advantages, challenges and innovation. In this era of global software engineering, it is vital to provide updated findings to the professionals and students and this book aims to deliver that.

Shuib B. Basri
University Technology PETRONAS, Malaysia

Preface

INTRODUCTION

The 21st century has seen a rapid growth in the globalization of every business particularly software engineering (Herbsleb & Moitra, 2001). Within software engineering sphere, the globalization and the Personal Computer (PC) revolution of 1990s has introduced Global Software Engineering (GSE) (Carmel, 1999; Lanubile, Damian & Oppenheimer, 2003; Šmite et al., 2010). GSE is also known as Distributed Software Engineering (DSE) or Distributed Software Development (DSD) or Global Software Development (GSD) (Verner et al., 2012). According to Herbsleb and Mockus (2003), it involves the engineering of application software with the help of interactions between people, organizations, and technology. The development of the software in GSE takes place across nations with individuals of different backgrounds, languages, and working styles.

Global software engineering is rapidly becoming the norm for software projects. It is a growing practice within software companies with an increasing number of software engineers working in a GSE environment. Consequently, today, GSE has become not only one of the most widely adopted model but a norm in software industry. Hence, it has gained importance not only amongst practitioners but also the researchers. The advantages of GSE, due to which it has become a norm in software industry, are manifold such as (1) accessibility to cheaper but highly skilled software engineers in low cost places like Eastern Europe, Latin America, and Far East; (2) an opportunity to conduct round the clock operations by utilizing software teams in different time zones, decreased development time and cost; (3) conducting operations in closer proximity to the emerging markets; (4) a chance to take a business opportunity from anywhere in the globe by forming global software teams and the advancement in communication technology (i.e., growing usage of E-mail and instant messaging as well as cheaper international telecommunication).

Apart from the advantages of GSE, there are quite a number of challenges that the very field faces, such as geographic, socio-cultural, temporal distance, historical, technical and political. Moreover, GSE projects also face communication challenges such as tardy feedbacks, bad video bandwidth, constrained, asynchronous communication, lack of shared project understanding, lack of trust and confidence between sites, difficulty of expression due to language barriers including the proficiency in the language and incomprehensible accents. Consequently, these issues have resulted in higher rate of failure of GSE projects. However, regardless of these issues, it seems that the benefits of GSE outweigh the issues. Having said that, the field has not matured yet and substantial work needs to be done to understand various aspects of GSE.

As software industry is getting more matured, vast majority of software community is reaching a consensus that people involved in the software development process deserve more attention than technologies. Human factors in software engineering is one of the growing areas of research. The central role of humans in software engineering is aptly described by Capretz, Ahmed and Da Silva (2017) in the words that, "software is developed by people and for people". It is considered to be a *'make or break'* issue or the determining factor for the success or failure of software projects (Acuna, Gomez & Juristo, 2008; Capretz, 2014). This central role of humans in software development can be understood by their involvement in all the phases of development e.g. as developers, humans influence the overall development process; as customers, they affect the software market; and as managers or administrators they also have a significant impact on the success and performance of the software process. Furthermore, it can also be understood by their impact on software development at different levels such as organizational, interpersonal and individual (Pirzadeh, 2010). However, despite its importance, human factors in software engineering are often ignored and are often not given equal attention compared to the technical factors. Prior research has focused on merely few concepts which were applied to limited areas of development and hence, there are several knowledge gaps in the research of human factors in software engineering. It can be concluded that research work on human factors in software engineering has only *scratched the surface*.

With careful selection of articles from globally acclaimed scholars, this book has mainly focused on human factor to cope the challenges at a human, social, organizational, cultural, technological and ergonomic level in Global Software Engineering (GSE). Diversified topics in this book investigate how the processes and tools used to create systems can be efficiently utilized to ensure the amplification of ingenuity and smarts of human, as opposed to letting them spend their valuable intellectual exertion on managing mundane or unnecessary problems. Furthermore, the book focuses on techniques and latest trends in various dimensions of robust security testing; cost estimation and capability mature models in GSE; knowledge management and study mapping; and adaptation of modern agile practices in the context of GSE.

The objective of this book is to improve the quality of software development processes by primarily focusing on the 'human' aspect of it. The book aims to provide solutions for various aforementioned problems which GSE faces. It provides solutions concerning task management and efficient selection of the team, knowledge management in GSE and how it can effect competitive advantage, adaptation of agile software development, reliability and safety of the software, cultural issues, cost, process predictability as well as the communication and socialization among GSE teams.

The major intended target audience of this book are students and practitioners of software engineering in general and in GSE, as well as researchers and educators who are interested in the human side of software engineering. For the practitioners, it provides solutions for important human related issues in software engineering which can improve the efficiency and success rate of software development. Specifically for the practitioners working in a GSE environment, the book provides useful insight into the matters such as team formation, communication as well as socialization. For researchers, the book instigates a trend in research towards exploring different facets of human involvement, issues and challenges. For educators, it aims to become a reference to inculcate in students the awareness of human factors and challenges.

ORGANIZATION OF THE BOOK

The book is organized into 13 chapters. A brief description of each of the chapters follows:

Chapter 1 discusses the technical requirements of the task along with personality preferences to sort the task list at the developer end for efficient selection. This not only reduces the burden from platform but also increases the effectiveness in the submissions.

Chapter 2 proposes executive and technical recommendations to be applied by the business environment's knowledge officers, architects, analysts and engineers to enable solutions to knowledge-based global software engineering paradigms' development and maintenance.

Chapter 3 is about developing a user-centered software by jointly applying the tools of axiomatic design and TRIZ. It is expected that this software provides more comfort and information reliability than the before versions.

Chapter 4 reviews the distribution of the studies over past years, source of publication, type of the research, knowledge types been used, technology usage, purposes, benefits and problems related to knowledge sharing in Software Engineering. Furthermore, snowballing and direct search for the studies published by researchers of the previously selected studies were performed.

Chapter 5 is about hoe knowledge is treated as a cornerstone for software companies to achieve sustainable competitive advantage. In addition, role of knowledge management in ASD which generate both positive and negative effects are also part of this chapter.

Chapter 6 highlights High-Performance Analytics (HPA) which is driven by the business world with broad necessities to figure out the fruition as snappy as possible on the greatest dataset. The improvement in HPA ends up imaginable with creative progression vast memory, 64bit location, Grid Computing and moderateness of gear costs, value: execution marker.

Chapter 7 provides a platform to the reader to investigate in the domain of adaptation of agile software development practices in global software engineering. In addition, this chapter also submits a comprehensive review on the scope, strengths, and limitation of adaptation of agile software development practices in global software engineering domain.

Chapter 8 aim to find the factors that affect innovative behavior and check the effect of those factors on employee innovative behavior covering both individual and organizational perspectives in Sri Lankan software companies.

Chapter 9 help evaluators and beginners to plan a security development lifecycle. This is done to enhance the reliability and safety of the software. In-depth research into safety checking out strategies and techniques is also part of this chapter.

Chapter 10 discusses different techniques that are currently being used for security testing in SDLC and detecting vulnerabilities within the application. In order to understand this and give the general idea of SDLC, chapter summarizes software engineering and different type of testing techniques which include static and dynamic approaches.

Chapter 11 discuss regarding effort to develop a software through global software development, cultural issues, software development cost and software process predictability.

Chapter 12 propose an approach for scenario dependency testing. Dependency graphs are generated against all the dependencies present on an activity diagram under test. The test paths extracted from these dependency graphs help in testing.

Chapter 13 demonstrates the importance of communication and socialization among global Software Engineering teams, with a specific focus on agile distributed teams. The technological advancement of communication tools encourages team members to communicate and socialize actively.

Baber Sheikh Fazalellahi
Sukkur IBA University, Pakistan

REFERENCES

Acuña, S. T., Gómez, M., & Juristo, N. (2008). Towards understanding the relationship between team climate and software quality—A quasi-experimental study. *Empirical Software Engineering, 13*(4), 401–434. doi:10.100710664-008-9074-8

Capretz, L. F. (2014). Bringing the human factor to software engineering. *IEEE Software, 31*(2), 104–104. doi:10.1109/MS.2014.30

Capretz, L. F., Ahmed, F., & da Silva, F. Q. B. (2017). Soft sides of software. *Information and Software Technology, 92*, 92-94.

Herbsleb, J. D., & Mockus, A. (2003). An empirical study of speed and communication in globally distributed software development. *IEEE Transactions on* Software Engineering, *29*(6), 481–494.

Herbsleb, J. D., & Moitra, D. (Eds.). (2001). Special Issue on Global Software Development. *IEEE Software, 18*(2).

Carmel, E. (1999). *Global software teams: Collaborating across borders and time zones*. Prentice Hall PTR.

Lanubile, F., Damian, D., & Oppenheimer, H. L. (2003). Global software development: Technical, organizational, and social challenges. *Software Engineering Notes, 28*(6), 2–2. doi:10.1145/966221.966224

Pirzadeh, L. (2010). *Human Factors in Software Development: A Systematic Literature Review* (Unpublished Master's thesis). Department of Computer Science and Engineering Division of Networks and Distributed Systems Chalmers University of Technology, Göteborg, Sweden.

Šmite, D., Wohlin, C., Gorschek, T., & Feldt, R. (2010). Empirical evidence in global software engineering: A systematic review. *Empirical Software Engineering, 15*(1), 91–118. doi:10.100710664-009-9123-y

Verner, J. M., Brereton, O. P., Kitchenham, B. A., Turner, M., & Niazi, M. (2012). Systematic Literature Reviews in Global Software Development: A Tertiary Study. *16th International Conference on Evaluation & Assessment in Software Engineering (EASE 2012)*, 2 – 11. 10.1049/ic.2012.0001

Chapter 1
Task Assignment and Personality:
Crowdsourcing Software Development

Abdul Rehman Gilal
Sukkur IBA University, Pakistan

Muhammad Zahid Tunio
Beijing University of Posts and Telecommunication, China

Ahmad Waqas
Sukkur IBA University, Pakistan

Malek Ahmad Almomani
 https://orcid.org/0000-0002-3890-9792
University Technology PETRONAS, Malaysia

Sajid Khan
Sukkur IBA University, Pakistan

Ruqaya Gilal
Universiti Utara Malaysia, Malaysia

ABSTRACT

An open call format of crowdsourcing software development (CSD) is harnessing potential, diverse, and unlimited people. But, several thousand solutions are being submitted at platform against each call. To select and match the submitted task with the appropriate worker and vice versa is still a complicated problem. Focusing the issue, this study proposes a task assignment algorithm (TAA) that will behave as an intermediate facilitator (at platform) between task (from requester) and solution (from worker). The algorithm will divide the tasks' list based on the developer's personality. In this way, we can save the time of both developers and platform by reducing the searching time.

DOI: 10.4018/978-1-5225-9448-2.ch001

INTRODUCTION

Crowdsourcing has become an emerging trend for the quick software development due to the parallel and micro-tasking. It is also cost efficient based on the knowledge of the crowd or "wisdom of the crowd". CSD uses an open call format. This process involves three kinds of roles: 1) requester, 2) platform (i.e., the service provider) and 3) crowd-source developer (i.e., the person for coding and testing). This type of call format enables large numbers of task accessibility and self-selection. On the platform, a number of developers can register and choose a task from available set. Once after the submission of the task from developers, the platform is required to evaluate the submission to decide for the best solution from developers, to pay the rewards. Based on the Ke Mao et al. studies (Mao, Capra, Harman, & Jia, 2017; Mao, Yang, Wang, Jia, & Harman, 2015), selection of an appropriate task to reward from the extensive large set of tasks is a very hectic work for the developers. Besides, it is also a tiring and time-consuming job for the platform to evaluate thousands of submitted tasks from developers. Ye Yang and M.C Yuen (Yang, Karim, Saremi, & Ruhe, 2016; Yuen, King, & Leung, 2011) mentioned that from the task requester perspective, it is very hard to match the developer with the task and it is also very difficult to monitor the risk of the reliability of the CSD developers.

In the same view, Chilton and Eman Aldhahri (Aldhahri, Shandilya, & Shiva, 2015; Chilton, Horton, & Miller, 2010) continued to claim that matching of the improper task to improper CSD developer may not only decrease the quality of the software deliverables but it also overburdens both platform and developers. They further mentioned that most workers view a minimum number of recent tasks that are posted at the platform because tasks are posted in hundreds. By considering the low level of skills and expertise level of the crowdsourced software developers, unrealistic matching of CSD worker and the task may have an effect on the software quality. Latoza et al. (Latoza & Hoek, 2015) also emphasized on the matching of workers with their expertise and knowledge and to get maximum benefit from the CSD worker is an issue. Similar is the case is discussed in the (Geiger & Schader, 2014; Gilal, Jaafar, Omar, Basri, & Din, 2016; Gilal, Jaafar, Omar, Basri, & Waqas, 2016; Gilal, Omar, & Sharif, 2013; Tunio et al., 2017) studies that while keeping extrinsic and intrinsic choice of CSD workers self-identification principle for individual contributors to select those tasks which are the best match with their psychological preferences (i.e., personality). Psychological is an important factor to compliance with the choice and individual capabilities with the respective task requirements. Moreover, to choose a few best submissions out of thousand submissions is really a hectic job at CSD platform level. Every CSD worker is not supposed to give the best solution for each task (Dang, Liu, Zhang, & Huang, 2016). More seriously, malicious workers can also submit the tasks for reviews to increase the complexity at the platform (Carmel, de Souza, Meneguzzi, Machado, & Prikladnicki, 2016; Carpenter & Huang, 1998; Nawaz, Waqas, Yusof, Mahesar, & Shah, 2017; Nawaz, Waqas, Yusof, & Shah, 2016; Waqas, Yusof, Shah, & Khan, 2014; Waqas, Yusof, Shah, & Mahmood, 2014). Keeping it in view, Leticia Machado, et al.(Howe, 2006) stated that CSD model does not only deal with technology issues but economic as well as personal issues that make the model more complex.

According to (Fernando Capretz, 2014; Gilal, Jaafar, Basri, Omar, & Abro, 2016; Gilal, Jaafar, Basri, Omar, & Tunio, 2016; Gilal, Jaafar, Omar, Basri, & Waqas, 2016; Gilal, Omar, et al., 2017; Tunio et al., 2018), the key complexities pertinent to the development of software are concerned with human aspects from their social and cognitive point of view. According to Martínez et al., (Martínez, Rodríguez-Díaz, Licea, & Castro, 2010), though the technical aspects maintain principal importance to obtain good performance in a software development process but the human or soft aspects (i.e., personality types) cannot be ignored. Personality refers to internal psychological patterns such as feelings and thoughts that carve the behavior of a person (Fu, Chen, & Song, 2015). Personality can create healthy behavior of an employee that can lead the overall project to success. On the other side, it can also cause damages within project development if it is improperly managed. Numerous studies have been carried out in the past that applies many theoretical frameworks adopted from the domain of psychology to better understand the personality of software developers (Basri et al., 2017; Gilal, Jaafar, Omar, Basri, & Waqas, 2016; Tunio et al., 2017). Thus, human aspects should be emphasized to cope up with the challenges while developing projects under the umbrella of software engineering.

The aim of this study is to propose and formulate a Crowdsourcing software development task assignment algorithm (TAA) based on the type of task and personality types. This study would extend the literature and guidelines for the researchers who are willing to contribute to improve the crowd source algorithms for software development in which human factor is involved. By applying the discussed advancements, future algorithms can reduce the task selection burdens from developers and platforms.

RELATED WORK

There are different dimensions of human factors in software engineering. Studies have been conducted from different perspectives (Capretz & Ahmed, 2010b; Hazzan & Hadar, 2008) such as the investigation of human factors in different phases of software life cycle, the effect of team work in software development, how can a personality profile suit a particular task like code review, or about some other miscellaneous issues. The word personality has been the center of discussion for many psychologists and the number of definitions has been suggested in the past to elaborate this word. Due to its abstract nature, different psychologists have defined this word differently. However, personality is often defined with two classical definitions that have widely accepted among psychologists. The first definition is given by Allport (1961) in which he defines personality as person characteristics that consist of dynamic of behavior, thought and feelings. The second most important definition is given by Child (1968), which refers personality as internal factors that differentiate a person's behavior for particular situations. It can be inferred from these two definitions given by Allport and Child that personality is solely internal process that carves and mold the attitude of people. Though the personality has been considered and discussed under the umbrella of psychology, but the recent finding of the research studies reveal the fact that personality is also shaped and molded due to the biological and genetic inheritance. In the same vein, Child defines personality as stable or relatively stable that does not bring radical change in weeks but it takes time that can be predicated.

The main difference between these two definitions given by Child and Allport is that the first definition reveals consistency within individuals, and difference between individuals, whereas later definition emphasizes characteristic patterns that show the nature of behaviour within individuals. In a nutshell, both definitions shows that personality forms our actions, feelings, thoughts and consistence and it also varies from person to person for different people maintain different attitude and temper having different personalities.

In the conclusion, this study follows the definition of personality given by Allport and Child. In which personality is defined that ——the personality is solely internal process that carves and molds the attitude of people.

For the last 50 years, the Myers-Brigs Type Indicator (MBTI) (Myers, McCaulley, Quenk, & Hammer, 1998) has been used as a source for identification of personality preferences and personality type of an individual. This personality type indicator is used for making theories of Jung applicable and useful in everyday life. An individual's personality type in MBTI is assessed on four dimensions: social interaction (extroversion (E) and introversion (I)), decision making (thinking (T) and feeling (F)), information gathering (sensing (S) and intuition (N)), and dealing with the external world (judging (J) and perceiving (P)). Both Katharine Cook Briggs and her daughter, Isabel Briggs Myers are considered as pioneer of MBTI who not only extensively studied the work of Jung but they also explored and inter-related different theories of human behavior i.e., theory of psychological types into practical use.

The MBTI test allows individual personality type preferences to be classified according to the 16 types with the results reported as a combination of four dimensional pairs, which are Introversion (I) and Extroversion (E); Thinking (T) and Feeling (F); Sensing (S) and Intuitive (N) ; and Judging (J) and Perceiving (P). The 16 possible personality combinations are formed from these four dimensions. Table 1 shows 16 combinations of personality types based on MBTI.

A person can be classified into one of the 16 personality types based on the largest score obtained. For example, a person scoring higher on Introversion (I) than Extroversion (E); Sensing (S) than Intuition (N); Thinking (T) than Feeling (F); and Judging (J) than Perceiving (P), would be classified as an ISTJ.

Personality is a backbone that carves either negative or positive behaviour of individual towards different things. There are number of personality traits exhibited by people on different occasions influenced by different factors as well. These factors have been illuminated by Goldberg (1990), which are profusely followed and admitted. These factors are put into five broad categories: Extraversion, Neuroticism, Agreeableness, Openness to experience and conscientiousness. Though these five factors can be taken into account to form team for software engineering, but there is also another factor (Block, 1995) i.e., cognitive ability that is also very crucial and important whose importance cannot be denied while forming software engineering team that ensures good results.

The cognitive faculty of an individual covers abstract thinking, mindset, visualization capability and analytic and so on. Though five factors described by Goldberg (1990) are profusely used for the personality assessment in teamwork in software engineering, but the inclusion of cognitive faculty into these five factors prove to be lucrative to assess and point out an ideal personality suitable for SE team group (Block, 1995).

Neuroticism refers to the negative aspects of an individual's emotions that can be highlighted in the form of anxiety, depression, hostility, impulsiveness and self- consciousness. The opposite of neuroticism can be defined with self-control and emotional stability that one maintains despite of facing toughness in terms of working in an environment against to one's nature. People who suffer from this factor in abundance expose following features: they lose cognitive power due to facing constant pressure and depression emerging from surroundings or they commit errors and mistakes in numbers for having anxiety while performing assigned tasks.

Table 1. MBTI 16 personality types

ISTJ	ISFJ	INFJ	INTJ
ISTP	ISFP	INFP	INTP
ESTP	ESFP	ENFP	ENTP
ESTJ	ESFJ	ENFJ	ENTJ

This personality trait refers to the recreational aspects of individual who love to enjoy working with people and enjoy their company. Extrovert individuals are sociable, energetic, assertive, enthusiastic, adventurous, and they also show warmth in performing tasks. People who develop extraversion expose following features: they do not like the monotony for being sensitive. Thus, they love working under changing environment-having variety of works. Moreover, the people having an element of consciousness appear to be law abiding, dutiful, showing acute self-discipline and they also strive harder for achievements. These people show following features: they do not hesitate to make thorough decisions to benefit organization. Similarly, the people having this personality trait show much flexibility and compassions for others and they never become antagonist with any one. Such people exhibit tolerance, tactfulness, trust, respect, modesty and sympathy. These people also show following features: they are generally easy to be worked with.

People having this personality trait are more inclined to welcome new learning so as to enhance their experience and ideas. Such people are mostly curious, imaginative, broadminded, cultured and unconventional. These people also show following features: they are curious and immensely interested in learning. Additionally, they love to make improvisations and experimentations while performing assigned tasks. For the requirement of software engineering, cognitive ability factor and its importance cannot be nullified at any point. People having strong cognitive ability show following features: they possess high level of abstract thinking that begets novel ideas and concepts without being involved practically performing the things.

In addition, there are studies conducted in order to investigate the relationship between human skills and the software life cycle phases and indeed human is the key determinant of success to software development (Almomani, Basri, & Gilal, 2018). Human beings' activities for instance analyzing, thinking, decision making, designing, collaborating, communicating, implementing and even personnel morale swing etc. are consisted a lot in the software development. Variety of engineering methodologies to solve the software crisis and each with its own recognized strengths and weaknesses have evolved over years for decades. As a matter of fact, one software development methodology framework is not necessarily applicable to be used by all projects. Thus, researchers and practitioners have jumped into conclusion that there is no silver bullet for software engineering (Hazzan & Hadar, 2008). Over a century, with mobile development technologies and a boom of cloud-based application (Waqas, Gilal, et al., 2017; Waqas, Rehman, Gilal, & Khan, 2016; Waqas, Rehman, et al., 2017), as well as the appearance of e-commerce which brings people's daily life to cyberspace, human factor research has become a crucial topic in software engineering research especially for the field of software development. Similarly, Karn and Cowling (2006) emphasized that decision making process and group processes are always influenced by the personalities of the members involved in team. Additionally, personality can be measured keeping in account the traits and the types of individuals. Defining the traits and the types of individuals, Karen and Cowling also maintain that traits are associated with behaviour of individuals that can be seen through characteristics exposed into different and variety of situations. Whereas, type can be narrated as a category of fixed patterns of traits that reveal the actual characteristics of one's personality.

To recommend Crowdsourcing software development task, a content-based technique was used by Ke Mao, Capra et al., (Mao et al., 2017). This approach used a historical record of registration and winning for the CSD for automatically matching the task and developer. Snow et al., (Snow et al., 2008) proposed bias correction in crowd data in the form of modeling. They used a gold standard data set to estimate the CSD workers model accuracy. However, this method is used in micro-tasking. Ambati et al., (Ambati, Vogel, & Carbonell, 2011) used an implicit model based on skills and interest of CSD worker to recommend the classification based task. Yuen et al. (Yuen et al., 2011) mentioned and proposed an approach based on task matching which will encourage CSD workers to do a task on the continuous and long run. This approach is focused on the recommendation of the tasks to be best matched with the workers. Sheng et al., (Sheng, Provost, & Ipeirotis, 2008) stated that, for a task matching, labeling is used as a technique but it also evident a limitation. Whitehall et al., (Whitehill, Ruvolo, Wu, Bergsma, & Movellan, 2009), and Raykar et al., (Raykar, 2009) used EM algorithm to calculate the accuracy of the CSD worker, and answer matrix to relate and mapping the quality of the CSD worker. Determination of single labeling is focused on these studies (Capretz & Ahmed, 2010a; Dawid & Skene, 2006; Dempster, Laird, & Rubin, 2018; Gentle, McLachlan, & Krishnan, 2006; Gupta, 2011). According to (Howe, 2006), by ignoring the task requirements and the relationship between CSD worker's non-technical skills these approaches may get undesired results. Therefore, a new approach is needed to relate the human skills with the technical skills of the CSD workers. A comparison of other author's work and TAA is presented in 2.

The Existing model of crowdsourcing software development is working on open call format

As shown in Figure 1, initially the requester requests the platform to post the problem. The platform then sort out the problems and made its micro-tasking to post. CSD developers register themselves to participate in the various tasks. They are required to submit their solutions to the platform before deadlines. The platform initiates the review process over the submissions as soon the deadlines ended. After reviewing the submissions, platform publishes the results of prize-winning tasks. Moreover, developers also have the right of appeal against the rejection of their submission. At the end, the reward is given to the winner of submission.

Table 2. Comparison of TAA with other techniques

Authors	Techniques Used	TAA
Ke Mao, Capra et al., (Mao et al., 2017).	This approach used a historical record of registration and winning for the CSD for automatically matching the task and developer	TAA for Crowdsourcing software development algorithm will match the past task preferences and personality types to update the selection list for the developer or other way around for platform. As a result, the quality and efficiency of software deliverables will be increased with minimum efforts.
Snow et al., (Tratz et al., 2016)	Used a gold standard data set to estimate the CSD workers model accuracy. However, this method is used in micro-tasking	
Ambati et al., (Ambati et al., 2011)	Used an implicit modeling based on skills and interest of CSD worker to recommend the task.	
Sheng et al., (Sheng et al., 2008)	For a task matching, labeling is used as a technique.	
Liu et al., (Liu et al., 2012) Whitehall et al., (Whitehill et al., 2009), and Raykar et al., (Raykar, 2009).	Used EM algorithm to calculate the accuracy of the CSD worker, by using EM algorithm and answer matrix to relate and mapping the quality of the CSD worker	

Figure 1. Existing CSD process

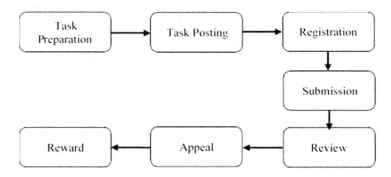

RESEARCH METHODOLOGY

The proposed approach will work the same as the open call format but the proposed task assignment CSD model includes the personality based categorization. Once, after the requester prepared a request for the task, the platform shortlists the posts of tasks for competition based on personality types. In this case, the registration of developer requires the personality measurement test to know the type of personality of developers. Meanwhile, this proposal also suggests that the task should also be included with a specific explanation that can be used to define the required traits of personality for the task. For example, the social networking based tasks may require a developer with the extrovert trait. Since the extrovert developer can understand and work on the task with interest as they involve themselves in social activities. Hence, the task will be directly available for the developers, if the developers are already registered with the platform along with their personality types (i.e., by using MBTI). The classification of individual personality types is classified on the MBTI test that allows the combination of four-dimensional pairs and from those four combinations, there are the 16 possible personality combinations that are already discussed in Table 1. To evaluate a personality of the CSD worker, this study, will use MBTI personality type as an instrument because this instrument is widely used in the research of software engineering (Almomani et al., 2018; Gilal, Jaafar, Abro, et al., 2017; Gilal, Jaafar, Omar, et al., 2017; Jaafar et al., 2017; Kazai, Kamps, & Milic-Frayling, 2011).

This study devised the CSD task assignment algorithm based on personality types and three categories of tasks: design, development and testing. To describe better CSD task matching domain the relationships among the CSD developer, the task, the requester, and platform are to be defined. Following is the definition of the relationships which are basically adapted from the study of Yuen et al.,(Yuen et al., 2011). The mathematical description of TAA is used to sort the available tasks to best matching, sorting and assigning the tasks to developers.

TAA in CSD consists of 5 kinds of tuple {L, M, O, P, Q}

1. Where L: L= {lx\x =1 ….. U_N} is a set of CSD requester who wants to post the tasks on the platform.
2. Where M: M= {my\y=1 …..M_N} is a set of developers on CSD platform and M_N is the maximum number of the CSD developer.
3. Where O: O= {oi\i=1 …….O_N} is a set of categories of CSD task available on CSD platform for example (development, design, f2f) whereas O_N is a maximum number of categories of the task.
4. Where P: P= {pi\i=1…….P_N} is a set of personality traits of the CSD developer. Where P_N is the total number of personality types.
5. Where Q: Q = {qi\i=1 ……Q_N} is a set of the task in all categories of CSD, whereas, the Q_N is the total number of the task in each category.

The following attributes are in A task category Oi:

r i,j is the requester of the task Q1, Q2 where $r_{i,j} =\exists_L x \in L$.
Dij = {d,i,j,k \ k =1 ….. Dn } is a set of CSD developers who haveparticipated on task q1,q2..qn j, and DN is the number of developers who participate on task q1,q2.qn where Di, jk $=\exists$ My $\in$ M.

e i,j is the personality types of worker wi, k to

mi,j is the reward by the platform r i, j for developer D ij k to complete task Qij

```
Algorithm
Procedure Match the Task (Developer my, personality record
PR(my))
{run when CSD developer my log into the CSD platform}
Input: Q, the set of available tasks in all categories
ON, the number of task categories
QN, the number of available tasks in category qi
Algorithm: for i = 1 → O_N do
  for j = 1 → Q_N do
Based on Q and PR(My)
Compute   PR of each available developer for my
  j ← j + 1
  end for i ← i + 1
end for
 Output: the available tasks with personality type matching in
all categories will be sorted for developers.
```

We carried out empirical experiments to collect data on the final year students of bachelors program of Computer Systems Engineering at Dawood University of Engineering and Technology Karachi, Pakistan. Students were taught the fundamental concepts of crowdsourcing in the initial classes. Later, they were required to create an account on the prototype developed for the experiment that replicated the crowdsourcing environment (i.e., Topcoder). The prototype recorded participants' personality and choices. There were 91 students involved in the experiment; 49 were male and 42 were female.

Two rounds of experiments were carried out. In the first round, participants selected tasks based on their own choice from the random list of total 100 small tasks. After the first round, the tasks were computed based on the given algorithm above to evaluate the results. The first round helped us to 1) compute the initial results for the comparison with second round and 2) use the results to update the user profile for second round list. However, in the second round, the task list was shown to the participants based on their technical skills and personality types.

RESULTS AND DISCUSSION

Based on the results, it was found that results from round 2 were better than round 1. For instance, out of total 91 submitted tasks of round 1 only 37 were appeared effective. Whereas, total 61 tasks were classified into effective class in round 2. It could have happened due to a huge list of tasks in round 1. However, optimized task list have surely shown effective choices made by the same participants. Figure 2 shows the comparison between both classes.

It was further observed from the results of round 1 that developers selected the tasks from the top 20-30 and bottom 80-100 visible tasks from the list. This is mentioned due the reason that only few 5 tasks were selected between 30-80. Figure 3 shows the overall distribution of the selection style of the participants.

However, by applying the selected algorithm on the task list based on the task type and personality in round 2, the task selection behavior of the participants appeared quite different. Each participant got different task list based on his or her skills. Therefore, the submitted tasks fulfilled the requirements effectively.

Moreover, based on the effective results, it was found that each category of task is appealing different type of personality. For instance, ESFP and ENFJ personality types were more attracted towards designing tasks. Similarly, ISFJ, INFJ, INFP and INTP were completely invisible to be working effectively on design projects. Table 3 summarizes the results of all types of tasks against each personality types.

Figure 2. Effective and ineffective submissions in both rounds

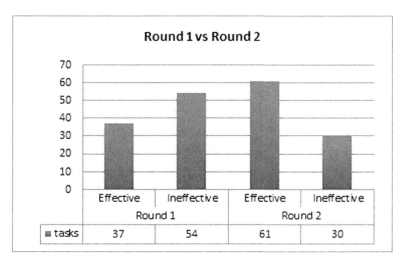

Figure 3. Round 1 selected tasks out of 100

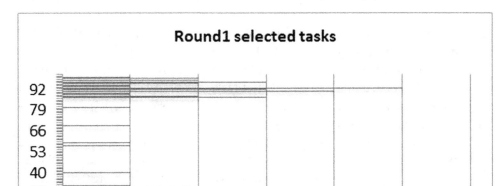

Table 3. Tasks and personality in effective class of both rounds

	Design	Development	Testing
ISTJ	1	11	1
ISFJ	0	2	0
INFJ	0	1	0
INTJ	2	0	3
ISTP	2	1	0
ISFP	1	2	2
INFP	0	0	8
INTP	0	2	0
ESTP	1	3	3
ESFP	9	1	0
ENFP	3	1	0
ENTP	2	0	0
ESTJ	1	5	0
ESFJ	1	1	5
ENFJ	9	0	4
ENTJ	3	6	1

In the same vein, ISTJ, ESTJ and ENTJ personality types were classified effective in both rounds. Capretz and Faheem (Capretz & Ahmed, 2010a) also produced similar results for the programmer personality. In the very study, ISTJ was the most frequent personality type for programmer role whereas our study also denotes "TJ" pair with I or E is effective. Moreover, INTJ, INFP, ENTP and ENFJ were not found in the effective development projects. Lastly, INFP and ESFJ were prominent personality types in both effective rounds. Whereas, ISFJ, INFJ, ISTP, INTP, ESFP, ENFP, ENTP and ESTJ were as disappeared as zero. Figure 4 summarizes the personality types in the effective submissions.

At the end, ISTJ, ENFJ, ESFJ and ESFP personality types were found most frequent in the experiment.

CONCLUSION

Crowdsourcing business approach is still facing crucial challenges in terms of assessing and selecting appropriate tasks as solution. Available techniques, methods or

Figure 4. Effective tasks and personality types

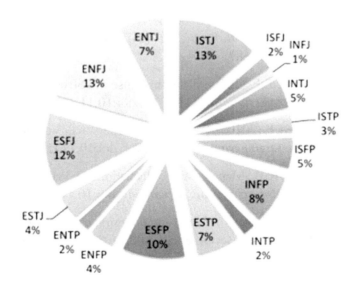

Personality types and effective frequency

algorithms in CSD are yet to obtain the satisfactory outcomes. Technical requirements of the task along with personality preferences can sort the task list at the developer end for efficient selection. This way cannot only reduce the burden from platform but also increases the effectiveness in the submissions.

REFERENCES

Aldhahri, E., Shandilya, V., & Shiva, S. (2015). Towards an effective crowdsourcing recommendation system: A survey of the state-of-the-art. *Proceedings - 9th IEEE International Symposium on Service-Oriented System Engineering, IEEE SOSE 2015*. 10.1109/SOSE.2015.53

Allport, G. W. (1961). *Pattern and growth in personality*. Academic Press.

Almomani, M. A., Basri, S., & Gilal, A. R. (2018). Empirical study of software process improvement in Malaysian small and medium enterprises: The human aspects. *Journal of Software: Evolution and Process*. doi:10.1002mr.1953

Ambati, V., Vogel, S., & Carbonell, J. (2011). Towards Task Recommendation in Micro-Task Markets. *Human Computation AAAI Workshop*.

Basri, S., Omar, M., Capretz, L. F., Aziz, I. A., Jaafar, J., & Gilal, A. R. (2017). Finding an effective classification technique to develop a software team composition model. *Journal of Software: Evolution and Process*. doi:10.1002mr.1920

Block, J. (1995). A contrarian view of the five-factor approach to personality description. *Psychological Bulletin*, *117*(2), 187–215. doi:10.1037/0033-2909.117.2.187 PMID:7724687

Capretz, L. F., & Ahmed, F. (2010a). Making sense of software development and personality types. *IT Professional*, *12*(1), 6–13. doi:10.1109/MITP.2010.33

Capretz, L. F., & Ahmed, F. (2010b). Why do we need personality diversity in software engineering? *Software Engineering Notes*, *35*(2), 1. doi:10.1145/1734103.1734111

Carmel, E., de Souza, C. R. B., Meneguzzi, F., Machado, L., & Prikladnicki, R. (2016). *Task allocation for crowdsourcing using AI planning*. doi:10.1145/2897659.2897666

Carpenter, B., & Huang, Z. (1998). *Multilevel bayesian models of categorical data annotation*. Unpublished Manuscript. doi:10.1023/A:1009769707641

Child, I. L. (1968). Personality in culture. Handbook of Personality Theory and Research, 82–145.

Chilton, L. B., Horton, J. J., & Miller, R. C. (2010). Task search in a human computation market. *Proceedings of the ACM SIGKDD Workshop on Human Computation*, 1–9. 10.1145/1837885.1837889

Dang, D., Liu, Y., Zhang, X., & Huang, S. (2016). A Crowdsourcing Worker Quality Evaluation Algorithm on MapReduce for Big Data Applications. *IEEE Transactions on Parallel and Distributed Systems*, *27*(7), 1879–1888. doi:10.1109/TPDS.2015.2457924

Dawid, A. P., & Skene, A. M. (2006). Maximum Likelihood Estimation of Observer Error-Rates Using the EM Algorithm. *Applied Statistics*. doi:10.2307/2346806

Dempster, A. P., Laird, N. M., & Rubin, D. B. (2018). Maximum Likelihood from Incomplete Data Via the EM Algorithm. *Journal of the Royal Statistical Society. Series B. Methodological*. doi:10.1111/j.2517-6161.1977.tb01600.x

Fernando Capretz, L. (2014). Bringing the human factor to software engineering. *IEEE Software*, *31*(2), 104. doi:10.1109/MS.2014.30

Fu, Y., Chen, H., & Song, F. (2015). STWM: A solution to self-adaptive task-worker matching in software crowdsourcing. Lecture Notes in Computer Science. doi:10.1007/978-3-319-27119-4_27

Geiger, D., & Schader, M. (2014). Personalized task recommendation in crowdsourcing information systems - Current state of the art. *Decision Support Systems*, *65*(C), 3–16. doi:10.1016/j.dss.2014.05.007

Gentle, J. E., McLachlan, G. J., & Krishnan, T. (2006). The EM Algorithm and Extensions. *Biometrics*. doi:10.2307/2534032

Gilal, A. R., Jaafar, J., Abro, A., Umrani, W. A., Basri, S., & Omar, M. (2017). Making programmer effective for software development teams: An extended study. *Journal of Information Science and Engineering*. doi:10.6688/JISE.2017.33.6.4

Gilal, A. R., Jaafar, J., Basri, S., Omar, M., & Abro, A. (2016). Impact of software team composition methodology on the personality preferences of Malaysian students. *2016 3rd International Conference on Computer and Information Sciences, ICCOINS 2016 - Proceedings*. 10.1109/ICCOINS.2016.7783258

Gilal, A. R., Jaafar, J., Basri, S., Omar, M., & Tunio, M. Z. (2016). Making programmer suitable for team-leader: Software team composition based on personality types. *2015 International Symposium on Mathematical Sciences and Computing Research, iSMSC 2015 - Proceedings*. doi:10.1109/ISMSC.2015.7594031

Gilal, A. R., Jaafar, J., Omar, M., Basri, S., Aziz, I. A., Khand, Q. U., & Hasan, M. H. (2017). *Suitable Personality Traits for Learning Programming Subjects: A Rough-Fuzzy Model. International Journal of Advanced Computer Science and Applications.*

Gilal, A. R., Jaafar, J., Omar, M., Basri, S., & Din, I. (2016). Balancing the Personality of Programmer: Software Development Team Composition. *Malaysian Journal of Computer Science, 29*(2), 145–155. doi:10.22452/mjcs.vol29no2.5

Gilal, A. R., Jaafar, J., Omar, M., Basri, S., & Waqas, A. (2016). A Rule-Based Model for Software Development Team Composition: Team Leader Role with Personality Types and Gender Classification. *Information and Software Technology, 74*, 105–113. doi:10.1016/j.infsof.2016.02.007

Gilal, A. R., Omar, M., Jaafar, J., Sharif, K. I., Mahesar, A. W., & Basri, S. (2017). Software Development Team Composition: Personality Types of Programmer and Complex Networks. In *6th International Conference on Computing and Informatics (ICOCI-2017)* (pp. 153–159). Academic Press.

Gilal, A. R., Omar, M., & Sharif, K. I. (2013). Discovering personality types and diversity based on software team roles. In *International Conference on Computing and Informatics, ICOCI 2013* (pp. 259–264). Academic Press.

Goldberg, L. R. (1990). An alternative" description of personality": The big-five factor structure. *Journal of Personality and Social Psychology, 59*(6), 1216–1229. doi:10.1037/0022-3514.59.6.1216 PMID:2283588

Gupta, M. R. (2011). Theory and Use of the EM Algorithm. *Foundations and Trends® in Signal Processing.* doi:10.1561/2000000034

Hazzan, O., & Hadar, I. (2008). Why and how can human-related measures support software development processes? *Journal of Systems and Software, 81*(7), 1248–1252. doi:10.1016/j.jss.2008.01.037

Howe, J. (2006). *The Rise of Crowdsourcing. Wired Magazine.*

Jaafar, J., Gilal, A. R., Omar, M., Basri, S., Abdul Aziz, I., & Hasan, M. H. (2017). A Rough-Fuzzy Inference System for Selecting Team Leader for Software Development Teams. In *Advances in Intelligent Systems and Computing* (Vol. 661, pp. 304–314). Cham, Switzerland: Springer.

Karn, J. S., & Cowling, A J. (2006). Using ethnographic methods to carry out human factors research in software engineering. *Behavior Research Methods, 38*(3), 495–503. Retrieved from http://www.ncbi.nlm.nih.gov/pubmed/17186760

Kazai, G., Kamps, J., & Milic-Frayling, N. (2011). *Worker types and personality traits in crowdsourcing relevance labels*. doi:10.1145/2063576.2063860

Latoza, T. D., & Van Der Hoek, A. (2015). A Vision of Crowd Development. *Proceedings - International Conference on Software Engineering.* 10.1109/ICSE.2015.194

Liu, X., Lu, M., Ooi, B. C., Shen, Y., Wu, S., & Zhang, M. (2012). Cdas: A crowdsourcing data analytics system. *Proceedings of the VLDB Endowment International Conference on Very Large Data Bases*, 5(10), 1040–1051. doi:10.14778/2336664.2336676

Mao, K., Capra, L., Harman, M., & Jia, Y. (2017). A survey of the use of crowdsourcing in software engineering. *Journal of Systems and Software*, *126*, 57–84. doi:10.1016/j.jss.2016.09.015

Mao, K., Yang, Y., Wang, Q., Jia, Y., & Harman, M. (2015). Developer recommendation for crowdsourced software development tasks. *Proceedings - 9th IEEE International Symposium on Service-Oriented System Engineering, IEEE SOSE 2015.* 10.1109/SOSE.2015.46

Martínez, L. G., Rodríguez-Díaz, A., Licea, G., & Castro, J. R. (2010). Big five patterns for software engineering roles using an ANFIS learning approach with RAMSET. In *Advances in Soft Computing* (pp. 428–439). Springer. doi:10.1007/978-3-642-16773-7_37

Myers, I. B., McCaulley, M. H., Quenk, N. L., & Hammer, A. L. (1998). *MBTI manual: A guide to the development and use of the Myers-Briggs Type Indicator* (Vol. 3). Palo Alto, CA: Consulting Psychologists Press.

Nawaz, N. A., Waqas, A., Yusof, Z. M., Mahesar, A. W., & Shah, A. (2017). WSN based sensing model for smart crowd movement with identification: An extended study. *Journal of Theoretical and Applied Information Technology.*

Nawaz, N. A., Waqas, A., Yusof, Z. M., & Shah, A. (2016). WSN based sensing model for smart crowd movement with identification: a conceptual model. *Multi Conference on Computer Science And Information Systems 2016.*

Raykar, V. (2009). *Supervised Learning from Multiple Experts : Whom to trust when everyone lies a bit.* doi:10.1145/1553374.1553488

Sheng, V. S., Provost, F., & Ipeirotis, P. G. (2008). *Get another label? improving data quality and data mining using multiple, noisy labelers.* doi:10.1145/1401890.1401965

Snow, R., Connor, B. O., Jurafsky, D., & Ng, A. Y. (2008). Cheap and Fast - But is it Good? Evaluating Non-Expert Annotations for Natural Language Tasks. *Proceedings of EMNLP*. 10.3115/1613715.1613751

Tratz, S., Hovy, E., Nulty, P., Costello, F., Verhoeven, B., Daelemans, W., … Han, J. (2016). *Cheap and fast - but is it good? Evaluation non-expert annotiations for natural language tasks*. doi:10.3115/1119282.1119287

Tunio, M. Z., Luo, H., Cong, W., Fang, Z., Gilal, A. R., Abro, A., & Wenhua, S. (2017). Impact of Personality on Task Selection in Crowdsourcing Software Development: A Sorting Approach. *IEEE Access: Practical Innovations, Open Solutions*, *5*, 18287–18294. doi:10.1109/ACCESS.2017.2747660

Tunio, M. Z., Luo, H., Wang, C., Zhao, F., Gilal, A. R., & Shao, W. (2018). Task Assignment Model for crowdsourcing software development: TAM. *Journal of Information Processing Systems*. doi:10.3745/JIPS.04.0064

Waqas, A., Gilal, A. R., Rehman, M. A., Uddin, Q., Mahmood, N., & Yusof, Z. M. (2017). C3F: Cross-Cloud Communication Framework for Resource Sharing amongst Cloud Networks: An Extended Study. *International Journal of Computer Science and Network Security*, *17*(8), 216–228.

Waqas, A., Rehman, M. A., Gilal, A. R., & Khan, M. A. (2016). CloudWeb: A Web-based Prototype for Simulation of Cross-Cloud Communication Framework (C3F). *Bahria University Journal of Information & Communication Technology*, *9*(2), 65–71.

Waqas, A., Rehman, M. A., Gilal, A. R., Khan, M. A., Ahmed, J., & Yusof, Z. M. (2017). A Features-based Comparative Study of the State-of-the-Art Cloud Computing Simulators and Future Directions. *International Journal of Advanced Computer Science and Applications*, *8*(8), 51–59. doi:10.14569/IJACSA.2017.080807

Waqas, A., Yusof, Z. M., Shah, A., & Khan, M. A. (2014). ReSA : Architecture for Resources Sharing Between Clouds. In *Conference on Information Assurance and Cyber Security (CIACS2014)* (pp. 23–28). Academic Press. 10.1109/CIACS.2014.6861326

Waqas, A., Yusof, Z. M., Shah, A., & Mahmood, N. (2014). Sharing of Attacks Information across Clouds for Improving Security: A Conceptual Framework. In *IEEE 2014 International Conference on Computer, Communication, and Control Technology* (pp. 255–260). IEEE. 10.1109/I4CT.2014.6914185

Whitehill, J., Ruvolo, P., Wu, T., Bergsma, J., & Movellan, J. (2009). Whose Vote Should Count More: Optimal Integration of Labels from Labelers of Unknown Expertise. *Advances in Neural Information Processing Systems.*

Yang, Y., Karim, M. R., Saremi, R., & Ruhe, G. (2016). Who Should Take This Task?: Dynamic Decision Support for Crowd Workers. *Proceedings of the 10th ACM/IEEE International Symposium on Empirical Software Engineering and Measurement.* 10.1145/2961111.2962594

Yuen, M. C., King, I., & Leung, K. S. (2011). Task matching in crowdsourcing. *Proceedings - 2011 IEEE International Conferences on Internet of Things and Cyber, Physical and Social Computing, iThings/CPSCom 2011.* 10.1109/iThings/CPSCom.2011.128

Chapter 2

The Business Transformation Framework and Enterprise Architecture Framework for Managers in Business Innovation:
Knowledge Management in Global Software Engineering (KMGSE)

Antoine Trad
IBISTM, France

ABSTRACT

The KMGSE offers a real-life case for detecting and processing an enterprise knowledge management model for global business transformation, knowledge management systems, global software engineering, global business engineering and enterprise architecture recurrent problems solving. This global software engineering (GSE) subsystem is a driven development model that offers a set of possible solutions in the form of architecture, method, patterns, managerial and technical recommendations, coupled with an applicable framework. The proposed executive and technical recommendations are to be applied by the business environment's knowledge officers, architects, analysts and engineers to enable solutions to knowledge-based, global software engineering paradigms' development and maintenance.

DOI: 10.4018/978-1-5225-9448-2.ch002

INTRODUCTION

This Global Software Engineering (GSE) subsystem is a driven development model that offers a set of possible solutions in the form of architecture, method, patterns, managerial and technical recommendations, coupled with an applicable framework. The proposed executive and technical recommendations are to be applied by the business environment's knowledge officers, architects, analysts and engineers to enable solutions to knowledge-based global software engineering paradigms' development and maintenance.

BACKGROUND

This work's background combines Knowledge Management (KM), GSE, enterprise architecture, heuristics/ mathematical models, technology management, business transformation and business engineering fields. Building a KMGSE based on a Decision Making System (DMS) should be the major strategic goal for business companies, as shown in Figure 1 (Lanubile, Ebert, Prikladnicki, & Vizcaíno, 2010; Cearley, Walker, & Burke, 2016; Thomas, 2015).

The proposed KMGSE model or pattern is: 1) a generic and cross-business and a global technology modelling concept; 2) engineering and reasoning engine that contains basically GSE modelling techniques; 3) qualitative research methods that manage sets of factors; and 4) a framework that can be used by any type of Business Transformation Project (BTP). The authors based their over-all research method on intelligent neural networks and driven development, where both methods resemble to the human empiric brain processing that is very much influenced by the authors' previous works and more specifically by the chapter related to the Knowledge and Intelligence Driven Development (KIDD) (Trad & Kalpić, 2018a). The KMGSE concept is business and technology driven one and is agnostic to a specific application and business environment, as shown in Figure 2. The KMGSE is founded on a research framework that in turn is based on the industry architecture standard, the Architecture Development Method (ADM) (The Open Group, 2011a). Enterprise architecture is a methodology used to develop BTPs, requirements, architecture, intelligence modules, knowledge modules and its technology software engineering components. The Business Transformation Manager (BTM) or an enterprise architect can integrate a KMGSE in the global architecture and its underlying software modelling of a BTP to support the DMS system (Trad & Kalpić, 2017b; Trad & Kalpić, 2017c; Thomas, 2015; Tidd, 2006). This KMGSE proposal's goal is to deliver recommendations for managing aligned GSEs with synchronised KM(s) and DMS(s). The applied research methodology is based on literature review, a qualitative methodology and on a proof

Figure 1. Technology trends
Source: Cearley, Walker, & Burke, 2016

of concept for the proposed hypotheses. In a holistic knowledge management and software architecture, the BTM's role is important and his or her (for simplicity, in further text – his) decisions are aided by using factors within the AMM subsystem. A large set of factors can influence such an AMM, like: a) the role of the knowledge management subsystem; b) enterprise business critical success factors; c) enterprise budget and resources; d) DMS capabilities; e) audit and technological conditions; f) financial predispositions; and g) security, financial and legal control mechanisms using a collaborative tools for GSE (Lanubile, Ebert, Prikladnicki, Vizcaíno, & Vizcaino, 2010). A systems approach is the optimal choice to model such a KMGSE (Daellenbach & McNickle, 2005; Trad & Kalpić, 2016a). As shown in Figure 2, the decision model interacts with the external world via an implemented framework to manage the KMGSE's factors and that is this chapter's focus.

Adapting simplistic agilization methodologies to the underlined islands of technologies is not enough and the main problem can arise due to the lack of company's holistic synchronized agility approach, that can be insured by the KMGSE Pattern (Thomas, 2015; Cearley, Walker, & Burke, 2016).

Figure 2. The research framework's concept
Source: Trad & Kalpić, 2016a

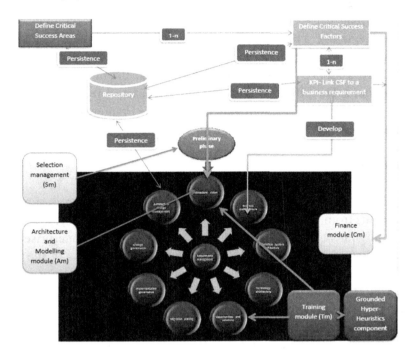

FOCUS OF THE ARTICLE

The Research Processes

This research's main topic is related to BTPs and the ultimate research question is: "Which business transformation manager characteristics and which type of support should be assured in the implementation phase of a business transformation project?" Decision making concepts based on critical success areas are their main research component.

Critical Success Areas, Factors and Decision Making

Critical Success Area (CSA) is a set of Critical Success Factors (CSF) where the CSF is a set of Key Performance Indicators (KPI), where each KPI corresponds to a single KMGSE or BTP requirement and/or knowledge feature. For a given problem, an enterprise architect can identify the initial set of CSFs for the KMGSE. Hence the CSFs are important for the mapping between the knowledge constructs, organisational items and KMGSE (Peterson, 2011). Therefore, CSFs reflect performance areas that must meet strategic BTP goals and defined constraints. Measurements are used to evaluate performance in each of the CSA sets, where CSFs can be internal or external to the environment; like: 1) knowledge item or gap analysis is an internal CSF; and 2) decisions-making in real time and in minimal time is also an internal one. Once the initial set of CSFs has been identified, then the BTP can use the KMGSE to propose a knowledge item. The proposed KMGSE delivers a set of recommendations and solutions for an aligned architecture that is part of the Framework (Trad & Kalpić, 2018a; Trad & Kalpić, 2017b; Trad, & Kalpić, 2017c).

The Framework

The BTM or the enterprise architect's decisions can be made in a just-in-time manner by using outputs from various credible knowledge management stores. The defined knowledge alignment strategy should asses and govern the enterprise's global knowledge sphere that is formalized and implemented by means of the KMGSE pattern. The proposed research framework supports such a pattern, as shown Figure 2. Unfortunately, an immense set of methodologically (?) archaic factors can influence such a complex process, like: 1) the influence of knowledge and intelligence management on BTPs; 2) working with complex systems and defining the granularity of knowledge items; 3) management of large and global software engineering projects; and 4) the complex implementation of existing architecture standards. A global concept for the management of the KMGSE approach is optimal for BTPs (Daellenbach & McNickle, 2005). In this research chapter, the focus is on the KMGSE module that supports the global knowledge management on many levels. The KMGSE can be applied to various types of BTPs and other general fields and it is a part of the Knowledge management module (Km) and the Decision module (Dm). In this chapter the authors propose a set of KMGSE managerial and technical recommendations and a reusable real-world module (Trad 2018a; Trad 2018b; Trad 2018c; Trad 2018d).

The KMGSE component is supported by The Open Group's Architecture Framework (TOGAF) architecture development method's phases, where each KMGSE pattern item circulates through its phases. The KMGSE patterns contain their private set of CSFs, where these CSFs can be applied to (Peterson, 2011): a) select the important knowledge management factors and items; b) detect the KMGSE's most important assets; c) estimate the actual assets of the BTP using the KM system's interface; and to eventually take a decision on BTP's continuation; d) control and monitor the needed KMGSE pattern instances; e) upgrade the BTP's KM skills; and f) support the BTP management activities. The Framework or the *Environment* is composed of the following modules denoted by corresponding abbreviations:

Figure 3. The implementation environment that enables knowledge management

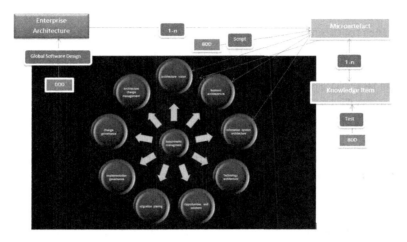

- **"Sm":** For the selection management of the Framework.
- **"Am":** For the architecture and modelling strategy that can be applied by the Framework.
- **"Cm":** For the control and monitoring strategy that can be applied by the Framework.
- **"Dm":** For the decision-making strategy that can be applied by the Framework.
- **"Tm":** For the training management of the Framework.
- **"Pm":** For the project management strategy that can be applied by the Framework.
- **"Fm":** For the financial management's support to the Framework.
- **"Gm":** For the Geopolitical mind-mining of the Framework.
- **"Km":** For Knowledge management in the Framework and it was introduced in this chapter.

This chapter is a part of years-long research cluster that has produced many articles, literature reviews, usable items and research artefacts. In this chapter, parts of previous works are reused for the better understanding of this complex research. This work can be considered as a pioneering one, in the field of global transformation and architecture projects. For that purpose, this phase's research sub-question is: "How should knowledge management and global software engineering be managed in transformation projects?".

The KMGSE is business-driven and is founded on a research framework that in turn is based on enterprise architecture and information and communication technology (The Open Group, 2011a).

The Research's Uniqueness

The uniqueness of this research promotes a holistic unbundling process, the alignment of standards and strategies to support *Projects* (Farhoomand, 2004). The uniqueness of this research project is based on its holistic approach that combines: 1) *Project*; 2) AHMM4BT; 3) software auditing, modelling and architecture; 4) business engineering; 5) financial analysis; 6) iCTM's profile; 6) holistic urban and EA; and 7) it offers a methodology and Framework.

Review's and Check of the Critical Success Factors/Critical Success Areas

This chapter promotes the transformation through the use of Critical Success Area (CSA) that contains a set of CSFs, where a CSF is a set of Key Performance Indicators (KPI), where each KPI corresponds to a single *Projects* requirement and/or an item that can be a profile requirement or skill that has a column in each evaluation table (Peterson, 2011; Trad & Kalpić, 2018a). Where for a each CSA an Excel Workbook (WB) is created and in which all its CSFs are stored. The WB has a scripts in the background that are automated to calculate the weightings and ratings. This research project proposes a standardized and automated manner to evaluate literature reviews that is an evolution in regards to just the subjective method it does or (doesn't) make sense. If the automated literature review's evaluation is successful, only then the experiment is done.

A *Project* starts with the first phase called the feasibility phase to check the basic CSFs, to check if the *Project* makes sense; that is based on WB evaluation. Based on the KMGSE literature review and related evaluation processes known as the Qualitative(1), the most important extracted CSFs that are used and evaluated using the following rules (Trad & Kalpić, 2018a):

- Stored WB references should be credible and are estimated by the authors and follow a classification supported by the CSF management system.
- *Projects* like mergers are the result of organisational changes in companies to act as a single enterprise with consolidated WB CSFs, resources and business interests.
- Applied modelling language should be limited in order to make the *Projects* manageable and not too complex.
- The ADM is considered to be mature if it has been in use for more than ten years and that it has been reported as successful to enforce the interest in using the ADM.

- The ADM is appropriate for any project's local conditions and manages the *TKM&F's* iterations and CSFs with WB tuning scripts.
- If the aggregations of all the *Project's* CSA/CSF WB tables/sheets are positive and exceed the defined minimum, the *Projects* continues to its PoC or can be used for problem solving.
- This evaluation concept will be applied to seven different CSAs that are presented in tables.

INFORMATION AND COMMUNICATION TECHNOLOGY

Modelling and Patterns

A KMGSE pattern expresses a fundamental structural concept or schema for the BTP's global software system's implementations: 1) it offers a set of predefined knowledge and intelligence templates to instantiate items; 2) it describes their responsibilities and content; 3) it defines the software artefacts for these KM modules; 4) it defines a global software engineering model; and 5) it includes the description of the relationships between the different KMGSE templates. A KMGSE pattern is a schema that can be used to refine the Architecture Development Method (ADM) cycle. A KMGSE pattern describes the common structure for a general design problem within a BTP implementation context by using the "1:1" concept or a holistic GSE pattern. A KMGSE pattern is a set of idioms, where an idiom is a basic KM pattern that is not specific to any environment. An idiom describes the aspects of an artefact and its relationships with other BTP artefacts. KMGSE patterns refer to patterns that are used to develop KM models or modules using an enterprise agile implementation model.

Agility Concept

Global enterprise agility is achieved by combining various business, technology and software methodologies that promote global enterprise agility to be used on various levels of the BTP, in order to unbundle and maintain the existing enterprise environment and glue its innovated KM items using a dynamic Information System's (IS) components and KMGSE patterns as shown in Figure 4. Using a mixed bottom-up approach, the BTM can design an IS GSE concept that can handle various types of software modules to be used in the KMGSE microartefacts.

The agility is supported by the following items:

Figure 4. The information system's interaction with various modules

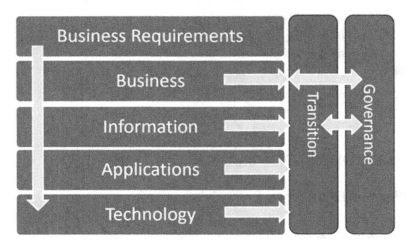

- Methodology and implementation: in most of BTPs various types of methodologies and implementation environments are used. For this chapter the ADM is applied as an architecture methodology and Microsoft's Visual Studio backed-up with Oracle's NetBeans are used.
- Change management and integration: in most of BTPs, various types of change management and integration environments are aligned, for this chapter Maven and Jenkins are applied as change management and integration environments (Seth & Khare, 2015).
- Integration tests: in most of BTPs various types of integration, tests are integrated, for this chapter Mockito is used (Shafique & Labiche, 2010).

Microartefacts / Building Blocks

KMGSE's microartefact that interacts with a multitude of different BTP microartefacts in a synchronized manner and uses the ADM to assist it in the coordination of GSE activities (The Open Group, 2011a). The KMGSE includes various types of pattern scenarios that uses heuristics scenarios to make the BTP's integration more flexible (Trad & Kalpić, 2017a). KMGSE components support the BTP by offering microartefacts to handle various types of knowledge and intelligence endpoints. The usage of knowledge and intelligence endpoints provides some of the mechanisms needed to make KMGSE tuneable with critical success factors.

The Information Technology's Critical Success Factors

Based on the literature review, the most important IT's CSFs that are used are shown in Table 1.

The Modules Chained Link to the Software Engineering and Design Methodologies

This section's deduction is that global software engineering is central for the KMGSE subsystem in which it has its fundaments.

GLOBAL SOFTWARE ENGINEERING STANDARDS AND DESIGN

Today many GSE standards exist and they are very advanced; these standards and their related tooling and development environments can help in an iterative unbundling of the traditional business and its technology environments, through the execution of an agile approach for software development. An agile concept may drive the business company to become a part of dynamic knowledge and intelligence ecosystem.

Global Software Development and Choreography

Actual global software integration and development environments are skeletons that enclose various technologies and methodologies representing a unified implementation strategy for the BTP's needs. The *Environment* offers a high level interpreted language environment that can be used to enable fast business transformation development iterations and supports its KMGSE. Such a development environment must respect existing standards, and its main characteristics are:

Table 1. The critical success factors that have an average of 4.33

Critical Success Factors	KPIs	Weightings
CSF_IT_Modelling	Complex ▼	From 1 to 10. **6 Selected**
CSF_IT_AgilityConcept	InitialLevel ▼	From 1 to 10. **4 Selected**
CSF_IT_Microartefacts	NotReady ▼	From 1 to 10. **3 Selected**

- It delivers functional language building blocks that hang to the enterprise's organisational node.
- It uses the company's standard development environment(s) and does not alter any aspect of its global engineering.
- It delivers the needed knowledge and intelligence microartefacts to be used in the BTP development.

The KMGSE pattern is based on existing proven standards as shown in Figure 5. Standard architectures are based on service oriented architecture to support KMGSE. This research chapter presents a solution in the form of a proof of concept for such an approach, using existing standards and the mapping concept for a global software design.

Global Software Design

Defining granularity is a very complex undertaking in the implementation phase of the KMSGE in addition to the complexity in implementing the "1:1" mapping and classification of the discovered knowledge and intelligence microartefacts in the development of the business environments which have limited resources. This software design concept uses complex communication buses to interact with various KMGSE's instances. Mapping of a requirement to a software artefact is done by the use of a range of KMGSE patterns that can be modelled using the *Environment's* internal heuristic language and functions. This mapping concept is supported by a set of microartefacts where the *Environment's* functional language consists of

Figure 5. Existing set of standards

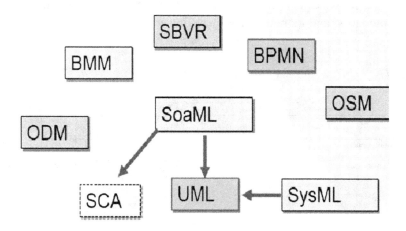

building microartefacts to dynamically evaluate compound expressions, according to applied mathematical principles. The KMGSE patterns use the internal mathematical model to evaluate the BTP's requirements and to deliver knowledge in a just in time manner (Neumann, 2002).

A Holistic Knowledge Management Model

The enterprise's holistic KMGSE model is a set of multiple coordinated knowledge management patterns that correspond to various just-in-time processing neural scenarios (Cearley, Walker, & Burke, 2016). Knowledge manipulation and intelligence are holistic and empiric human mental capabilities that combine reflex, information management and processing that coordinate and control various processing activities. Related and networked information coordination manages knowledge patterns, data, extracts and correlates them in space and time to detect heuristic patterns to deliver various types of problem solving (Gardner, 1999). These KMGSE patterns and their underlined mechanics are used to generate sets of factors' weightings for possible actions that are called knowledge/intelligence microartefacts that are the stub of this research's *Environment*. Weightings' concept enables the KMGSE patterns to build a knowledge subsystem that delivers answers in the form of knowledge values. In many cases, fast change requests may generate an important set of corresponding knowledge solutions that can be ambiguous and make the KM actions uncertain and complex to implement. The KM is responsible for a rational heuristic approach for enterprise knowledge extraction, as shown in Figure 6. The KMGSE's concept is based on a holistic systemic approach to use all the *Environment's* microartefacts (Daellenbach & McNickle, 2005; Trad & Kalpić, 2016a). A DMS can give a company the most important competitive business advantages that may insure its future and it is not a secret that intelligent knowledge artefacts are the basis of any successful BTP (Trad, 2015a; Trad, 2015b; Trad, 2015c). Major research and advisory firms like Gartner, confirm that knowledge services will leverage business ISs' components from various enterprise departments. Gartner confirms also that services are the dominating business enablers for Fortune 500 companies who need dynamic business intelligence support (Clark, Fletcher, Hanson, Irani, Waterhouse, & Thelin, 2013).

Major characteristics of such a KMGSE patterns' model are:

- Predict and design performance feasible solutions.
- Predict and design fallout feasible and stable solutions.
- Take the weakest platform in the global environment as a target, like for example an Android operating system; and align the architectures.

Figure 6. The neural network enterprise architecture component tree

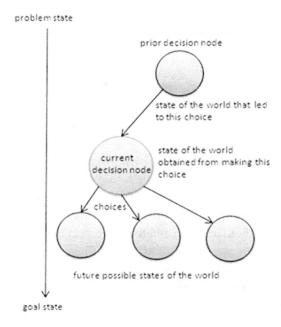

- Use different languages to support different features. C/C++ for backend operations, Java or .NET for the human client interfaces; to support an n-tier architecture.

An N-Tier Architecture

An important CSF in the BTP is the role of the n-tier architecture's model and applied strategy; where the integration of KMGSE patterns is the base of the future n-tiered business system. KMGSE patterns are crucial for the future of any KM system and an integration strategy has to be defined using a standardized methodology like Archimate, as shown in Figure 7 (MID, 2014). Architecture methodologies improve the robustness of a KM system by simplifying their design, development, integration and maintenance; that insures the GSE lifecycle. The KM system of a business transformation process is based on a hands-on holistic approach (Greefhorst, 2009).

The Global Software Engineering Standards Success Factors

Based on the literature review, the most important global software engineering CSFs that are used are shown in Table 2.

Figure 7. Archimate modelling environment
Source: Greefhorst, 2009

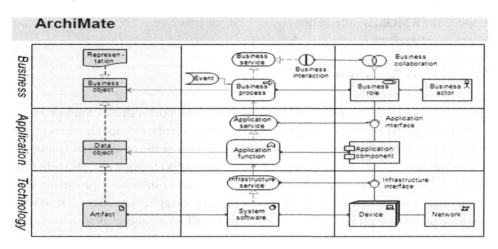

Table 2. The critical success factors that have an average of 7.0

Critical Success Factors	KPIs		Weightings
CSF_GSE_GlobalSoftDev&Choreography	LimitedUsability	▼	From 1 to 10. **4 Selected**
CSF_GSE_GlobalSoftwareDesign	ComplexToApply	▼	From 1 to 10. **6 Selected**
CSF_GSE_KnowledgeIntelligenceModel	Applicable	▼	From 1 to 10. **9 Selected**
CSF_GSE_nTierArchitecture	Integrated	▼	From 1 to 10. **9 Selected**

The Modules Chained Link to the Architecture Aspects

This section's deduction is that the application of an architecture is central for the KMGSE subsystem in which it has its fundaments.

ARCHITECTURE AND GLOBAL SOFTWARE INTEGRATION

Architecture Development Method's Integration

The ADM's integration in the KMGSE and the BTP enables the automation of their activities, throughout all the ADM iterations. The ADM encloses cyclic iterations; where information about all its phases is logged. DMS platforms are not dedicated to any specific business and they offer: 1) knowledge management components' management; 2) performance and reliability prediction and stabilization; and 3) GSE integration in the ADM. The ADM is controlled and monitored in real-time and supports the KMGSEs' interactions using GSE various types of tests and integration driven developments.

Test Driven Developments

The Test Driven Development (TDD) is a global manual approach and a concept where software developers design the test first and then do the development; whereas the Design Driven Development (DDD) that is also known as the model-first approach, is based on patterns and it can manage various types of BTP requirements including the KMGSE requirements (Selic, 2003). TDD is used in testing processes that evaluate the design for a given set of requirements and verifies its status. For BTPs, the implementation phase is very complex and it offers a concept that delivers the KM microartefacts status which assists the KMGSE's development. Concerning the KMGSE the dilemma is: which type of development driven method is more suitable, TDD or DDD or any other. Even if both methods are usable, TDD is more adapted for building KM microartefacts. BTP's are in general large GSEs, where the tests are developed later in future. The integration of KMGSE microartefacts needs the DDD methodology that in halts various technologies. The DDD is optimal for GSE projects like a BTP. It has to be assisted by an Acceptance Test Driven Development (ATDD) methodology (Design Patterns, 2015).

Acceptance Test Driven Development

Similar to TDDs, Acceptance Test Driven Development (ATDD) methodology is based also on developing tests where tests represent the results of the behaviour of various KMGSE microartefacts. In the ATDD's approach, the BTP team creates acceptance level tests, then they implement the end KM system. Later, the results are checked to improve the KM system. ATDD is today used for defining specifications by a concrete example, following similar practices that have existed since the 1990s. Kent Beck and Martin Fowler mentioned the ATDD concept in 2015 even if they remarked that it was very difficult to implement acceptance criteria using standard unit tests in various phases of the GSE. Unit tests are not the unique way to develop ATDD tests, were business users contribute to define workable acceptance tests or use behaviour driven development techniques (Koskela, 2007).

Behaviour Driven Development

In Behaviour Driven Development (BDD) approach that includes acceptance tests that offer the jumpstart for the GSE and serve as a concept for communication between the BTM, the business users and the BTP's developers. The used agile approach and acceptance tests are implemented in prose so that business system users can understand the business system that is assisted by a KM system. The BDD comprises an internal mapping subsystem to link prose to GSE code. The prose scenarios contain information to automate the linkage of the needed GSE classes and the BTP's team-members. This can assist in adding code snippets to the generated microartefact. The BDD enables a semi-automatic acceptance tests integration with the architecture iterations that map to the GSE's project Design Driven Development concept (Lazar, Motogna, & Parv, 2010).

The Architecture Critical Success Factors

Based on the literature review, the most important architecture CSFs that are used are shown in Table 3.

The Modules Chained Link to the Knowledge Aspects

This section's deduction is that the application of a knowledge and intelligence unit driven development is central for the KMGSE.

Table 3. The critical success factors that have an average of 7.2

Critical Success Factors	KPIs	Weightings
CSF_ArchInt_Method	ComplexToImplement ▾	From 1 to 10. **5 Selected**
CSF_ArchInt_TDD	Mature ▾	From 1 to 10. **10 Selected**
CSF_ArchInt_ATDD	Laborious ▾	From 1 to 10. **8 Selected**
CSF_ArchInt_BDD	NotAdapted ▾	From 1 to 10. **4 Selected**
CSF_ArchInt_DDD	Essential ▾	From 1 to 10. **9 Selected**

KNOWLEDGE AND INTELLIGENCE UNITS DRIVEN DEVELOPMENT

Unit of Work

To define the KMGSE's unit of work, the alignment and classification of all the BTP's resources must be enabled using the "1:1" mapping concept. In this research the KMGSE microartefact is used that can be represented with a class diagram and can be represented by means of extensible Mark-up Language (XML). Such a mapping concept is based on a naming convention that links all the BTP's resources. These resources can be one of the following artefacts' standard formats:

- The Unified Modelling Language's (UML) format to describe static or dynamic BTP artefacts.
- Architecture and design patterns and using their XML interfaces to be used to structure the microartefacts.
- The Entity Relational Modelling (ERM) using the XML Scheme Diagrams (XSD) format to model the KMGSE global data model.
- Test Driven Development (TDD) and other driven development formats to implement the GSE's global tests.
- Behaviour Driven Development (BDD) format to describe the microartefacts behaviour.

Standard Engineering Patterns

Defining the unit of work for a GSE using the "1:1" concept, serves as a concrete microartefact that can be represented with a class diagram, where mapping supports the interoperability between all the BTP's microartefacts that are compatible with the following standards:

- Knowledge management XML standard to import and export knowledge items (Feljan, Karapantelakis, Mokrushin, Liang, Inam, Fersman, & Souza, 2017).
- The Unified Modelling Language's (UML) and the System Modelling XML (SysML) for the design of the KMGSE microartefacts.
- Design patterns and their XML interfaces for the structural design of the KMGSE microartefacts.
- The Project Management XML (PMXML) for the project coordination of the KMGSE microartefacts.

- The Service Oriented Architecture XML (SoaML) and the Web Services XML (WSDL) for the communication between the KMGSE microartefacts.
- The Business Process Modelling Notation (BPMN) and the Business Process Execution Language (BPEL), can be used for the design of the KMGSE microartefacts.
- The client-side frameworks to build dynamic front-ends.

Knowledge Patterns

The knowledge pattern contains a mapping concept in XML format that insures the interoperability between all the KMGSE microartefacts; these resources can conform to the following standards:

- The Project Management XML (PMXML) part is used by the project management to synchronize the project development cycles.
- The Architecture XML (ArchiXML) format to interchange between various phases.
- The Information Technology Infrastructure Library (ITIL) that uses the Data Centre XML (DCML) format to describe the microartefacts platform characteristics.
- The Control Objectives for Information and Related Technology (COBIT) using the Governance, Risk, and Compliance XML (GRC-XML) format to control the BTP's IS.
- The Business Reporting XML (XBRL) format for the accounting of the KMGSE microartefacts.

Functional Environments

Many functional development environments, libraries exist, like for example the (Moore, 2014; North, 2010):

- Artificial intelligence and expert systems for various application domains.
- Features that are supported by BDD supports concepts of Neuro Linguistic Programming (NLP) and hard systems thinking.
- NLP supports neural network that forms the business intelligence application's infrastructure.

KMGSEs uses BDD and NLP like interpreted scripts that are compiled and executed in real-time; such operations can be done by business professionals with no prior computer science background. That is why the authors recommend an interpretable NLP based KMGSE microartefacts.

The Knowledge Management Success Factors

Based on the literature review, the most important knowledge CSFs that are used are shown in Table 4.

The Modules Chained Link to the Intelligence or Decision System Aspects

Due to the CSFs, this section's deduction is that decision making is central for the KMGSEs.

INTELLIGENCE AND DECISION SYSTEMS

Complex systems modelling refers to classical operational research, systems analysis and global systems engineering; which is optimal for KM systems, enterprise architecture and BTPs. Complex systems modelling is an approach for solving complex problems in KM and operational situations and it replaces science experimentation labs with a set of applied mathematics/heuristics models that simulate project KM requests and deliver information and/or decisions in the form of solutions. The Complex systems KM requests are adapted to BTP problems and requests (Daellenbach & McNickle, 2005). BTP KM requests are processed by using the *Environment's* heuristics module, as shown in Figure 8 that in turn are based on the selected critical success areas and factors.

Table 4. The critical success factors that have an average of 7.7

Critical Success Factors	KPIs	Weightings
CSF_KM_UnitOfWork	Exist	From 1 to 10. **8 Selected**
CSF_KM_StandardEngineeringPatterns	Usable	From 1 to 10. **7 Selected**
CSF_KM_FunctionalDevelopment	Operational	From 1 to 10. **9 Selected**
CSF_KM_KnowledgePatterns	NeedsHolisticModelling	From 1 to 10. **6 Selected**

Figure 8. Complex system's approach
Source: Daellenbach & McNickle, 2005

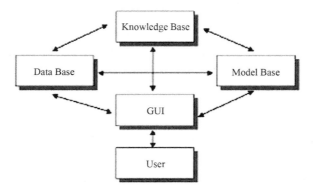

Knowledge Management Resources, Artefacts and Factors

The *Environment's* mapping concept is used to relate and assemble the BTP's resources. This concept is used to manage autonomic KM microartefacts' instances in all of the GSE's phase; and it is based on an iterative model that maps all the KM's items to CSFs (The Open Group, 2011a). The BTP's KM system has to identify the initial set of CSFs to be used, as shown in Figure 9.

Figure 9. The knowledge management subsystem

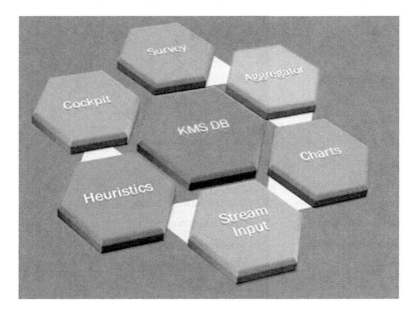

The Microartefacts' Distributed Model

The proposed KMGSE integrates the AMM nomenclature that is presented to the reader in a simplified form to be easily understandable on the cost of a holistic formulation vision. The KM uses the AMM that is formalized as shown in Figure 10.

As shown in Figure 10, the symbol $\sum$ indicates summation of all the relevant named set members, while the indices and the set cardinality have been omitted. The summation should be understood in a broader sense, more like set unions.

The Knowledge Management Requests Processing

A KMGSE must be managed by the existing *Environment*, where the KM officer configures the types of KM microartefacts to be involved; these microartefacts are orchestrated by the AMM actions to deliver possible information. The KMGSE actions map to the various processes, found in TOGAF's phases, which are responsible for the implementation of mechanisms needed to deliver the infrastructure. The KMGSE pattern is implemented in all of the BTP's components and the implementation of KM mechanisms should be able to deliver the requested knowledge resources; such a set of actions can be modelled and managed by the AMM (The Open Group, 2011a; Trad & Kalpić, 2017a; Trad & Kalpić, 2017b; Trad & Kalpić, 2017c).

Figure 10. The applied mathematical model's nomenclature
Source: Trad, & Kalpić, 2017a

AMM

$$mcRequirement = KPI \tag{1}$$

$$CSF = \sum KPI \tag{2}$$
$$CSA = \sum CSF \tag{3}$$
$$Requirement = \sum mcRequirement \tag{4}$$

$$(e)neuron = action + mcIntelligenceArtefact \tag{5}$$

$$mcArtefact = \sum (e)neurons \tag{6}$$
$$mcEnterprise = \sum mcArtefact \tag{7}$$
$$(e)Enterprise = \sum mcEnterprise \tag{8}$$

$$mcArtefactScenario = \sum mcArtefactDecisionMaking \tag{9}$$

$$IntelligenceComponent = \sum mcArtefactScenario \tag{10}$$

$$OrganisationalIntelligence = \sum IntelligenceComponent \tag{11}$$

$$AMM = ADM + OrganisationalIntelligence \tag{12}$$

A Quantitative-Qualitative Research Mixed Model

A problem, RQ, CSF or phenomenon are examined in iterations relating breadth and depth, using heuristics/beam search, which is specialized for unknown problems or the ones that appear in a preliminary phase or first iterations. Then, the *TKM&F* qualitative research module input data stream(s) consist(s) of sets of numbers that are collected from sets generated by using designed/structured and approved/validated data object-collection modules and statistically processed.

The Applied Enterprise Mathematical Model

The DMS is based on the KMGSE concept which in turn applies the AMM. The DMS is a part of the *Environment* that uses [2] to support just-in-time decision-making. The DMS, as shown in Figure 11, is based on a light version of the ADM.

The Enterprise AMM (EAMM) is the combination of an enterprise architecture and transformation methodologies.

The Applied Transformation Model

The transformation is the combination of an enterprise architecture methodology like the Open group's methodology and the AMM that can be modelled after the following formula for the Transformational Model (TM):

TM = Enterprise Architecture + AMM (1).

Figure 11. The enterprise model

Model's nomenclature

mcEnterprise	A micro enterprise component
mcRequirement	A micro requirement
mcArtefact	A microartefact
action (or action)	An atomic service (or neuron) execution scheme
mcIntelligenceArtefact	A set that contains: dynamic basic intelligence + governance + persistence+ traceability + data_xsd + resources
mcArtefactDecisionMaking	A microartefact_decision making entity
mcArtefactScenario	A microartefact scenario

(KMGSE):
KMGSE = Knowledge database + AMM (2).

The KMGSE is based on a concurrent and synchronized framework which uses threads that can make various models run in parallel and exchange dynamically knowledge resources through a mathematical choreography.

The Applied Decision System's Critical Success Factors

Based on the literature review, the most important DMS CSFs that were used are shown in Table 5.

The table 5 shows that the KMGSE implementation is very risky and that a positive domain is the DMS.

THE MODEL IMPLEMENTATION

The Proof of Concept

The KMGSE Proof of Concept (PoC) was implemented using the research's *Environment* that had been developed using the Microsoft Visual Studio .NET and Java. The PoC is based on the DMS and the CSFs' binding to a specific research resources, where the KM system was designed using an enterprise architecture tool. The KM processing model represents the relationships between this research's requirements, knowledge microartefacts (or building blocks), unique identifiers and the CSFs.

The proof of concept was achieved using the development environment and the research framework that is shown in Figure 12. The KMGSE uses services that make calls to DMS as shown in Figure 13.

Table 5. The critical success factors that have an average of 9.0

Critical Success Factors	KPIs		Weightings
CSF_DMS_KM_CSFs	Integrated	▼	From 1 to 10. **10 Selected**
CSF_DMS_KM_MicroartefactsModel	Synchronized	▼	From 1 to 10. **8 Selected**
CSF_DMS_KM_RequestsProcessing	Built	▼	From 1 to 10. **9 Selected**
CSF_DMS_KM_AMM	Built	▼	From 1 to 10. **10 Selected**
CSF_DMS_KM_TM	Built	▼	From 1 to 10. **10 Selected**

Figure 12. The Environment frontend

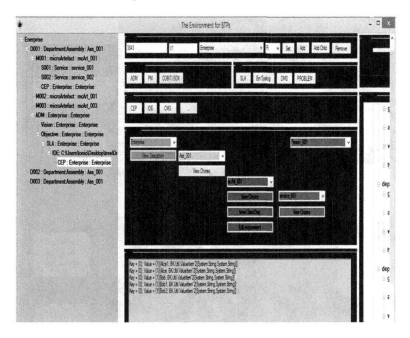

KM related CSFs were selected as demonstrated previously in this article's tables and the result of the processing of the DMS, as illustrated in Table 6, shows clearly that the KMGSE is not an independent component and in fact it is strongly bonded to the BTP's overall risk architecture.

The model's main constraint is that CSAs, having an average result below 8.5, will be ignored. This fact keeps the Standards Mapping and Architecture's CSAs (marked in green) that helps to make this work's conclusion; and drops the information system, knowledge management's and architecture' CSAs marked in red. It means that such a KMGSE transformation will surely face failure and that the KMGSE must be done in multiple transformation projects, where the first one should try to transform the base systems, the information system and the architecture paradigm.

SOLUTION AND RECOMMENDATIONS

In this article that is related to the KMGSE transformation, the authors propose the following set of architecture, technical and managerial recommendations:

- A GSE concept must be established and tried for its feasibility.

Figure 13. The research flow

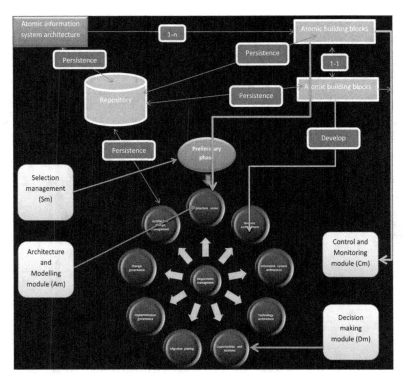

Table 6. The knowledge management research's outcome

CSA Category of CSFs/KPIs	Influences Knowledge management	Average Result
The Information System	Built on silos/difficult to transform ▾	From 1 to 10. 4.33
The global software engineering standards	Complex to adaopt ▾	From 1 to 10. 7.00
The Knowledge Management	Difficut to implement ▾	From 1 to 10. 7.70
The Architecture	Very heavy ▾	From 1 to 10. 7.2
The DMS	Implementable ▾	From 1 to 10. 9.00

- A BTP must build a global knowledge management concept that is a part of the DMS.
- Enormous efforts must be applied to integrate underlying global information system to support the knowledge management. Here the main problem is alignment because software blocks are silos.
- KM should replace traditional obsolete knowledge management systems.
- The architecture development method's integration in a KM system enables the automation of all its knowledge and decision activities.
- The BTP must be separated in multiple transformation projects, where the first one should attempt to transform the information system and the global architecture.

FUTURE RESEARCH DIRECTIONS

The *Environment* future research efforts will focus on the various software engineering domains like configuration management and automated tests in transformational initiatives in a cross-functional environment.

CONCLUSION

This research phase is part of a series of publications related to BTPs and enterprise architectures. This research is based on mixed action research model; where critical success factors and areas are offered to help BTP architects to diminish the chances of failure when building knowledge systems. In this article, the focus is on knowledge management systems. KMGSE describes a structured inter-relationship development of various knowledge fields and the implementation of knowledge artefacts and mechanisms. The KMGSE component's global software engineering is an important factor for the business information system's evolution. The most important managerial recommendation that was generated by the previous research phases was that the business transformation manager must be an architect of adaptive business systems.

The PoC was based on the CSFs' binding to a specific research resources and the reasoning model represents the relationships between this research's requirements, microartefacts and the CSFs. The result implies that an attempt of transformation is dangerously prone to failure. To avoid this scenario, we recommend to perform the BTP through multiple independent transformation projects, where the task of the first ones is to transform the information system and global architecture.

ACKNOWLEDGMENT

In a work as large as this research project, technical, typographical, grammatical, or other kinds of errors are bound to be present. Ultimately, all mistakes are the authors' responsibility. Nevertheless, the authors encourage feedback from readers, identifying errors in addition to comments on the work in general. It was our great pleasure to prepare this work. Now our greater hopes are for readers to receive some small measure of that pleasure.

REFERENCES

Cearley, D., Walker, M., & Burke, B. (2016). Top 10 Strategic Technology Trends for 2017. *Gartner.* Retrieved from https://www.gartner.com/doc/3471559?plc=ddp

Daellenbach, H., & McNickle, D. (2012). *Management Science - Decision-making through systems thinking* (2nd ed.). Palgrave Macmillan.

Design Patterns. (2015). Design Patterns for TDD and DDD. Retrieved from https://8408bcbcd6613c300fa58123cb291b2defe56766.googledrive.com/host/0Bwf9odcK3Cu0bFAzS3kzTDI4Tms/

Feljan, A. V., Karapantelakis, A., Mokrushin, L., Liang, H., Inam, R., Fersman, E., & Souza, R. S. (2017). *A Framework for Knowledge Management and Automated Reasoning Applied on Intelligent Transport Systems.* Academic Press.

Gardner, H. (1999). *Intelligence Reframed: Multiple Intelligences for the 21st Century.* New York, NY: Basic Books.

Greefhorst, D. (2009). *Using the Open Group's Architecture Framework as a pragmatic approach to architecture.* Informatica.

Gunasekare, U. (2015). Mixed Research Method as the Third Research Paradigm: A Literature Review. *International Journal of Science and Research, 4*(8).

Koskela, L. (2007). *Test driven: practical tdd and acceptance tdd for java developers.* Greenwich, CT: Manning Publications.

Lanubile, F., Ebert, C., Prikladnicki, R., & Vizcaíno, A. (2010). Collaboration Tools for Global Software Engineering. *IEEE Journals & Magazines, 27*(2).

Lazar, I., Motogna, S., & Parv, B. (2010). Behaviour-Driven Development of Foundational UML Components. Department of Computer Science. Cluj-Napoca, Romania: Babes-Bolyai University. doi:10.1016/j.entcs.2010.07.007

MID. (2014). *Enterprise Architecture Modeling with ArchiMate*. MID GmbH.

Moore, J. (2014). *Java programming with lambda expressions-A mathematical example demonstrates the power of lambdas in Java 8*. Retrieved from http://www.javaworld.com/article/2092260/java-se/java-programming-with-lambda-expressions.html

Neumann, G. (2002). Programming Languages in Artificial Intelligence. In Bidgoli (Ed.), Encyclopedia of Information Systems (pp. 31-45). San Diego, CA: Academic Press.

North, N. (2010). *Behaviour-Driven Development Writing software that matters*. DRW Publications.

Peterson, S. (2011). *Why it Worked: Critical Success Factors of a Financial Reform Project in Africa*. Faculty Research Working Paper Series. Cambridge, MA: Harvard Kennedy School.

Selic, B. (2003). The pragmatics of model-driven development. *IEEE Software, 20*(5).

Seth, N., & Khare, R. (2015). ACI (Automated Continuous Integration) using Jenkins: Key for successful embedded software development. In *Recent Advances in Engineering & Computational Sciences (RAECS), 2015 2nd International Conference on* (pp. 1-6). IEEE.

Shafique, M., & Labiche, Y. (2010). *A systematic review of model based testing tool support*. Carleton University.

The Open Group. (2011a). *Architecture Development Method*. The Open Group. USA. Retrieved from http://pubs.opengroup.org/architecture/togaf9-doc/arch/chap05.html

Thomas, A. (2015). *Gartner, Innovation Insight for Microservices*. Stamford, CT: Gartner.

Tidd, J. (2006). *From Knowledge Management to Strategic Competence* (2nd ed.). London, UK: Imperial College. doi:10.1142/p439

Trad, A. (2018a). *The Business Transformation Framework's Resources Library. Internal project*. IBISTM.

Trad, A. (2018b). *The Transformation Framework Proof of Concept. Internal project and paper*. IBISTM.

Trad, A. (2018c). The Transformation Framework's Resources Library. IBISTM.

Trad, A. (2018d). *The Transformation Framework Proof of Concept*. IBISTM.

Trad, A., & Kalpić, D. (2017a). *An Intelligent Neural Networks Micro Artefact Patterns' Based Enterprise Architecture Model*. Hershey, PA: IGI-Global.

Trad, A., & Kalpić, D. (2017b). *A Neural Networks Portable and Agnostic Implementation Environment for Business Transformation Projects. The Basic Structure*. Annecy, France: IEEE. doi:10.1109/CIVEMSA.2017.7995318

Trad, A., & Kalpić, D. (2017c). *A Neural Networks Portable and Agnostic Implementation Environment for Business Transformation Projects. The Framework*. Annecy, France: IEEE. doi:10.1109/CIVEMSA.2017.7995319

Trad, A., & Kalpić, D. (2018a). *The Business Transformation Framework and Enterprise Architecture Framework for Managers in Business Innovation-Knowledge and Intelligence Driven Development (KIDD)*. In Encyclopedia of E-Commerce Development, Implementation, and Management. Hershey, PA: IGI-Global.

Trad, A., & Kalpić, D. (2018a). *An applied mathematical model for business transformation-The Holistic Critical Success Factors Management System (HCSFMS)*. In Encyclopaedia of E-Commerce Development, Implementation, and Management. Hershey, PA: IGI-Global.

ADDITIONAL READING

Capgemini (2007). *Trends in Business transformation - Survey of European Executives*. Capgemini Consulting and the Economist Intelligence Unit. France.

Daellenbach, H., McNickle, D., & Dye, Sh. (2012). *Management Science. Decision-making through systems thinking* (2nd ed.). USA: Palgrave Macmillian.

Farhoomand, A. (2004). *Managing (e)business transformation*. UK: Palgrave Macmillan. doi:10.1007/978-1-137-08380-7

IBM. (2009). *TOGAF or not TOGAF: Extending Enterprise Architecture beyond RUP*. USA: IBM Developer Works.

Maier, R. (2009). *Knowledge Management Systems: Information and Communication Technologies for Knowledge Management Paperback*. Germany: Springer.

KEY TERMS AND DEFINITIONS

ADM: Architecture development method.

Critical Success Factors: Can be used to manage the statuses and gaps in various project plans and give projects the capacity to proactively and automatically recognize erroneous building blocks and to just-in-time reschedule the project plan(s).

DMS: Decision making systems.

EMS: Enterprise knowledge management.

Environment: Is this research's framework.

GSE: Global software engineering.

KIDP: Knowledge and intelligence design pattern.

KMGSE: Knowledge management and global software engineering.

KMS: Knowledge management system.

Manager: Business transformation manager.

Project: Business transformation project.

TOGAF: The Open Group's architecture framework.

Chapter 3

Software Development for Ergonomic Compatibility Assessment of Advanced Manufacturing Technology

Arturo Realyvásquez
iD https://orcid.org/0000-0003-2825-
2595
*Instituto Tecnológico de Tijuana,
Mexico*

Aide Aracely Maldonado-Macías
*Autonomous University of Ciudad
Juárez, Mexico*

Guadalupe Hernández-Escobedo
iD https://orcid.org/0000-0002-7516-972X
*Tecnológico Nacional de México, Mexico & Instituto Tecnológico de Tijuana,
Mexico*

ABSTRACT

Ergonomic assessment of advanced manufacturing technology (AMT) involves several attributes. Most of these attributes can be assessed only subjectively. Several models have been developed to assess AMT from an ergonomic approach. However, these models have several deficiencies, such as 1) assessment for all alternatives in all their ergonomic attributes should be done in a single period. It lacks time pauses when decision-makings include several decisors and alternatives, 2) every person can access the information and change it, and 3) they lack the propriety of correcting mistakes once users (or decisors) have entered an unwished data. Then, the objective of this research is to develop a software for the ergonomic assessment of AMT that deletes these deficiencies. As method, axiomatic design (AD) was applied jointly with the TRIZ methodology. Software was validated with results of a previous case study. Finally, authors developed a software that removed the deficiencies of previous models.

DOI: 10.4018/978-1-5225-9448-2.ch003

INTRODUCTION

Currently, ergonomic assessment covers several aspects, such as physical and psychological characteristics of employees, workstations design, physical environment conditions, organizational conditions, and technology (Carayon et al., 2006; Realyvásquez, Maldonado-Macías, García-Alcaraz, & Arana, 2018). Specifically, for the ergonomic assessment of advanced manufacturing technology (AMT), Maldonado-Macías (2009) developed a mathematical model. This model helps in the planning and selection of AMT and it includes the ergonomic attributes shown in Figure 1. Also, this model includes an Ergonomic Compatibility Evaluation Questionnaire (ECEC), which contains questions to determine the relative weighting of attributes by means of the Analytic Hierarchy Process (AHP) methodology.

However, this model has the deficiency that calculations must be done by hand, that is, there is no software that allows to calculate the weightings of the ergonomic attributes and make a decision to select AMT alternatives. Because of this, Maldonado-Macías, Guillén-Anaya, Barrón-Díaz, & García-Alcaraz (2011) created a software to calculate the weightings of ergonomic attributes of AMT. This software allows to decide for the best AMT alternative from and ergonomic perspective. Later, Realyvásquez-Vargas, Maldonado-Macías, García-Alcaraz, & Alvarado-Iniesta (2014) developed an expert system based on fuzzy rules. Nevertheless, both the software proposed by Maldonado-Macías et al. (2011) and the expert system developed by Realyvásquez-Vargas et al. (2014) have the following disadvantages:

Figure 1. Ergonomic attributes for AMT
Source: (Maldonado-Macías, 2009)

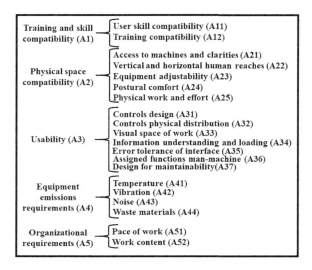

1) assessment for all alternatives in all their ergonomic attributes should be done in a single period, it lacks time pauses when decision-makings include several decisors and alternatives, 2) every person can access to the information and change it, and 3) they lack the propriety of correcting mistakes once users (or decisors) have entered an unwished data. All these characteristics represent a disadvantage in the demand of the current pace of life and work. Then, the objective of this research is to develop a software for the ergonomic assessment of AMT that provides the following advantages:

- Provide pauses and password for the assessment process, so this process can be done in different periods and information is saved and secured.
- Close sessions after a specific inactive time.
- Mistakes can be corrected.
- Users have different roles: administrator, creator of evaluation, and evaluator.
- Provide the result in a graphical way.

To achieve this objective, the technique of axiomatic design (AD) can be applied.

LITERATURE REVIEW

Axiomatic Design

Currently, axiomatic design (AD) is one of the most frequently applied engineering theories and methodologies in the academic literature and industrial practices (Farid, 2016; Tomiyama et al., 2009). It was proposed by Nam P. Suh due to the need to make the field of design more than a science rather than an art (Farid, 2016; Suh, 1990, 2001). The most distinguishing characteristic of AD is the use of design axioms, which guide the designer through the engineering process. At the beginning, AD was applied only in Suh's home field, i.e., mechanical engineering of products (Farid, 2016; Suh, 1990). Today, AD has expanded to other disciplines, including software and complex systems in the twenty first-century (Do & Suh, 1999; Farid, 2016; Kim, Suh, & Kim, 1991; Suh, 1995), to support the design of a wide variety of systems (software, manufacturing systems, organizations, and products, for instance). This successful expansion into new design applications of ever larger system scale has suggested a degree of universality to AD as a theory (Farid, 2016). The main objective of AD is to determine the best designs among the proposed design, to increase creativity, to minimize the iterative trial-and-error process, and to reduce the random search process. It requires a continuous interplay between what customers/designers want to achieve and how they want to achieve it (Hirani & Suh, 2005; Suh, 1990, 2001).

According to (Suh, 2001), the world of design is made up of four domains: 1) the customer domain, 2) the functional domain, 3) the physical domain, and 4) the process domain. Figure 2 shows the domain structure. The domain on the left represents "what we want to achieve", whereas the domain on the right represents the design solution, "how we propose to satisfy the requirements specified by the customers". The design process begins with the customer domain and finishes with the process domain. However, as design process is iterative, the designer can go back to the customer domain. Firstly, in the customer domain, AD establishes the customer needs (CNs) that the is looking for to satisfy in a product, process, system, or material. Then, in the functional domain, functional requirements (FRs) and constraints (Cs) of the system to be designed are determined to meet CNs. The next step is to match these FRs to design parameters (DPs), which are conceive in the physical domain. This step allows to identify and choose the DPs necessary for the design of the system. Once the DPs are chosen, designers must go to the process domain and identify the process variables (PVs) based on the creation of a new process or the use of an existing process (Suh, 1998).

AD theory is composed of two key axioms: 1) independent axiom and 2) information axiom. The first axiom refers that independence of functional requirements must be always preserved. When there are two or more FRs, one of the FRS should not affect the other FRs. In this manner, designer has to select the proper DPS to satisfy the FRs independently. This is done one to one in a mapping process between one FR and the corresponding DP (Won & Joon, 2005).

Accordingly, the application of this axiom determines coupled, decoupled and uncoupled designs. An ideal design is an uncoupled design, where one DP can satisfy each FR independently. However, these designs are commonly difficult to achieve, and decoupled designs can be acceptable designs as well. Both uncoupled and coupled designs satisfy the independence axiom. In the other hand, a coupled

Figure 2. Domains of AD
Source: (Suh, 2001)

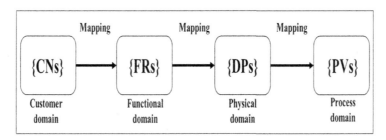

design exists when DPs and FRs cannot be satisfied independently. In this case, designers must work creatively to change the product to a decoupled or uncoupled design. Once the first axiom is accomplished, the second axiom is also required for better designs. The information axiom explains that in all good designs information content must be the minimum. This axiom establishes the idea that the success of a design is determined by the probability associated with achieving the FRs. This probability decreases with the amount of information necessary to fulfill the FRs (Lenz & Cochran, 2000).

AD theory has been applied successfully to the design of products, organizations and systems. For instance, (O Kulak, Cebi, & Kahraman, 2010) present a literature review of AD applications. Among these applications, they mention that 20 authors, such as (Ferrer, Rios, & Ciurana, 2009; Gumus, Ertas, Tate, & Cicek, 2008; Tang, Zhang, & Dai, 2009), applied AD to product design; whereas 9 authors, included (Bang & Heo, 2009; Helander, 2007; Lo & Helander, 2007) applied AD to system design. Also, literature review mention that 7 authors applied AD to manufacturing system design. Some of these authors are (Durmusoglu & Kulak, 2008; Nakao, Kobayashi, Hamada, Totsuka, & Yamada, 2007; Schnetzler, Sennheiser, & Schönsleben, 2007). Similarly, AD was applied by 11 authors, such as (Lindkvist & SÖDerberg, 2003; Togay, Dogru, & Tanik, 2008; Yi & Park, 2005), to software design. Finally, 13 authors applied AD to decision making. These authors include (Celik, 2009a, 2009c; Celik, Cebi, Kahraman, & Er, 2009a). Appendix 1 (Table 4) shows a more complete literature review of applications of AD (O Kulak et al., 2010).

Despite its multiple applications, some authors claim that to solve design problems, AD by itself is not enough, so it requires the support of several techniques and methodologies for FRs determination and enhance creative solutions; so it has been applied in combination with Failure Mode Error Analysis (FMEA), Design for six sigma (DFSS), TRIZ (Theory of inventive problem solving technique) and decision support multiattribute methods, among others (Dickinson, 2006; Realyvásquez, Hernández-Escobedo, & Maldonado-Macías, 2018).

TRIZ

TRIZ is a Russian acronym for the Theory of Inventive Problem Solving. It was proposed by Altshuller and originated from several technical and patent information studies. The latter showed that only 1% of the solutions were truly pioneering inventions; the rest represented the use of previously known ideas and concepts but in a novel way (Altshuller, 1984; Yang & Zhang, 2000a). This led to the conclusion that the idea of a design solution to a problem might be already known. But where and how this idea can be found? Based on a systematic view of the technical world,

TRIZ provides different techniques and tools that help designers create a new design idea and avoid numerous trials and errors during the problem solving process (Yang & Zhang, 2000a).

According to several authors, TRIZ is a powerful systematic ideation methodology for technical problem solving that leads to the enhancement of existent techniques (Kremer et al., 2012; Savransky, 2000). Moreover, TRIZ is a human-oriented knowledge-based systematic methodology of inventive problem solving (Savransky, 2000). In TRIZ, every factor that affects a system can be defined as a parameter, and there is a dependency relationship among system parameters. TRIZ structures a problem into a "contradiction statement" and derives solutions that address the problem statement both from technical and system perspectives. Hence, the ideality of the design increases as a parameter is improved without worsening the other parameter. In this sense, TRIZ demonstrates its capability as a support tool for original idea creation.

Despite the success of TRIZ in aiding idea generation, if implemented alone, TRIZ falls short in selecting the most appropriate idea. Therefore, using it in unison with appropriate tools – such as AD, in this study – is strongly recommended (Kremer et al., 2012).

TRIZ comprises 40 inventive principles to guide the TRIZ practitioner in developing useful concepts of solution for inventive situations (Yang & Zhang, 2000a). Each solution represents a recommendation to make a specific change in a system and eliminate technical contradictions. The literature provides a contradiction table that recommends which principles should be considered in solving approximately 1,250 contradictions. Five of these 40 inventive principles are stated below (Altshuller, 2002; Technical Innovation Center, 2013):

- **Segmentation:** Divide an object into independent parts, make an object sectional (for easy assembly or disassembly) or increase the degree of an object's segmentation.
- **Local quality:** Each part of an object should be placed under conditions that are most favorable for its operation.
- **Nesting:** One object is placed inside another. That object is placed inside a third one, and so on.
- **Prior action:** Place objects in advance so that they can go into action immediately from the most convenient location.
- **Periodic action:** Replace a continuous action with a periodic one (impulse). If the action is already periodic, change its frequency. Use pauses between impulses to provide additional action.

In the last decade, various works have illustrated the advantages of combining TRIZ and AD and have reported how these techniques complement each other (Realyvásquez, Hernández-Escobedo, et al., 2018). AD analyzes the problem and structures it in the most suitable way, whereas TRIZ can solve the minimum number of design conflicts that are intrinsically present in a case study (Borgianni & Matt, 2016). That said, when TRIZ is combined with AD, it can analyze a complex problem and deduce the most relevant conflicts, since TRIZ uses AD to appropriately structure the problem. Similarly, AD is useful for analyzing the system and its requirements, but it completely lacks means to identify technical solutions. These solutions, according to the axioms that guide the design process, should be appropriately characterized by satisfying performances for each requirement and high controllability of the system. In conclusion, both methods – TRIZ and AD – can be applied jointly thanks to the not contradictory objectives they have. Appendix 2 (Table 5) shows a more complete literature review of applications of TRIZ (Shirwaiker & Okudan, 2008).

METHODOLOGY

To design the software, authors propose a cross-sectional, non-experimental methodology that comprises six stages. The following sections review the used instruments and thoroughly discuss the methodology stages.

Instruments

Authors rely on the following instruments to design the software and satisfy the users' needs:

- **Computer Equipment:** Laptop Toshiba Satellite C645d and Dell Inspiron 7567
- **Visual Studio 2015**
- **Server AWS**

Method

As previously mentioned, the methodology followed to design the software comprises six stages as depicted in Figure 3.

Stage 1. State User' Needs (UNs): Authors define the user's needs (UNs) that had to be satisfied by the software. These UNs are defined based on deficiencies of before versions of the software.

Figure 3. Methodology proposed to design the software
Source: Prepared by the authors (2018)

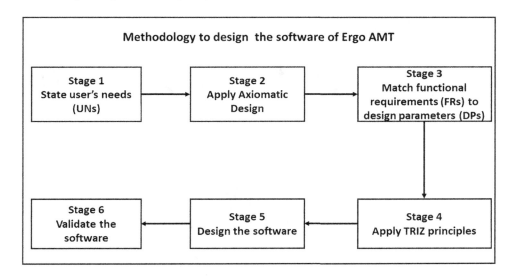

Stage 2. Apply Axiomatic Design: Once the UNs are identified, authors define the FRs of the design that have to satisfy such UNs. Also, authors set the constraints that will limit the design of the software.

Stage 3. Match FRs to DPs: At this stage, each FR is assigned a DP that will allow the software to meet the said FR. The DPs correspond to buttons that perform a specific function that helps to meet the UNs.

Stage 4. Apply TRIZ Principles: Once authors have defined the UNs, FRs, Cs, and DPs, they apply the five TRIZ principles mentioned above. These principles help to find an easy way that DPs can meet the FRs.

- **Segmentation:** This principle is applied to divide the evaluation process performed by users (decisors). In the Matlab version developed by Realyvásquez-Vargas et al. (2014) there is only one line of waiting (as shown in Figure 4a). This line includes all the users, and then, if there are n users, user n has to wait for the $n – 1$ user to finish. Now, by applying the segmentation principle, this line of waiting is divided individually, (as shown in Figure 4b) and users do not have to wait another user finishes the evaluation to perform their one. Figure 4 shows a graphical analogy of before and after applying the segmentation principle.

Figure 4. The case of the segmentation principle: a) waiting line for evaluation before applying the principle, b) no waiting line after applying the principle
Source: Prepared by the authors (2018)

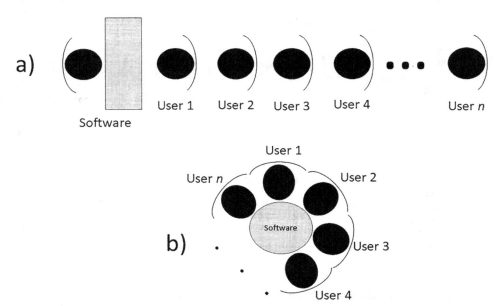

- **Local Quality:** This principle is used to placed buttons and specific commands in parts on where the user is familiar to find them. For example, the button Save button is placed up on the left, whereas the command "Close the window (×)" is placed up on the right. Figure 5 shows the example of this principle.
- **Nesting:** Authors apply this principle to place the ergonomic sub-attributes inside the attributes. Also, this principle is applied to place some commands inside other commands. For instance, the command Save and the command Close are placed inside the command File. Figure 6 shows the example of this principle.
- **Prior Action:** This principle is applied together with the local quality principle, since most commonly known buttons (for instance Save, Close) are placed strategically so the users can find them easily, as users are familiar with them in other softwares.
- **Periodic Action:** This principle is applied to replace a continuous evaluation, i.e., replace an evaluation that has to be performed at only one moment, with an evaluation that can be performed in pauses when required.

Figure 5. Example of the local quality principle for the command "Close the window (×)"
Source: Prepared by the authors (2018)

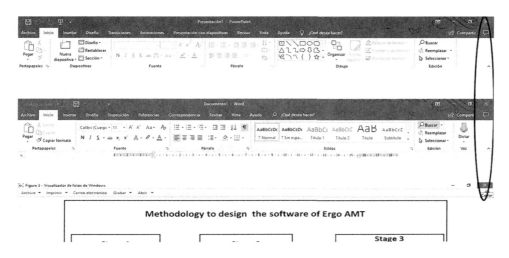

Figure 6. Example of the nesting principle for different commands and subcommands
Source: Prepared by the authors (2018)

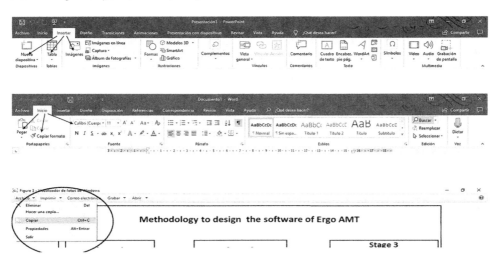

Stage 5. Design the Software: Once materials, UNs, FRs, Cs, and DPs were available, authors begin to design the software. Firstly, a planning of the structure of the software and the database is carried out. Then, the database is created according to the FRs. The next step is to codify the software. Once software is codified, a user-friendly graphical interface is designed. Later, the database is inserted in a server and connected in the cloud to a desktop application. Finally, pilot tests were performed.

Stage 6. Validate the Software: Validation of the software is performed by means of contrasting the results of a previous case study performed by Realyvásquez-Vargas et al. (2014) with the results given by the software. The previous case study is the case of Computer Integrated Manufacturing (CIM). In this case, two alternatives were assessed by three experts. Table 1 shows the linguistic assessment inputs provided by the three experts on the two alternatives. In Table 1, P = Poor, R = Regular, G = Good, VG = Very Good, E = Excellent, VL = Very Low, L = Low, M = Medium, H = High, VH = Very High.

Table 2 shows the results obtained by for the case study of CIM. In Table 2, EIC = ergonomic incompatibility content, therefor, the best alternative is the one with the less value of EIC, i.e., the alternative Y.

If final decision is the same, the software is validated.

Table 1. Assessments given by the experts in the case of CIM

Sub-attributes	Alternatives	Experts' assessments		
		E1	E2	E3
A111		G	VG	G
A112		R	G	R
A121		R	G	VG
A122		G	G	VG
A123		G	G	VG
A124		R	G	VG
A125		M	L	L
A131	X	G	G	G
A132		G	VG	VG
A133		G	VG	VG
A134		G	VG	G
A135		G	G	G
A136		R	VG	G
A137		R	G	P
A141		L	L	VL

continued on following page

Table 1. Continued

Sub-attributes	Alternatives	Experts' assessments		
		E1	E2	E3
A142		L	M	L
A143		M	M	M
A144		M	M	L
A151		G	VG	G
A152		G	VG	VG
A111		G	VG	G
A112		G	VG	R
A121		G	E	R
A122		G	VG	G
A123		G	VG	G
A124		R	VG	G
A125		M	L	L
A131		G	VG	G
A132		G	VG	G
A133	Y	R	VG	G
A134		G	VG	G
A135		R	G	G
A136		G	VG	G
A137		R	VG	P
A141		L	VL	VL
A142		L	L	L
A143		M	M	M
A144		L	M	L
A151		G	VG	G
A152		G	VG	G

Source: (Realyvásquez-Vargas et al., 2014)

Table 2. Results for the case of CIM

	Alternative	
	X	Y
EIC	0.9117	0.8383

Source: (Realyvásquez-Vargas et al., 2014)

RESULTS

The results of the proposed design methodology are mentioned below:

Results for Stage 1

Along the before versions (paper and Matlab®) of the model to evaluate the ergonomic compatibility of AMT, the following UNs were identified:

- Perform the evaluation at any time and at any place.
- Have the option to perform the complete evaluation at only one time or by several times (evaluation with pauses).
- Correct the mistakes at any time before completing the evaluation.
- View results in a graphical way to have a comparison view.

Results for Stage 2

To satisfy the UNs, the following FRs were defined:

- FR_0 = Efficiency.
- FR_1 = Easy access to the evaluation software.
- FR_2 = Save information and start/close session (login).
- FR_3 = Answer questions at an undefined order by selecting options.

FR_1 will help users to perform the evaluation at every moment and place. On the other hand, FR_2 will allow the users to perform the complete evaluation at only one moment or at different moments, since they will be able to start session, introduce and save the data, and close session. Finally, FR_3 will provide a question/answer framework where users can answer questions at a customized order, even change the answers if they change of opinion (i.e. correct mistakes). The answers will be registered only if the user answer all of them and activate the submit button.

Together, FR_1, FR_2, and FR_3 achieve FR_0 = efficiency, as they provide comfortable mental workload and help to have an efficient use of time. However, designs also imply constraints. In this work, authors identified two constraints that may prevent the design from being carried out: a lack of experience in designing the software and a lack of money to constantly pay a web server. In this sense, Figure 7 shows the mapping between the UNs (customer domain) and the FRs (functional domain) and the design constraints.

Figure 7. Design constraints and mapping from user (or customer) domain to functional domain
Source: Prepared by the authors (2018)

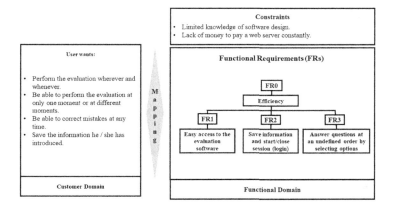

Results for Stage 3

Since the before versions of the software (paper and Matlab®) were poorly available for users, FR_1 – easy access to the evaluation software – was related to DP_1 = create a desktop software compatible with the most widely used operative system: Windows. On the other hand, since sometimes the users do not have enough time to perform completely the evaluation (they have little free time, they have more important activities), FR_2 – save information and start/close session (login) – was associated with DP_2 = Create an account by providing a user name and a password and create a close session button and a save button. This DP_2 will allow users to perform the evaluation at only one moment or gradually, at different moments. Finally, to meet FR_3 – answer questions at an undefined order by selecting options – authors considered DP_3 = Design a question/answer framework with an ordinal scale. At this ordinal scale, the users can select only one option of the answers.

Then, the design matrix is given by equation (1):

$$\begin{bmatrix} FR_1 \\ FR_2 \\ FR_3 \end{bmatrix} = \begin{bmatrix} A_{11} & 0 & 0 \\ 0 & A_{22} & 0 \\ 0 & 0 & A_{33} \end{bmatrix} \times \begin{Bmatrix} DP_1 \\ DP_2 \\ DP_3 \end{Bmatrix} \tag{1}$$

where A_{ij} represents non-zero elements and 0 represents a zero element.

The design equations for the matrix stated above are given by equation (2), equation (3), and equation (4) as follows:

$$FR_1 = A_{11} \times DP_1 \tag{2}$$

$$FR_2 = A_{22} \times DP_2 \tag{3}$$

$$FR_3 = A_{44} \times DP_3 \tag{4}$$

The design is uncoupled since the design matrix is diagonal. Therefore, the information content is zero, and it does not violate the information axiom (Cochran, Eversheim, Kubin, & Sesterhenn, 2000; Y.-S. Kim & Cochran, 2000). Hence, to obtain the best design, the sequence must be the following:

1. Create a desktop software compatible with the most widely used operative system: Windows.
2. Create an account by providing a user name and a password and create a close session button and a save button.
3. Design a question/answer framework with an ordinal scale.

Figure 8 shows the Register/Log in components, whereas Figure 9 shows the Save, Log out and Finish buttons, and the question/qualification framework.

Figure 8. Register and log in components of the software
Source: Prepared by the authors (2018)

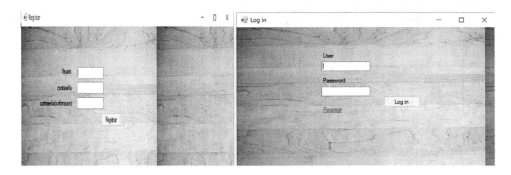

Figure 9. Save, log out and finish buttons, and the question/qualification framework
Source: Prepared by the authors (2018)

Results of Stage 4

Results of stage 4 can be easily detected in Figure 8 and Figure 9. The segmentation principle is applied with the Register, Log in and Log out options. Local quality, Nesting and Prior action principles are achieved by the location of the different commands and buttons. Finally, the Periodic action principle is achieved by the Save, Log out and Log in options.

Results of Stage 5

Figure 8 and Figure 9 demonstrate the results of stage 5.

Results of Stage 6

Results of stage 6 showed that software validation was achieved. As mentioned above, this validation was performed by means of contrasting the results of a previous case study with the results given by the software. In the previous case study, two CIM alternatives (X and Y) were evaluated (see Table 2). In this case study, the best alternative was Y, with an EIC = 0.8383. By introducing the same data of the case study (see Table 1) in the software, results indicated that alternative X had an

EIC = 1.205, and alternative y had an EIC = 1.052. Then, Y is the best alternative. Table 3 shows the comparison of the previous case study and the software.

FUTURE WORK

As future work, authors will seek to promote and implement the software at a local, national and international level. To do this, authors will contact middle and senior managers of manufacturing companies, and with researchers around the world. Software implementation in different case studies around the world will allow to know the different ergonomic attributes more demanded and applied in the AMT. Also, software implementation will allow to perform a comparative analysis about the EIC of AMT by countries, or regions, so manufacturing companies will have the opportunity to select an AMT alternative with low EIC.

CONCLUSION

This research has achieved developing a user-centred software by jointly applying the tools of axiomatic design and TRIZ. Then, the main objective was achieved. It is expected that this software provides more comfort and information reliability than the before versions.

This research argues AD is conceived as a tool that helps designers stay on the right track to reach their design goals. User needs, functional requirements, and design parameters serve as guidelines to the design process. Similarly, when implemented from an ergonomic point of view, TRIZ increases creative problem solving. Then, this research has also demonstrated that combining AD and TRIZ is an excellent strategy to solve problems and perform innovative designs.

Table 3. Validation of the software

CIM alternatives' EIC		
Alternative	Case study	Software
X	0.9117	1.205
Y	0.8383	1.052
Best alternative	Y	Y

Source: Prepared by the authors (2018)

REFERENCES

Altshuller, G. (1984). *Creativity as an exact science: the theory of the solution of inventive problems.* New York, NY: Gordon and Breach Science Publishers. Retrieved from http://cds.cern.ch/record/450367

Altshuller, G. (2002). *40 principles: TRIZ keys to innovation (3rd ed.).* Worcester, MA: Technical Innovation Center. Retrieved from https://books.google.com.mx/books?id=mqlGEZgn5cwC&dq=triz&lr=&hl=es&source=gbs_navlinks_s

Bae, S., Lee, J. M., & Chu, C. N. (2002). Axiomatic Design of Automotive Suspension Systems. *CIRP Annals, 51*(1), 115–118. doi:10.1016/S0007-8506(07)61479-6

Bang, I. C., & Heo, G. (2009). An axiomatic design approach in development of nanofluid coolants. *Applied Thermal Engineering, 29*(1), 75–90. doi:10.1016/j.applthermaleng.2008.02.004

Bariani, P. F., Berti, G. A., & Lucchetta, G. (2004). A Combined DFMA and TRIZ approach to the simplification of product structure. *Proceedings of the Institution of Mechanical Engineers. Part B, Journal of Engineering Manufacture, 218*(8), 1023–1027. doi:10.1243/0954405041486091

Borgianni, Y., & Matt, D. T. (2016). Applications of TRIZ and Axiomatic Design: A Comparison to Deduce Best Practices in Industry. In Procedia CIRP, 39. doi:10.1016/j.procir.2016.01.171

Carayon, P., Hundt, A., Karsh, B. T., Gurses, A. P., Alvarado, C. J., Smith, M., & Flatley Brennan, P. (2006). Work system design for patient safety: The SEIPS model. *Quality & Safety in Health Care, 15,* i50–i58. doi:10.1136/qshc.2005.015842 PMID:17142610

Cascini, G., & Rissone, P. (2004). Plastics design: Integrating TRIZ creativity and semantic knowledge portals. *Journal of Engineering Design, 15*(4), 405–424. doi:10.1080/09544820410001697208

Cavallucci, D., Lutz, P., & Thiébaud, F. (2002). Methodology for bringing the intuitive design method's framework into design activities. *Proceedings of the Institution of Mechanical Engineers. Part B, Journal of Engineering Manufacture, 216*(9), 1303–1307. doi:10.1243/095440502760291853

Celik, M. (2009a). A hybrid design methodology for structuring an Integrated Environmental Management System (IEMS) for shipping business. *Journal of Environmental Management, 90*(3), 1469–1475. doi:10.1016/j.jenvman.2008.10.005 PMID:19038488

Celik, M. (2009b). Designing of integrated quality and safety management system (IQSMS) for shipping operations. *Safety Science, 47*(5), 569–577. doi:10.1016/j.ssci.2008.07.002

Celik, M. (2009c). Establishing an Integrated Process Management System (IPMS) in ship management companies. *Expert Systems with Applications, 36*(4), 8152–8171. doi:10.1016/j.eswa.2008.10.022

Celik, M., Cebi, S., Kahraman, C., & Er, I. D. (2009a). An integrated fuzzy QFD model proposal on routing of shipping investment decisions in crude oil tanker market. *Expert Systems with Applications, 36*(3), 6227–6235. doi:10.1016/j.eswa.2008.07.031

Celik, M., Cebi, S., Kahraman, C., & Er, I. D. (2009b). Application of axiomatic design and TOPSIS methodologies under fuzzy environment for proposing competitive strategies on Turkish container ports in maritime transportation network. *Expert Systems with Applications, 36*(3), 4541–4557. doi:10.1016/j.eswa.2008.05.033

Celik, M., Kahraman, C., Cebi, S., & Er, I. D. (2009). Fuzzy axiomatic design-based performance evaluation model for docking facilities in shipbuilding industry: The case of Turkish shipyards. *Expert Systems with Applications, 36*(1), 599–615. doi:10.1016/j.eswa.2007.09.055

Cha, S.-W., & Cho, K.-K. (1999). Development of DVD for the Next Generation by Axiomatic Approach. *CIRP Annals, 48*(1), 85–88. doi:10.1016/S0007-8506(07)63137-0

Chen, K.-Z., Feng, X.-A., & Zhang, B.-B. (2003). Development of computer-aided quotation system for manufacturing enterprises using axiomatic design. *International Journal of Production Research, 41*(1), 171–191. doi:10.1080/00207540210161687

Chen, S.-J., Chen, L.-C., & Lin, L. (2001). Knowledge-based support for simulation analysis of manufacturing cells. *Computers in Industry, 44*(1), 33–49. doi:10.1016/S0166-3615(00)00071-3

Cochran, D. S., Eversheim, W., Kubin, G., & Sesterhenn, M. L. (2000). The application of axiomatic design and lean management principles in the scope of production system segmentation. *International Journal of Production Research, 38*(6), 1377–1396. doi:10.1080/002075400188906

Deo, H. V., & Suh, N. P. (2004). Mathematical Transforms in Design: Case Study on Feedback Control of a Customizable Automotive Suspension. *CIRP Annals, 53*(1), 125–128. doi:10.1016/S0007-8506(07)60660-X

Dickinson, A. L. (2006). Integrating Axiomatic Design Into a Design for Six Sigma Deployment (DFSS). *Design*, 2–7.

Do, S.-H., & Suh, N. P. (1999). Systematic OO programming with axiomatic design. *Computer*, *32*(10), 121–124. doi:10.1109/2.796146

Donnarumma, A., Pappalardo, M., & Pellegrino, A. (2002). Measure of independence in soft design. *Journal of Materials Processing Technology*, *124*(1–2), 32–35. doi:10.1016/S0924-0136(01)01135-9

Durmusoglu, M., & Kulak, O. (2008). A methodology for the design of office cells using axiomatic design principles. *Omega*, *36*(4), 633–652. doi:10.1016/j.omega.2005.10.007

Farid, A. M. (2016). An Engineering Systems Introduction to Axiomatic Design. In A. M. Farid & P. Suh Nam (Eds.), *Axiomatic Design in Large Systems* (pp. 3–47). Cham, Switzerland: Springer International Publishing. doi:10.1007/978-3-319-32388-6_1

Ferrer, I., Rios, J., & Ciurana, J. (2009). An approach to integrate manufacturing process information in part design phases. *Journal of Materials Processing Technology*, *209*(4), 2085–2091. doi:10.1016/j.jmatprotec.2008.05.009

Gazdík, I. (1996). Zadeh's extension principle in design reliability. *Fuzzy Sets and Systems*, *83*(2), 169–178. doi:10.1016/0165-0114(95)00388-6

Goel, P. S., & Singh, N. (1998). Creativity and Innovation in Durable Product Development. *Computers & Industrial Engineering*, *35*(1–2), 5–8. doi:10.1016/S0360-8352(98)00006-0

Gonçalves-Coelho, A. M., & Mourão, A. J. F. (2007). Axiomatic design as support for decision-making in a design for manufacturing context: A case study. *International Journal of Production Economics*, *109*(1–2), 81–89. doi:10.1016/j.ijpe.2006.11.002

Gumus, B., Ertas, A., Tate, D., & Cicek, I. (2008). The Transdisciplinary Product Development Lifecycle model. *Journal of Engineering Design*, *19*(3), 185–200. doi:10.1080/09544820701232436

Gunasekera, J. S., & Ali, A. F. (1995). A three-step approach to designing a metal-forming process. *JOM*, *47*(6), 22–25. doi:10.1007/BF03221198

Harutunian, V., Nordlund, M., Tate, D., & Suh, N. P. (1996). Decision Making and Software Tools for Product Development Based on Axiomatic Design Theory. *CIRP Annals*, *45*(1), 135–139. doi:10.1016/S0007-8506(07)63032-7

Helander, M. G. (2007). Using design equations to identify sources of complexity in human–machine interaction. *Theoretical Issues in Ergonomics Science, 8*(2), 123–146. doi:10.1080/14639220601092442

Heo, G., & Lee, S. K. (2007). Design evaluation of emergency core cooling systems using Axiomatic Design. *Nuclear Engineering and Design, 237*(1), 38–46. doi:10.1016/j.nucengdes.2006.06.001

Hirani, H., & Suh, N. P. (2005). Journal bearing design using multiobjective genetic algorithm and axiomatic design approaches. *Tribology International, 38*(5), 481–491. doi:10.1016/j.triboint.2004.10.008

Houshmand, M., & Jamshidnezhad, B. (2006). An extended model of design process of lean production systems by means of process variables. *Robotics and Computer-integrated Manufacturing, 22*(1), 1–16. doi:10.1016/j.rcim.2005.01.004

Huang, G. Q. (2002). Web-based support for collaborative product design review. *Computers in Industry, 48*(1), 71–88. doi:10.1016/S0166-3615(02)00011-8

Huang, G. Q., & Jiang, Z. (2002). Web-based design review of fuel pumps using fuzzy set theory. *Engineering Applications of Artificial Intelligence, 15*(6), 529–539. doi:10.1016/S0952-1976(03)00010-1

Jang, B.-S., Yang, Y.-S., Song, Y.-S., Yeun, Y.-S., & Do, S.-H. (2002). Axiomatic design approach for marine design problems. *Marine Structures, 15*(1), 35–56. doi:10.1016/S0951-8339(01)00015-6

Kahraman, C., & Çebi, S. (2009). A new multi-attribute decision making method: Hierarchical fuzzy axiomatic design. *Expert Systems with Applications, 36*(3 PART 1), 4848–4861. doi:10.1016/j.eswa.2008.05.041

Kim, D.-E., Chung, K.-H., & Cha, K.-H. (2003). Tribological design methods for minimum surface damage of HDD slider. *Tribology International, 36*(4–6), 467–473. doi:10.1016/S0301-679X(02)00236-0

Kim, S.-J., Suh, N. P., & Kim, S.-G. (1991). Design of software systems based on axiomatic design. *Robotics and Computer-integrated Manufacturing, 8*(4), 243–255. doi:10.1016/0736-5845(91)90036-R

Kim, Y.-S., & Cochran, D. S. (2000). Reviewing TRIZ from the perspective of Axiomatic Design. *Journal of Engineering Design, 11*(1), 79–94. doi:10.1080/095448200261199

Kremer, G., Chiu, M.-C., Lin, C.-Y., Gupta, S., Claudio, D., & Thevenot, H. (2012). Application of axiomatic design, TRIZ, and mixed integer programming to develop innovative designs: A locomotive ballast arrangement case study. *International Journal of Advanced Manufacturing Technology, 61*(5-8), 827–842. doi:10.100700170-011-3752-1

Kulak, O. (2005). A decision support system for fuzzy multi-attribute selection of material handling equipments. *Expert Systems with Applications, 29*(2), 310–319. doi:10.1016/j.eswa.2005.04.004

Kulak, O., Cebi, S., & Kahraman, C. (2010). Applications of axiomatic design principles : A literature review. *Expert Systems with Applications, 37*(9), 6705–6717. doi:10.1016/j.eswa.2010.03.061

Kulak, O., Durmuşoğlu, M. B., & Kahraman, C. (2005). Fuzzy multi-attribute equipment selection based on information axiom. *Journal of Materials Processing Technology, 169*(3), 337–345. doi:10.1016/j.jmatprotec.2005.03.030

Kulak, O., Durmusoglu, M. B., & Tufekci, S. (2005). A complete cellular manufacturing system design methodology based on axiomatic design principles. *Computers & Industrial Engineering, 48*(4), 765–787. doi:10.1016/j.cie.2004.12.006

Kulak, O., & Kahraman, C. (2005a). Fuzzy multi-attribute selection among transportation companies using axiomatic design and analytic hierarchy process. *Information Sciences, 170*(2–4), 191–210. doi:10.1016/j.ins.2004.02.021

Kulak, O., & Kahraman, C. (2005b). Multi-attribute comparison of advanced manufacturing systems using fuzzy vs. crisp axiomatic design approach. *International Journal of Production Economics, 95*(3), 415–424. doi:10.1016/j.ijpe.2004.02.009

Lee, H., Seo, H., & Park, G.-J. (2003). Design enhancements for stress relaxation in automotive multi-shell-structures. *International Journal of Solids and Structures, 40*(20), 5319–5334. doi:10.1016/S0020-7683(03)00291-9

Lee, J., & Shin, H. (2008). Parameter design of water jet nozzle utilizing independence axiom. *Proceedings of the Institution of Mechanical Engineers. Part E, Journal of Process Mechanical Engineering, 222*(3), 157–169. doi:10.1243/09544089JPME202

Lenz, R. K., & Cochran, D. S. (2000). The application of axiomatic design to the design of the product development organization. Academic Press.

Liang, S. F. M. (2007). Applying axiomatic method to icon design for process control displays. In R. N. Pikaar, E. Koningsveld, & P. J. M. Settels (Eds.), *Meeting Diversity in Ergonomics* (pp. 155–172). Amsterdam, The Netherlands: Elsevier Science. doi:10.1016/B978-008045373-6/50011-8

Lindkvist, L., & SÖDerberg, R. (2003). Computer-aided tolerance chain and stability analysis. *Journal of Engineering Design, 14*(1), 17–39. doi:10.1080/0954482031000078117

Lo, S., & Helander, M. G. (2007). Use of axiomatic design principles for analysing the complexity of human–machine systems. *Theoretical Issues in Ergonomics Science, 8*(2), 147–169. doi:10.1080/14639220601092475

Maldonado-Macías, A. (2009). *Modelo de evaluación ergonómica para la planeación y selección de tecnología de manufactura avanzada*. Instituto Tecnológico de Ciudad Juárez.

Maldonado-Macías, A., Guillén-Anaya, L., Barrón-Díaz, L., & García-Alcaraz, J. L. (2011). Evaluación Ergonómica para la Selección de Tecnología de Manufactura Avanzada: una Propuesta de Software. *Revista de La Ingeniería Industrial, 5*, 1–11. Retrieved from https://s3.amazonaws.com/academia.edu.documents/36650920/ MandonadoIE2011_6029-89.pdf?AWSAccessKeyId=AKIAIWOWYYGZ2Y53UL 3A&Expires=1516140763&Signature=7nYcphKAorNP1QNm%2F7jlwjcgKQo%3 D&response-content-disposition=inline%3Bfilename%3DEvaluacion_Ergonomica

Melvin, J. W., & Suh, N. P. (2002). Simulation Within the Axiomatic Design Framework. *CIRP Annals, 51*(1), 107–110. doi:10.1016/S0007-8506(07)61477-2

Monplaisir, L., Jugulum, R., & Mian, M. (1998). Application of TRIZ and Taguchi methods: Two case examples. In *Proceedings of the Taguchi methods conference, 4th total product development symposium*. Retrieved from http://www.triz-journal.com

Nakao, M., Kobayashi, N., Hamada, K., Totsuka, T., & Yamada, S. (2007). Decoupling Executions in Navigating Manufacturing Processes for Shortening Lead Time and Its Implementation to an Unmanned Machine Shop. *CIRP Annals - Manufacturing Technology, 56*(1), 171–174. doi:10.1016/j.cirp.2007.05.041

Ng, N. K., & Jiao, J. (2004). A domain-based reference model for the conceptualization of factory loading allocation problems in multi-site manufacturing supply chains. *Technovation, 24*(8), 631–642. doi:10.1016/S0166-4972(02)00125-6

Pappalardo, M., & Naddeo, A. (2005). Failure mode analysis using axiomatic design and non-probabilistic information. *Journal of Materials Processing Technology, 164–165*, 1423–1429. doi:10.1016/j.jmatprotec.2005.02.041

Realyvásquez, A., Hernández-Escobedo, G., & Maldonado-Macías, A. A. (2018). Ergonomic Bench to Decrease Postural Risk Level on the Task of Changing Forklift's Brake Pads: A Design Approach. In J. L. Hernández-Arellano, A. A. Maldonado-Macías, J. A. Castillo-Martínez, & P. Peinado-Coronado (Eds.), Handbook of Research on Ergonomics and Product Design (pp. 28–47). Hershey, PA: IGI Global. doi:10.4018/978-1-5225-5234-5.ch002

Realyvásquez, A., Maldonado-Macías, A., García-Alcaraz, J. L., & Arana, A. (2018). Macroergonomic Compatibility Index for Manufacturing Systems. A Case Study. In S. Trzcielinski (Ed.), *Advances in Ergonomics of Manufacturing: Managing the Enterprise of the Future* (pp. 179–189). Los Ángeles, CA: Springer International Publishing; doi:10.1007/978-3-319-60474-9_17

Realyvásquez-Vargas, A., Maldonado-Macías, A., García-Alcaraz, J. L., & Alvarado-Iniesta, A. (2014). Expert System Development Using Fuzzy If–Then Rules for Ergonomic Compatibility of AMT for Lean Environments. In J. L. García-Alcaraz, A. A. Maldonado-Macías, & G. Cortés-Robles (Eds.), *Lean Manufacturing in the Developing World. Methodology, Case Studies and Trends from Latin America* (pp. 347–369). Cham, Switzerland: Springer International Publishing. doi:10.1007/978-3-319-04951-9_16

Savransky, S. (2000). *Engineering of creativity : introduction to TRIZ methodology of inventive problem solving*. Boca Raton, FL: CRC Press. doi:10.1201/9781420038958

Schnetzler, M. J., Sennheiser, A., & Schönsleben, P. (2007). A decomposition-based approach for the development of a supply chain strategy. *International Journal of Production Economics*, *105*(1), 21–42. doi:10.1016/j.ijpe.2006.02.004

Shin, M. K., Lee, H. A., Lee, J. J., Song, K. N., & Park, G. J. (2008). Optimization of a nuclear fuel spacer grid spring using homology constraints. *Nuclear Engineering and Design*, *238*(10), 2624–2634. doi:10.1016/j.nucengdes.2008.04.003

Shirwaiker, R. A., & Okudan, G. E. (2008). Triz and axiomatic design: A review of case-studies and a proposed synergistic use. *Journal of Intelligent Manufacturing*, *19*(1), 33–47. doi:10.100710845-007-0044-6

Stratton, R., & Mann, D. (2003). Systematic innovation and the underlying principles behind TRIZ and TOC. *Journal of Materials Processing Technology*, *139*(1–3), 120–126. doi:10.1016/S0924-0136(03)00192-4

Stratton, R., & Warburton, R. D. (2003). The strategic integration of agile and lean supply. *International Journal of Production Economics*, *85*(2), 183–198. doi:10.1016/S0925-5273(03)00109-9

Su, J. C.-Y., Chen, S.-J., & Lin, L. (2003). A structured approach to measuring functional dependency and sequencing of coupled tasks in engineering design. *Computers & Industrial Engineering*, *45*(1), 195–214. doi:10.1016/S0360-8352(03)00031-7

Suh, N. P. (1990). *The principles of design. Oxford series on advanced manufacturing: 6*. New York, NY: Oxford University Press.

Suh, N. P. (1995). Designing-in of quality through axiomatic design. *IEEE Transactions on Reliability*, *44*(2), 256–264. doi:10.1109/24.387380

Suh, N. P. (1995a). Design and operation of large systems. *Journal of Manufacturing Systems*, *14*(3), 203–213. doi:10.1016/0278-6125(95)98887-C

Suh, N. P. (1995b). Design and operation of large systems. *Journal of Manufacturing Systems*, *14*(3), 203–213. doi:10.1016/0278-6125(95)98887-C

Suh, N. P. (1997). Design of Systems. *CIRP Annals*, *46*(1), 75–80. doi:10.1016/S0007-8506(07)60779-3

Suh, N. P. (1998). Axiomatic Design Theory for Systems. *Research in Engineering Design*, *10*(4), 189–209. doi:10.1007001639870001

Suh, N. P. (2001). *Axiomatic Design: Advances and Applications*. Oxford University Press.

Suh, N. P. (2005). Complexity in Engineering. *CIRP Annals*, *54*(2), 46–63. doi:10.1016/S0007-8506(07)60019-5

Suh, N. P., Cochran, D. S., & Lima, P. C. (1998). Manufacturing System Design. *CIRP Annals*, *47*(2), 627–639. doi:10.1016/S0007-8506(07)63245-4

Suh, N. P., & Do, S.-H. (2000). Axiomatic Design of Software Systems. *CIRP Annals*, *49*(1), 95–100. doi:10.1016/S0007-8506(07)62904-7

Suh, N. P., & Sekimoto, S. (1990). Design of Thinking Design Machine. *CIRP Annals*, *39*(1), 145–148. doi:10.1016/S0007-8506(07)61022-1

Tang, D., Zhang, G., & Dai, S. (2009). Design as integration of axiomatic design and design structure matrix. *Robotics and Computer-integrated Manufacturing*, *25*(3), 610–619. doi:10.1016/j.rcim.2008.04.005

Technical Innovation Center. (2013). *40 Principles*. Retrieved from http://triz.org/index.php/triz/principles

Thielman, J., & Ge, P. (2006). Applying axiomatic design theory to the evaluation and optimization of large-scale engineering systems. *Journal of Engineering Design*, *17*(1), 1–16. doi:10.1080/09544820500287722

Thielman, J., Ge, P., Wu, Q., & Parme, L. (2005). Evaluation and optimization of General Atomics' GT-MHR reactor cavity cooling system using an axiomatic design approach. *Nuclear Engineering and Design*, *235*(13), 1389–1402. doi:10.1016/j.nucengdes.2004.11.015

Togay, C., Dogru, A. H., & Tanik, J. U. (2008). Systematic Component-Oriented development with Axiomatic Design. *Journal of Systems and Software*, *81*(11), 1803–1815. doi:10.1016/j.jss.2007.12.746

Tomiyama, T., Gu, P., Jin, Y., Lutters, D., Kind, C., & Kimura, F. (2009). Design methodologies: Industrial and educational applications. *CIRP Annals*, *58*(2), 543–565. doi:10.1016/j.cirp.2009.09.003

Tsai, C. C., Chang, C. Y., & Tseng, C. H. (2004). Optimal design of metal seated ball valve mechanism. *Structural and Multidisciplinary Optimization*, *26*(3–4), 249–255. doi:10.100700158-003-0342-3

Tseng, M. M., & Jiao, J. (1997). A module identification approach to the electrical design of electronic products by clustering analysis of the design matrix. *Computers & Industrial Engineering*, *33*(1–2), 229–233. doi:10.1016/S0360-8352(97)00081-8

Won, K., & Joon, Y. (2005, November). Mutual Compensation of TRIZ and Axiomatic Design. *Design*, 1–12.

Yang, K., & Zhang, H. (2000a). A Comparison of TRIZ and Axiomatic Design. In *First International Conference on Axiomatic Design* (pp. 235–243), Cambridge, MA: Academic Press. Retrieved from http://moodle.stoa.usp.br/file.php/1359/TRIZ_AD.pdf

Yang, K., & Zhang, H. (2000b). *Compatibility analysis and case studies of axiomatic design and TRIZ*. Retrieved from https://triz-journal.com/compatiability-analysis-case-studies-axiomatic-design-triz/

Yi, J.-W., & Park, G.-J. (2005). Development of a design system for EPS cushioning package of a monitor using axiomatic design. *Advances in Engineering Software*, *36*(4), 273–284. doi:10.1016/j.advengsoft.2004.06.016

KEY TERMS AND DEFINITIONS

Advanced Manufacturing Technology: Technology that helps perform in an easy and fast way operations in manufacturing processes, so the companies meet the requirements of quantity and quality.

Assessment: Comparison of the state of a variable in a specific condition with the standard value of such variable for that condition. Such comparison helps determine if the state of the variable is acceptable or not.

Axiomatic Design: A design discipline that serves as guide to designers since it considers users' needs, design's functional requirements, and design parameters.

Ergonomic Compatibility: Human interaction with other elements of a work system in which it facilitates the achievement of objectives in a safe, comfortable and healthy way

Ergonomics: A discipline aimed to provide safety, health, and comfort to employees, so they improve their individual performance at short term, and the organizational performance at long term.

Software: An informatic tool that can perform the following tasks: analyze and process information in a fast way and save this information.

TRIZ: A Russian technique that contains forty principles which can be applied to solve different engineering problems in an easy and cheap way.

APPENDIX 1

See Table 4.

APPENDIX 2

See Table 5.

Table 4. Literature review of applications of AD

Source	Axiom		Application area						Method			Type of evaluation	
	Independence	Information	Product design	System design	Manufacturing system design	Software design	Decision making	Others	An application of AD	An integrated method	Theoretical development	Crisp	Fuzzy
(Celik, 2009b)		✓					✓	✓					✓
(Celik, 2009c)		✓					✓	✓					✓
(Celik, 2009a)		✓					✓	✓					✓
(Celik, Cebi, Kahraman, & Er, 2009b)		✓					✓						✓
(Celik, Cebi, et al., 2009a)		✓					✓						✓
(Celik, Kahraman, Cebi, & Er, 2009)		✓					✓						✓
(Kahraman & Çebi, 2009)		✓					✓				✓		✓
(Tang et al., 2009)	✓		✓									✓	
(Gumus et al., 2008)	✓		✓								✓	✓	
(Durmusoglu & Kulak, 2008)	✓				✓				✓			✓	
(Lee & Shin, 2008)	✓		✓									✓	
(Togay et al., 2008)	✓					✓			✓			✓	
(Ferrer et al., 2009)	✓		✓									✓	
(Shin, Lee, Lee, Song, & Park, 2008)	✓		✓									✓	
(Bang & Heo, 2009)	✓			✓					✓			✓	
(Lo & Helander, 2007)	✓	✓	✓	✓							✓	✓	
(Helander, 2007)	✓	✓	✓	✓					✓			✓	
(Gonçalves-Coelho & Mourão, 2007)	✓	✓					✓		✓			✓	

continued on following page

Table 4. Continued

Source	Axiom		Application area						Method			Type of evaluation	
	Independence	Information	Product design	System design	Manufacturing system design	Software design	Decision making	Others	An application of AD	An integrated method	Theoretical development	Crisp	Fuzzy
(Nakao et al., 2007)	✓				✓				✓			✓	
(Schnetzler et al., 2007)	✓				✓				✓			✓	
(Liang, 2007)	✓	✓	✓						✓			✓	
(Heo & Lee, 2007)	✓			✓					✓			✓	
(Thielman & Ge, 2006)	✓			✓								✓	
(Houshmand & Jamshidnezhad, 2006)	✓				✓				✓			✓	
(Kulak & Kahraman, 2005a)		✓					✓				✓	✓	✓
(Kulak & Kahraman, 2005b)		✓					✓				✓	✓	✓
(Kulak, 2005)		✓					✓					✓	
(Kulak, Durmuşoğlu, & Kahraman, 2005)	✓								✓				✓
(Kulak, Durmusoglu, & Tufekci, 2005)	✓		✓		✓				✓				
(Pappalardo & Naddeo, 2005)	✓							✓				✓	
(Yi & Park, 2005)	✓					✓						✓	
(Hirani & Suh, 2005)	✓		✓									✓	
(Thielman, Ge, Wu, & Parme, 2005)	✓			✓								✓	
(Suh, 2005)	✓							✓			✓	✓	
(Ng & Jiao, 2004)	✓							✓			✓	✓	

continued on following page

Table 4. Continued

Source	Axiom		Application area						Method			Type of evaluation	
	Independence	Information	Product design	System design	Manufacturing system design	Software design	Decision making	Others	An application of AD	An integrated method	Theoretical development	Crisp	Fuzzy
(Chen, Feng, & Zhang, 2003)	✓		✓									✓	
(Deo & Suh, 2004)	✓			✓							✓	✓	
(Lindkvist & SöDerberg, 2003)	✓		✓			✓						✓	
(Chen et al., 2003)	✓					✓			✓			✓	
(Su, Chen, & Lin, 2003)	✓							✓			✓	✓	
(Kim, Chung, & Cha, 2003)	✓		✓						✓			✓	
(Lee, Seo, & Park, 2003)	✓		✓									✓	
(Melvin & Suh, 2002)	✓							✓				✓	
(Huang & Jiang, 2002)	✓					✓					✓		✓
(Jang, Yang, Song, Yeun, & Do, 2002)	✓	✓	✓				✓		✓			✓	
(Huang, 2002)	✓					✓					✓	✓	
(Bae, Lee, & Chu, 2002)	✓		✓						✓			✓	
(Donnarumma, Pappalardo, & Pellegrino, 2002)	✓	✓						✓			✓	✓	
(Chen, Chen, & Lin, 2001)	✓					✓			✓			✓	
(Suh & Do, 2000)	✓					✓						✓	
(Cochran et al., 2000)	✓				✓				✓			✓	
(Cha & Cho, 1999)	✓		✓						✓			✓	
(Goel & Singh, 1998)	✓	✓	✓	✓			✓		✓			✓	

continued on following page

Table 4. Continued

Source	Axiom		Application area						Method			Type of evaluation	
	Independence	Information	Product design	System design	Manufacturing system design	Software design	Decision making	Others	An application of AD	An integrated method	Theoretical development	Crisp	Fuzzy
(Suh, Cochran, & Lima, 1998)	✓				✓				✓			✓	
(Tseng & Jiao, 1997)	✓											✓	
(Suh, 1997)	✓			✓					✓				
(Gazdik, 1996)	✓											✓	✓
(Harutunian, Nordlund, Tate, & Suh, 1996)	✓					✓			✓			✓	
(Suh, 1995b)	✓										✓	✓	
(Suh, 1995)	✓			✓							✓	✓	
(Gunasekera & Ali, 1995)	✓					✓			✓			✓	
(Kim et al., 1991)	✓					✓			✓			✓	
(Suh & Sekimoto, 1990)	✓	✓	✓						✓			✓	

Source: Kulak et al. (2010)

81

Table 5. Literature review of applications of TRIZ

	Design problem	TRIZ system for problem definition	TRIZ system for problem solution	Suggested parameters	Potential solutions
Manufacturing systems	Modifying supply chain management for a fashion apparel manufacturer (Stratton & Warburton, 2003)	• Physical contradiction	• Separation principle	• Separation in time	• Supply chain focus shifted from efficiency of production to speed of response. • Early runs will be production focused and later orders will be delivery speed focused
	Principle of flexible manufacturing systems and group technology	• Physical contradiction	• Separation principle	• Separation in space • Separation in time	• The machine setups can be designed according to the part family designs. • Batches of different families can be manufactured in the same cell
Manufacturing processes	Improvement of fluorination process (Monplaisir, Jugulum, & Mian, 1998)	• Physical contradiction • Su-Field Analysis	• 76 Standard solutions	• Separation in space • Class II Condensed standards	• Making use of gravity to induce uniformity into the fluorination process by placing gas port on the top
	Improvement of the ampoule sealing process (Yang & Zhang, 2000b)	• Technical contradiction • Physical contradiction	• Contradiction matrix • Separation principle	• Previously placed pillow • Other way round • Segmentation	• Keeping the part of ampoule containing drug, immersed in water while sealing its ends with a burner
	Improvement in bottle-filling process (Cavallucci, Lutz, & Thiébaud, 2002)	• Technical contradiction	• Contradiction matrix	• Separation in space • Segmentation	• Splitting the main tank into two smaller tanks to reduce water pressure
				• Replace a mechanical system	• Use acoustics or optical level gauging system instead of physical contact
				• Physical or chemical properties • Feedback	• Chemical sterilized Nozzle
Design for manufacturing	Design of a 500 passengers supersonic air plane (Stratton & Mann, 2003)	• Technical contradictions • Physical contradictions	• Contradiction matrix • Separation principles	• Dynamism • Preliminary action • Copying • Separation in time	• Variable Wing Geometry— perform as boosters during takeoff and maneuvers while flying
	Design of a metal seated ball valve mechanism (Tsai, Chang, & Tseng, 2004)	• Technical contradictions • Su-Field analysis	• Contradiction matrix • 76 Standard solutions	• Design of a metal seated ball valve mechanism (Tsai et al., 2004) • Segmentation • Asymmetry • Spheriodality • Porosity • Class II and III condensed standards	Use of magnets, electro-magnets or magnetic fluid for sealing for three designs illustrated in Tsai, Chang, & Tseng (2004)
	Design of motorscooter wheel using plastics (Cascini & Rissone, 2004)	• Technical contradictions • Su- Field analysis	• Contradiction matrix • 76 Standard solutions	• Segmentation • Optical changes • Dimensionality change • Replacing a mechanical system • • Class I condensed standards • Local quality	• Two-piece assembly • Three-dimensional web • Strengthening hollow rim with a high viscosity substance like foam for energy dissipation

continued on following page

Table 5. Continued

	Design problem	TRIZ system for problem definition	TRIZ system for problem solution	Suggested parameters	Potential solutions
	Design of a satellite antenna (Bariani, Berti, & Lucchetta, 2004)	• Technical contradictions • Physical contradictions	• Contradiction matrix • Separation principles	• Local quality • Previously placed pillow • Preliminary action • Optical changes • Separation in space	• Making the antenna out of plastic and coating the reflector surface with a metal • Properly designed rib/web to reduce the material volume but maintain stiffness

Source: Shirwaiker & Okudan (2008)

Chapter 4
Knowledge Sharing Initiatives in Software Companies:
A Mapping Study

Shanmuganathan Vasanthapriyan
 https://orcid.org/0000-0002-0597-0263
Sabaragamuwa University of Sri Lanka, Sri Lanka

ABSTRACT

This mapping study aims to investigate knowledge sharing initiatives in software companies based on existing studies from 2005 to 2017. Initially, search string was applied in seven digital repositories. Snowballing and direct search on publications were conducted to reduce the limitation of accessing specific databases. Regarding 15 selected studies, a variety of aspects; publication year and source, research type, purpose, and types of knowledge been used; were concerned. According to findings, a majority of studies have been focused on factors affecting knowledge sharing and point out organizational commitment as the most undergoing influencer on knowledge sharing. Findings further prove criticality of knowledge sharing for sustainability of software companies. Contrary to that, findings provide convincing evidence on improper knowledge sharing systems as the highly referred problem associated with knowledge sharing in software companies and provide new directions to future research.

DOI: 10.4018/978-1-5225-9448-2.ch004

INTRODUCTION

Knowledge is a critical organizational resource and the management of this knowledge is key to long-term sustainability and success of organizations. Efficient management of knowledge is not possible without a proper process of knowledge sharing (Paulin and Sunneson, 2012; Andreasian and Andreasian, 2013). Knowledge sharing is the process which integrates and merges knowledge among each individual and teams in an organization by exchanging each other's tacit knowledge, and explicit knowledge (Paulin and Sunneson, 2012; Andreasian and Andreasian, 2013). Most of the issues arising in the software companies are identified as a result of inefficient knowledge sharing. To improve the organizational performance knowledge should be shared in a structured way that the right knowledge is conveyed to the right person at the right time.

Knowledge sharing in software companies has been attained a considerable attention of researchers in recent years. This paper focuses on identifying current literature about knowledge sharing in software companies by employing a mapping study. The contribution of this mapping study consists of baseline data and recommendations which could be a source of general guidance for academic researchers in stimulating future research in the context of knowledge sharing. In this mapping study, includes previous studies published since 2005 to 2017. Research studies related to knowledge sharing which are conducted outside the software industry are also taken into account in certain situations. This paper addresses the following aspects: distribution of the studies over past years, source of publication, type of the research, knowledge types been used, technology usage, purposes, benefits and problems related to knowledge sharing. Furthermore, snowballing and direct search for the studies published by researchers of the previously selected studies were performed (Erica et al., 2014).

The rest of this paper presents the background of this mapping, discussion of the research method, results, implications and limitations of the study, and finally conclusion and future research possibilities of the study.

BACKGROUND

Knowledge Sharing

Knowledge sharing could be identified as a process between units, teams and organizations where people exchange their knowledge with others (Andreasian and Andreasian, 2013; Anthony, 2013). Knowledge sharing starts at the individual level, since every person has tacit and explicit knowledge to share with others. Sharing tacit knowledge is more challenging as it cannot be easily expressed (Kharabsheh et al., 2016). Previous literature (Lin, 2006; Yi, 2009) view knowledge sharing as an organizational innovation, which supports dissemination of innovative ideas to improve business processes and new business opportunities. But this costs money, time and energy which are limited resources (Block, 2012).

Knowledge Sharing in Software Companies

Software industry is much younger and knowledge intensive industry. (Kukko and Helander, 2012). It creates a lack in well-structured knowledge sharing processes in software industry. In software companies, independent, competent and creative people with a high level professional knowledge shape the business and knowledge and innovativeness are critical to stay competitive and growth (Kukko, 2013). Hence, knowledge sharing is a cornerstone for software companies for their growth and sustainability. It can be seen that many issues are arisen in knowledge sharing domain in software companies due to inefficient knowledge sharing (Ranasinghe and Jayawardana, 2011; Kharabsheh et al., 2016). If there is not available a proper knowledge sharing process, employees would proceed with the knowledge that they already have or with the knowledge that is most easily available. Even that knowledge is accurate and of good quality, sometimes it may not be good enough to achieve the success of the projects or the sustainability of today's market (Zammit et al., 2016).

Related Work

Mapping studies are generally conducted with the intention of providing a broad overview of a specific topic and investigating the need of more primary studies related to derived sub-topics. This secondary study focuses on identifying and classifying all the previous research related to a broad knowledge management-based topic 'Knowledge sharing in software companies'. A tertiary study was conducted as the first step of this mapping study to search existing secondary studies in knowledge sharing. The purpose of this tertiary study is to explore the state of art in knowledge sharing in software companies in general. Also, knowledge management related secondary studies were searched with the intention of obtaining comprehensive understanding of the subject. Therefore, secondary studies were investigated with the aid of knowledge management and knowledge sharing separately.

In order to perform this tertiary study, search string depicted in Table 1 was applied for searching studies in knowledge sharing, and title of the study, abstract and the keywords were used as the metadata fields to apply the search string.

Table 1. Search terms of the tertiary study on knowledge sharing in software companies

Areas	Search terms
Knowledge sharing	*"knowledge sharing", "knowledge transfer"*
Software companies	*"software companies", "software industry"*
Review	*"systematic literature review", "systematic review", "systematic mapping", "mapping study", "systematic literature mapping"*
Search string	*("knowledge sharing" OR "knowledge transfer") AND ("software companies" OR "software industry") AND ("systematic literature review" OR "systematic review" OR "systematic mapping" OR "mapping study" OR "systematic literature mapping")*

Then the search string was applied in seven electronic databases; IEEE Xplore, Springer Link, Science Direct, Emerald Insight, Research Gate, ACM Digital Library and PIM Sri Lankan Journal of Management. Regarding the tertiary study which conducted on searching for the secondary studies in knowledge management, search string depicted in Table 2 was used and applied it into the same seven databases.

RESEARCH METHOD

Research method of this mapping study is defined according to the guidelines described by Kitchenham and Charters (2007), which consists of three major phases; planning, conducting and reporting. In the planning phase, pre-review activities are performed and establishes an evaluation protocol describing sources of studies, research questions, selection criteria; inclusion criterion and exclusion criteria; search string, and mapping processes. According to Kitchenham and Charters (2007), in conduction phase, studies are searched and selected for extracting data from them.

Table 2. Search terms of the tertiary study on knowledge management in software companies

Areas	Search terms
Knowledge management	*"knowledge management"*
Software companies	*"software companies", "software industry"*
Review	*"systematic literature review", "systematic review", "systematic mapping", "mapping study", "systematic literature mapping"*
Search string	*("knowledge management") AND ("software companies" OR "software industry") AND ("systematic literature review" OR "systematic review" OR "systematic mapping" OR "mapping study" OR "systematic literature mapping")*

Moreover, additional relevant studies are identified by snowballing the lists of references in the selected studies and direct searches were performed to identify studies of important researchers as well. These researchers were pointed out from the papers which were selected using search strings and snowballing. Additional studies support to overcome limitation of accessing a limited set of electronic databases. As suggested by Kitchenham and Charters, results are articulated in the reporting phase and these results and findings are used to provide answers to research questions (2007).

This section discusses about main steps followed in this mapping study including research questions, study selection, data extraction and synthesis, classification schema and eventually, limitations of the mapping.

Research Questions

The objective of this mapping study is to represent an overall view of the current status of research studies in knowledge sharing in software companies. Table 3 shows the research questions which focused in this mapping study and the reasoning for considering them.

Study Selection

A selection process was performed in order to retrieve the appropriate studies. In this selection process, following selection aspects were concerned.

1. Definition of search string
2. Sources for searching
3. Definition for inclusion and exclusion criteria
4. Method of storing data

These major aspects of the selection criteria, and the method of assessing the study selection are discussed follow.

Terms and Search String

The search string consists of two different areas; knowledge sharing and knowledge management. Title, abstract and keywords were used as the three metadata fields in applying the search string. Table 4 represents the search string applied in databases.

Table 3. Research questions and their rationales

No.	Research question	Rationale
RQ1	What are the years and sources that research been published?	This question provides knowledge on sources of publication and publication years of selected studies.
RQ2	Which types of facets have been treated as the focal point in the studies from the knowledge sharing perspective?	This question investigates different aspects of knowledge sharing that have been obtained much attention when applying knowledge sharing into software companies.
RQ3	What types of research have been done?	Scientific papers present different types of research. This question points out the type of research that have been used in selected studies.
RQ4	What kind of problems have been reported by software companies about knowledge sharing?	This question investigates the major problems that have been gained the attention of researchers in the domain of knowledge sharing in software companies.
RQ5	What are the reasons of using knowledge sharing in software companies?	This question points out reasons and purposes that have been described in the previous studies for employing knowledge sharing activities in software companies.
RQ6	What types of knowledge are generally managed in knowledge sharing?	Aims to find out different types of knowledge which have been managed in knowledge sharing and define the more important knowledge type in knowledge sharing.
RQ7	What are the technologies used to provide better knowledge sharing in software companies?	This question aims to highlight the technologies currently used in knowledge sharing activities in software companies. This information supports to fill the existing gaps in knowledge sharing by guiding their future research towards new technologies.
RQ8	What are the major conclusions reported related to the application of knowledge sharing in software companies?	Highlights the major conclusions regarding benefits of current studies and remaining problems to be addressed in the future research as reported in studies related to knowledge sharing in software companies.

Table 4. Search terms of the mapping study on knowledge sharing in software companies

Areas	Search terms
Knowledge management	*"knowledge management"*
Knowledge sharing	*"knowledge sharing", "knowledge transfer"*
Software companies	*"software companies", "software industry"*
Search string	*("knowledge management" OR "knowledge sharing" OR "knowledge transfer") AND ("software companies" OR "software industry")*

Sources

According to the tertiary study accomplished previously, seven electronic databases were identified as the most relevant databases which contains studies more appropriate to the research topic. Hence, the searching criteria was performed in the following seven electronic databases.

1. IEEE Xplore (http://ieeexplore.ieee.org)
2. Springer Link (https://link.springer.com)
3. Science Direct (https://www.sciencedirect.com)
4. Emerald Insight (http://emeraldinsight.com)
5. Research Gate (https://www.researchgate.net)
6. ACM Digital Library (https://dl.acm.org)
7. PIM Sri Lankan Journal of Management (https://www.sljm.pim.sjp.ac.lk)

Inclusion and Exclusion Criteria

The selection criteria is constructed with one inclusion criterion and five exclusion criteria. Table 5 and Table 6 depict the inclusion criterion and exclusion criteria used in the selection process respectively.

Table 5. Inclusion criterion in selection process

No.	Inclusion criterion (IC)
IC1	The paper discusses knowledge sharing in software companies

Table 6. Exclusion criteria in selection process

No.	Exclusion criteria (EC)
EC1	The paper does not contain an abstract
EC2	The paper is published just as an abstract
EC3	The language used in writing the paper is not English
EC4	The paper is a previous version of a study already selected
EC5	The paper is not a primary study. It is either an editorial or a summary

Data Storage

All the studies retrieved through the searching phase were systematized and stored properly, for the purpose of using in classification and analysis processes. Then all the relevant data regarding the identified studies were extracted such as id and bibliographic references.

Assessment

The mapping protocol was tested before performing the mapping, in order to verify the adequacy and feasibility of the protocol. Furthermore, a set of search terms were employed iteratively until the most accurate search string was developed to retrieve the studies which are more relevant to the investigation.

Data Extraction and Synthesis

In this study, publications since 2005 to 2017 were considered. In the search process, a total of 480 publications were returned as the searching result. Out of the total search result, 7 from IEEE Xplore, 87 from Springer Link, 118 from Science Direct, 74 from Emerald Insight, 20 from Research Gate, 171 from ACM Digital Library, and 3 from PIM Sri Lankan Journal of Management were found. Then, the selection process was performed on the selected publications to extract the most relevant studies. Figure 1 depicts the five stages of the selection process.

In the first phase of selection process, selection criteria were applied over the title of the study, abstract and keywords of the selected studies. Aim of this step is to eliminate studies which are clearly irrelevant to the subject. Application of selection criteria; inclusion criterion and exclusion criteria; in this stage eliminated totally 432 studies returning 48 papers. It resulted in approximately 90% reduction of the selected set of studies. 1 paper was eliminated by EC3 (The language used in writing the paper is not English) and other 431 papers were eliminated for not satisfying IC1 (The paper discusses knowledge sharing in software companies).

In the second stage, looked for the papers which exist in more than one databases regarding the remained 48 papers, and duplications were eliminated. Total of 5 papers were identified as duplicated papers. These 5 papers were eliminated resulting 43 papers in remain and it showed approximate 10.4% reduction.

These 43 papers which remained after removing duplications were taken to the third stage of the selection process. In this stage, selection criteria were employed considering the full text with the intention of eliminating papers with incomplete and unrelated contents. This process eliminated total of 32 papers resulting 11 papers. 12 papers were eliminated by EC2 (The paper is published just as an abstract), 1 paper

Figure 1. The five stages of the selection process

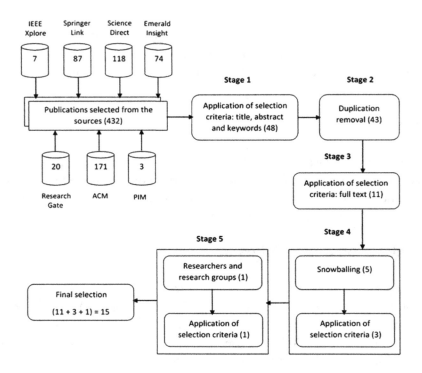

was eliminated by EC4 (The paper is a previous version of a study already selected), 6 papers were eliminated by EC5 (The paper is not a primary study. It is either an editorial or a summary), and other 13 papers were eliminated for not satisfying IC1 (The paper discusses knowledge sharing in software companies). This elimination resulted in approximately 74.4% reduction of the study set.

In order to overcome the limitation of accessing only specific number of databases, stage 4 was performed focusing on papers outside the selected sources. In fourth stage, 5 additional papers were selected by snowballing previous 11 papers. Then, the selection criteria were employed over these 5 papers. In this process, no papers were eliminated by applying selection criteria over title of the study, abstract and keywords, due to they were allied with the concerned subject. But, when the selection criteria; inclusion criterion and exclusion criteria; were applied concerning the complete text, 2 papers were eliminated for not satisfying IC1 (The paper discusses knowledge sharing in software companies), resulting approximately 40% of reduction.

Finally, 14 papers selected until then, were taken into account in the fifth stage. In this stage, searched for publications of the researchers mentioned in remained studies, in digital libraries. Using results of this searching, a paper which was identified as more appropriate to this subject was selected as a direct search. Total of 15 papers were retrieved as the final result of this searching process, including, 11 from the sources, 3 from snowballing and 1 from directly searching the researchers.

Summary of each selection stage and their results are shown in Table 7. Table 7 clearly emphasizes the progressive elimination of the studies during the selection process. Table 8 provides bibliographic references of the studies selected. Each study has been provided with a unique identifier (#id) and these identifiers are used in the rest of this paper to represent each study.

Classification Scheme

A classification scheme was conducted on different aspects of the research questions except the last research question (RQ8).

Research Focus From the Knowledge Sharing Perspective (RQ2)

Selected studies of knowledge sharing have been focused on different facets of knowledge sharing. Based on selected studies, categories described below are considered in this mapping study: (i) Knowledge sharing in software development, (ii)

Table 7. Results of the selection stages

Stage	Applied criteria	Analyzed content	Initial number of studies	Final number of studies	Reduction (%)
1st	IC1 and EC3	Title, abstract and keywords	432	48	90.0
2nd	Duplicate removal	Title, abstract and keywords	48	43	10.4
3rd	IC1, EC2, EC4 and EC5	Full text	43	11	74.4
4th(a)	Snowballing	Title, abstract and keywords	5 (added by snowballing)	5 (added by snowballing)	-
4th(b)	Snowballing, IC1	Full text	5 (added by snowballing)	3 (added by snowballing)	40.0
5th	Research groups	Full text	1 (added by research groups)	1 (added by research groups)	-
Final Result			432 (sources) + 5 (snowballing) + 1 (research groups) = 438	11 (sources) + 3 (snowballing) + 1 (research groups) = 15	96.6

Table 8. Selected studies

ID	Bibliographic reference
#1	Amayah T A (2013) Determinants of knowledge sharing in a public sector organization. Journal of Knowledge Management 17(3), 454-471.
#2	Endres M and Chowdhury S (2013) The Role of Expected Reciprocity in Knowledge Sharing. International Journal of Knowledge Management 9(3), 1-19.
#3	Ranasinghe G and Jayawardana A K L (2011) Impact of knowledge sharing on project success in the Sri Lankan software industry. Sri Lankan Journal of Management 16(1).
#4	Heeager L and Nielsen P A (2013) Agile Software Development and the Barriers to Transfer of Knowledge: An Interpretive Case Study. In Proceedings of the Nordic Contributions in IS Research (SCIS), Lecture Notes in Business Information Processing (Aanestad M and Bratteteig T, Eds), p 18-39, Springer Publications, Berlin, Heidelberg.
#5	Seba I, Rowley J and Lambert S (2012) Factors affecting attitudes and intentions towards knowledge sharing in the Dubai Police Force. International Journal of Information Management. 32(1), 372-380.
#6	Zammit J P, Gao J and Evans R (2016) A Framework to Capture and Share Knowledge Using Storytelling and Video Sharing in Global Product Development. In Proceedings of the 12th IFIP International Conference on Product Lifecycle Management (PLM), (Bouras A, Eynard B, Foufou S and Thoben K D, Eds), p 259-268, IFIP Advances in Information and Communication Technology, Doha, Qatar.
#7	Park J and Lee J (2012) Knowledge sharing in information systems development projects: Explicating the role of dependence and trust. International Journal of Project Management 32(1), 153–165.
#8	Lin H F (2006) Impact of organizational support on organizational intention to facilitate knowledge sharing. Knowledge Management Research & Practice 4(1).
#9	Lin, H. F., "Effects of extrinsic and intrinsic motivation on employee knowledge sharing intentions", Journal of Information Science, 33, 135–149, 2007.
#10	Kukko M and Helander N (2012) Knowledge sharing barriers in growing software companies. In Proceedings of the Hawaii International Conference on System Sciences, IEEE Publications, Maui, HI, USA.
#11	Kukko M (2013) Knowledge sharing barriers in organic growth: A case study from a software company. Journal of High Technology Management Research 24(1), 18-29.
#12	Vasanthapriyan S, Xiang J, Tian J and Xiong S (2017) Knowledge synthesis in software industries: a survey in Sri Lanka. Knowledge synthesis in software industries: a survey in Sri Lanka. Knowledge Management Research & Practice, 15(3), 413-430.
#13	Phung V D, Hawryszkiewycz I and Binsawad M H (2016) Classifying knowledge sharing barriers by organizational structure in order to find ways to remove these barriers. In Proceedings of the Eighth International Conference on Knowledge and Systems Engineering (KSE), IEEE Publications, Hanoi, Vietnam.
#14	Wickramasinghe V and Widyaratne R (2012) Effects of interpersonal trust, team leader support, rewards, and knowledge sharing mechanisms on knowledge sharing in project teams. The Journal of Information and Knowledge Management Systems 42(2), 214-236.
#15	Hau Y S, Kim B, Lee H and Kim Y G (2013) The effects of individual motivations and social capital on employees' tacit and explicit knowledge sharing intentions. International Journal of Information Management 33(2), 356-366.

Knowledge sharing barriers, (iii) Factors affecting knowledge sharing, (iv) Knowledge sharing model, and (v) General. The General category is used to categorize papers which discuss knowledge sharing in software companies in a general aspect instead of focusing on other categories mentioned above. One study can range more than one facet from the knowledge sharing perspective.

Research Type (RQ3)

As argued by Wieringa et al. (2006) and Petersen et al. (2008), a scientific research could be in different research approaches. Therefore, in this study, existing classification of research types as proposed by Wieringa et al. (2006) and Petersen et al. (2008) are concerned which are namely: validation research, solution proposal, opinion paper, evaluation research and experience paper etc. Moreover, Wieringa et al. (2006) points out that combinations of some categories are not likely to be happened, since, one study can span more than one category. In this study, only some of the categories were found to be adopted by the selected studies. Hence, the categories which showed zero studies in classification of selected studies were not concerned in this mapping study. The categories used in this mapping study, after disregarding irrelevant categories are shown below: (i) Evaluation research, (ii) Solution proposal.

Reported Problems (RQ4)

In this facet, major problems related to knowledge sharing in software companies are concerned as described in selected studies. Based on selected studies, following nine major aspects of problems have been extracted: (i) Poor employee attitude in sharing knowledge, (ii) Lack of employee motivation to share knowledge, (iii) Problems related to trust among employees, (iv) Problems related to available time, (v) Willingness of power relationships, (vi) Employee expectation on returning a value for sharing knowledge, (vii) Lack of communication skills, (viii) Lack of organizational commitment, and (ix) Problems related to technologies available . A study can span more than one category.

Purposes (RQ5)

This facet focuses on recognizing the purposes of organizations for leveraging knowledge sharing activities. Selected studies emphasize four major categories of purposes: (i) Better knowledge management, (ii) Competitive advantage, (iii) Project success, and (iv) Organizational learning. One study can range more than one category.

Types of Knowledge (RQ6)

This facet aims to recognize knowledge types that have been taken part in the research. Nonaka and Takeuchi (1995) proposed two types of knowledge which are tacit knowledge and explicit knowledge as the major distinguish between knowledge. In this mapping, classification of knowledge presented by Nonaka and Takeuchi (1995) was adopted. A study can span more than one category.

Technologies Used (RQ7)

This facet concerns over the technologies that have been used in software companies to incorporate knowledge sharing. Selected studies suggest different technological categories such as electronic knowledge repositories and conventional technologies (internet, intranet). But these studies do not provide a clear classification regarding technological methods that have been employed in organizations.

Limitations of the Mapping

In this section, limitations of the mapping study are discussed. This study is performed by just one author and major steps of this study; selecting studies and extracting data; are also performed by a single author. Therefore, this study may have some embedded subjectivity regarding selected studies and extracted data.

Also search string may include problems in the terminology. In such situations, it may have caused missing of certain primary studies. In the search string, term "Knowledge management" was included in order to investigate the research area more widely. In retrieving studies, only specific amount of databases were selected. In order to reduce this limitation, snowballing the references of studies selected from sources and direct search of researchers and research groups were performed. But, there may have considerable possibility of missing some valuable studies from the analysis performed.

Eventually, regarding the classification of research type, classification scheme proposed by Wieringa et al. (2006) was adopted. But, some of the other researchers point out this classification scheme as an inappropriate scheme to classify research types in secondary studies. This scheme is proposed to apply in requirement engineering processes. Hence, it may not fit with the context used in this study. Also, due to classification's dependency over background and expertise of researcher, there may have classification bias.

RESULTS

In this section, findings and results derived through the mapping study are discussed under each research question mentioned in the previous section. Identifiers depicted in Table 8 were used to represent each study whenever needed.

Classification by Publication Year and Source (RQ1)

In order to provide an outline view of the effort done by researchers in the field of knowledge sharing in software companies Figure 2 presents the distribution of selected papers over the year of publication. In this study, only the papers published since 2005 to 2017 were taken into account. According to Figure 2 researchers have focused on knowledge sharing in the software field considerably, in the recent decade, since, there have been published 13 papers out of 15 selected papers in 2011-2017 period of time and research in this duration is relatively stable. Before year 2010, a gap in the research related to the subject can be seen according to this study. Selected studies were published in Journals and Conferences. Majority of the papers have been published in Journals which is approximately 66.7% of publications. Other 33.3% of the papers have been published as Conference Papers.

When considering the sources of publication, there is a variance of the publication sources. Selected 15 papers have been published in 14 different sources. Two papers could be seen published in International Journal of Information Management. Therefore, it can be identified that there is no well-structured and well-established forum to discuss the topic. Moreover, publication vehicles in the area of Knowledge Management, Technology Management, Information Management, Project Management, System Science and System Engineering seem to be more approachable sources of publishing studies on this topic. Table 9 provides the information related to publication sources and types of the selected studies.

Research Focus From the Knowledge Sharing Perspective (RQ2)

According to the data shown in Table 10, each study discusses one or more facets of knowledge sharing: (i) Knowledge sharing in software development, (ii) Knowledge sharing barriers, (iii) Factors affecting knowledge sharing, and (iv) Knowledge sharing model. One study found which is not discussing any of the above mentioned aspects of knowledge sharing and it discusses the general background of knowledge sharing as one of the knowledge management phases. Therefore, it was categorized under General aspect. Most of the papers (44.4%) appeared to describe the factors affecting knowledge sharing. Only one paper found establishing a model for capturing and

Figure 2. Distribution of the selected studies over the years

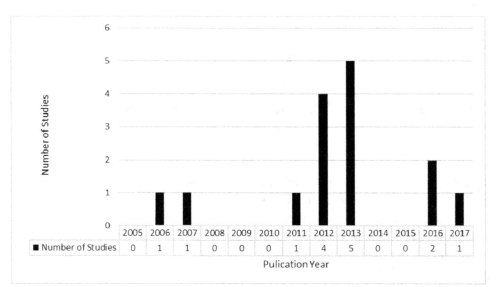

Table 9. Sources of publication

#ID	Source of publication	Type
#1	Journal of Knowledge Management	Journal
#2	International Journal of Knowledge Management	Journal
#3	Sri Lankan Journal of Management	Journal
#4	Nordic Contributions in IS Research (SCIS)	Conference papers
#5	International Journal of Information Management	Journal
#6	12th IFIP WG 5.1 International Conference, PLM	Conference papers
#7	International Journal of Project Management	Journal
#8	Knowledge Management Research & Practice	Journal
#9	Journal of Information Science	Journal
#10	Hawaii International Conference on System Sciences	Conference papers
#11	Journal of High Technology Management Research	Journal
#12	Knowledge Management Research & Practice	Journal
#13	Eighth International Conference on Knowledge and Systems Engineering (KSE)	Conference papers
#14	The Journal of Information and Knowledge Management Systems	Journal
#15	International Journal of Information Management	Journal

Table 10. Distribution of research focus from knowledge sharing perspective

Research Focus	2005	2006	2007	2008	2009	2010	2011	2012	2013	2014	2015	2016	2017	Total (%)
Knowledge sharing in software development							#3	#7 #14	#4					4 (22.2)
Knowledge sharing barriers								#10	#4 #11			#13		4 (22.2)
Factors affecting knowledge sharing		#8	#9					#5 #7 #14	#1 #2 #15					8 (44.4)
Knowledge sharing model												#6		1 (5.6)
General													#12	1 (5.6)

sharing knowledge. Three studies published by Heeager and Nielsen (2013) (#4), Park and Lee (2012) (#7), and Wickramasinghe and Widyaratne (2012) (#14) cover more than one aspects of the mentioned knowledge sharing aspects.

Research Type (RQ3)

Table 11 depicts the distribution of studies regarding the research type used. According to the classification of research types presented by Wieringa et al. (2006), in this mapping, selected studies have used only two research approaches; Evaluation research and Solution proposal. All 15 papers were classified into evaluation research (100%). Only two papers present solution proposals (approximately 13.3%). Other types were not followed by the selected studies.

Table 11. Distribution of research type

Research type	2005	2006	2007	2008	2009	2010	2011	2012	2013	2014	2015	2016	2017	Total (%)
Evaluation research		#8	#9				#3	#5 #7 #10 #14	#1 #2 #4 #11 #15			#6 #13	#12	15 (100)
Solution paper								#4				#6		2 (13.3)

Reported Problems (RQ4)

Table 12 represents the distribution of problems in software companies related to knowledge sharing. This section aims to make future directions for researchers and motivate research in this subject. According to the findings of this mapping, 'Lack of organizational commitment', has the highest representativeness, which is 10 papers out of 15 selected papers. It is computed as approximately 25.6%. Many sub sections such as leadership, reward systems and organizational culture etc. have been mentioned in different papers under organizational commitment. Next highest representativeness was 'Problems related to trust among individuals' (approximately 17.9% and 7 out of 15).

Table 12. Distribution of discussed problems

Problems	2005	2006	2007	2008	2009	2010	2011	2012	2013	2014	2015	2016	2017	Total (%)
Poor employee attitude in sharing knowledge			#9						#5					2 (5.1)
Lack of employee motivation to share knowledge									#1 #2 #4			#13		4 (10.3)
Problems related to trust among employees								#5 #7 #14	#4 #11 #15			#13		7 (17.9)
Problems related to available time								#5 #10	#4 #11					4 (10.3)
Willingness of power relationships									#11			#13		2 (5.1)
Employee expectation on returning a value for sharing knowledge								#5 #10	#1 #2					4 (10.3)
Lack of communication skills									#4					1 (2.6)
Lack of organizational commitment		#8					#3	#5 #14	#1 #4 #11			#6 #13	#12	10 (25.6)
Problems related to technologies available								#5	#4 #11			#6 #13		5 (12.8)

Purposes (RQ5)

Table 13 establishes the distribution of organizations' purposes of employing knowledge sharing in software companies. 12 studies have identified the purpose of applying knowledge sharing as achieving the competitive advantage. It represents 60% contribution of selected studies. Due to software companies majorly focus on large development projects, achieving project success, also has become one of the major purposes of applying knowledge sharing. It has 20% representativeness, which is 4 papers out of 15 selected papers.

Types of Knowledge (RQ6)

In order to classify studies under the types of knowledge considered in knowledge sharing, the classification proposed by Nonaka and Takeuchi (1995) was adopted. This proposes two types of knowledge; tacit and explicit knowledge as the fundamental types of knowledge. When considering selected papers, all the papers have mentioned tacit knowledge as the most important type of knowledge when sharing knowledge. Tacit knowledge is concerned in all 15 selected papers (100%). Only one study authored by Kukko (2013) has discussed both explicit and tacit knowledge. Though, Kukko further argues tacit knowledge as the most difficult and important knowledge to be shared. Therefore, explicit knowledge only represented 6.7% application in knowledge sharing as mentioned by selected papers. Table 14 represents the distribution of knowledge types.

Table 13. Distribution of purposes

Purposes	2005	2006	2007	2008	2009	2010	2011	2012	2013	2014	2015	2016	2017	Total (%)
Better knowledge management												#12		1 (5)
Competitive advantage		#8	#9					#5 #7 #10 #14	#1 #2 #4 #11 #15			#13		12 (60)
Project success							#3	#14	#4			#6		4 (20)
Organizational learning									#4			#6	#12	3 (15)

Table 14. Distribution of knowledge types

Knowledge type	2005	2006	2007	2008	2009	2010	2011	2012	2013	2014	2015	2016	2017	Total (%)
Tacit knowledge		#8	#9				#3	#5 #7 #10 #14	#1 #2 #4 #11 #15			#6 #13	#12	15 (100)
Explicit knowledge									#11					1 (6.7)

Technologies Used (RQ7)

Among 15 selected studies, only five studies (#4, #5, #6, #11, and #13) address the technological aspect of knowledge sharing. Other papers (#1, #2, #3, #7, #8, #9, #10, #11, #12, #14, and #15) do not give attention on this issue. Papers which focus on technological aspect have mentioned a gap in technologies used. While they point out usage of many technologies in software companies, they have also emphasized a lack in skills on these technologies. Even though, studies discuss about technological usage in knowledge sharing, they do not have mentioned a clear classification of technologies that have been employed in organizations.

Benefits and Problems Reported on Knowledge Sharing in Software Companies (RQ8)

This mapping provides information regarding both benefits and problems of implementing knowledge sharing processes in software companies. Benefits and problems which grasped in the selected studies are discussed below.

Benefits Reported on Knowledge Sharing in Software Companies

1. Competitive advantage

As a result of rapid competition in IT industry, organizations fail to be stable in their position in the market. Knowledge sharing makes the knowledge available all through the organization by transferring existing knowledge among employees. This shapes the knowledge resource in organizations and supports in achieving a sustainable competitive advantage.

2. Project success

In software companies, employees generally work as teams in medium to large scale projects where knowledge of each team member should be applied in. Therefore, success of the project is a dependence of the appropriateness of knowledge sharing among team members.

3.   Organizational learning

Organizational learning is the process of creating knowledge, capturing knowledge and transferring knowledge within an organization. When this takes place over many years, organization improves by gaining a vast range of experience.

Problems Reported on Knowledge Sharing in Software Companies

1.   Employees' unwillingness to share knowledge

Most of the employees do not share their experiences and insights. Therefore, this knowledge remains personal to the knowledge owner disabling sharing of that knowledge.

2.   Lack of time due to increased workload

Knowledge sharing is sometimes become an additional stuff to be done by employees. In their schedules which are already rushed, it may increase workload as well as costs.

3.   Unavailability of proper knowledge sharing processes

Most of the software companies are still under development. Therefore, SMEs mostly do not have well-structured knowledge sharing processes. This fact becomes an obstacle in implementing knowledge sharing activities.

DISCUSSION

As a summary of results, knowledge is treated as a cornerstone for software companies to achieve sustainable competitive advantage. However, knowledge sharing in software companies generate both positive and negative effects.

In this study, a selection criteria was conducted to identify most appropriate set of studies regarding this subject. At the initial stage, search string was applied in seven digital repositories and retrieved all the available studies related to this topic. Secondly, applying different selection criteria on selected studies retrieved 11 studies as the most appropriate studies regarding the topic. Thirdly, this content was increased up to 15 by adding 4 more studies which were identified as important to this subject, by snowballing and direct searching for publications by researchers of selected studies.

Selected 15 studies emphasize different facets of knowledge sharing in software companies. Each study focuses at least on one aspect of knowledge sharing either as a whole or sub section of knowledge sharing. With respect to different aspects of knowledge sharing, 'Factors affecting knowledge sharing', has received much attention from majority of studies.

Studies point out lack of organizational commitment as a major problem of knowledge sharing. Knowledge sharing begins at the bottom level of the hierarchy which is the individual level. Moving knowledge from individual level to organizational level is the most difficult to be performed, unless, the organization does not facilitate required enablers such as leadership, reward systems etc. to enable the sharing of knowledge, even all the other catalysts are available.

When considered the research types which were employed by selected studies, evaluation research was found the most leading research type. All the selected papers have employed an evaluation research while 2 papers out of 15 selected papers present solution proposals.

When considering the types of knowledge that have been managed in knowledge sharing, all most all studies have suggested tacit knowledge as the most prominent type of knowledge to be managed. Only one study was found mentioning both tacit and explicit knowledge. In order to categorize knowledge types, the classification established by Nonaka and Takeuchi (1995) was taken into account, focusing on the most general classification of knowledge into tacit and explicit knowledge.

With reference to technologies, only five papers (#4, #5, #6, #11 and #13) were found addressing the technological aspect of knowledge sharing. Even though, these studies widely talk about barriers and problems regarding leveraging technologies in knowledge sharing, they do not clearly grasp specific types of technologies that have been implemented in software companies to corporate in knowledge sharing. Eventually, this mapping points out achieving competitive advantage in the competitive business world as the major purpose of implementing knowledge sharing activities in software companies.

CONCLUSION

This paper contributes a mapping study of knowledge sharing in software companies based on following facets: (i) distribution of selected papers over years, (ii) research focus from knowledge sharing perspective, (iii) research type, (iv) reported problems in selected studies, (v) purposes of employing knowledge sharing in software companies, (vi) knowledge types managed in knowledge sharing, (vii) technologies used in knowledge sharing, and (viii) benefits and problems reported in selected studies.

As knowledge sharing is a well-known research area to conduct future research focusing on different facets of knowledge sharing, this mapping points out several knowledge sharing aspects. Among them majority of studies have been discussed on knowledge sharing barriers and factors affecting knowledge sharing. Even though, there is a considerable contribution of research related to knowledge sharing in recent years, there found a gap in research regarding knowledge sharing models and frameworks. Therefore, more future research might be necessary to propose appropriate frameworks in knowledge sharing. The key problems identified from this study are organizational commitment, trust and availability of technologies. Even technology usage in knowledge sharing has been discussed in certain literature, they have not mentioned types of technologies that have been employed in organizations. So, technology usage in knowledge sharing could be a broad field to direct future research. Also, all the studies have been focused on tacit knowledge as the most important type of knowledge when sharing knowledge. And there is a lack in research regarding sharing of explicit knowledge. Hence, future researchers could be able to conduct their research focusing on explicit knowledge sharing. In the context of results and findings of this mapping, following conclusions are highlighted:

1.   Knowledge sharing in software companies has gained much attention in research recently.
2.   Majority of research focused on factors affecting knowledge sharing.
3.   Lack of organizational commitment is the major problem in knowledge sharing.
4.   Achieving competitive advantage is the main purpose of employing knowledge sharing in software companies.
5.   Tacit knowledge is the most concerned knowledge type in the context of sharing knowledge.
6.   Technology usage in knowledge sharing has been recognized as more important to successful knowledge sharing.

REFERENCES

Amayah, T. A. (2013). Determinants of knowledge sharing in a public sector organization. *Journal of Knowledge Management, 17*(3), 454–471. doi:10.1108/JKM-11-2012-0369

Andreasian, G., & Andreasian, M. (2013). *Knowledge Sharing and Knowledge Transfer Barriers* (Dissertation).

Anthony, P., & Ezeh, A. (2013). Factors Influencing Knowledge Sharing in Software Development: A Case Study at Volvo Cars IT Torslanda. Gothenburg, Sweden: Gothenburg University Publications Electronic Archive.

Block, M. (2012). Knowledge Sharing as the Key Driver for Sustainable Innovation of Large Organizations. In *Sustainable Manufacturing* (pp. 337-342). Berlin, Germany: Springer.

Endres, M., & Chowdhury, S. (2013). The Role of Expected Reciprocity in Knowledge Sharing. *International Journal of Knowledge Management, 9*(3), 1–19. doi:10.4018/jkm.2013040101

Erica, F. D. S., Ricardo, D A F., & Nandamudi, L. V. (2014). Knowledge management initiatives in software testing: A mapping study. *Information and Software Technology, 57*(1), 378–391.

Hau, Y. S., Kim, B., Lee, H., & Kim, Y. G. (2013). The effects of individual motivations and social capital on employees' tacit and explicit knowledge sharing intentions. *International Journal of Information Management, 33*(2), 356–366. doi:10.1016/j.ijinfomgt.2012.10.009

Heeager, L., & Nielsen, P. A. (2013). Agile Software Development and the Barriers to Transfer of Knowledge: An Interpretive Case Study. In M. Aanestad, & T. Bratteteig (Eds.), *Proceedings of the Nordic Contributions in IS Research (SCIS), Lecture Notes in Business Information Processing* (pp. 18-39). Berlin, Germany: Springer Publications.

Joseph, B., & Jacob, M. (2011). Knowledge sharing intentions among IT professionals in India. Information Intelligence, Systems. *Technology and Management, 141*(1), 23–31.

Kharabsheh, R., Bittel, N., Elnsour, W., Bettoni, M., & Bernhard, W. (2016). A Comprehensive Model of Knowledge Sharing. In *Proceedings of the 17th European conference of KM*. Ulster University.

Kitchenham, B., & Charters, S. (2007). *Guidelines for performing Systematic Literature Reviews in Software Engineering.* Academic Press.

Kukko, M. (2013). Knowledge sharing barriers in organic growth: A case study from a software company. *The Journal of High Technology Management Research, 24*(1), 18–29. doi:10.1016/j.hitech.2013.02.006

Kukko, M., & Helander, N. (2012). Knowledge sharing barriers in growing software companies. In *Proceedings of the Hawaii International Conference on System Sciences.* IEEE Publications. 10.1109/HICSS.2012.407

Lin, H. F. (2006). Impact of organizational support on organizational intention to facilitate knowledge sharing. *Knowledge Management Research and Practice, 4*(1), 26–35. doi:10.1057/palgrave.kmrp.8500083

Lin, H. F. (2007). Effects of extrinsic and intrinsic motivation on employee knowledge sharing intentions. *Journal of Information Science, 33*(2), 135–149. doi:10.1177/0165551506068174

Nonaka, I., & Takeuchi, H. (1995). *The knowledge-creating company: How Japanese companies create the dynamics of innovation.* New York, NY: Oxford University Press.

Park, J., & Lee, J. (2012). Knowledge sharing in information systems development projects: Explicating the role of dependence and trust. *International Journal of Project Management, 32*(1), 153–165. doi:10.1016/j.ijproman.2013.02.004

Paulin, D., & Sunneson, K. (2012). Knowledge Transfer, Knowledge Sharing and Knowledge Barriers – Three Blurry Terms in KM. *Electronic Journal of Knowledge Management, 10*(1), 81–91.

Petersen, K., Feldt, R., Mujtaba, S., & Mattsson, M. (2008). Systematic mapping studies in software engineering. In *Proceedings of the 12th international conference on Evaluation and Assessment in Software Engineering.* BCS Learning & Development Ltd.

Phung, V. D., Hawryszkiewycz, I., & Binsawad, M. H. (2016). Classifying knowledge-sharing barriers by organizational structure in order to find ways to remove these barriers. In *Proceedings of the Eighth International Conference on Knowledge and Systems Engineering (KSE).* IEEE Publications. 10.1109/KSE.2016.7758032

Ranasinghe, G., & Jayawardana, A. K. L. (2011). Impact of knowledge sharing on project success in the Sri Lankan software industry. *Sri Lankan Journal of Management, 16*(1).

Sandhu, M., Jain, K., & Ahmad, I. (2011). Knowledge sharing among public sector employees: Evidence from Malaysia. *International Journal of Public Sector Management, 24*(1), 206–226. doi:10.1108/09513551111121347

Seba, I., Rowley, J., & Lambert, S. (2012). Factors affecting attitudes and intentions towards knowledge sharing in the Dubai Police Force. *International Journal of Information Management, 32*(1), 372–380. doi:10.1016/j.ijinfomgt.2011.12.003

Teddlie, C., & Tashakkori, A. (2006). A general typology of research designs featuring mixed methods. *Research in the Schools, 13*(1), 12–28.

Vasanthapriyan, S., Xiang, J., Tian, J., & Xiong, S. (2017). Knowledge synthesis in software industries: a survey in Sri Lanka. *Knowledge Management Research & Practice, 15(3), 413-430*.10.105741275-017-0057-7

Wickramasinghe, V., & Widyaratne, R. (2012). Effects of interpersonal trust, team leader support, rewards, and knowledge sharing mechanisms on knowledge sharing in project teams. *The Journal of Information and Knowledge Management Systems, 42*(2), 214–236.

Wieringa, R., Maiden, N., Mead, N., & Rolland, C. (2006). Requirements engineering paper classification and evaluation criteria: A proposal and a discussion. *Requirements Engineering, 11*(1), 102–107. doi:10.100700766-005-0021-6

Yi, J. (2009). A measure of knowledge sharing behavior: Scale development and validation. *Knowledge Management Research and Practice, 7*(1), 65–81. doi:10.1057/kmrp.2008.36

Zammit, J. P., Gao, J., & Evans, R. (2016). A Framework to Capture and Share Knowledge Using Storytelling and Video Sharing in Global Product Development. In *Proceedings of the 12th IFIP International Conference on Product Lifecycle Management (PLM)*. IFIP Advances in Information and Communication Technology. 10.1007/978-3-319-33111-9_24

Chapter 5
Knowledge Management Initiatives in Agile Software Development:
A Literature Review

Shanmuganathan Vasanthapriyan
(iD) https://orcid.org/0000-0002-0597-0263
Sabaragamuwa University of Sri Lanka, Sri Lanka

ABSTRACT

Agile software development (ASD) is a knowledge-intensive and collaborative activity and thus Knowledge Management (KM) principals should be applied to improve the productivity of the whole ASD process from the beginning to the end of the phase. The goal is to map the evidence available on existing researches on KM initiatives in ASD in order to identify the state of the art in the area as well as the future research. Therefore, investigation of various aspects such as purposes, types of knowledge, technologies and research type are essential. The authors conducted a systematic review of literature published between 2010 and December 2017 and identified 12 studies that discuss agile requirements engineering. They formulated and applied specific inclusion and exclusion criteria in two distinct rounds to determine the most relevant studies for their research goal. Reuse of knowledge of the team is the perspective that has received more attention.

DOI: 10.4018/978-1-5225-9448-2.ch005

INTRODUCTION

Software development is a process which is a collection of steps like analyzing, designing, programming, documenting, testing, maintaining and bug fixing (Vasanthapriyan, Tian, & Xiang, 2015). It is clear that software development has organized to deliver final better-quality solutions to the end users or customers. When the term "software development" converts to the term "agile software development", ASD has become a new turning point in the world. Although development teams have habituated traditional software methods like waterfall and prototyping, it is a good forethought to use agile for the development teams worldwide (Dybå & Dingsøyr, 2008).

There's a big focus in the ASD community on collaboration and the self-organizing team. That doesn't mean that there aren't managers. It means that teams have the ability to figure out how they're going to approach things on their own. It means that those teams are cross-functional. Those teams don't have to have specific roles involved so much as that when you get the team together, you make sure that you have all the right skill sets on the team.

Software development is a knowledge intensive and collaborative process which mainly depends on knowledge and experience of software engineers (Bjørnson & Dingsøyr, 2008; Vasanthapriyan et al., 2015). Therefore, the knowledge of the members of a team and the outside team within the organization should be properly managed by capturing, storing and reusing when needed. Even though traditional software methods use detailed specifications and design upfront and rigorous documentations (Abrahamsson, Salo, Ronkainen, & Warsta, 2017) to manage the knowledge, agile methods and principals (Petersen, Feldt, Mujtaba, & Mattsson, 2008) emerge to the software development which brings collaboration and interaction within the team and the outside of the team. It helps to manage the knowledge more efficiently and effectively by presenting the right knowledge in the right form to the right person at the right time.'

KM is about making the right knowledge available to the right people. It is about making sure that an organization can learn, and that it will be able to retrieve and use its knowledge assets in current applications as they are needed. In the words of Peter Drucker it is "the coordination and exploitation of organizational knowledge resources, in order to create benefit and competitive advantage" (Drucker, 1999). Where the disagreement sometimes occurs is in conjunction with the creation of new knowledge. Wellman (2009) limits the scope of KM to lessons learned and the techniques employed for the management of what is already known. He argues that knowledge creation is often perceived as a separate discipline and generally falls under innovation management. Williams and Bukowitz (1999) link KM directly to tactical and strategic requirements. Its focus is on the use and enhancement of knowledge-based assets to enable the firm to respond to these issues. According to this view, the answer to the question "what is knowledge management" would be significantly broader.

A similarly broad definition is presented by Davenport and Prusak (1970), which states that KM "is managing the corporation's knowledge through a systematically and organizationally specified process for acquiring, organizing, sustaining, applying, sharing and renewing both the tacit and explicit knowledge of employees to enhance organizational performance and create value". The knowledge must be constructed in a social and evolutionary process involving all stakeholders during the software development. Nakamori introduced a generic knowledge construction framework "Theory of knowledge construction systems" which is a systems approach to synthesize a variety of knowledge and to justify new knowledge (Nakamori, 2013).

Alahyari reported that only a substantial amount of papers has been published in recent years topics related to agile software development. Most of them were related to particular agile methods or comparing agile and other development processes (Alahyari, Svensson, & Gorschek, 2017). However, no recent study was found to have a dedicated focus on the concept of knowledge management. Previous reviews and investigations have been conducted for KM in ASD in different perspectives such as principals, methods, pros and cons, opportunities (Neves, Rosa, Correia, & de Castro Neto, 2011) and supporting agile practices (Fowler & Highsmith, 2001). However, what are the influences of KM in ASD and what kind of tools help to proceed with KM in ASD is not well understood. To identify and address this gap, mapping study has been performed to determine that there is research evidence on a relevant topic. Results of the mapping study help to recognize the gaps in order to suggest of future research and give the direction to a suitable position new research activity (Boden & Avram, 2009; Dorairaj, Noble, & Malik, 2012; Razzak & Ahmed, 2014). Further, in the context of ASD, KM can be used to capture knowledge and experience generated during the development process. Knowledge sharing is viewed as an important set of processes that can contribute to effective agile software development projects (Razzak, 2015).

The rest of this paper presents as below. Section 2 presents a background of KM and ASD and also related research. Section 3 discusses the research method applied to perform the mapping study. Results and discussions are presented in Section 4. Section 5 presents the conclusion and possibilities and directions for future works.

BACKGROUND

In this section, the main concepts related to the topic addressed namely: KM and ASD. Moreover, we briefly discuss related research, i.e. secondary studies that are related to these topics.

Knowledge Management

Knowledge is the possession of the information within its context. Knowledge is one of the most valuable assets for most organizations. That is, organizational knowledge is considering as the most valuable and the important asset the organization has. They are tacit and explicit. Tacit knowledge is derived from the experience which can be difficult to define and also to write down. For example, tacit knowledge covers knowledge that is unarticulated and associated to the senses, movement skills, physical experiences, intuition, or implicit rules of thumb. Explicit knowledge, in turn, represents the objective and rational knowledge that can be documented, and, thus can be accessed by multiple individuals. Explicit knowledge is very formal and can be documented (Begoña Lloria, 2008). Therefore, explicit knowledge can be shared and communicated easily (Dingsoyr & Smite, 2014). When approaching the KM, simply we can describe this as making the availability of the right knowledge to the right people in an organization. But in broadly KM can be identified as systematic management of the most valuable and important assets of the organization on behalf of creating value and meeting strategic requirements (Kavitha & Ahmed, 2011). KM can be viewed as the development and leveraging of organizational knowledge to increase organization's value (Begoña Lloria, 2008). KM is a method that simplifies the process of sharing, distributing, creating, capturing, and understanding of an organization's knowledge that should be employed (Davenport and Prusak (1970). ''The Knowledge-Creating Company'' by Nonaka and Takeuchi seeks in explaining the success of Japanese companies by their skills in ''organizational knowledge creation'' (Nonaka, Toyama, & Konno, 2000). According to Alavi and Leidner, the basic generic KM activities are known as "knowledge creation", "knowledge transfer" and "knowledge application" (Alavi & Leidner, 2001). Bhatt stated that KM process can be categorized into knowledge creation, knowledge validation, knowledge presentation, knowledge distribution, and knowledge application (Vasanthapriyan, Xiang, Tian, & Xiong, 2017). KM can be a formal process of determining what internally held information could be used to benefit an organization and ensuring that this information is easily made available to those who need it. Vasanthapriyan considered knowledge identification, knowledge acquisition, knowledge creation, knowledge sharing, knowledge storage, and knowledge application as KM activities to use in their study context (Vasanthapriyan et al., 2017). The importance of such

KM becomes critical for some key positions, who manage daily activities, especially when it requires critical decision makings with their know-how experiences. Further, models like SECI process which stands for Socialization, Externalization, Combination, and Internalization, can be used for knowledge transfer and creation within the organizations.

Agile Software Development

In 2001, failures of the waterfall model were identified and the Agile methodology was introduced (Schwaber & Beedle, 2002). The term agile has been presented in 2001 when seventeen software developers met to explore and share new and improved ways of software development (Fowler & Highsmith, 2001). Agile development methodologies consist with a set of software development practices that are defined by well experienced practitioners (Schwaber & Beedle, 2002). ASD has become an efficient and effective way of software development which is used to build software or the final output iteratively and incrementally. ASD is used to build software in multiple iterations and increments (Abrahamsson et al., 2017). Each iteration is ending up with a workable product which is getting early feedback of the customer or the end user. As well this helps in delivering the product more reliably and timely.

These agile development practices reacts to traditional or plan driven methods which emphasize ''an engineering based, rationalized approach'' (Dorairaj et al., 2012). Agile software development is more than frameworks such as Scrum, Extreme Programming or Feature-Driven Development (FDD) (Schwaber & Beedle, 2002). Agile methods share few common characteristics which include iterative development process, adaptive which means accept changes, less documentation, interact with customer, focus on delivery, frequent testing, communication and collaboration among team members, improve motivation, high quality codes, knowledge transfer through openness and high-quality products with customer satisfaction (Schwaber & Beedle, 2002). Agile practices involved in software engineering field are simple design, small releases, pair programming, test driven development, daily stand-up meetings, task boards, product backlog, user stories, and on-site customer. Agile practitioners have perceived benefits which include cost reduction, quality improvements, improve flexibility among development teams, improve productivity, and improve customer satisfaction and reduction of time to market. Those benefits are achieved in software development phase and it is needed to investigate that these benefits are addressed in software maintenance phase (Vasanthapriyan, 2017).

Agile is the ability to create and respond to change. It is a way of dealing with, and ultimately succeeding in, an uncertain and turbulent environment. ASD is more than practices such as pair programming, test-driven development, stand-ups, planning sessions and sprints. ASD is an umbrella term for a set of frameworks and practices based on the values and principles expressed in the Manifesto for ASD and the 12 Principles behind it. When you approach software development in a particular manner, it's generally good to live by these values and principles and use them to help figure out the right things to do given your particular context (Vasanthapriyan et al., 2017). On the other hand, activities such as informal communication, face-to-face meetings, and knowledge sharing through social practices can create a more flexible and unstructured environment (Vasanthapriyan, 2017).

Knowledge Management in Organizations

Knowledge in organizations takes many forms such as the competencies and capabilities of employees, the knowledge about its customers and suppliers, know-how of conducting certain processes, the systems used in the company for leveraging performance and intellectual properties owned by the company such as; copyrights, licenses, patents and so on (North & Kumta, 2018). All the knowledge intensive organizations rely on making the most effective use of the available knowledge within the organization in order to compete and survive. If there is not available a proper knowledge sharing process within the organization, software practitioners would proceed with the knowledge that they already have or with the knowledge that is most easily available. Even that knowledge is accurate and of good quality, sometimes it may not be good enough to achieve the success of the projects or the sustainability of today's market (Zammit, Gao, & Evans, 2016). Omotayo states the important factors that drives KM requirement for an organization, as; organizational survival, competitive differentiation, globalization effects and aging of workforce. As his explanation, it is an undisputed fact that organizations have to compete on the basis of knowledge, since products and services are becoming increasingly complex and competitive (Omotayo, 2015).

Focusing on the question 'Is knowledge management important for an organization?', Omotayo (2015) suggests, 'when you know better, you do better'. Therefore, in order to succeed in the corporate world and put your business on top, the company needs to possess the best management of knowledge (Omotayo, 2015).

Common KM practices of the organizations are as follows (Murali & Kumar, 2014)

1. Knowledge repositories: Store and manage the various knowledge artefacts like white papers, articles, videos and other knowledge materials created by the employees.
2. Communities of knowledge: Especially through cross functional teams containing experts from different departments.

3. Knowledge sharing sessions: Share the knowledge gained in training sessions or by other knowledge sources such as courses offered by the company. They are recorded and made available through knowledge repositories.
4. Mentoring: Share the skills or knowledge of an expert in a certain domain to others who don't possess that knowledge.

As a result of the above definitions, it can thus be concluded that management of knowledge is promoted as an important and necessity factor for organizational survival (Omotayo, 2015). Further, Teamwork and collaboration among software developers produce significant amount of knowledge, which makes the sense of effective knowledge sharing among individuals (Vasanthapriyan et al., 2017). In addition, the knowledge management processes that transitioned to agile (requirements and domain knowledge, continuous learning, knowledge repositories) concentrate on tacit knowledge (Cram & Marabelli, 2018). Knowledge sharing could be identified as a process between units, teams and organizations where people exchange their knowledge with others ((Andreasian & Andreasian, 2013). Knowledge sharing starts at the individual level, since every person has tacit and explicit knowledge to share with others. Sharing tacit knowledge is more challenging as it cannot be easily expressed (Vasanthapriyan et al., 2015).

Related Works

This paper presents a secondary study which is based on analyzing primary studies (Kitchenham, Budgen, & Brereton, 2011). Mapping studies are intended to provide an overview of a topic area and identify whether there are sub-topics where more primary studies are needed (Kitchenham et al., 2011). At the beginning of this study, a tertiary study has been performed to look for secondary studies investigating the state of art in KM in ASD. Because of having a research gap in research studies related to the software development in Sri Lanka, this study has been conducted on all the research studies related to the field of KM and ASD regardless of the country to get the clear and wide view of KM in ASD. Consequently, the country has not been considered in the search string and other used search string is shown in Table 1 which has been applied in three metadata fields (title, abstract and keywords). The search string has been applied in the following electronic databases: IEEE Xplore, ACM Digital Library, Springer Link, Science Direct, Emerald Insight, and Research Gate. Since some of the electronic databases don't have any secondary study which is addressed KM in ASD, another investigation has been done to search KM and ASD separately. For that tertiary study, used search strings are shown in Table 2 and Table 3. After searching the six databases, returning 404 results. After eliminating duplications and applying the selection criteria, 147 studies are presenting secondary studies which are related to the KM and ASD both. Regarding the study which has been conducted on searching for the secondary studies, at last, 12 studies have been selected.

RESEARCH METHOD

Research method of this mapping study is defined according to the guidelines described by Brereton, Kitchenham, Budgen, Turner, and Khalil (2007). Under the research method section, this paper discusses the main steps followed in the mapping study including research questions, study selection, data extraction and synthesis,

Table 1. Search terms of the study on KM in ASD

Areas	Search terms
ASD	"ASD ", "agile and software development"
Review	"systematic literature review", "systematic review", "systematic mapping", "mapping study", "systematic literature mapping"
Search string	("Agile software development) AND ("systematic literature review" OR "systematic review" OR "systematic mapping" OR "mapping study" OR' 'systematic literature mapping")

Table 2. Search terms of the study on ASD

Areas	Search terms
ASD	"ASD ", "agile and software development"
KM	"Knowledge Management"
Review	"systematic literature review", "systematic review", "systematic mapping", "mapping study", "systematic literature mapping"
Search string	("Agile software development" OR "Agile and software development") AND ("knowledge management") AND ("systematic literature review" OR "systematic review" OR "systematic mapping' 'OR "mapping study" OR "systematic literature mapping")

Table 3. Search terms of the study on KM

Areas	Search terms
KM	"Knowledge Management"
Review	"systematic literature review", "systematic review", "systematic mapping", "mapping study", "systematic literature mapping"
Search string	("Agile software development") AND ("systematic literature review" OR "systematic review" OR "systematic mapping" OR "mapping study" OR "systematic literature mapping")

Table 4. Inclusion and exclusion criteria

No.	Inclusion criterion (IC)
IC1	The study EKR use and project success in software companies
No.	Exclusion criteria (EC)
EC1	The study does not contain an abstract
EC2	The study is published just as an abstract
EC3	The language used in writing the study is not English
EC4	The study is an older version of a study already selected previously
EC5	The study is not a primary study. The study is either an editorial or a summary

classification schema that have been used in mapping and eventually, limitations of the mapping study. In the first selection stage, we looked for the current status of the research studies regarding in KM applied to ASD in organizations. In the second selection stage, a selection process has been performed to retrieve the studies. Here, following selection criteria were addressed:

1.   Definition of the search string and terms
2.   Sources for searching
3.   Definition for inclusion and exclusion criteria (shown in Table 4) and
4.   Way of storing data.

In the third selection stage, publications until December 2017 were considered. In the search process, as the searching result, a total of 404 publications were returned. Out of the total search result, 43 from IEEE Xplore, 107 from ACM Digital Library, 73 from Springer Link, 63 from Science Direct, 51 from Emerald Insight and 67 from Research Gate were found. To extract the most relevant studies, the selection process was performed on the selected publications. In the first stage, we eliminated duplications (publications that appear in more than one source), achieving 257 publications (reduction of approximately 63%). In the second stage, we applied the selection criteria (inclusion and exclusion criteria) over the title, abstract and keywords, resulting in 17 papers (reduction of 93%). 5 papers were eliminated by EC5 (The study is not a primary study) and 235 for not satisfying IC1 (The study discusses a KM initiative in ASD). In the third stage, the selection criteria were applied considering the full text, resulting in a set of 10 studies (reduction of approximately 41%). 1 paper was eliminated by EC4 (The study is an older version of another study already considered), and 6 papers were eliminated for not satisfying IC1 (The study discusses KM initiatives in ASD). Over these 10 studies considered relevant, the 4th stage, snowballing was performed which resulted in 6 papers. After applying the selection criteria over title, abstract and keywords, 3 papers remained (reduction of 50% over the 6 papers selected by snowballing). For the remaining, the selection criteria were applied considering the full text and only one paper remained (reduction of approximately 67% over the 3 previously selected papers).

Finally, we have selected 11 papers and in the 5th stage, we have looked for publications authored by the researchers and research groups involved in these studies. As a result of this searching, 2 papers identified and after analyzing the full text 1 paper was identified as more appropriate to the subject were selected as a direct search. Total of 12 papers was retrieved as the final result of this searching process, including, 10 from the sources, 1 from snowballing and 1 from direct searching researchers and research groups. Summary of each selection stage and their results are shown in Table 5. Table 5 clearly emphasizes the progressive elimination of the studies during the selection process. Table 6 provides the bibliographic references of the studies selected. Each study has been provided with a unique identifier (#id) and these identifiers are used in the rest of this paper to represent each study. When systematic mapping is conducting, a classification scheme is necessary to be defined (Petersen et al., 2008). The main finding of the selected research is; Factors affect KM using in ASD reported by the selected studies.

In this section, different kinds of limitation of this mapping study are discussed.

Table 5. Results of the selection stages

Stage	Applied criteria	Analyzed content	Initial number of studies	Final number of studies	Reduction
1st	Duplicate removal	Title, abstract and keywords	404	257	36.0
2nd	IC1 and EC3	Title, abstract and keywords	257	17	93.0
3rd	IC1, EC1, EC2, EC4 and EC5	Full text	17	10	41.0
4th (a)	Snowballing	Title, abstract and keywords	6 (added by snowballing)	3 (added by snowballing)	50.0
4th (b)	Snowballing and IC1	Full text	3 (added by snowballing)	1 (added by snowballing)	67.0
5th	Research groups	Full text	2 (added by research groups)	1 (added by research groups)	-
Final Result			404 (sources) + 6 (snowballing) + 2 (research groups) = 412	10 (sources) + 1 (snowballing) + 1	97.0

Table 6. Selected studies

ID	Bibliographic reference
#1	G. Borrego, A. L. Morán, R. R. P. Cinco, O. M. Rodríguez-Elias, and E. García-Canseco, "Review of approaches to manage architectural knowledge in Agile Global Software Development," IET Software, vol. 11, no. 3, pp. 77–88, Jan. 2017.
#2	J. Paredes, C. Anslow, and F. Maurer, "Information Visualization for Agile Software Development," 2014 Second IEEEWorking Conference on Software Visualization, 2014.
#3	M. A. Razzak and D. Mite, "Knowledge Management in Globally Distributed Agile Projects -- Lesson Learned," 2015IEEE 10th International Conference on Global Software Engineering, 2015
#4	Y. Andriyani, R. Hoda, and R. Amor, "Understanding Knowledge Management in Agile Software DevelopmentPractice," Knowledge Science, Engineering and Management Lecture Notes in Computer Science, pp. 195–207, 2017.
#5	M. Alawairdhi, "Agile development as a change management approach in software projects: Applied case study," 20162nd International Conference on Information Management (ICIM), 2016.
#6	Y. Andriyani, "Knowledge Management and Reflective Practice in Daily Stand-Up and Retrospective Meetings," LectureNotes in Business Information Processing Agile Processes in Software Engineering and Extreme Programming, pp. 285–291, 2017.
#7	F. O. Bjørnson and T. Dingsøyr, "A Survey of Perceptions on Knowledge Management Schools in Agile and TraditionalSoftware Development Environments," Lecture Notes in Business Information Processing Agile Processes in SoftwareEngineering and Extreme Programming, pp. 94–103, 2009.
#8	S. Dorairaj, J. Noble, and P. Malik, "Knowledge Management in Distributed Agile Software Development," 2012 AgileConference, 2012.
#9	A. R. Y. Cabral, M. B. Ribeiro, and R. P. Noll, "Knowledge Management in Agile Software Projects: A SystematicReview," Journal of Information & Knowledge Management, vol. 13, no. 01, p. 1450010, 2014.
#10	R. Vallon, B. J. D. S. Estácio, R. Prikladnicki, and T. Grechenig, "Systematic literature review on agile practices in globalsoftware development," Information and Software Technology, vol. 96, pp. 161–180, 2017.
#11	S. Ghobadi and L. Mathiassen, "Perceived barriers to effective knowledge sharing in agile software teams," InformationSystems Journal, vol. 26, no. 2, pp. 95–125, 2014.
#12	A. C. A. Menolli, M. A. Cunha, S. Reinehr, and A. Malucelli, "Old theories, New technologies: Understanding knowledge sharing and learning in Brazilian software development companies," Information and Software Technology, vol. 58, pp. 289–303, 2015.

This study may have some embedded subjectivity regarding selected studies and extracted data since major steps of this mapping study like selecting studies and extracting data is performed by one author.

1. This study is performed by just one author and major steps of this study; selecting studies and extracting data; are also performed by a single author. Therefore, this study may have some embedded subjectivity regarding selected studies and extracted data.

2. Also search string may include problems in the terminology. In such situations, it may have caused missing of certain primary studies. In the search string, term "Knowledge management" was included in order to investigate the research area more widely.

3. Only specific numbers of databases were selected for retrieving data. Snowballing technique is used to the references of studies selected from sources in order to reduce this limitation. Direct search of researchers and research groups were performed for selected studies but there may have the considerable possibility of missing some valuable studies from the analysis performed.

4. For some databases limitations on publication, the year was applied in order to select most updated research studies. Most of the times publications during 2010-2017 were searched so some important studies which were published before 2010 may have missed.

5. Hence, it may not fit with the context used in this study. Also, due to classification's dependency over background and expertise of researcher, there may have classification bias.

6. This study is used classification scheme proposed by Wieringa, Maiden, Mead, and Rolland (2006). But some researchers suggest that this method is inappropriate scheme to classify research types in secondary studies. So, there can be classification bias due to the expertise of the researchers and classification dependency over the background.

RESULTS AND DISCUSSION

In this section, findings and results derived through the mapping study are discussed. All the results were summarized in a table with the identifier of the paper, its bibliographic reference and that table were used as the source of extracting information to answer each research question. Figure 1 is represented to elaborate the distribution of selected papers over the year of publication. Only the papers published from 2009 to December 2017 were taken into account in order to get an updated view of the study area. According to Figure 1, researchers have focused on KM in ASD in recent years, since, there have been published 10 papers out of 12 selected papers in a 2014-2017 period of time.

That is 83% of the total selected studies. The selected studies were published in Journals and conferences. Most of the papers have been published in journals which is approximately 67% of publications. Other 33% of the papers are conference papers. As an overall view, it seems these publications covered the area of KM, ASD. According to the data shown in Table 7, distribution of the studies which are relevant to the research focuses from the ASD perspective. Most of the papers are

Figure 1. Distribution of the selected studies over the years

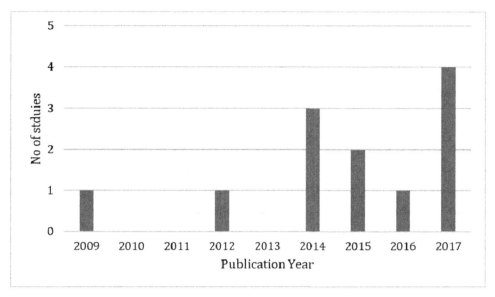

addressing KM in ASD without focusing on any aspects of ASD (7 out of 12). As well the papers which are addressing KM in ASD process are also showing high value (5 out of 12). Table 8 shows, most of the studies are discussing the aspects which are related to the KM process as a whole or focusing on one of its activities. Most of the papers (83.33%) discuss knowledge representation to provide KM support in ASD. Table 9 shows the distribution of research types. All the selected 12 studies propose some solution for KM in ASD.

Evaluation research and Solution proposal were the two types of research types. 8 papers out of 12 were classified into evaluation research (66.67%) and four papers present solution proposals (approximately 33.33%). Considering the distribution

Table 7. Research focus from the ASD perspective along the years

Research Focus	2009	2010	2011	2012	2013	2014	2015	2016	2017	Total
KM in ASD Process				#8		#11	#3	#1, #4		5 (41.6.7%)
KM in various kind of ASD phases							#3			1 (8.33%)
KM in ASD in general without focusing on any aspects of ASD	#7					#2, #9	#12	#5	#6, #10	7 (58.33%)

Table 8. Distribution over research focus regarding the KM perspective

Research Focus	2009	2010	2011	2012	2013	2014	2015	2016	2017	Total
KM Model						#9			#1	2 (16.67%)
Knowledge Representation	#7			#8		#9, #11	#3, #12	#5	#1, #4, #6	10 (83.33%)
Knowledge Elicitation				#8			#3		#1	3 (25%)
Knowledge Evolution				#8			#3			2 (16.67%)
Knowledge Management Systems (KMS)				#8		#2			#10	3 (25%)

Table 9. Distribution over research type

Research Focus	2009	2010	2011	2012	2013	2014	2015	2016	2017	Total
Evaluation Research	#7			#8		#9, #11	#3		#1, #4, #10	8 (66.67%)
Proposal Solution						#2	#12	#5	#6	4 (33.33%)

over the years, Table 10 shows the problems reported by software organizations related to knowledge in ASD. As well as we think these problems as a motivation for performing a research in KM to ASD. When we consider the results in Table 10, "Barriers in transferring ASD knowledge" and "ASD knowledge is not properly shared" are showing similar and the largest percentages (6 out of 12, corresponding to 50%). Table 11 shows the distribution of the purposes of the organization in managing ASD knowledge. When we consider the results, we can notice that "Organizational Learning" (8 studies-66.67%) has the largest value. "Process of knowledge in ASD" (6 studies-50%) and "Competitive advantages" (5 studies-41.67%) are showing next large percentages. Although "Reuse of knowledge related to ASD" (3 studies-25%) and "Cost reduction" (1 study) are showing some less percentage, all the purposes help to manage the knowledge in ASD.

Table 12 shows the distribution of the knowledge types in ASD over the years. Here the research focus fact "General" (3 studies- 25%) has got the largest percentage from the selected studies. "Product knowledge" (2 studies -16.7%), "Project knowledge" (3 studies-25%) and "Process knowledge" (1 studies-8.33%)

Table 10. Distribution of related problems (Motivation)

Research Focus	2009	2010	2011	2012	2013	2014	2015	2016	2017	Total
Barriers to transferring ASD knowledge				#8		#9, #11	#3		#1, #4	6 (50%)
Loss of ASD Knowledge	#7							#5	#10	3 (25%)
ASD knowledge is not properly shared	#7					#2, #9, #11	#12		#6	6 (50%)

Table 11. Distribution of purposes

Research Focus	2009	2010	2011	2012	2013	2014	2015	2016	2017	Total
Reuse of knowledge related to ASD						#2			#1, #10	3 (25%)
Knowledge Representation				#8		#9, #11			#1, #4, #10	6 (50%)
Knowledge Elicitation						#11				1 (8.33%)
Knowledge Evolution				#8		#9, #11	#3		#6	5 (41.67%)
Knowledge Management Systems (KMS)	#7			#8		#9	#12, #3	#5	#6, #4	8 (66.67%)

are having the percentages among the selected studies as given. The distributions of the technologies which are used to implement KM in ASD are shown in Table 13. Here, we have presented three different technologies in the research. It should be noticed that 2 studies do not address this question (#2, #5), representing 16.67%. The majority of the below studies uses conventional technologies (5 in 12 studies, corresponding to 41.67%). This category concerns IT conventional technologies such as databases, intranets, and internet.

According to the results of this mapping, there are many benefits to implementing KM in organizations for managing ASD knowledge.

Increasing the Effectiveness

It is necessary to increase the effectiveness of the ASD since knowledge and experience about the domain and the system which is going to develop are directly affecting to the effectiveness.

Table 12. Distribution of knowledge

Research Focus	2009	2010	2011	2012	2013	2014	2015	2016	2017	Total
Product knowledge						#2			#4	2 (16.67%)
Project knowledge							#3		#1, #4, #10	3 (25%)
Process knowledge									#4	1 (8.33%)
General	#7			#8		#9, #11	#12	#5	#6, #10	8 (66.67%)

Table 13. Distribution of technologies used

Research Focus	2009	2010	2011	2012	2013	2014	2015	2016	2017	Total
Ontology	#7					#11			#1	3 (25%)
Recommendation Systems				#8			#3		#4	3 (25%)
Process knowledge						#9, #11	#12		#6, #10	5 (41.67%)

Selection and Application of Suited Techniques and Methods

It is not a doubt that experience plays a key role in ASD and managing the past experience of the whole team members helps to effectively tailor the techniques and methods to the on-going project.

Competitive Advantages

KM is now seen as a strategic factor and knowledge is also identified as a factor of cost savings and competitive advantage. The ability to transfer best practices in the organization helps to bring a competitive advantage to the organization.

Cost Reduction

In ASD, the cost is strongly related with the time. Here the experience of all the team members helps to develop the product according to the timeline. As well development team decreases the risk of cost overruns and avoids costly activities that do not provide value by focusing on business value with every activity.

Increase the Productivity

It can be considered that there will be a new understanding of KM in ASD that it involves managing three different types of knowledge which are identified as process, project, and product. These three are helping to implement KM strategies like discussions, artifacts and visualizations during every day agile process in a business organization. Therefore, these strategies will help agile practitioners to become aware of and enable those to manage the knowledge in every agile practice productively.

Table 14 shows how the benefits are accommodating by the selected studies. Two of these benefits which are mentioned above are cited by over half of the studies. Although there are many benefits in KM in ASD, there are problems also. Those problems are,

KM Systems Are Not Appropriated

There are many difficulties in implementing the KM strategies such as knowledge acquisition, coding, storage, and searching functionalities effectively in KM systems because it involves all the problems mentioned above such as how to represent knowledge and time and interest of the employees.

Increased Workload

Since there are short timelines, it is a potential risk to incorporate the principles of KM in ASD because knowledge sharing can imply in increasing the team members' workload and costs. Table 15 shows how the problems are distributed in the selected studies.

CONCLUSION

As a summary of results, knowledge is treated as a cornerstone for software companies to achieve sustainable competitive advantage. However, knowledge management in ASD generate both positive and negative effects.

The study describes the results of ten research questions which have done investigations of the following points:

1. Distribution of the selected studies over the years;
2. Research focus from the software testing perspective;
3. Research focus from the KM perspective;

Table 14. Distribution of the identified benefits

Research Focus	2009	2010	2011	2012	2013	2014	2015	2016	2017	Total
A				#8		#9	#3	#5	#1, #4, #10	7 (58.33%)
B							#3		#1, #4	3 (25%)
C				#8		#2	#12		#1, #4	5 (41.67%)
D	#7			#8		#9, #11	#3, #12	#5	#4, #6, #10	10 (83.33%)

Table 15. Distribution of problems

Research Focus	2009	2010	2011	2012	2013	2014	2015	2016	2017	Total
A	#7			#8		#9, #11	#3, #12	#5	#1, #4, #10	10 (83.33%)
B						#2, #11			#6	3 (25%)

4. Research type;
5. Reported problems;
6. Purposes of employing in ASD;
7. Purposes to employ KM in ASD;
8. Types of knowledge typically managed in ASD;
9. Technologies used in KM in ASD;
10. Main conclusions (benefits and problems) reported on the KM in ASD.

The major problem in organizations are low reuse rate of knowledge and barriers in knowledge transfer in ASD is a recent research;

1. Knowledge types which are used in ASD are not identified correctly in the organizations;
2. Reuse of development knowledge is the main purpose of applying KM in ASD;
3. There is a great concern with explicit knowledge using in ASD, although tacit knowledge has been also recognized as a very useful knowledge item;
4. Advanced technologies used to provide KM in ASD.

Hence, future software engineering-based researchers could be able to conduct their research focusing on tacit and explicit knowledge management. In the context of results and findings of this mapping, following future research topics are highlighted:

1. Tacit Knowledge Management in globally distributed agile software development.
2. Investigating the scope of agile project management to be adapted by software companies.
3. Analysis of KM involvement in Kanban and Scrum for software development projects.
4. Understanding architectural knowledge sharing in agile software development.

According to these specific dimensions of knowledge will help agile practitioners have become aware of and enable them to manage, the knowledge in everyday agile practices effectively.

ACKNOWLEDGMENT

We thank some of the key officials from the Sri Lankan software companies to motivate us for this kind of study. We also thank the Sabaragamuwa University of Sri Lanka to encourage this research.

REFERENCES

Abrahamsson, P., Salo, O., Ronkainen, J., & Warsta, J. (2017). *Agile software development methods: Review and analysis.* arXiv preprint arXiv:1709.08439

Alahyari, H., Svensson, R. B., & Gorschek, T. (2017). A study of value in agile software development organizations. *Journal of Systems and Software, 125,* 271–288. doi:10.1016/j.jss.2016.12.007

Alavi, M., & Leidner, D. E. (2001). Review: Knowledge management and knowledge management systems: Conceptual foundations and research issues. *Management Information Systems Quarterly, 25*(1), 107–136. doi:10.2307/3250961

Andreasian, G., & Andreasian, M. (2013). *Knowledge Sharing and Knowledge Transfer Barriers. A Case Study.* Academic Press.

Begoña Lloria, M. (2008). A review of the main approaches to knowledge management. *Knowledge Management Research and Practice, 6*(1), 77–89. doi:10.1057/palgrave. kmrp.8500164

Bjørnson, F. O., & Dingsøyr, T. (2008). Knowledge management in software engineering: A systematic review of studied concepts, findings and research methods used. *Information and Software Technology, 50*(11), 1055–1068. doi:10.1016/j. infsof.2008.03.006

Boden, A., & Avram, G. (2009). *Bridging knowledge distribution-The role of knowledge brokers in distributed software development teams.* Paper presented at the Cooperative and Human Aspects on Software Engineering, 2009. CHASE'09. ICSE Workshop on. 10.1109/CHASE.2009.5071402

Brereton, P., Kitchenham, B. A., Budgen, D., & et al, . (2007). Lessons from applying the systematic literature review process within the software engineering domain. *Journal of Systems and Software, 80*(4), 571–583. doi:10.1016/j.jss.2006.07.009

Cram, W. A., & Marabelli, M. (2018). Have your cake and eat it too? Simultaneously pursuing the knowledge-sharing benefits of agile and traditional development approaches. *Information & Management, 55*(3), 322–339. doi:10.1016/j. im.2017.08.005

Davenport, T., & Prusak, L. (2000). *Working knowledge: How organizations manage what they know.* Brighton, MA: Harvard Business Press.

Dingsoyr, T., & Smite, D. (2014). Managing knowledge in global software development projects. *IT Professional, 16*(1), 22–29. doi:10.1109/MITP.2013.19

Dorairaj, S., Noble, J., & Malik, P. (2012). *Knowledge management in distributed agile software development.* Paper presented at the Agile Conference (AGILE), 2012. 10.1109/Agile.2012.17

Drucker, P. F. (1999). Knowledge-worker productivity: The biggest challenge. *California Management Review, 41*(2), 79–94. doi:10.2307/41165987

Dybå, T., & Dingsøyr, T. (2008). Empirical studies of agile software development: A systematic review. *Information and Software Technology, 50*(9), 833–859. doi:10.1016/j.infsof.2008.01.006

Fowler, M., & Highsmith, J. (2001). The agile manifesto. *Software Development, 9*(8), 28–35.

Kavitha, R., & Ahmed, M. I. (2011). *A knowledge management framework for agile software development teams*. Paper presented at the Process Automation, Control and Computing (PACC), 2011 International Conference on. 10.1109/PACC.2011.5978877

Kitchenham, B. A., Budgen, D., & Brereton, O. P. (2011). Using mapping studies as the basis for further research–a participant-observer case study. *Information and Software Technology, 53*(6), 638–651. doi:10.1016/j.infsof.2010.12.011

Murali, A., & Kumar, S. K. (2014). Knowledge Management and Human Resource Management (HRM): Importance of Integration. *FIIB Business Review, 3*(1), 3–10.

Nakamori, Y. (2013). Knowledge and systems science: enabling systemic knowledge synthesis. Boca Raton, FL: CRC Press. doi:10.1201/b15155

Neves, F. T., Rosa, V. N., Correia, A. M. R., & de Castro Neto, M. (2011). *Knowledge creation and sharing in software development teams using Agile methodologies: Key insights affecting their adoption*. Paper presented at the Information Systems and Technologies (CISTI), 2011 6th Iberian Conference on.

Nonaka, I., Toyama, R., & Konno, N. (2000). SECI, Ba and leadership: A unified model of dynamic knowledge creation. *Long Range Planning, 33*(1), 5–34. doi:10.1016/S0024-6301(99)00115-6

North, K., & Kumta, G. (2018). *Knowledge management: Value creation through organizational learning*. Springer. doi:10.1007/978-3-319-59978-6

Omotayo, F. O. (2015). Knowledge Management as an important tool in Organisational Management: A Review of Literature. University of Nebraska-Lincoln.

Petersen, K., Feldt, R., Mujtaba, S., & Mattsson, M. (2008). *Systematic Mapping Studies in Software Engineering*. Paper presented at the EASE.

Razzak, M. A. (2015). *Knowledge Management in Globally Distributed Agile Projects--Lesson Learned*. Paper presented at the Global Software Engineering (ICGSE), 2015 IEEE 10th International Conference on, Sri Lanka.

Razzak, M. A., & Ahmed, R. (2014). *Knowledge sharing in distributed agile projects: Techniques, strategies and challenges*. Paper presented at the Computer Science and Information Systems (FedCSIS), 2014 Federated Conference on. 10.15439/2014F280

Schwaber, K., & Beedle, M. (2002). Agile software development with Scrum (Vol. 1). Upper Saddle River, NJ: Prentice Hall.

Vasanthapriyan, S. (2017). Agile and scrum in a small software development project: a case study. In *Proceedings of 7th International Symposium*. South Eastern University of Sri Lanka.

Vasanthapriyan, S., Tian, J., & Xiang, J. (2015). *A survey on knowledge management in software engineering.* Paper presented at the Software Quality, Reliability and Security-Companion (QRS-C), 2015 IEEE International Conference on, Vancouver, Canada. 10.1109/QRS-C.2015.48

Vasanthapriyan, S., Xiang, J., Tian, J., & Xiong, S. (2017). Knowledge synthesis in software industries: a survey in Sri Lanka. Knowledge Management Research & Practice, 15(3), 413-430. doi:10.105741275-017-0057-7

Wellman, J. (2009). *Organizational learning: How companies and institutions manage and apply knowledge.* Springer. doi:10.1057/9780230621541

Wieringa, R., Maiden, N., Mead, N., & Rolland, C. (2006). Requirements engineering paper classification and evaluation criteria: A proposal and a discussion. *Requirements Engineering, 11*(1), 102–107. doi:10.100700766-005-0021-6

Williams, R. L., & Bukowitz, W. R. (1999). *The knowledge management field book.* London, UK: FT Management.

Zammit, J., Gao, J., & Evans, R. (2016). Capturing and sharing product development knowledge using storytelling and video sharing. *Procedia CIRP, 56*, 440–445. doi:10.1016/j.procir.2016.10.081

Chapter 6
Big Data and Global Software Engineering

Ramgopal Kashyap
https://orcid.org/0000-0002-5352-1286
Amity University Chhattisgarh, India

ABSTRACT

A large vault of terabytes of information created every day from present-day data frameworks and digital innovations, for example, the internet of things and distributed computing. Investigation of this enormous information requires a ton of endeavors at different dimensions to separate learning for central leadership. An examination is an ebb-and-flow territory of innovative work. The fundamental goal of this paper is to investigate the potential effect of enormous information challenges, open research issues, and different instruments related to it. Subsequently, this article gives a stage to study big data at various stages. It opens another skyline for analysts to build up the arrangement in light of the difficulties, and open research issues. The article comprehended that each large information stage has its core interest. Some of this is intended for bunch handling while some are great at constant scientific. Each large information stage likewise has explicit usefulness. Unique procedures were utilized for the investigation.

INTRODUCTION

The world has changed into information society that very relies upon data. Since information structures make proportions of records every day, reliably, it shows up the world is accomplishing the dimension of data overweight. It is apparent now that remembering the real objective to process such volumes of data an enormous

DOI: 10.4018/978-1-5225-9448-2.ch006

limit required in regards to amassing and figuring resources. Even though the improvement of limit confined by the headway of hardware and advances getting progressively specific, nowadays various affiliations have grasped and widely use information structures running on mechanical stages, various their inspiration has pushed toward acquiring to be subject to data. In the built-up affiliation's evidence explicitly impact the justification of business shapes; information has transformed into a focal point of their business or business end. Along these lines, the business asks for the data, other than the availability of specific data specifically time. Progressively unusual likewise, unsafe fundamental administration process relies upon rightness and straightforwardness of data.

Motivation

Interesting driver related to this subject says that the advancement of data is limitless. What is the overall population going to do about the data overweight? The best strategy to manage and moreover to process all the data? It seems like we are having an enormous information issue. Another driver for this subject is recuperating the information not to collect all data for further examination. Among all of the data, how to recover the appropriate information and inside a required time? Which test should associate with data? What is the agreement between the expense of recuperation and estimation of that information? What are the costs of capacity to recuperate needed information? It seems like it is about the advantage, the trade-off between the opinion of the information, what's more, the expense to get it. Besides the two drivers, the test is to picture the information to such an extent that its regard is expansive and legitimate. The essential issue is the information overweight. Examination in the ordinary mode, to the area the enormous information, is anchoring data that might require for consideration. All need an original point of view, the other methodology, structure or system, accepting any. The unrivaled examination is one of them. Grasping new advancements requires processing, finding and separating these large instructive lists that can't be overseen using traditional databases and models were given the nonattendance of limit resources to the extent computation and limit. Tip top examination addresses one of the creative techniques that can associate with the extending volumes, speed, and collection of data.

Goals

Colossal information wonder, which is portrayed by brisk advancement of volume, combination, and speed of data information assets, thrives the adjustment in the context in logical data getting ready. Superior Analytics can be one of the philosophies. The purpose of the hypothesis is an investigation layout, request, and chats on issues and challenges on the initiating state of a forte of forefront examination utilizing different procedures HPA strategies that could raise and enhance the count execution of the test.

Outcome

The degree of the hypothesis resolved to research and procedures of extensive information and superior Analytics. Speculative bit of the theory is an aftereffect of finish examine that shortens a state of craftsmanship graph for this issue, describes the drivers and consequences of huge information marvel, and gives approaches for managing great information, in explicit methodology in perspective of High-Performance Analytics. Especially the aftereffect of the examination arranged on an audit of HPA, request, characteristics and central purposes of a specific procedure for HPA utilizing the distinctive blend of system resources. A useful bit of the proposition is an aftereffect of exploratory errand that joins illustrative getting ready of the large dataset using insightful stage from SAS Institute. The investigation displays sound taking care of for particular HPA systems that discussed in speculative part. One a player in the examination consolidates shaping different consistent circumstances on which the inclinations and settlement of HPA organize are delineated.

PROBLEM IDENTIFICATION AND SUMMARY

As said in the introduction a fundamental issue of this hypothesis is data, data getting ready, removing information and stuff around it. Let us initially start with the general methodology of matter.

Theoretical Problem

The data volume addresses a test everything considered, not just like that, should be put inside a set. The open data like customer data in their business setting that creates in all estimations are point by point in portions later, and the associated data with explanatory and execution limit (Kuner, Cate, Millard and Svantesson, 2012), outlined in Figure 1.

Pondering the authentic examples, when all of the lines are building up, the openness of data has overburdened ability to separate data examination, and what's more a capacity to use the investigation either to run inspection or store investigation enlisting and limit. A data opening conveys the weakness to separate data given the limited interpretive techniques may fuse data mining computations, trademark tongue taking care of, etc., e.g., pushed feeling examination of printed comments

Figure 1. The information volume challenge

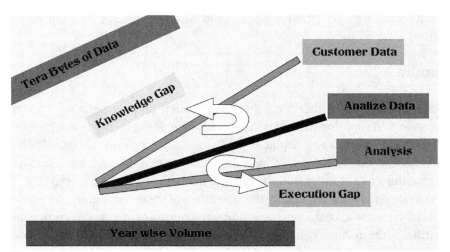

of online life (Hassani-Mahmooei, Berecki-Gisolf, and Collie, 2017). An execution opening imparts inability to utilize inspection as a result of the confined openness of advantages may fuse taking care of units, data reserves, etc. for the requested period, e.g., undertaking to process the throughout the step by step trade at a bank in the required design of the clearinghouse over one night.

Where Is the Issue?

While an execution limits the extent that gear is creating at a stable rate, data volumes are growing exponentially. Along these lines, the learning gap is getting progressively broad, and the domain of the lost information openings in a set of available data containing the information noteworthy as to the information needs. The fact of the matter is to support the course of action of essential data that possibly includes the gainful information. Henceforth, the volume and availability of data are not an issue rather than the getting ready and relationship of data.

Enormous Information and Examination

Colossal data poses the two openings and troubles for associations to remove regard from extensive data, it must be arranged and inspected advantageously, and the results require being available to have the ability to affect positive change or affect business decisions. The ampleness furthermore relies upon an affiliation having the right blend of people, process and development by unadulterated definition, examination is the divulgence and correspondence of vital precedents in data anyway for business, consideration should e viewed as the extensive use of data, authentic additionally, quantitative examination, using useful and farsighted models to drive reality-based business organization decisions and exercises. Examination streamlines key strategies, limits and parts it very well may be used to add up to both inside and external data investigation process is appeared in figure 2. It engages relationship to meet accomplice declaring demands, supervise enormous data volumes, publicize inclinations, regulate danger, upgrade controls and, in the long run, enhance multiple leveled execution by transforming information into learning (Ahmadvand and Goudarzi, 2017). The examination can recognize innovative open entryways in key methodology, limits, and parts. It makes a catalyst for headway and change and by testing the standard; it can create new possible results for the business and its customers. Propelled strategies can empower associations to discover primary drivers, analyze small-scale portions of their business areas, change methods and influence correct assumptions regarding future events or customers' tendency to buy, to unsettle or secure.

It is never again enough for associations to appreciate current process or errands with a view on upgrading what starting at now exists when there is by and by the capacity to address if a procedure is material to the business, or whether there is another strategy for handling a specific issue. The key driver for improvement

Figure 2. Analytics process

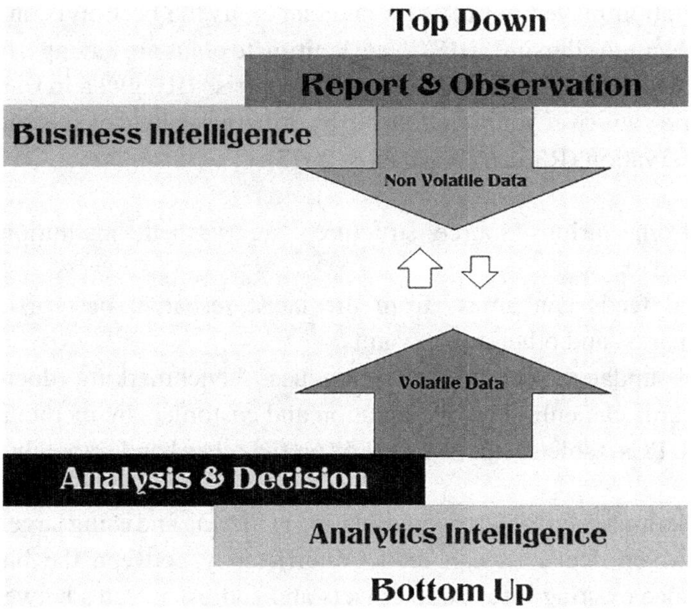

inside affiliations is to test existing practices rather than dependably recognizing the equivalent ceaselessly. Most associations have many-sided and partitioned structure scenes that make the substantial similarity and dispersing of data troublesome. The critical objective of picture division is to fragment the data picture into critical non-covering districts areas for help examination or observation. There is an arrangement of philosophies keeping an eye on this endeavor, abusing different picture properties to achieve the given goal (Kashyap and Gautam, 2017a). They cross from low-level strategies using power limits, edge following or region creating, over outline based and quantifiable procedures, to demonstrate based computations additionally, other increasingly lifted sum systems. The blend based game plan has Tbeen introduced, where the last bundle is molded using a mix of eventual outcomes of a couple of division methods and like this quelling their insufficiencies (Kashyap, Gautam and Tiwari, 2018). Notwithstanding the dependable push to develop incredible division estimations, there has not been any comprehensive division strategy examined. Under these conditions, there is a situation which procedure to choose for given explicit educational accumulation and whether the blend of division results would be valuable (Kashyap, Gautam, 2017b). This undertakings to answer these request for portrayed grouping of picture taking care of data set of images of little photos the execution of a couple of division systems on pictures of moment models in three one of a kind modalities was penniless down. The course of action often quality records were used to achieve evaluation as objective gave the idea that there was no single division procedure which out and out beat the others in the straight set. The symbolic execution of the systems was by then surveyed with an end that Mean Shift computation played out the best and can en as the best division strategy all around (Kashyap, Anderson, 2018). New legitimate plans are having a fundamental influence in enabling a practical Intelligent Enterprise (IE) given in figure 2. An IE makes a single view over your relationship by utilizing a blend of standard itemizing and data observation (Rho and Vasilakos, 2017):

- Data from various source structures are washed, institutionalized and requested
- External feeds can amass from the latest research, best practice tenets, benchmarks, and other online vaults
- Use of updated recognition techniques, benchmarking documents and dashboards can enlighten organization and customers by methods for mobile phones, PCs, tablets, etc. in-house or on the other hand remotely.

All associations need to start contemplating gathering and using large tremendous data. Data-driven decisions can reduce inefficiency between the business, real and IT, advance existing information assets and address isolates between different components of an affiliation. Regardless, it is imperative that the best data and the most dynamic logical gadgets and frameworks add up to nothing if they not used by people who are asking the correct request. Gigantic data, rising accumulating advancement stages, and the latest indicative computations are enabling impacts to business accomplishment not an affirmation of it.

HUGE INFORMATION DRIVERS

The points of interest and threats of large data while there is in all likelihood that the massive data upset has made liberal preferences to associations and clients alike, there are proportionate perils that go with using large data huge information drivers given in figure 3.

The need to stay sensitive data, to guarantee private information and to administer data quality, exists whether instructive accumulations are gigantic or little (Rey-del-Castillo and Cardeñosa, 2016). In any case, the specific properties of immense data volume, variety, speed, and integrity make new sorts of risks that require a full methodology to engage an association to utilize large data while avoiding the devices. It should be done in a sorted out way with the objective that associations can start to comprehend the upsides of significant data in the endeavor with managing the perils.

Figure 3. Big data drivers

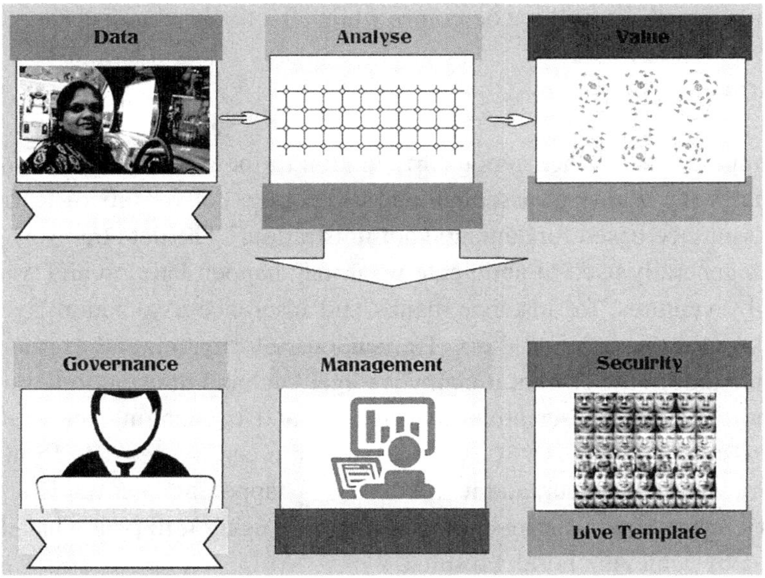

The going with pages look at the possible results and risks related to extensive data and give instances of how large data is being used to comprehend a segment of the erratic issues associations stand up to today. We recognize regular and new risks and considerations for the seven key advances to advance: organization, organization, building, usage, quality, security and insurance (Waterman and Hendler, 2013). The idea of instructive accumulations and the conclusion drawn from such enlightening collections are continuously ending up progressively essential what's more; affiliations need to create quality and checking limits and parameters for significant data. For example, altering a data error can be extensively more over the top than getting the data right the first run through and getting the data wrong can be cataclysmic what's more, inherently increasingly costly to the affiliation if not cured. For quite a while the human administration's condition has gotten a handle on extensive data. With the ability to reach every patient touch point, the proportion of data inside the social protection natural framework has exploded. The advancement of new data sources and the knowledge to squash that data with existing data sources is progressing colossal information is making the probability of new positive patient outcomes.

A part of these new data sources consolidate the mix of disease libraries, tissue vaults, and genomic information, and a short time later altering them to imperative uses clinical models. It is portraying fundamental consideration treatment approaches in light of new inherited bits of learning and clinical tradition organizing estimations, and describing focused patient consideration treatment bits of information earlier inside the consideration movement process. The impetus from these new colossal data bits of information will be valuable for the patient. The nature of the data will in a like manner straightforwardly influence driving new key social protection bits of information in making brilliant outcomes while effectively administering expenses.

Analytics

The examination is another famous articulation in the development business and it "insinuates our ability to assemble and use data to deliver bits of learning that instruct assurance based fundamental administration." The data that was destitute down was generally used to anticipate what may happen later on and was wholly clutched by ventures, for instance, banks and insurance associations, yet not by relationship, for example, retailers. Tremendous information and examination go as the same unit in the current imaginative age. Gigantic information examination uses a thorough and prescriptive investigation and is changing the examination scene (Hussain and Roy, 2016). An accurate examination uses data from the past to envision what may occur, and its likelihood is happening later on. However, the customary inspection is taking data from the past, using it to pick what should be done close by achieving perfect results.

Methodologies

The issue has assorted settling approaches hypothetically; the data opening can be closed by compelling or reducing the advancement of data. The logical limit is settled and subject to investigate bleeding edge examination. Everything considered, having created a dimension of inquiry might be an OK approach except if the study is physically possible to continue running on exchange advancements and hardware. The execution opening It can close by growing use limit, for instance, dispersed or parallel getting ready confined by a dimension of the division of undertaking running with additional units for planning CPU, RAM and securing data. This methodology has a disadvantage in generally limited resources and won't handle the issue as a result of first extent supply: request of data. Beside limit, another perspective of enhancing may be input itself. Is all the data required? Imperative to separate or store? Given the requirements the dull or unimportant data that holds small, accepting any, information can be filtered through, with the peril of lost information opportunity in missing data yet we don't understand what we don't have the foggiest thought. By applying "beast compel" count on the whole dataset the issue is beginning once again from the earliest starting point.

Insights to Foresight

Advanced Analytics can be fitting for various business examination regarding explore customer designs lead, contention, deception acknowledgment, inefficiency in process Capacity Maturity Model (CMMI), grandstand carton examination conditions, causalities, relations in things' arrangements, etc. (Weber, Königsberger, Kassner, and Mitschang, 2017). All that truly matters is different examination usages can be orchestrated by the speed of data with time conditions ceaseless, aggregate planning, or to the collection of data sorted out, semi-organized, unstructured.

Specify that examination can recuperate helpful information from data that may address bits of learning. With encourage, the test can move into hunches — new creating district of the survey addressed by unstructured data content with broad use of online life (Lomotey and Deters, 2015). Content examination recognizes and isolates the vital information and deciphers mines and structures it to reveal precedents, ends, and associations inside and among records.

- The automated content request makes information looks far speedier and afterward some fruitful than manual or survey naming techniques.
- Ontology organization consolidates content storage facilities, approving data quality with unsurprising and purposely described associations.

- Sentiment examination usually finds and perceives presumption conveyed in online materials, for instance, individual to individual correspondence goals, comments, and sites on the Web, and from inside electronic documents.
- Text mining gives dangerous ways to deal with explore unstructured data gatherings and discover officially darken thoughts and models.

Business Intelligence

Business Intelligence (BI) and OLAP ordinarily invest critical energy in addressing, declaring, and separating chronicled data to grasp and balance happens with a date or for specific times beforehand. Affiliations can use BI and OLAP tallies to broaden a point of view of what the numbers say is likely going to happen later on (Kekwaletswe and Lesole, 2016). Regardless, the advanced examination can give an extensively progressively significant perception of why what more, a deductively based, the insightful viewpoint is without limits. The advanced examination enables customers to research various variables to refine understanding. Advanced investigation consistently needs to explore unrefined, bare essential data instead of tinier precedents and collections, which typically used for BI and OLAP.

BI frameworks offer client connections through dashboard interfaces that incorporate information get to what's more, representations, for example, diagrams and charts with cautions, pointers, and different changes trackers. Current BI frameworks can revive information in dashboards all the more much of the time, enabling clients to track measurements that can caution spikes, plunges, or different deviations from anticipated standards in something closer to constant. What BI frameworks need is both the more profound, more exploratory point of view that best in the class examination can give and the bits of knowledge driven by prescient and other systematic models. By connecting with dashboard gateways, BI clients can devour progressed investigation through representations, and utilize information disclosure capacities to pick up a "why" comprehension of what the BI execution measurements are appearing. Associations can go further and make progressed investigation tasks themselves the drivers, and execute BI dashboards and measurements to give sees into the consequences of the logical tasks. Illustrations incorporate examination that gives understanding into consumer loyalty, an accomplishment in extortion anticipation (Arbel, 2015). A vital piece of huge information investigation capacities is access to enormous information. Business associations are ending up increasingly mindful of the estimation of information. Five information composes distinguished: open information, private information, information debilitate, network information, and self-evaluation information. The meanings of this information write they are particular source information, e.g., nonindividual information when they characterize the accompanying information composes (Tromp, Pechenizkiy & Gaber, 2017).

Public information regularly free information gave by legislative establishments, private associations or people. Private information is association claimed information. Data deplete speaks to information with no, or little incentive in its unique situation yet may give valuable Intel when associated with other information. Community information is, for example, Facebook, Twitter, and other web-based social networking created information. Self-measurement information is information produced from wearable advancements like savvy watches, wellness groups and so forth (N. Smith, 2015). Information can come additionally into outside and personal information: Internal information is hierarchical information made by the authoritative procedures. Illustrations are stock updates, deals, exchanges or other inside procedures. External information is information from outside sources, open, private yet achievable through purchasing or exchanging, network information among others.

Huge Data Analytics

Enormous Data Analytics can be portrayed with the accompanying chain of activities with information to reveal groupings or connections and uncover useful perceptions (Figure 4).

Huge data analytics offers an organization an understanding perspective inside its structure and acquires radiant data for present and future business arrangements. The objective for big data researchers is to pick up learning, got from the information preparing. Ongoing information alludes to floods of information that are conveyed specifically after information accumulation. So, there exists no deferral in the change from raw information accumulation to the data given from continuous information. Beside continuous information, organizations additionally confer assets to extricate an incentive from present and correct information. Over the top accentuation on constant information can lead bring about difficulties and disappointment of

Figure 4. Handling ventures of big data analytics

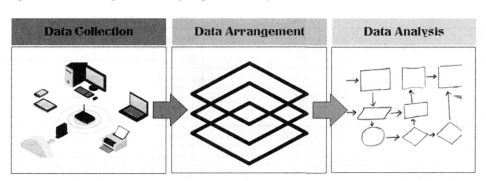

information-driven central leadership (Diesner, 2015)? The accessibility of present and correct information is important to position consistent information into the set of examples and patterns. Further, "right time information" and unique information should be given to help central leadership. Henceforth, applicable information should e assembled and incorporated for particular necessities or situations, types, and source of data is provided in Table 1.

The Principle of Work

As demonstrated by the arrangement, the exchange between enormous information and the association is depicted by the going with advances:

1. The creation data, delivered in the midst of the amassing of the Intelligent Engineering Products, is sent to the association's ERP where the data secured in the standard databases. Furthermore, the Case Company ensures customer's analysis into the ERP too.
2. Next, the ERP programming normally transmits unrefined data to the enormous information Analytics Tool that disperses it in the SQL Server and makes the examination to demonstrate the working adequacy of the vendor in various zones: mechanical assembly use, time use, execution rate, false coefficient, quality degree, etc (Tromp, Pechenizkiy and Gaber, 2017).
3. Finally, the Case Company can follow and streamline the work procedure, manage the business methods and finish new upgrades in the establishment strategy.

Table 1. Sort of data and data sources

S.N.	Types of Data	
1.	Organized Data	Table and Records
2.	Unstructured Data	Human Language, Audio and Video
3.	Semi-Structured Data	XML and Similar Standards
4.	Occasion Data	Messages (typically in Real Time)
5.	Complex Data	Hierarchical or Legacy Sources
6.	Spatial Data	Long/Lat Coordinates and GPS Output
7.	Online networking Data	Blogs, Tweets and Social Networks
8.	Logical Data	Astronomy, Genomes, and Physics
9.	Machine Generated Data	Sensors, RFID and Devices
10.	Metadata	Data that depicts the substance of other information

The examination result can be challenging to get with one original additional data examination works can be repeated for a couple of times by affirming the conclusion and choosing the estimation of the examination result. The methodology of tremendous data examination may yield in each examination strategy with the goal that the incredible outcome can be gotten just by repeated displays of various techniques.

Methodological ideal models and troubles of great information methodologically, large data empowers us to utilize both desire and causal examination. Best in class gigantic data research and practice draws on a collection of frameworks from machine learning, built up estimations, and econometrics, to plan of tests industry calls this A/B or multivariate testing to test existing hypotheses and hypotheses, making new theories, and making colossal scale business regard (Yu, Yurovsky and Xu, 2011). Researchers can layout and lead investigations and accumulate the data anticipated that would procure answers to a grouping of the request including:

(1) Effects of partner affect, (2) impacts of the impact of dynamic ties, (3) has implications of anonymity on online associations, (4) comes to fruition from elective assessing strategies for cutting-edge media, (5) the impact of meticulously created front line recommender systems, and (6) the changing tendency structures of Generation Y and Z customers. Separating these issues completely present methodological troubles, anyway, we see the challenges as open entryways for able investigators.

The colossal data strategies indicated above have in like manner raised disputes. Late revelations from two surely understood destinations, Facebook and OkCupid, the two of which investigated diverse roads in regards to their customers, have begun eagerness for the subject of what, assuming any, fitting applications exist for the use of the online social space as an examination place for advancing our perception of human direct (Davalos and Merchant, 2015). The critical inquiry is whether such experimentation by associations or conceivably by scholastics as a group with associations offers favorable circumstances to society all over the place, and, accepting this is the situation, what proper examination is legitimate and implementable? We battle that there is a strong case for such experimentation, not just to keep up a vital separation from costly terrible decisions, yet also for the journey for a better understanding of what drives human social correspondences. Dreadful decisions hurt all that genuinely matters of associations, and even they cost society since poor choices result in a misallocation of essential resources. As far back as that phlebotomy was a valuable therapeutic practice, correctly made experimentation has driven legitimate examination and learning revelation. Directly, with the openness of immense scale experimentation yielding large data, the potential for inspection, testing, and new learning enhancement are dazzling.

Past updated essential authority in business settings, we fight great societal favorable position from such experimentation. We by and by have remarkable digitization of conventional techniques (Soltani and Navimipour, 2016). The enormous proportion of little-scale level tremendous data about human interchanges offers openings never available in the physical world in light of expense or infeasibility of similar data gathering. We as of now have opportunities to deliver new causal encounters, to test the suitability of age-old reliable rules and norms that speak to social cooperation's. We can thoroughly test existing speculations and collect and test new theories. So, we can go where social scientists could merely dream of going previously. It passes on us to the need to exactly address the issue of paying little mind to whether such broad-scale field investigations would cause more societal insidiousness than extraordinary. This clear idea of preferred societal standpoint is irrefutable of essential excitement for our individual universities' ethics and human subjects warning gatherings generally called institutional review sheets. Associations need to remove a leaf from, or perhaps collaborate with, the insightful network and set up near ethics warning gatherings overseeing human subjects. In case, as an overall population, we place stock in enthusiasm about us as a creature assortments, by then we need to pick up from what testing them on the web social graph tells us. Of course, we require our establishments to compensate for lost time for development. Using large data and examination goes with a huge gathering of challenges, countless are ready ground for future research. Immense data is a larger number of brains boggling to regulate than standard corporate data. Already, associations generally administered very much organized data. Regardless, associations by and by the need to manage a great deal of internal and external data that in many cases will be unstructured or around sorted out. Counting appropriate what's increasing, innovative survey data from any of the about inescapable review decisions, firms presently can go up against a large display of inside, external, and diagram data.

Pervasive Informing

Today, individuals and associations record what they find interesting, store this information for themselves or others, also, share the data for individual and furthermore business purposes. For ease, we imply this wonder as ubiquitous lighting up since a specific target is to instruct someone about something reaching out from a beautiful dish, someone's pulse, the video gets, social cooperation's, vehicle assignments, and street observation in every practical sense any bit of information. General enlightening is possible in light of mechanical pushes in flexible enlisting, video spouting, social sorting out, astute vehicles, and the Internet of things. Information grabbing and exchanging are without a doubt basic; the test is to find a motivator in putting aside the chance to complete such assignments (Ding, Erickson, Kellogg and

Patterson, 2011). The issue is whether one can use large data and data examination to get authentic regard. Can an association turn out to be increasingly familiar with its customers better? Can the association recognize its by and large critical clients and enhance benefits through giving these customers with more modified customer associations or better customer organizations? Will the association use information to build a more grounded publicize position? The troubles from inescapable prompting fuse are becoming much better large data building and examination to manage and utilize extensive data to pass on business regard.

Usage Environments

From an unadulterated amassing perspective, stack circumstances, for instance, Hadoop have been familiar with administer large data 3D shapes. Similarly, as with any new development, such making things should be moved nearer with clear vision and sound input. As noted (Nurika, Hassan and Zakaria, 2017), in any case, great the philosophy, one should now and again look at the results. Much of the time, stack circumstances remain overwhelmingly underutilized with the risk of showing one more costly legacy inconvenience and endangering future tremendous data-driven advancements. Progressively moderate in-memory setups could display an exciting choice in the movement towards the create gigantic data affiliation.

COORDINATION ISSUES

A key gigantic data challenge for any firm is to recognize and disentangle the interrelationships of the large data shape and draw out the regard recommendations by interfacing the distinctive data streams using appropriately described unique identifiers; it may wind up possible to get an increasingly add up to picture of customer lead (Mynarz, 2014). In a security setting, an arrangement of associated components, for instance, claims, candidates, policyholders, automobiles, locally available diagnostics contraptions, auto fix shops, charge cards, and small numbers might be worked to unveil an unusual perspective on complex interest practices or blackmail plans.

Esteem Assessment

The troublesome impact and creative uses of large data because certified challenges for the descriptive frameworks and models that will make. These models generally start from customary estimations, econometrics, machine learning, or artificial thinking. A key typical for these illustrative systems is that they fixate on enhancing a specific exactness worldview or experiences based target work, e.g., constraining a mean squared bungle or expanding likelihood. Commonly, execution is condensed using looking at official estimates that can be troublesome to understand for end customers or no specialists (Thompson, Varvel, Sasinowski and Burke, 2016). As analytic models gain and more effective in the critical decisions of a firm, it is essential to associate this correspondence opening to make critical trust. Specifically, to get trust in an insightful model, the two data scientists and boss should get a most generally utilized dialect in which the possibility of enormous worth accept an essential part. Different as unadulterated authentic execution e.g., assessed using misclassification rates, mean squared missteps, twists, top decile, certified regard based criteria transform into the shared segments. The reasonable standards are uncommonly poor upon the specific business setting.

Expository Models Ought to Be Justifiable to Chiefs

Unmistakably, this has an emotional part to it and depends upon both the depiction and precise multifaceted nature of the deliberate model and moreover the guidance or establishment of the end customer. Black box analytical models in light of extraordinarily complex logical formulas are likely not going to be trusted to reinforce key business systems, for instance, credit risk estimation, distortion ID, or even remedial finding. In any case, if a revelation procedure passes on exact therapeutic dissect, again and again, would the patient-driven expert select for less correct yet easily sensible decisions? Regard based execution premise concerns operational efficiency including model evaluation, indicate checking, and show reviving. The first of these implies the benefits that are relied upon to collect the critical data follow up on the obtained yield. Consistently original initiative settings, brisk model appraisal are a key essential. Consider the instance of charge card distortion area, where frequently a decision ought to be made in less than five seconds after the trade began. Recommender systems are another situation where any customer action or event, for example, recorded using zone-based organizations (Angelis and Kanavos, 2013). Despite model evaluation tries, operational capability in like manner includes the advantages anticipated that would screen, backtest, and, where relevant, extend test the logical models. Finally, the model must be stimulated or revived as new data creates or business conditions change. The association that can perceive changing conditions and quickly modify its models is the association that will succeed.

Overseeing Analytic Decisions

Drawing out decision arranged determinations from large data examination impacts and enhances the affiliation's first initiative. With examination, we will see more decisions being automated, as such influencing the decision systems and commitments all through the association. With decisions being motorized potentially in light of gigantic data examination, administering and exhibiting business decisions is a rising test. Alliances are sharply drawn in with enhancing their business frames and engaging quick and convincing reaction to new troubles, openings, or controls. By explicitly exhibiting decisions and the basis behind them, arrangements can be directed freely from the strategies, radically growing business spryness. It requires reasonable decision examination techniques for business (Ploskas, Stiakakis, and Fouliras, 2014) and what's more methodologies and measures to delineate, appear, additionally, direct business essential administration. The decision demonstrates what's more, documentation is such a standard for decision showing, gotten by the Object Management Group, to overcome any obstacle between business process blueprint and business decisions.

Quantifiable Profit and Trust

Finally, an asymptomatic model ought to incorporate economic motivating force by either delivering advantages or cutting costs or both. A benefit driven evaluation of an indicative model is crucial to make trust transversely over various dimensions and claim to fame units in any affiliation. Regulatory decisions are customarily in perspective of money related return, rather than a truthfully basic logical model. Besides, that is the place examination can deliver the question and subsequently miss the mark. It is our firm conviction this should be catalyzed by more research in no under two domains, To begin with, innovative systems should e made to accurately quantify the landing on endeavor of an analytical model thinking about the low expense of model proprietorship, including distorted and opportunity costs, and covering a satisfactorily long and fitting time horizon. As a next subject on the investigation plan, the consequent money related bits of learning and measures should e explicitly introduced into a deliberate model building process, instead of essentially used as ex-post appraisal measures (Batarseh, Yang and Deng, 2017). Specifically, legitimate models ought to never again aimlessly revolve around enhancing a likelihood work or constraining a misclassification rate, anyway go for including business regard where it is vital, thinking about all the recently referenced criteria. At precisely that point will the fundamental trust be gained over every decision level and claim to fame units in a firm?

METHODOLOGIES FOR ANALYZING BIG DATA: A NEW APPROACH

When you use SQL request to investigate cash related numbers or OLAP gadgets to make bargains gauges, you generally appreciate what kind of data you have and what it can tell you. Salary, geography and time all relate to one another in distinct ways. You don't generally fathom what the proper reactions are in any case you do know how the diverse segments of the instructive accumulation relate to one another. BI customers routinely run standard reports from sorted out databases that have been purposely shown to utilize these associations. Gigantic data examination incorporates making "sense" out of immense volumes of moving data that in its unrefined edge does not have a data model to portray what each segment infers concerning the others. There are a couple of new issues you should consider as you set out on this new kind of examination: Discovery in various cases you don't go by and large fathom what you have and how individual instructive files relate to one another. You should understand it through a methodology of examination and divulgence. Cycle because the real associations are not commonly known early, uncovering understanding is every now and again an iterative procedure as you find the appropriate reactions that you search. The possibility of accentuation is that it all overdrives you down a way that winds up being a halt. That is okay experimentation is a bit of the strategy. Various examiners and industry experts prescribe that you start with close to nothing, notably portrayed endeavors, gain from each cycle, and persistently continue forward to the accompanying idea or field of demand (Yang and Yecies, 2016). Adaptable Capacity due to the iterative thought of extensive data examination is set up to contribute more vitality and utilize more resources to deal with issues. Mining and anticipating huge data examination isn't very differentiating. You don't, for the most part, know how the distinctive data segments relate to one another. As you mine the data to discover models and associations, a thorough examination can yield the encounters that you search. Choice Management thinks about trade volume and speed. In case you are using gigantic data examination to drive various operational decisions, for instance, redoing a site or inciting call center masters about the affinities and activities of purchasers by then you need to consider how to motorize and enhance the execution of all of those exercises.

For example, you may do not understand paying little respect to whether social data uncovers knowledge into arrangements designs. The test accompanies comprehending which data segments relate to which other data parts, and in what limit. The strategy of exposure not directly incorporates examining the data to perceive how you can use it yet likewise choosing how it relates to your regular undertaking data. New sorts of demand include what occurred, and also why. For example, a critical measurement for a few, and associations are customer unsettle. Assessing blend is straightforward. However, for what reason does it occur? Customer support asks for, web-based life examination, and other customer info would all have the capacity to help clear up why customers blemish (Pan, Wang, and Han, 2016). Near strategies can be used with various sorts of data and in multiple conditions. For what reason did bargains fall in a given store? For what reason do certain patients endure longer than others? Attempt to find the right data, discover the covered associations, and analyze it precisely.

Huge Data Analysis Requirements

In the past fragment, Techniques for breaking down great information, we discussed some of the methodologies you can use to find which means and find covered associations in large data. Here are three immense necessities for coordinating this demand essentially:

1. Limit data improvement
2. Use existing aptitudes
3. Deal with data security

Restricting data improvement is tied in with directing figuring resources. In standard examination circumstances, data is passed on to the PC, dealt with, and after that sent to the accompanying objective. For example, creation data might be isolated from e-business systems, changed into social data compose, and stacked into an operational data store sorted out for enumerating. However, the volume of data builds up; this sort of ETL designing pushes toward winding up continuously less viable. There's essentially an unreasonable measure of data to move around. It looks good to store and process the data in a similar place. With new data and new data sources comes the need to acquire new capacities. The present scope of capabilities will make sense of where examination ought to and should be conceivable (Horton and Tambe, 2015). Right when the necessary capacities are insufficient concerning, a blend of getting ready, securing and new instruments will address the issue. Since most affiliations have more people who can analyze data using SQL than using MapReduce, it is necessary to have the ability to help the two sorts of taking care. Data security is fundamental for some corporate applications. Data appropriation focus customers are accustomed not solely to intentionally described estimations and estimations and properties, yet moreover to a regular course of action of association techniques and security controls. These exhaustive methodologies are consistently absent from unstructured data sources and open source examination instruments. Concentrate on the security and data organization necessities of each examination adventure and make without question that the gadgets you are using can oblige those requirements.

Database Processing With Oracle Advanced Analytics

Most Oracle customers are incredibly familiar with SQL as a vernacular for inquiry, declaring, and examination of sorted out data. It is the acknowledged standard for testing and the development that underlies most BI mechanical assemblies. R is a pervasive open source programming dialect for verifiable examination. Agents, data analysts, researchers, and scholastics by and considerable use R, provoking a creating pool of R programming engineers. At the point when data has stacked into Oracle Database, customers can benefit themselves of Oracle Advanced Analytics (OAA) to uncover covered associations in the data. Prophet Advanced Analytics, an option of Oracle Database Enterprise Release, offers a blend of extraordinary in database estimations and open source R figurings, accessible through SQL and R tongues. It joins first-class data mining limits with the open source R vernacular to engage thorough examination, data mining, content mining, quantifiable examination, advanced numerical counts and original plan all inside the database (Jin, Liu, and Qi, 2012). Prophet Advanced Analytics gives all middle logical limits and lingos on extraordinary in database designing. These illustrative limits fuse data mining figurings realized in the database, nearby SQL capacities with regards to fundamental critical techniques, and joining with open source R for quantifiable programming and access to a progressively broad plan of measurable strategies.

This serious analytic condition offers a large extent of abilities to Oracle Database customers dealing with large data stretches out by restricting data improvement and ensuring internal security, adaptability, and execution. It consolidates data mining devices that let you make complex models and pass on them on sweeping instructive accumulations. You can utilize the outcomes of these perceptive models inside BI applications. For example, you can use backslide models to predict customer age in perspective of acquiring behavior and measurement data. You can in like manner collect and apply insightful models that help you center around your best customers, make bare essential customer profiles, find and check distortion, and comprehend various other logical troubles.

Productive Data Mining

The data mining instruments in OAA enable data examiners to work explicitly with data inside the database, explore the data graphically, make and evaluate various data mining models, and send gauges and bits of information all through the endeavor. It consolidates data burrowing counts for portrayal, grouping, promotes compartment examination, deception ID, and substance mining that can be associated with settle a broad assortment of data-driven issues. It furthermore consolidates twelve figurings that you can use to manufacture and send insightful applications that like this mine star chart data to pass on consistent results and desires. Since the data, models, and results remain in the Prophet Database, data improvement is wiped out, information torpidity is restricted, and security is kept up. Using standard SQL charges you can get to tip top figurings in the database to mine tables, sees, star developments, and esteem based and unstructured data (Bacardit and Llorà, 2013). Any person who can get to dataset away in an Oracle Database can get to OAA occurs, desires, recommendations, and disclosures using standard reports and BI instruments.

Factual Analysis With R

Prophet Advanced Analytics has been expected to engage examiners to use R on huge instructive lists. Insightful models can be made in R. The related tables, and points of view in Oracle Database appear as R objects SQL declarations. Inspectors can create an R code to control the data in the database. By running R programs right in the database, there is no convincing motivation to move data around. This organized designing ensures unprecedented security and execution since you can apply huge, flexible gear advantages for complex issues. OAA supports existing R substance and pariah packages as well. All present R enhancement capacities, gadgets, and element can run clearly with OAA, and scale against dataset away in Oracle Database 11g. The powerful blend between R, Oracle Database, and Hadoop engages inspectors to stay in contact with R content that can continue running in three unmistakable conditions: a workstation running open source R, Hadoop running with Oracle enormous information connectors, and Oracle Database (Duque Barrachina and O'Driscoll, 2014). It is not hard to associate the outcomes of the examination to business examination gadgets, for instance, Prophet Business Intelligence and Oracle Analytics, as depicted in the going with the region.

Connecting Hadoop and Oracle Database

There are two distinct options for associating data and interim achieves Hadoop with your Oracle data dissemination focus. Dependent upon your use case, you may need to stack Hadoop data into the data stockroom, or forsake it set up and request it using SQL. Prophet Loader for Hadoop gives an essential technique to accumulate HDFS data into an Oracle data stockroom. MapReduce to make progressed enlightening accumulations that can capably e stacked into Oracle Database. Not in any way like other Hadoop loaders, has it made Oracle interior designs, enabling it to accumulate data speedier with fewer system resources. When stacked, the data can get to with ordinary SQL based Business Intelligence gadgets (Hossen, Moniruzzaman, and Hossain, 2015). Prophet SQL Connector for HDFS is a quick connector for getting to HDFS data clearly from Oracle Database, overcoming any prevention among HDFS and data conveyance focus conditions. The dataset away in HDFS can by then addressed by methods for SQL, joined with dataset away in Oracle Database, or stacked into Oracle Database.

Prophet's Big Data Platform

Prophet has three assembled structures that light up particular parts of the significant data issue. Each stage fuses all the first gear and programming critical for remarkable data dealing. All pieces are pre-composed what's increasing, readied to send and work. Prophet has done the tireless work of incorporating these constructed structures so you can remove an impetus from your data by methods for extensive advanced data arrange with the facilitated examination. This complete course of action fuses unique systems managing data acquirement, stacking, limit, organization, analysis, blend, and presentation so you can quickly expel a motivation from large data with the composed examination. Prophet enormous information Appliance consolidated a mix of open source programming and focused programming made by Oracle to address immense data essentials. It is expected to anchor and mastermind gigantic data capable, and to be the savviest stage to run Hadoop (AlMahmoud, Damiani, Otrok and Al-Hammadi, 2017). For extra information on the sufficiency of this methodology, see the white paper "Getting genuine about huge information: Build Versus Buy" from the Enterprise Strategy Group. Prophet Exadata Database Machine passes on phenomenal execution and flexibility for an extensive variety of database applications. It is the speediest stage open for running Oracle Database and the detailed examination discussed in this section.

Prophet examination is an assembled system that consolidates an undertaking BI organize, in memory examination writing computer programs, also, gear updated for the broad-scale survey. With mechanical assemblies for frontline data discernment and study, it enables customers to gain great comprehension from a great deal of data. Right, when Oracle Analytics used with Prophet Advanced Analytics, customers have an expansive stage that passes on understanding into important business subjects, for instance, beat figure, thing recommendations, end examination, and deception disturbing.

Analytics for the Enterprise

The relationship in every industry are trying to grasp the enormous storm of astronomical data, and furthermore to make demonstrative stages that can arrange customary sorted out data with semi-composed and unstructured wellsprings of information. Right when fittingly got and researched, extensive data can give interesting bits of learning into promote designs, outfit frustrations, obtaining practices, bolster cycles and various diverse business issues, cutting down costs, and engaging centered around business decisions. To get a motivating force from extensive data, you require a solid game plan of answers for getting, dealing with, and separating the data, from acquiring the data and finding new bits of information to settling on repeatable decisions and scaling the related information structures. Prophet progressed investigation is ideal for uncovering covered associations in large data sources. Notwithstanding whether you need to anticipate customer lead, imagine cross/up offer openings, upgrade displaying exertion response rates, check disturb, analyze "publicize holders" to discover affiliations, precedents and associations, use influencers in relational associations, decline deception, or predict future demand, Oracle Advanced Analytics can help (Ravada, 2015). Correctly when used as a piece of combination with open source instruments, for instance, Hadoop and MapReduce. This excellent orderly course of action passes on all that you need to get, deal with, separate and extend the estimation of large data inside the endeavor while fulfilling essential requirements for constraining data improvement, using existing scopes of capacities, and ensuring lifted measures of security.

- A unique data examination game plan includes organizations or estimations that experience both machine capacity data-driven organizations and human information cooperation driven organizations.
- To support and ensure the compromise of machine limit and human learning, joining driven organizations are required to enable customers to associate with the two data-driven organizations and joint exertion is driven organizations and offer instruments to fuse the delayed consequence of two sorts of organizations.
- All organizations or computations together help the large data change from an unrefined association to adapting thing (base up) or from hypothesis to resources (top-down) (Kuiler, 2014).
- Human learning should be related to the whole technique of data change, including planning data-driven organizations, interpreting the eventual outcome of data-driven organizations, cooperating with various authorities on deciphering and sharing the results.
- As showed up in the plan chart, there are three sorts of portions:
- Data-driven organizations, which misuse significant data taking care of advancement to look, separate and aggregate data from heterogeneous data sources. The commitment of the data-driven organizations is sorted out or possibly unstructured data from different data sources. The yield of data-

driven organizations s looked, or private information discovered models or records, etc. The data-driven organizations hope to improve the systems of individual sense-making (Luo, Zhang, Zukerman, and Qiao, 2014).

The comments among individuals, so to support the total appreciation of the issues related to data examination. The commitment of the joint exertion driven organizations could be the yield of data-driven organizations, and moreover, the participation's comments, disputes and talks, etc. (Luo, Zhang, Zukerman, and Qiao, 2014) figure 5 demonstrated this idea for online networking. The adapting thing hypothesis, methods, etc. should be the aftereffect of their affiliation. The joint exertion driven organizations mean to help synergistic sense-making.

Coordination driven organizations are to ensure and support the steady coordination of the independent organizations made. Related limits consolidate UI, data storing and coordination segments, etc. (Dafferianto Trinugroho, 2014).

This methodology opens up an extra station to necessities showing and examination, which relies upon changing and separating speculative models from humanism and emotional science to an arrangement knick-knack. The investigation work reported in this area gives a depiction of how theoretical models were picked and associated with the examination and blueprint of the structure has appeared in figure 5. We believe this inconspicuous undertaking at bringing human science or mental science models into essential structuring will enhance the natural need showing process. Significantly more work is relied upon to refine to meet the practical necessities of essentials master.

Approaches to Deal With Big Data

Colossal information can be seen as an issue, of course as luck this zone contains systems of dealing with the large relative data from the perspective of plan, methods, establishment, and headways.

Approaches

The regular BI designing can start stage for structures with its procedure tallying masterminding an area, data conveyance focus, data stores, ETL, etc. One may find that it is most likely not going to store all data in central, adventure data dispersion focus and not all data are critical to being secured. There has been new structure approaches created: Hybrid Storage Architecture blend of reserves for various data makes and arranges, temporary data reserves, data stream taking care. Upstream Intelligence sensible and quantifiable limits are associated immediately in the process in the anchoring of data that consolidates specific Stream and occasion moreover

Figure 5. Conceptual Architecture for Big Data Analytics in Social Media Monitoring

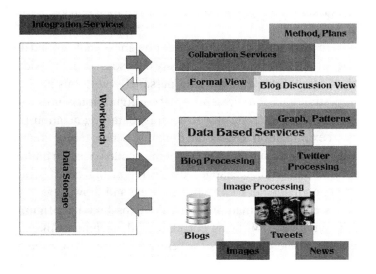

getting ready based oversee based systems, plan to recognize evidence (Askitas, 2016). As results of this advancement, Post current BI Architecture addresses a complicated course of action that has procured, generally from ordinary Business Intelligence and incorporates the possibility of blend storing structure, upstream understanding, and stream an event getting ready. Postmodern BI Architecture includes circled data circulation focus, consolidated Metadata layer, made an organization out of data streams and composed exertion learning organization.

Post Current Bi Architecture

Due to an arranged assortment of necessities from business symmetrical BI models propelled: a Top Down and Bottom Up building. The Top Down designing stressed a report drove or a data-driven methodology where a data stockroom show is made first in perspective of the business/declaring necessities. Methods of this methodology start with an ETL routine to move data from the source system to the data conveyance focus, and a short time later continues with making reports and dashboards to address data in DW. This methodology generally satisfies accommodating customers with periodical uncovering and checking. Besides that, affiliation's advantages control customers to wear down extraordinarily delegated examination or endeavors in imaginative work division. With past methodology control customers are left aside to use uniquely designated spreadsheets, free/neighborhood database events, SQL and data mining workbenches with Top Down methodology control customers find

BI instruments relentless and an information warehousing structure too much obliged for their stresses (Kekwaletswe and Lesole, 2016). Open entryway for Bottom-Up configuration approach has appeared.

The Bottom Up methodology suits better for business analysts and data scientists who require the off the cuff examination of any data source, both inside and outside corporate points of confinement, working personally with business executives to enhance existing strategies. Post present day BI configuration is an eventual outcome of improvement of data warehousing structures, data organization programs and adding advanced examination to alter the dynamic between best down and base up necessities. This compositional thought is generally called creamer building depicted. Colossal Data and HPA don't change data warehousing or BI structures. They fundamentally supplement them with new headways and show signs of improvement handcrafted to meet the information essentials. Crossbreed configuration can, on the other hand, contain the following correlative advancements like:

Hadoop clusters to help to amass for semi-sorted out data, used as a piece of orchestrating district or of course interpretive sandboxes. Streaming and Complex Event Processing Engines to encourage predictable understanding, used as brilliant sensors that can associate with streams. Analytical Sandbox to help examination dealing with, extraordinarily delegated inquiries, to satisfy transient examination needs, used as a section for other BI structures. A nonsocial database system to store unstructured or unrefined data, used as a piece of the descriptive sandbox, or masterminding locale •Data focus point to support unique systems and applications rather than to have uncovering or examination applications explicitly, data stockroom used as a middle (Shmueli, 2017).

Big Data Analytics Tools

BDA structures, passed on Cloud or in-house server farm, have to wind up essential to going up against the computational demand errands. In the going with, we show a survey of the most used BDA mechanical assemblies in composing.

Apache Hadoop

Apache Hadoop is an open source passed on preparing the structure for moving on the limit and gathering treatment of large educational accumulations on clusters worked from product gear using fundamental programming models, i.e., MapReduce. It is planned to scale up from single to a large number of servers, all of which offers both neighborhood count and limit. It grants getting huge ready data by using group dealing. Rather than rely upon hardware to pass on high openness, the library itself is planned to perceive, what's more, handle disillusionments at the application layer (Mavridis and Karatza, 2017). Hadoop focus sections offer organizations to work arranging, a passed on record system and data dealing with MapReduce, huge information investigation for clump examinations.

Apache Kafka

Apache Kafka is a snappy, flexible, dependable, and fault tolerant distribute in advising system. Kafka routinely used as a piece of the place of regular message vendors like JMS and AMQP because of its higher throughput, resolute quality and replication [Kafka] exhibiting the structure spilling examination. Apache Kafka can work in the mix with different systems for regular examination and the rendering of spouting data, for instance, Apache Storm, Apache HBase or Apache Spark. As a rule, it is used for two sorts of usage, developing consistent data work forms, exchanging messages between structures or applications reliably, and continuous spilling applications that change or react to the data stream (Shaheen, 2017). Kafka is a message delegate on a dimension plane versatile, and fault tolerant. In spite of the usage case, Kafka operator's enormous surges of messages for low dormancy examination in the Apache Hadoop natural framework.

DISCUSSION

Tremendous information wonder has delineated in this section with its causalities, definitions, effects, and impacts. Notice that the adjustment in context from data drove methodology towards information-driven methodology may be seen perilously on the conventional idea of central data stockroom and physically approved data decency and consistency. Rather than that, it makes required courses of action that satisfy necessities for versatility and adaptability supporting data examination. Information Driven Approach is a starting stage for Upstream Insight. Tremendous information adjusts building in that way that Post Modern BI Architecture made in mélange of Hybrid Storage Architecture Analytical Sandboxes, Hadoop, NoSQL, RDBMS, Upstream Intelligence mainly supported by Complex Event Processing and standard data warehousing (Omidi and Alipour, 2016). Another superb idea, following the Hybrid Storage Architecture, is Information Federation that inclinations to discover data on various mechanical assemblies in different structures what's more, plans. In any case, it supports examination and ensures giving of consistent access to data by methods for primarily united data get to having the BI configuration completely extended post current BI Architecture; there are anyway propels that twist for imaginative approaches to manage to handle Big Data. Area of high execution examination isn't broadly portrayed and mapped. The progression of HPA is generally dictated by business enthusiasm for having information delayed consequences of data taking care of immediately and by the availability of benefits structure figuring, free memory with facilitating.

Analytic phases of HPA move among the traders and principle speaking realized as prohibitive courses of action. Specialization of stages relies upon business requirements and business applications. Moreover extraordinary particular drivers impact the use of phase, which can be for instance a number of clients/supporters with respect to applications and customers, data volumes, sort of data, fit in the overall structure of BI plan, e.g. organizing domain, information distribution center, subordinate/self-sufficient data bazaars, off the cuff look into and prototyping office. Information storage facilities are moving towards pooled resources where data are independent as demonstrated by the data essentialness require planning; data orchestrate composed, semi-sorted out, unstructured. Establishment and plan of data examination and organization structure are moving from being execution tuned towards being specifically versatile in linkage with scattered parallel getting ready, arrange to figure, and in memory examination (Hamoud and Obaid, 2013). Flexibility goads another perspective that developments on premises association towards cream standard and devices arranged a game plan, where adaptability can be adaptable with private cloud.

CONCLUSION

Since the huge information has endlessly perceived for a long time, there is an important measure ask about done in composing, white papers, and online references. In this hypothesis, the critical information Phenomenon delineated in a survey including its causalities, definition, effect, and impacts. It addresses a starting stage and driver for High-Performance Analytics concerning rough material that contains covered information, precedents, and regard. Shutting from investigating, enormous information, with its dynamic estimations, should not be considered as an issue, instead of the situation to change it into a preferred standpoint. Analytics is comprehensively asked about in this proposition as a methodology towards dealing with great information as a result of this area. It is so far rising, being refined and formalized among vendors, investigate on HPA is taking a stab at remembering the ultimate objective to bring outline, the portrayal of HPA techniques and strategies database examination and parallel enrolling their traits, and appropriate usage. HPA is driven by the business world with broad necessities to figure to fruition as snappy as possible on the greatest dataset. The improvement HPA ends up imaginable with creative progression vast memory, 64bit location, Grid Computing and moderateness of gear costs, value: execution marker. Until further notice, HPA can see as an answer compared to the Business Intelligence, yet exceedingly on premises, the progression will continue further. The exploration could be extended to bounce into HPA game plans from different vendors differentiating distinctive prohibitive strategies in unobtrusive components. Test assignments as it has been laid out, show the execution of HPA approach on massive datasets. Unmistakable intellectual exercises and their blends have displayed the upsides of the consistent stage in light of In-Memory Analytics approach. In Memory Analytics building has found as supportive for the count different exercises association, inclined lines, checking, percentile, since all data are stacked in memory and can be explicitly tended. There are a couple of imperatives of preliminary assignments. For the future work, the analytical exercises can attempt on informative stages that realize other HPA approaches, n addition against common methodology in Business Intelligence, e.g., OLAP. Now and again, merchants offer the formative stage that would complete all discussed HPA approaches and in case, it is trying to perform them on a comparable system establishment. The examinations are satisfactory for taking a gander at the execution of analytical action among one another, to perceive central focuses and points of interest of picked precise stage.

REFERENCES

Ahmadvand, H., & Goudarzi, M. (2017). Using Data Variety for Efficient Progressive Big Data Processing in Warehouse-Scale Computers. *IEEE Computer Architecture Letters, 16*(2), 166–169. doi:10.1109/LCA.2016.2636293

AlMahmoud, A., Damiani, E., Otrok, H., & Al-Hammadi, Y. (2017). Spamdoop: A privacy-preserving Big Data platform for collaborative spam detection. *IEEE Transactions On Big Data*, 1-1. doi:10.1109/tbdata.2017.2716409

Angelis, A., & Kanavos, P. (2013). A Multiple Criteria Decision Analysis Framework For Value-Based Assessment Of New Medical Technologies. *Value in Health, 16*(3), A53. doi:10.1016/j.jval.2013.03.302

Arbel, L. (2015). Data loss prevention: The business case. *Computer Fraud & Security, 2015*(5), 13–16. doi:10.1016/S1361-3723(15)30037-3

Askitas, N. (2016). Big Data is a big deal but how much data do we need?. *Asta Wirtschafts- Und Sozialstatistisches Archiv, 10*(2-3), 113-125. doi:10.100711943-016-0191-3

Bacardit, J., & Llorà, X. (2013). Large-scale data mining using genetics-based machine learning. *Wiley Interdisciplinary Reviews. Data Mining and Knowledge Discovery*, *3*(1), 37–61. doi:10.1002/widm.1078

Batarseh, F., Yang, R., & Deng, L. (2017). A comprehensive model for management and validation of federal big data analytical systems. *Big Data Analytics*, *2*(1), 2. doi:10.118641044-016-0017-x

Dafferianto Trinugroho, Y. (2014). Information Integration Platform for Patient-Centric Healthcare Services: Design, Prototype, and Dependability Aspects. *Future Internet*, *6*(1), 126–154. doi:10.3390/fi6010126

Davalos, S., & Merchant, A. (2015). Using Big Data to Study Psychological Constructs: Nostalgia on Facebook. *Journal of Psychology & Psychotherapy*, *05*(06). doi:10.4172/2161-0487.1000221

Diesner, J. (2015). Small decisions with big impact on data analytics. *Big Data & Society*, *2*(2). doi:10.1177/2053951715617185

Ding, X., Erickson, T., Kellogg, W., & Patterson, D. (2011). Informing and performing: Investigating how mediated sociality becomes visible. *Personal and Ubiquitous Computing*, *16*(8), 1095–1117. doi:10.100700779-011-0443-8

Duque Barrachina, A., & O'Driscoll, A. (2014). A big data methodology for categorizing technical support requests using Hadoop and Mahout. *Journal Of Big Data*, *1*(1), 1. doi:10.1186/2196-1115-1-1

Hamoud, A., & Obaid, T. (2013). *Building Data Warehouse for Diseases Registry: First Step for Clinical Data Warehouse*. SSRN Electronic Journal. doi:10.2139srn.3061599

Hassani-Mahmooei, B., Berecki-Gisolf, J., & Collie, A. (2017). Using Bayesian Model Averaging to Analyse Hierarchical Health Data: Model implementation and application to linked health service use data. *International Journal For Population Data Science*, *1*(1). doi:10.23889/ijpds.v1i1.89

Horton, J., & Tambe, P. (2015). Labor Economists Get Their Microscope: Big Data and Labor Market Analysis. *Big Data*, *3*(3), 130–137. doi:10.1089/big.2015.0017 PMID:27442956

Hossen, A., Moniruzzaman, A., & Hossain, S. (2015). Performance Evaluation of Hadoop and Oracle Platform for Distributed Parallel Processing in Big Data Environments. *International Journal Of Database Theory And Application*, *8*(5), 15–26. doi:10.14257/ijdta.2015.8.5.02

Hussain, A., & Roy, A. (2016). The emerging era of Big Data Analytics. *Big Data Analytics*, *1*(1), 4. doi:10.118641044-016-0004-2

Jin, C., Liu, N., & Qi, L. (2012). Research and Application of Data Archiving based on Oracle Dual Database Structure. *Journal of Software*, *7*(4). doi:10.4304/jsw.7.4.844-848

Kekwaletswe, R., & Lesole, T. (2016). A Framework for Improving Business Intelligence through Master Data Management. *Journal of South African Business Research*, 1-12. doi:10.5171/2016.473749

Kuiler, E. (2014). From Big Data to Knowledge: An Ontological Approach to Big Data Analytics. *The Review of Policy Research*, *31*(4), 311–318. doi:10.1111/ropr.12077

Kuner, C., Cate, F., Millard, C., & Svantesson, D. (2012). The challenge of 'big data' for data protection. *International Data Privacy Law*, *2*(2), 47–49. doi:10.1093/idpl/ips003

Lomotey, R., & Deters, R. (2015). Unstructured data mining: Use case for CouchDB. *International Journal of Big Data Intelligence*, *2*(3), 168. doi:10.1504/IJBDI.2015.070597

Luo, H., Zhang, H., Zukerman, M., & Qiao, C. (2014). An incrementally deployable network architecture to support both data-centric and host-centric services. *IEEE Network*, *28*(4), 58–65. doi:10.1109/MNET.2014.6863133

Mavridis, I., & Karatza, H. (2017). Performance evaluation of cloud-based log file analysis with Apache Hadoop and Apache Spark. *Journal of Systems and Software*, *125*, 133–151. doi:10.1016/j.jss.2016.11.037

Mynarz, J. (2014). Integration of public procurement data using linked data. *Journal Of Systems Integration*, 19-31. doi:10.20470/jsi.v5i4.213

Nurika, O., Hassan, M., & Zakaria, N. (2017). Implementation of Network Cards Optimizations in Hadoop Cluster Data Transmissions. *ICST Transactions On Ubiquitous Environments*, *4*(12). doi:10.4108/eai.21-12-2017.153506

Omidi, M., & Alipour, M. (2016). Why NoSQL And The Necessity of Movement Toward The NoSQL Data Base. *IOSR Journal Of Computer Engineering*, *18*(05), 116–118. doi:10.9790/0661-180502116118

Pan, E., Wang, D., & Han, Z. (2016). Analyzing Big Smart Metering Data Towards Differentiated User Services: A Sublinear Approach. *IEEE Transactions On Big Data*, *2*(3), 249–261. doi:10.1109/TBDATA.2016.2599924

Ploskas, N., Stiakakis, E., & Fouliras, P. (2014). Assessing Computer Network Efficiency Using Data Envelopment Analysis and Multicriteria Decision Analysis Techniques. *Journal Of Multi-Criteria Decision Analysis*, 22(5-6), 260–278. doi:10.1002/mcda.1533

Ravada, S. (2015). Big data spatial analytics for enterprise applications. *SIGSPATIAL Special*, 6(2), 34–41. doi:10.1145/2744700.2744705

Rey-del-Castillo, P., & Cardeñosa, J. (2016). An Exercise in Exploring Big Data for Producing Reliable Statistical Information. *Big Data*, 4(2), 120–128. doi:10.1089/big.2015.0045 PMID:27441716

Rho, S., & Vasilakos, A. (2017). Intelligent collaborative system and service in value network for enterprise computing. *Enterprise Information Systems*, 12(1), 1–3. doi:10.1080/17517575.2016.1238962

Shaheen, J. (2017). Apache Kafka: Real Time Implementation with Kafka Architecture Review. *International Journal Of Advanced Science And Technology*, 109, 35–42. doi:10.14257/ijast.2017.109.04

Shmueli, G. (2017). Research Dilemmas with Behavioral Big Data. *Big Data*, 5(2), 98–119. doi:10.1089/big.2016.0043 PMID:28632441

Smith, N. (2015). Wearable Tech: Smart Watches. *Engineering & Technology*, 10(4), 20–21. doi:10.1049/et.2015.0451

Soltani, Z., & Navimipour, N. (2016). Customer relationship management mechanisms: A systematic review of the state of the art literature and recommendations for future research. *Computers in Human Behavior*, 61, 667–688. doi:10.1016/j.chb.2016.03.008

Thompson, S., Varvel, S., Sasinowski, M., & Burke, J. (2016). From Value Assessment to Value Cocreation: Informing Clinical Decision-Making with Medical Claims Data. *Big Data*, 4(3), 141–147. doi:10.1089/big.2015.0030 PMID:27642718

Tromp, E., Pechenizkiy, M., & Gaber, M. (2017). Expressive modeling for trusted big data analytics: Techniques and applications in sentiment analysis. *Big Data Analytics*, 2(1), 5. doi:10.118641044-016-0018-9

Tromp, E., Pechenizkiy, M., & Gaber, M. (2017). Expressive modeling for trusted big data analytics: Techniques and applications in sentiment analysis. *Big Data Analytics*, 2(1), 5. doi:10.118641044-016-0018-9

Waterman, K., & Hendler, J. (2013). Getting the Dirt on Big Data. *Big Data*, 1(3), 137–140. doi:10.1089/big.2013.0026 PMID:27442195

Weber, C., Königsberger, J., Kassner, L., & Mitschang, B. (2017). M2DDM – A Maturity Model for Data-Driven Manufacturing. *Procedia CIRP*, *63*, 173–178. doi:10.1016/j.procir.2017.03.309

Yang, J., & Yecies, B. (2016). Mining Chinese social media UGC: A big-data framework for analyzing Douban movie reviews. *Journal Of Big Data*, *3*(1), 3. doi:10.118640537-015-0037-9

Yu, C., Yurovsky, D., & Xu, T. (2011). Visual Data Mining: An Exploratory Approach to Analyzing Temporal Patterns of Eye Movements. *Infancy*, *17*(1), 33–60. doi:10.1111/j.1532-7078.2011.00095.x

KEY TERMS AND DEFINITIONS

DM: Data mining or information mining is the route toward discovering plans in full instructive records including techniques at the union of machine learning, estimations, and database systems. An interdisciplinary subfield of software engineering, it is principal methodologies wherein adroit methodologies are associated with remove data designs the general goal of which is to isolate information from an educational file and change it into a reasonable structure for encouraging use. Aside from the unrefined examination step, it incorporates database and data organization points, data pre-taking care of, display and construing thoughts, interesting quality estimations, multifaceted nature considerations, post-getting ready of discovered structures, recognition, and web-based refreshing. Information mining is the examination adventure of the "learning disclosure in databases" process or KDD. The term is a misnomer, in light of the way that the goal is the extraction of precedents and gaining from a great deal of data, not merely the extraction (mining) of data.

HPDA: High-performance data analytics with data examination the methodology utilize HPC's usage of parallel taking care of to run notable logical programming at places higher than a teraflop or (a trillion skimming point assignments for each second). Through this methodology, it is possible to quickly investigate extensive enlightening lists, influencing conclusions about the information they to contain. Some examination remaining tasks at hand enhance the circumstance with HPC rather than standard figure structure. While some "gigantic data" errands proposed to executed on thing hardware, in "scale out" designing there are certain conditions where ultra-brisk, high-limit HPC "scale up" approaches are favored. It is the space of HPDA. Drivers consolidate a delicate time portion for examination (e.g., continuous, high-repeat stock trading or exceedingly complex examination issues found in legitimate research).

Chapter 7
Adaptation of Modern Agile Practices in Global Software Engineering

Moiz Mansoor
*Institute of Business Management,
Pakistan*

Syed Sajjad Hussain Rizvi
Hamdard University, Pakistan

Manzoor Ahmed Hashmani
*University Technology PETRONAS,
Malaysia*

Muhammad Waqar Khan
*Institute of Business Management,
Pakistan*

Muhammad Zubair
IQRA University, Pakistan

ABSTRACT

Software engineering has been an active working area for many decades. It evolved in a bi-folded manner. First research and subsequently development. Since the day of its inception, the massive number of variants and methods of software engineering were proposed. Primarily, these methods are designed to cater the time-varying need of modern approach. In this connection, the Global Software Engineering (GSE) is one of the growing trends in the modern software industry. At the same time, the employment of Agile development methodologies has also gained the significant attention in the literature. This has created a rationale to explore and adopt agile development methodology in GSE. It gained rigorous attention as an alternative to traditional software development methodologies. This paper has presented a comprehensive review on the adaptation of modern agile practices in GSE. In addition, the strength and limitation of each approach have been highlighted. Finally, the open area in the said domain is submitted as one of the deliverables of this work.

DOI: 10.4018/978-1-5225-9448-2.ch007

INTRODUCTION

Agile Software Development (ASD) and GSE are two rapidly growing fields in the software development industry (Cockburn 2002). This growth has translated into a significant advancement in both industry and academia. GSE is an extensive concept incorporating software development methods across both, organizational and geographical borders (Rodríguez,et. al. (2012). While ASD emphasis on the development of close collaboration between users and developers. It focuses on delivering software within timelines considering budget constraints. This process is repetitive, adaptive, and shortly defined (Kruchten, 2013).

During the last several years the trend of globalization of business has witnessed, that brought changes in industries. Most of the companies started working on Global Software Engineering (GSE), to get results more efficient, cheaper and faster. However, these benefices are not easy to accomplish. Culture, collaboration between teams, language, time zones, economic conditions, insufficient knowledge of client's interest and many more make the tasks harder to achieve. Researchers have investigated this issue and have identifies teamwork as a significant actuating parameter to handle the issues of GSE.

During the past decade, the hybridization of Agile Software Engineering (ASE) and Global Software Engineering (GSE) concept has submitted the significant change in software industry. This includes, but not limited to, rapid application development, round the clock development, taking the most eminent professional on board irrespective of their geographical location, reduced production cost, less time to launch etc. (Kaur, et. al. 2014). In spite of the fruitful benefits of agile GSD, it is faced with some challenges. One important challenge is the effective and adequate communication in between distributed teams and customers (Jalali, et. al. 2010). Poor communication is an extensive risk to agile GSD (e.g., delivering an inaccurate, incomplete or inefficient message (Abrahamsson, et. al. 2017). Knowledge sharing and communication is the constitutional concern of distributed global agile development environments (Èmite et. al. 2011). During the recent years organizations are moving to the development of Global Software Engineering. The Projects which are been developed by separate teams have been noted as more challenging as compare to those project which are been running at one platform (Kaur, et. al. 2014). Furthermore knowledge of all possible challenges and potential mitigation strategies of GSE is essential for running a successful project. The collected challenges may further arrange into checklists. Moreover the developed checklists separated into risk management process particularly risk identification and risk mitigation planning.

In recent literature, the researchers have investigated the hybridization of ASD and GSE (Wohlin, 2014). This has evolved a trend of implementing agile development in global software projects. Moreover, the hybridization of ASD and GSE has also accumulated their strengths. This includes, but not limited to, rapid development, optimum resource utilization, integration of global experts, better communication, reduce coordination issues, increased trust, improved productivity, etc (Kaur, st. al. 2014)

In addition, the implementation of the agile method in GSE is also encouraged by the fact that agile development gained huge attentiveness from industry (Kaur, st. al. 2014). In recent literature, although there is a growing interest in becoming agile and globalized for rapid and optimal software development. However, a few works have been reported in this connection.

The main goal of agile development focuses on face-to-face communication among collocated teams compared to geographically dispersed (Global Software Development) GSD teams (Šmite, et. al. 2010). The increase in the use of agile approaches in GSD along with the literature on communication challenges has recently become of interest (Lanubile et. al. 2010). Communication challenges in agile GSD are required to be studied and the tools, methods, and strategies to address these challenges need to be developed (Dullemond, et. al. 2010).

Due to the successful agile software development and implementation, its application in GSD is gaining momentum day by day. Apparently, the scenario looks benefiting however, distributed project team encountered some inherent constraints to apply agile practices (Nguyen-Duc et. al. 2015). One of the basic reason is the need for effective communication, to overcome the logical issue it essentially requires team members to be collocated. Other major difficulties faced are usually related to communication, personnel, culture, different time zones, trust, and knowledge management (Kaur, et. al. 2014). Nonetheless, several strategies, methods, and solutions are reported in the recent literature to handle these challenges.

In the subsequent part of this paper first, a comprehensive review of the existing well knows agile practices in global software development is presented. The discussion includes the strengths, limitations, and potential barriers of each ASD in GSE.

GSE has various potential advantages, including shortening time-to-showcase cycles by utilizing time-zone contrasts and enhancing the capacity to rapidly react to customers' needs (Singh et. al. 2015). Globally distributed software engineering also allows organizations to profit by access to a bigger qualified asset pool with the guarantee of reduced development costs(Kaur, et. al. 2014). Another conceivably positive effect of globally distributed engineering is creativity, as the blend of designers with various social cultures may trigger new thoughts (Casey, 2009, July). The mutual reason behind coming together was to lessen the production value and to attain something productive at the same time. Additional reasons included consumption of time effectively, the foundation of new business openings with new accomplices, adaptability as for the quantity of in-house assets and solving issues of accessibility of local assets (Wright et. al. 2010). Following are the main advantages of GSE

Less Costly

Maybe the first and most looked for after advantage of GSE has been that of decreased cost of development. The reason for this advantage is that organizations are globalizing their product improvement exercises to use less expensive workers situated in a more economical area (Nguyen-Duc et. al. 2013). This has been made possible by the fast communication links enabling the quick exchange of the essential item within reach (Abrahamsson, et. al. 2017). The difference in salaries crosswise over locales can be huge, with a US programming specialist's wage being greater than that of a man with an equal level of expertise in Asia or South America (Ågerfalk, 2008). It is true that companies are currently searching in areas where they offer more excellent execution in terms of getting the work done branched forward with the guarantee of less expensive work.

Intercultural Workforce

A large pool of skilled labor by coordinating across distance is a major catch in this for the companies where the activity of development may contain contributions from skilled worked located in any part of the world (Conchúir et, al. 2009). The organizations possess the opportunities to enhance the scope of thie software engineering activities. This could be managed by accumulating the contributions of diversified skilled workers. This is because the geographically disperse location have diverse skill set of software development. Moreover, the intercultural competency depends upon different factors like cognitive, affective, and behavioral aspects (Holmstrom et. al. 2006). In addition, the unified foreign language skills are also necessary to communicate in an culturally diverse environment (Abrahamsson, et. al. 2017). This facilitate the environment to set a common goal, and to enhance the trust level among team members.

Time-Zone Effectiveness

Having designers situated in various time-zones can enable associations to increment the quantity of day by day working. This is primarily because it based on 'follow-the-sun' working model. This also facilities to diminish process duration (Conchúir, 2006). In this connection, the organization can attain the maximum productivity for the constraint amount of time. (Šmite, 2010). In addition the approach facilitated the to drive out from the severe pressure to improve 'time-to-market 'parameter.

Skilled Workers

It is broadly realized that talented engineers have the best effect on advancement, efficiency, and quality.. GSE can possibly encourage access to a vast majority of exceptionally gifted engineers . Therefore, it has been suggested that due to the diverse backgrounds of GSE actors can lead to increased innovation and shared best practice amongst team members (Carmel et. all. 2001). The GSE also motivated the worker to enhance their skills for the competitive advantages

Closeness Towards the Market and Customers

Another benefit is the proximity it offers to market and customers. Not only is the whereabouts of the local market easily available for the customers to get their hands on but also for the businessmen and companies, it is accessible now to learn the location of their potential customers (Cimolini et. al. 2012). Subsequently, this can create new jobs can create goodwill with local customers. Indeed, it may be a business necessity to locate closer to customers in order to expand to other markets. By branching out into the local markets or in new countries where the customers are located, a more direct interaction becomes possible.

Accountability

A formal record of communication provides increased traceability and accountability. Also, Projects process maturity can be well monitored this way and each individual will be entitled to deliver on task this way. Requirements-related communication between two different entities from distant locations is mostly done through "formal" mediums, i.e. the bi-weekly meetings when the communication is focused merely on urgent matters (Conchúir, et. al 2006). Whenever work-related issues arise that required cross-site communication, including an email, making a phone call or waiting for formal requirements meeting to take place.

Improved Task

The product architecture should determine the team structure, rather than the other way around. The idea of GSE drives groups to part their work according to element content well-defined independent modules, without "stepping on each other's toes" (Conchúir, et. al 2006). This allows decisions to be made about each component by the experts of that particular realm. Partitioning tasks can result in efficient work (Conchúir, et. al 2006).

GUIDING PRINCIPLES OF THE MODERN AGILE MOVEMENT

In the recent era of software engineering and development, the Agile-based approaches have been proposed. Primarily, these approaches rendered the concept of rapid development in software engineering. Moreover, it limits many of the traditional and classical software design and development phase for fast application development (Mohammad et. al. 2013). Likewise, with the growth of Information and Communication Technology (ICT), the concept of Global Software Development (GSD) has gained significant attention. GSD is the process of structuring the software design and development team beyond the local and geographical boundaries.

Modern Agile's first true meaning comes from its four guiding principles. They are Make People Awesome; Make Safety a Prerequisite; Experiment & Learn Rapidly, and Deliver Value Continuously (Rao et. al. 2011). Following are the details of these principles:

Designing and developing software applications with the express purpose of empowering the users of those applications is known as "Make People Awesome". The software development company is also likely to transform its processes based on this principle (Phil 2015). The design of the software system also provides the fundamental platform to the software product

Make Safety a Prerequisite increases the issues of quality and safety to a foundational ingredient for success according to the creators of Modern Agile. Fear of failure tends to smother the effectiveness of software development teams. According to this principle, attaching fault is never a focus; everyone works together to solve hitches. With this safe environment, leads to the overall advanced quality level in software delivery (Wood et. al. 2013).

Experiment and Learn Rapidly cracks the elimination of the fear of failure into a system where experimentation and learning are supported. This is expressly vital bearing in mind the rapid rate of transformation in the software industry with new digital strategies and innovations happening on a regular basis. Speediness is of the essence of research (Phil 2015). If an experiment doesn't work, the developer simply moves on to another idea.

Deliver Value Continuously is an important principle for Modern Agile, and is vastly relevant for companies with a Continuous Delivery program. The emphasis is getting the value into the customer's hands as quickly as possible (Phil 2015). The other three principles of Modern Agile combine to make this last principle possible.

Modern Agile is a comparatively new concept and opinions on it are mixed. Implementing some of the principles as part of a traditional Agile or DevOps program makes perfect sense, especially for companies already doing Continuous Delivery (Wood et. al. 2013).

AGILE TESTING METHODOLOGY

Agile testing methodology is primarily a software testing approach. This approach is based on the fundamentals of agile software development system. The close collaboration between the client and the development is essential for executing the project towards the goal. Specifically, the collaboration, is an important ingredient for agile testing (Cockburn, 2002). Moreover, the supports to align the development of the stakeholders is well needs of smooth execution.

Following are some of the advantages of Agile Testing:

1.   Agile Testing saves time and money. As the matter of the fact the time and money are the two principle constraints for any business application
2.   Fewer documentations to fill out and write up. This make the process documented with little efforts.
3.   In Agile Testing the system contain the regular and intensive user feedback. This helps to establish a close and robust testing environment (Cockburn, 2002)
4.   In this approach the daily standup meetings are the integral part of this approach. This style of meeting support rapid resolution the problems. Moreover, it limit any bottleneck into the system

AGILE METHODOLOGY PHASES

The agile methodology process also consists of its own life cycle. There are six phases in agile methodology (Kruchten et. al. 2013). Following are the six phases:

1.   **Concept:** The problem statement and the rationale of solution is identified logically
2.   **Inception:** Gather the need resources of the and initiation of the project as a formal start
3.   **Construction:** The project team begins to work on the project's development using software implemented
4.   **Quality:** To identify the quality parameters and their corresponding measures
5.   **Production:** Development and optimization of the product
6.   **Retirement:** Closures of product.

RECENT AGILE METHODS

The strength of agile methodologies is its ability to accommodate any change in requirement during any stage of the SDLC. This makes the system driving it to be more convenient and flexible. Agile methods are highly recommended in dynamic forceful environments where there is a frequent change appear in requirements (Wood et. al. 2013). This approach is appropriate when customer and developers work together in a highly intractable environment; many of the software houses have published their successful experience of implementing agile methods in software development environment (Wood et. al. 2013). Nevertheless, a lot of challenges are linked with the implementation process, especially in global software engineering. The set of difficulties faced includes, but not limited to: communication, personnel, culture, different time zones, trust, and knowledge management, to overcome the challenges and to get it to work efficiently extensive efforts is a growing need (Ji et. al. 2011). In the following part of this section, a brief description of the above stated ASD is presented with their working principle, strength, and limitations.

Extreme Programming

Extreme Programming (XP) was first proposed in March 1996. First, it starts with conducting requirement gathering process. Subsequently, based on the requirements, the project is then decomposing into the small number of cycles/iteration. The cycles are set up using pair programming approach. Therefore, any change in user requirements can be accommodated during the development phase. The iteration plan shall be re-developed accordingly (Wood et. al. 2013). In the final stage the software quality assurance where the developed feature will be tested for bugs, if identified; the bugs shall be resolved in the next iteration. After completion of all acceptance testing, project tracing shall be executed in which feedback is taken from the project owner that how much job has already been done (Ji et. al. 2011). The pictorial illustration of XP is shown in Figure 1.

The following are the major advantages of XP

1. It is one of the most simplest ASD
2. XP save the time and money by limiting unnecessary documentation and other formalities
3. Close loop and constant feedback
4. XP contributes to ascend the employee satisfaction and retention
5. The entire process of XP is visible and accountable to every entity of the system

Despite the above advantages of XP following are some of the limitations of XP

1. XP relies on the code rather the design. It is a known fact that an optimum design will result in the quality product
2. XP does not guarantee the code quality assurance
3. Due to its intensive interaction with the team member, XP is not suggested for GSD

SCRUM

SCRUM founded in 1993 at the Easel Corporation, the structure of SCRUM mainly consists of sprints (Munassar et. al. 2010). In each sprint, the team finishes its tasks in a result of developing a small part of the product. The requirements initiated to go into a sprint and managed through a product backlog (Munassar et. al. 2010). Release backlog and sprint backlog is developed during sprint backlog meeting. The sprint is usually of timeframe, two to four weeks and is bound to end on time whether task achieved or not. If for somewhat reason some of the work is not completed they are shifted back to the product backlog. The complete sprint cycle is usually managed by the SCRUM master (Schwaber et. al. 2002), (Schwaber et. al. 2004).

The following are the major advantages of SCRUM

1. Up to the mark adaptively to project requirements changes within the project management cycle.
2. The product owner is constantly in coordination with the development team to sustain process transparency .
3. The testing phase takes place after each iteration, the bugs and unnecessary features are fixed quickly.

Figure 1. Extreme programming

Extreme Programming (XP) at a Glance

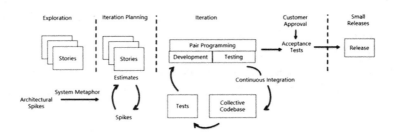

4.   Execution of a roll-back plan to a previous version is quite easy.

Despite the above advantages of SCRUM following are some of the limitations of SCRUM

1.   As the product requirement process is on-going and adjusted often, they are hardly documented. It means the development process can be the shift to some other dimension if the product owner is not absolutely clear of the product requirements.
2.   Experienced professionals are required to monitor and control such a project management model which will act as a Scrum Master and make sure the project is moving towards right direction.
3.   Initial timelines are adjusted quite frequently and delivering the expected product precisely on time is not a thing happening often.

Feature Driven Development (FDD)

Feature Driven Development (FDD) emphasis on design and development phases and doesn't go through the complete development life cycle. In the Development phase, a team of software developers and domain experts are formed to design the architecture and build the overall model of the domain to establish the scope of the system (Tirumala et. al. 2016). In a list down Features phase, the cross-functional team categorizes a required list of features, subsequently, the features are combined together to form a set of features.

List of features designed are then prioritized in a plan by feature phase and then high-level project plan is developed which includes the order in which feature sets will be developed (Tirumala et. al. 2016). In the next step, the Design by Feature and

Figure 2. SCRUM

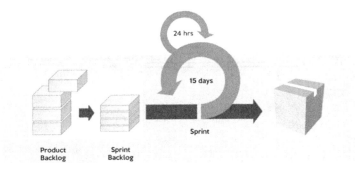

Build by Feature phase the series of iterations are practiced and assign to different feature teams to execute the design. The steps shall be repeated until all features are realized (Highsmith et. al. 2001).

The following are the major advantages of FDD (Palmer et. al. 2001):

1. It usually works great for extensively large-scale products with a number of modules requiring frequent updates and constantly delivers value .
2. The requirements and other supporting papers are well-documented; making easy for developers with any experience can easily jump in and find their role to work on the project.
3. The end product is always better than the initial ones.

Despite the above advantages of FDD following are some of the limitations of FDD (Palmer et. al. 2001)

1. The model is not feasible to be used for smaller projects with strict deadlines
2. The win-win situation in this model relies mainly on having the highly-skilled and experienced project leads monitoring the process throughout the development cycles
3. Documentation is unusual if any. The product owner gets the feature, yet its exact description is outside the scope of FDD model.

Figure 3. FDD processes with outcomes
(Source: Palmer, SR, Felsing, JM 2002. p 57)

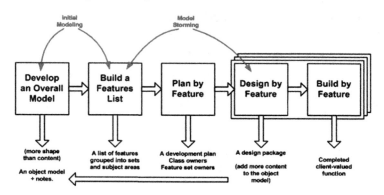

Dynamic Systems Development Method

Dynamic Systems Development Method (DSDM) is a verified method of agile project management and quick product delivery (Sani et. al. 2013). It includes a well-defined process area for effective monitoring and controlling at the same time. Requirements are then classified into must have, should have, could have, and want to have for prioritization, the technique is also called Moscow rule technique. The feasibility study and business study are the two phases that actually develop the scope of the project. Both of the studies shall be conducted sequentially (Chapram et. al. 2018). The actual development is done in the last three phases of the project, which are usually iterative and incremental. The problem statement is defined in the feasibility study and costs estimation and technical review of system development and project delivery is done which provides an output in the form of feasibility report and development scope plan. Business and technology analysis is conducted by a business analyst in the business study phase.

The output of this phase is designing system architecture and detailed development strategy that includes a plan for prototyping, testing, and configuration management (Sani et. al. 2013). Then it comes to the iterative phase of the development process in which analysis, coding and testing are executed which is also called 'functional model iteration' and is the first incremental and iterative phase of the process.

In Design and Build iteration, which is also called in UAT (user acceptance testing) phase, the system is handed over to the user securely to perform its testing (Chapram et. al. 2018). The objective of this phase is to resolve tweaking bugs and to cover the non-functional requirements of the user. The final step is the implementation phase in which the final product is delivered on the Live environment (Sani et. al. 2013). The pictorial representation of DSDM model is illustrated in Figure 4.

The following are the major advantages of DSDM:

1. The product owner/ Business users understand and get hands-on in the software development
2. The deliverables are quick in terms of functionality and achieving milestones.
3. Offers effective communication between end users and software developers.

Despite the above advantages of DSDM following are some of the limitations of DSDM:

1. The DSDM methodology is quietly costly as far as implementation is a concern.
2. It is not suitable for small sized organizations.

Figure 4. DSDM project lifecycle

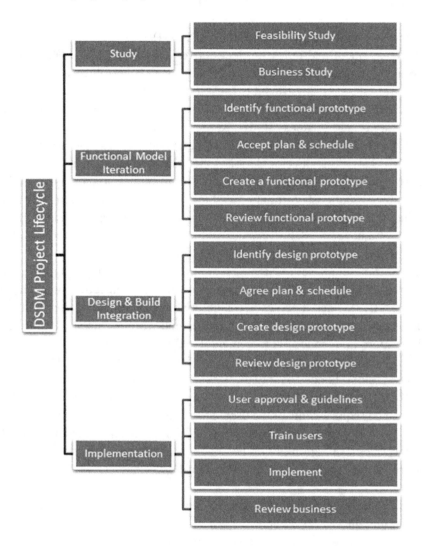

Adaptive Software Development

Adaptive Software Development is mainly focused on requirement as the creator of the method states that requirements may be fuzzy during the initiation of the project. It consists of developing objectives and mission, identifying requirements, gap analysis and Time box (Highsmith et. al. 2013). These are based on a fact of developing a set of requirements; define scope, estimates and resource allocation.

The span of iteration is depending on project size and level of uncertainty. The team defines the goal and develop an objective statement for each iteration and then time box is assigned to each iteration (Calinescu et. al. 2012). The developers along with the cross-functional team assign features for each iteration. Cooperation requires teamwork which is full of trust and respect (Agovic, et. al. 2014). The team must collaborate on quick decision making, requirements, and problems. In this phase, focus groups provide feedback, formal technical reviews, and analyses (Stoica et. al. 2013). The Adaptive Software Development method replaces the traditional waterfall model and real-world testing of the model is in progress (Jalali et. al. 2012).

IMPLEMENTATION OF AGILE METHODS IN GSE

Over the past few years, the repaid growth of information and communication technology (ICT) has been observed. This growth has played the catalytic role in business, education, health, finance, government, economics etc. Likewise, GSE and GSD are also the beneficiaries of this growth. This subsequent part of this session, a summarized view on the scope, benefits, and limitations of the hybrid GSE and GSD are presented .

XP

1. Small releases lower the complexity results quick validation of features by the global customer

Figure 5. Adaptive software development process

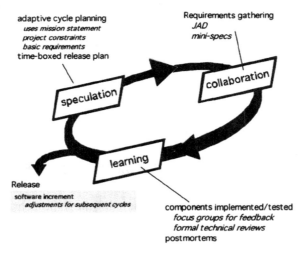

2.   Small iterations shall be practiced and executed weekly, ensuring developer would have enough task in hand so as to reduce to and fro.

3.   As global customers are not available on-site, story cards can be used to transfer the requirements to developers. Allowing it to communicate in pieces.

4.   The development team can work into two groups. One would be responsible for reverse engineering, developing the functional specification and communicating with off-site customers. The second group will put their efforts into the forward engineering process.

SCRUM

1.   Communication challenges can overcome by adjusting working hours so as to participate in daily scrums

2.   To overcome face-to-face meetings difficulty due to geographical distance, teams shall use tools for synchronous communication; such as teleconference; videoconference; web-conferencing; audio/video Skype; Team Viewer with Live Meeting; and/or desktop sharing

3.   Occasional visits and frequent communication by distributed team members for sprints reduces cultural misunderstandings

4.   Project kick-off sprint sometimes called as print "zero" can be used to understand vision, mission, strategy, and goals.

FDD

1.   FDD can be used for effective global software maintenance

2.   No notable implementation of FDD found in global software engineering

3.   Communication might act as a barrier in large scale global project.

4.   Global project teams should be compensated properly for dedication to the completion of the project.

5.   Informal communication shall be made part of the formal meetings to prevent conflicts due to lack of documentation.

DSDM

1.   Beneficial to be used for small size projects and will not support complex global projects.

2.   Privilege to enrich itself by composing with XP agile methodology, it inherits limitations of XP into DSDM

3.   Communication barriers can be overcome using the same techniques as SCRUM and XP

ASDM

1. The chief product owner should prioritize user stories align with business representatives during requirement exploration
2. The technical product owner should play an important role in a technical liaison between the onshore and offshore team.
3. The on-shore team should support and help offshore members to learn their culture, processes, and technology.
4. Daily scrum meeting should be conducted every day for 15 minutes during the development phase, it plays a vital role in global software development

CHALLENGES OF AGILE IN GSE

In the recent era of software engineering and development the Agile based approaches have been proposed. Primarily, these approaches rendered the concept of rapid development in software engineering. Moreover, it limit many of the traditional and classical software design and development phase for fast application development. Likewise, with the growth of Information and Communication Technology (ICT), the concept of Global Software Development (GSD) has gained the significant attention. GSD is the process of structuring the software design and development team beyond the local and geographical boundaries. In the recent literature, the researchers have proposed to employ Agile approaches in the GSD. Apparently, the scenario looks benefiting, however; it also turns into some challenges as a by-product. When there are collocation and frequent communication between the developers and the customers, agile methods are the most suitable. Incorporating agile methods in GSD requires an ample amount of effort (Jalali et. al. 2012). Following are the challenges of agile development in GSE

Communication

Communication is one of the main challenges in the agile GSD, it is considered as one of the most valuable element in Global Software Engineering especially in DS environments where the sharing of info between the members and understanding of the requirements of a customer is allowed (Jalali et. al. 2012). Communication between different developers located at different geological locations is necessary and this is a challenge . Various causes of the communication challenges are contrasting working hours, the absence of communication mediums, language barrier, insufficient face-to-face interaction, and greater communication costs .

Different Time Zones

The change in time zones increments the communication gap which is the communication in between distributed teams becomes arduous. Most common time zone difficulties occur when developers are located in countries like USA, India, Japan etc. "The difference is of 12.5 hours between USA and India, therefore communication within the distributed team members may prove difficult (Hanssen et. al. 2011)

Lack of Communication Tools

Applicable communication tools are required in agile projects between onshore and offshore development teams including the customers. The agile projects might fail if the proper communication tools are absent such as video conferencing etc. (Hanssen et. al. 2011). Therefore, it is required of distributed teams to have authorization to different communicational tools and employ them in accordance with their necessity for efficient communication.

Language Barrier

Associations among various members from various countries speaking various languages are usually hard due to their different native languages (Hanssen et. al. 2011). Members whose native language is not English often face problems when the mode of communication among members is in English making the meeting time longer than usual as it becomes harder to express the views. To increase the availability of intercultural collaboration, machine translations can be used (Dullemond et. al. 2009).

High Communication Cost

The tools used for communications are very costly, organizations are required to spend money so that they can administer better communicational facilities to their teams.

Lack of Teamwork

Collaboration among the team members in distributed agile development is of utmost importance so that high-quality products can be obtained (Dullemond et. al. 2009). It is important for each team member to know of the importance of contribution and teamwork, lack of communication may result in the fall in the morale of team members.

Cross-Cultural Diversity

A major issue in communication is Culture, an example of which is the pass of information between offshore and onshore members is only confirmed instead of critical (Dullemond et. al. 2009). Communication and collaboration between members may be affected if cultural issues are not handled properly (Dullemond et. al. 2009).

Personal Selection

The selection of personnel is highly important in agile development as requirement keeps on varying hence it becomes demanding to have cross-functional teams having developers, analysts, and testers. Usually, programmers who fail to implement plan-driven approaches and are unable to handle the dynamic requirements prove to be a liability for the team, accordingly pair programming is among agile practices which are used in development to pick a coding partner with common aims (Jalali et. al. 2010).

Feeling of Insecurity

Insecurity is often an issue faced by new team members or junior members which results in these members failing to easily communicate and put forward their concepts in team discussions. Due to this developing trust in a team becomes burdensome (Jalali et. al. 2010).

The Sense of Belonging to a Team

Poor team bonding is a result of the lack of constant face-to-face communication or any type of communication among members located at different geographical and geological locations. Another reason for lack of trust results from many socio-cultural differences and difference in languages of the distributed team members (Jalali et. al. 2010)

Temporal Distance

Admirably, face to face communication is most adequate means of communication in GSE. In GSE the project team is not only distribute geographically but it can be distribute into different adjoining time zones. Temporal distance add challenges to attain effective communication among distributed teams and shorten the communication (Paasivaara et. al. 2015).

Geographical Distance

One of the main benefit of implementing GSE is to employing from low cost developers from low wage countries (Inayat et. al. 2015). It means that software development process is not done in one platform. So it generates geographical distance. Thus face to face communication is seemed to effective communication process (Inayat et. al. 2015)

Socio-Cultural Distance

The team members which are working in GSE projects belongs to different nationalities. Cultural diversity can be develop factor in GSE. Cultural diversity in GSE projects can be develop factor. Cultural distance can be exist between two organizations, not always between two nationalities (Hoda et. al. 2017). Language difference is usually indicate as one of the challenges in communication caused by socio-culture distance (Hoda, et. al. 218). . Misconceive of message is usually happen when two communicating parties talking in foreign language. Moreover it causes mutual understanding between project members (Hoda et. al. 2017).

CONCLUSION

The current research literature on the recent trends of different agile methodologies practiced in Global Software Engineering was briefly described in this study. The implementation of agile in GSE is not yet well explored. However, it is clear that numerous challenges are associated with the process. There is not sufficient evidence found to conclude that agile was successfully implemented in large distributed global projects. In most of the studies that we reviewed, the customized agile method is explained. The main factor communication is found to play a vital role in practicing agile method in global software engineering also explained in this study. These results can be used towards proposing such a comprehensive framework for agile applicability in GSE. This study is fundamentally provides a logical platform to the researchers for further investigation in the domain of the adaptation of agile software development practices in global software engineering. The description present in this chapter strongly advocate for the adaptation of agile software development practices in global software engineering. In addition, this chapter also submit a comprehensive review on the limitations of this integration. This has created a pressing need to devise the new methods in agile development and software engineering to overcome these challenges.

REFERENCES

Abrahamsson, P., Salo, O., Ronkainen, J., & Warsta, J. (2017). *Agile software development methods: Review and analysis.* arXiv preprint arXiv:1709.08439

Ågerfalk, P. J., Fitzgerald, B., Olsson, H. H., & Conchúir, E. Ó. (2008, May). Benefits of global software development: the known and unknown. In *International Conference on Software Process* (pp. 1-9). Berlin, Germany: Springer. 10.1007/978-3-540-79588-9_1

Agovic, A., & Agovic, A. (2014). *U.S. Patent No. 8,719,781.* Washington, DC: U.S. Patent and Trademark Office.

Anwer, F., Aftab, S., Waheed, U., & Muhammad, S. S. (2017). Agile Software Development Models TDD, FDD, DSDM, and Crystal Methods: A Survey. *International Journal of Multidisciplinary Sciences and Engineering, 8*(2), 1-10.

Calinescu, R., Ghezzi, C., Kwiatkowska, M., & Mirandola, R. (2012). Self-adaptive software needs quantitative verification at runtime. *Communications of the ACM, 55*(9), 69–77. doi:10.1145/2330667.2330686

Carmel, E., & Agarwal, R. (2001). Tactical approaches for alleviating distance in global software development. *IEEE Software, 18*(2), 22–29. doi:10.1109/52.914734

Casey, V. (2009, July). Leveraging or exploiting cultural difference? In *2009 Fourth IEEE International Conference on Global Software Engineering* (pp. 8-17). Piscataway, NJ: IEEE. 10.1109/ICGSE.2009.9

Chapram, S. B. (2018). An Appraisal of Agile DSDM Approach. *International Journal of Advanced Studies in Computers. Science and Engineering, 7*(5), 1–3.

Cimolini, P., & Cannell, K. (2012). Agile Software Development. In Agile Oracle Application Express (pp. 1–13). New York, NY: Apress. doi:10.1007/978-1-4302-3760-0_1

Cockburn, A. (2002). *Agile software development.* Agile Software Development Series.

Conchúir, E. Ó., Ågerfalk, P. J., Olsson, H. H., & Fitzgerald, B. (2009). Global software development: Where are the benefits? *Communications of the ACM, 52*(8), 127–131. doi:10.1145/1536616.1536648

Conchúir, E. Ó., Holmstrom, H., Agerfalk, J., & Fitzgerald, B. (2006, October). Exploring the assumed benefits of global software development. In *2006 IEEE International Conference on Global Software Engineering (ICGSE'06)* (pp. 159-168). Piscataway, NJ: IEEE. 10.1109/ICGSE.2006.261229

Dullemond, K., van Gameren, B., & van Solingen, R. (2009, July). How technological support can enable advantages of agile software development in a GSE setting. In *2009 Fourth IEEE International Conference on Global Software Engineering* (pp. 143-152). Piscataway, NJ: IEEE. 10.1109/ICGSE.2009.22

Dullemond, K., Van Gameren, B., & Van Solingen, R. (2010, August). Virtual open conversation spaces: Towards improved awareness in a GSE setting. In *2010 5th IEEE International Conference on Global Software Engineering* (pp. 247-256). IEEE.

Èmite, D., & Wohlin, C. (2011). A whisper of evidence in global software engineering. *IEEE Software, 28*(4), 15–18. doi:10.1109/MS.2011.70

Hanssen, G. K., Šmite, D., & Moe, N. B. (2011, August). Signs of agile trends in global software engineering research: A tertiary study. In *2011 IEEE Sixth International Conference on Global Software Engineering Workshop* (pp. 17-23). Piscataway, NJ: IEEE. 10.1109/ICGSE-W.2011.12

Highsmith, J., & Cockburn, A. (2001). Agile software development: The business of innovation. *Computer, 34*(9), 20–127. doi:10.1109/2.947100

Highsmith, J. R. (2013). Adaptive software development: a collaborative approach to managing complex systems. Boston, MA: Addison-Wesley.

Hoda, R., Salleh, N., & Grundy, J. (2018). The rise and evolution of agile software development. *IEEE Software, 35*(5), 58–63. doi:10.1109/MS.2018.290111318

Hoda, R., Salleh, N., Grundy, J., & Tee, H. M. (2017). Systematic literature reviews in agile software development: A tertiary study. *Information and Software Technology, 85*, 60–70. doi:10.1016/j.infsof.2017.01.007

Holmstrom, H., Conchúir, E. Ó., Agerfalk, J., & Fitzgerald, B. (2006, October). Global software development challenges: A case study on temporal, geographical and socio-cultural distance. In *2006 IEEE International Conference on Global Software Engineering (ICGSE'06)* (pp. 3-11). Piscataway, NJ: IEEE. 10.1109/ICGSE.2006.261210

Inayat, I., Salim, S. S., Marczak, S., & et al, . (2015). A systematic literature review on agile requirements engineering practices and challenges. *Computers in Human Behavior, 51*, 915–929. doi:10.1016/j.chb.2014.10.046

Jalali, S., & Wohlin, C. (2010, August). Agile practices in global software engineering-A systematic map. In *2010 5th IEEE International Conference on Global Software Engineering* (pp. 45-54). IEEE. 10.1109/ICGSE.2010.14

Jalali, S., & Wohlin, C. (2010, August). Agile practices in global software engineering-A systematic map. In *2010 5th IEEE International Conference on Global Software Engineering* (pp. 45-54). Piscataway, NJ: IEEE. 10.1109/ICGSE.2010.14

Jalali, S., & Wohlin, C. (2012). Global software engineering and agile practices: A systematic review. *Journal of Software. Ecological Processes*, *24*(6), 643–659.

Ji, F., & Sedano, T. (2011, May). Comparing extreme programming and Waterfall project results. In *2011 24th IEEE-CS Conference on Software Engineering Education and Training (CSEE&T)* (pp. 482-486). Piscataway, NJ: IEEE. 10.1109/ CSEET.2011.5876129

Kaur, P., & Sharma, S. (2014). Agile software development in global software engineering. *International Journal of Computers and Applications*, *97*(4).

Kruchten, P. (2013). Contextualizing agile software development. *Journal of Software: Evolution and Process*, *25*(4), 351–361.

Lanubile, F., Ebert, C., Prikladnicki, R., & Vizcaíno, A. (2010). Collaboration tools for global software engineering. *IEEE Software*, *27*(2), 52–55. doi:10.1109/ MS.2010.39

Mohammad, A. H., & Alwada'n, T. (2013). Agile software methodologies: Strength and weakness. *International Journal of Engineering Science and Technology*, *5*(3), 455.

Munassar, N. M. A., & Govardhan, A. (2010). A comparison between five models of software engineering. *International Journal of Computer Science Issues*, *7*(5), 94.

Nguyen-Duc, A., & Cruzes, D. S. (2013, August). Coordination of Software Development Teams across Organizational Boundary--An Exploratory Study. In *2013 IEEE 8th International Conference on Global Software Engineering* (pp. 216-225). IEEE.

Nguyen-Duc, A., Cruzes, D. S., & Conradi, R. (2015). The impact of global dispersion on coordination, team performance and software quality–A systematic literature review. *Information and Software Technology*, *57*, 277–294. doi:10.1016/j. infsof.2014.06.002

Paasivaara, M., Blincoe, K., Lassenius, C., et al. (2015, May). Learning global agile software engineering using same-site and cross-site teams. In *2015 IEEE/ACM 37th IEEE International Conference on Software Engineering* (Vol. 2, pp. 285-294). Piscataway, NJ: IEEE. 10.1109/ICSE.2015.157

Palmer, S. R., & Felsing, M. (2001). A practical guide to feature-driven development. London, UK: Pearson Education.

Phil, M. (2015). Comparative analysis of different agile methodologies. *International Journal of Computer Science and Information Technology Research, 3*(1).

Portillo-Rodríguez, J., Vizcaíno, A., Piattini, M., & Beecham, S. (2012). Tools used in Global Software Engineering: A systematic mapping review. *Information and Software Technology, 54*(7), 663–685. doi:10.1016/j.infsof.2012.02.006

Rao, K. N., Naidu, G. K., & Chakka, P. (2011). A study of the Agile software development methods, applicability and implications in industry. *International Journal of Software Engineering and Its Applications, 5*(2), 35–45.

Sani, A., Firdaus, A., Jeong, S. R., & Ghani, I. (2013). A review on software development security engineering using dynamic system method (DSDM). *International Journal of Computers and Applications, 69*(25).

Schwaber, K. (2004). *Agile project management with Scrum.* Microsoft Press.

Schwaber, K., & Beedle, M. (2002). *Agile software development with Scrum* (Vol. 1). Upper Saddle River, NJ: Prentice Hall.

Singh, A., Singh, K., & Sharma, N. (2015). Agile in global software engineering: An exploratory experience. *International Journal of Agile Systems and Management, 8*(1), 23–38. doi:10.1504/IJASM.2015.068607

Šmite, D., Moe, N. B., & Ågerfalk, P. J. (Eds.). (2010). Agility across time and space: Implementing agile methods in global software projects. Berlin, Germany: Springer Science & Business Media. doi:10.1007/978-3-642-12442-6

Šmite, D., Wohlin, C., Gorschek, T., & Feldt, R. (2010). Empirical evidence in global software engineering: A systematic review. *Empirical Software Engineering, 15*(1), 91–118. doi:10.100710664-009-9123-y

Stoica, M., Mircea, M., & Ghilic-Micu, B. (2013). Software Development: Agile vs. Traditional. *Informatica Economica, 17*(4).

Tirumala, S., Ali, S., & Babu, A. (2016). A Hybrid Agile model using SCRUM and Feature Driven Development. *International Journal of Computers and Applications*, *156*(5), 1–5. doi:10.5120/ijca2016912443

Wohlin, C. (2014, May). Guidelines for snowballing in systematic literature studies and a replication in software engineering. In *Proceedings of the 18th international conference on evaluation and assessment in software engineering* (p. 38). New York, NY: ACM. 10.1145/2601248.2601268

Wood, S., Michaelides, G., & Thomson, C. (2013). Successful extreme programming: Fidelity to the methodology or good teamworking? *Information and Software Technology*, *55*(4), 660–672. doi:10.1016/j.infsof.2012.10.002

Wright, H. K., Kim, M., & Perry, D. E. (2010, November). Validity concerns in software engineering research. In *Proceedings of the FSE/SDP workshop on Future of software engineering research* (pp. 411-414). New York, NY: ACM. 10.1145/1882362.1882446

Chapter 8
Study of Employee Innovative Behavior in Sri Lankan Software Companies

Shanmuganathan Vasanthapriyan
 https://orcid.org/0000-0002-0597-0263
Sabaragamuwa University of Sri Lanka, Sri Lanka

ABSTRACT

Along with the advancement of the technology, software companies have to face a huge competition in the global market. To face this competition, innovations can be used as a strategic weapon. As employees are the main driving forces of innovation, their behavior can be a crucial factor in boosting innovation. Innovative behavior is referred as the introduction and application of new ideas, products, processes, and procedures to a person's work role or an organization. This behavior directly affects innovation performance of an organization. The main aim of this study is to identify the factors that affect employee innovative behavior and their effect in Sri Lankan software companies using a quantitative methodology. Apart from that, this study provides a conclusive summary of the current status of innovative behavior of employees. The initial step mapping study was done to find the past literature related to the research topic. From that study, 17 papers were identified as primary studies.

DOI: 10.4018/978-1-5225-9448-2.ch008

INTRODUCTION

Sri Lankan software companies have shown a rapid growth since last decades, with the advancement of the information technology (Balasooriya, 2014). Because of this, many local and global investors are willing to invest on this sector. All these software organizations have to operate in a global market where there is a huge competition (Balasooriya, 2014). Innovations are known as a strategic weapon to face this competition. The word "innovation "refers to "something freshly introduced". Innovation is about putting in ideas to make new results. This result may be a new product, a new approach or even a new application of an old product or approach. Innovation emerges due to new competitive demands (Baragde & Baporikar, 2017). Therefore, to survive in the modern economic climate, organizations must seek innovation to change processes, create different and more effective processes, or improve existing processes. Organizations may go for different types of innovations such as product innovation, process innovation, service innovation, business innovation and all contribute to strengthen the competitive advantage of a certain company (Gamal, Salah, & Elrayyes, 2011).

Employees are the main driving force of the innovation in the industry (Li & Zheng, 2014). So the employee innovative behavior, which can be defined as an act of generating, promoting and applying of innovative thinking in the organization for the purpose of personal and organizational performance is very crucial (Chatchawan, Trichandhara, & Rinthaisong, 2017; Li & Zheng, 2014). As software companies in Sri Lanka are constantly evolving, it is important to know how a company's ability to innovate can be improved. All innovative activities can be traced back to the behavior of employees. This absolutely makes the employee the center point of attention. It is difficult for innovation to be forged by an individual alone. As a result, a great deal of attention should be paid to the factors affecting innovative work behavior (Chatchawan et al., 2017). In order to understand the state of innovative behavior of employees, it is important to go through difficulties and obstacles which employees meet when they engage in innovative activities. For that we should consider the barriers in both internal and external factors regarding employees. The relationship between factors and barriers is that if a factor affects the subject negatively, it becomes a barrier.

Motivation

Nowadays, innovation plays a key role in facing the vast competition created with technology advancement. This huge competition among companies has created the need of understanding the factors behind the high performance of organizations (Abdel Aziz & Rizkallah, 2015). Many studies identified innovation as one of the key factors or practices behind the success of the organizations and the key factor for their competitive advantage. Intellectual capital and innovation are considered as the drivers of competitive advantage in many industries. The first stages of innovation is associated with the generation of new ideas, their promotion and their final realization at the workplace are the result of the expression of innovative behaviors.

When we look over the software engineering perspective we can clearly observe several examples of the innovative behavior exhibited by software engineers, with positive impacts at the individual, team, and organizational levels. For instance, during the completion of a huge software project there is need for a well-structured database. Developing and maintaining this database should be done manually. But a member in the software development team implements scripts to automate this manual work, thus both reducing errors and freeing up to perform other productive activities. Then was promoted the new idea to her manager, finally incorporating the solution into the company's routine protocol. What is relevant in this example is that he voluntarily took the initiative to develop the script automations during her spare time, but it was not among her duties or project tasks. So, this gives lots of benefits to the company. This example also shows that innovative behavior is not just an inventing a product, but it can be a simple idea to improve individual and organizational performance.

If we consider the innovations in the Sri Lankan context, there is a huge lack of attention towards this topic. Lots of software companies in Sri Lanka are giving services to foreign companies, but the problem is they do not try to invent new ideas. Most of the companies are trying to get service from employees throughout the whole day and they do not pay attention towards employee behavior and their satisfaction. This will negatively impact on the bond between the organization and employees. So as mentioned earlier, a great deal of attention should be paid to the factors affecting innovative work behavior. The benefits of innovative behavior in practice prompted us to look for factors that promote or inhibit this behavior at the individual, group, and organizational levels, from the perspective of software engineering. Therefore, this research topic should be more concerned.

Research Significance and Objectives

Most of the research has been done on investigating the effect of individual or organizational factors that affect innovative behavior of employees in organizations. Only a few researches were there addressing both individual and organizational factors in the same research. Another problem was that, 75% of the research were literature review-based studies and qualitative studies. Qualitative studies have been done by holding different types of interviews with employees. Problem with that was sample population was small. Literature review-based studies have focused in analyzing the previously done studies and other documents. They have not been focused on finding the current state of the employee innovative behavior in organizations. Considering the Sri Lankan context, no research was published addressing the employee innovative behavior in software companies. Some of research were found regarding innovations in organizations. Previously done quantitative studies also have considered few factors that affect innovative behavior. Even if they have focused on both individual and organizational factors, they haven't given more attention to the individual factors. Therefore, considering the above facts, there is need of comprehensive study regarding this research topic.

The main objective of this research is to find the factors that affect employee innovative behavior and the effect of those factors on innovative behavior of employees in Sri Lankan software companies using a survey based empirical research method. This study is aimed to cover both individual and organizational factors to investigate a broad area of the research topic. This study also provides a conclusive summary of those factors. This summary gives a clear idea about the current status of employee innovative behavior in Sri Lankan software companies. Furthermore, this study helps to identify areas to stimulate the innovation willingness of employees and to promote their innovative behavior.

Research Questions

As mentioned earlier, this study is aimed to investigate the effect of the factors that affect employee innovative behavior in Sri Lankan software companies. In order to achieve the above objectives following research questions (RQs) were proposed.

- **RQ1:** What is the current status of employee innovative behavior in Sri Lankan software companies?
- **RQ2:** What are the factors affecting innovative behavior of employees in Sri Lankan software companies?
- **RQ3:** How is the impact on the factors affecting employee innovative behavior in Sri Lankan software companies?
- **RQ4:** What areas should be mostly improved in order to improve employee innovative behavior in Sri Lankan software companies?

Throughout this study the above research questions have been answered. This study consists of a literature review that provide past important points related to the research topic and research questions, a methodology section with questionnaire design and proposed hypothesis, an analysis section with survey results, a discussion section of the study and finally conclusion section with future research possibilities.

LITERATURE REVIEW

Background

The current economy is based on the information technology as we can see IT dominates the business world (Baragde & Baporikar, 2017; Edison, Bin Ali, & Torkar, 2013). There has been big improvement in the industrial sector, which has created a huge competition. To compete with other parties, innovations become important and crucial (Baragde & Baporikar, 2017). Software companies are required to develop their knowledge in various fields to face the competition (de Souza Bermejo, Tonelli, Galliers, Oliveira, & Zambalde, 2016; Gourova & Toteva, 2012). Therefore, software companies should have the ability to identify and understand latent needs in areas that go beyond the boundaries of software knowledge and development technologies (de Souza Bermejo et al., 2016). Nowadays innovation has become the core pillar of achievement for every organization in the current business world (Ikeda & Marshall, 2016; Rose & Furneaux, 2016; Shahzad, Xiu, & Shahbaz, 2017). Therefore, innovations directly help organizations to gain large market share but if they fail to consistently innovate overtime they will lose their position to emerging firms that have innovative offerings (Linder, Jarvenpaa, & Davenport, 2003; Muller, Välikangas, & Merlyn, 2005). When we talk about innovation in software companies, it is not just software innovations, it also engages in the voluntary and intentional generation, promotion, and realization of new ideas for the benefit of individual performance, group effectiveness, or the organization (Monteiro, da Silva, & Capretz, 2016; Westerski, Iglesias, & Nagle, 2011). In considering innovation, organizations are required to capitalize on employees' innovative behavior which is the interested subject and consideration of both practitioner and researchers (Hakimian, Farid, Ismail, & Nair, 2016).

Innovations in Software Industry

The current economy is based on the information technology as we can see the IT dominates the business world (Baragde & Baporikar, 2017; Edison et al., 2013). There has been big improvement in the industrial sector, which has created a huge competition. To compete with other parties, innovations become important and crucial (Baragde & Baporikar, 2017). Software companies are required to develop their knowledge in various fields to face the competition (de Souza Bermejo et al., 2016; Gourova & Toteva, 2012). Therefore, software companies should have the ability to identify and understand latent needs in areas that go beyond the boundaries of software knowledge and development technologies (de Souza Bermejo et al., 2016). Nowadays innovation has become the core pillar of achievement for every organization in the current business world (Ikeda & Marshall, 2016; Rose & Furneaux, 2016; Shahzad et al., 2017). Therefore, innovations directly help organizations to gain large market share but if they fail to consistently innovate overtime they will lose their position to emerging firms that have innovative offerings (Linder et al., 2003; Muller et al., 2005). When we talk about innovation in software companies, it is not just software innovations, it also engages in the voluntary and intentional generation, promotion, and realization of new ideas for the benefit of individual performance, group effectiveness, or the organization (Monteiro et al., 2016; Westerski et al., 2011). Edison has stated that sustained innovation is very important in any business, so the problem is not innovation, but rather making it continuously on a regular basis (Edison et al., 2013).

Innovative Behavior of Employees

Innovative Work Behavior is defined as the intentional behavior of an individual to introduce or apply new ideas to their assigned work role. Successful innovation requires both generation and implementation of novel ideas. Employees in organizations are rarely able to implement ideas on their own and often receive permission from their managers to implement them. Lukes has stated that an important aspect of innovative behavior is to communicate ideas with colleagues and managers to receive their feedback. The motivation of employee's innovative behavior can be divided into two factors as internal and external factors. The added value of employees having positive commitment is that they tend to be more determined in their work, show relatively high productivity and are more proactive in offering their support. Psychological Capital means employees are willing to take the risk of innovation failure and actively participate in innovation within the organization (Li & Zheng, 2014). Psychological capital focus on personal psychological sources with their basic four components as mentioned below.

1.   Self-efficacy (confidence).
2.   Hope.
3.   Optimism (positive attitude).
4.   Resiliency (capacity of recovery) (Çavuş & Gökçen, 2015).

The organizational innovation atmosphere can be defined as the degree of supporting for creativity and innovation felt by members of the organization on the work environment (Li & Zheng, 2014; Pratoom & Savatsomboon, 2012). Considering above factors organizational innovation atmosphere can be sub divided into organizational strategy, organizational support, rewards (incentives) and resource availability (Chatchawan et al., 2017; Smith, Busi, Ball, & Van der Meer,

2008). Organizational factors are usually related to the internal organization culture. Therefore, factors such as the reward system, management support, culture of trust and risk taking, allocation of resources and specially the free time and finally the organizational structure and the related centralization of decision are directly related to the employees' idea generation.

Growth Types

Software companies can be divided into various types considering different indicators, where there are a few big players, some medium-sized companies, and a large number of small companies. If we consider the firm growth, revenue can be considered as a good indicator of viewing growth, because it is one of the basic measuring instruments of business. If we look through the perspective of a single company, growth can be considered as a way of seeking success, profitability and better competitiveness (Kukko, 2013). Kukko in his research has divided software companies into three types considering the growth type, they are organic, acquisition and network growth type. Growing organically is considered a better way to grow when compared with firms that have grown mainly through acquisitions. Organic growth can be defined as natural growth of revenue and personnel by adding sales of services or products. It is usually in small and newer companies. Acquisitioned growth is achieved through acquiring external resources. Through an acquisitioned growth a company acquires new personnel, new products and services, new processes and etc. This process is called outsourcing. Most of the companies belong to this growth type are medium size companies. Networked growth companies are having strategic relationships and this growth can be seen as a transitional form of organic and structural growth. This growth type can be seen as a mix of organic and acquisitioned growth. Most of the companies having this type growth type are large multinational companies (Kukko, 2013).

RESEARCH METHODOLOGY

Research Method

In order to examine the effect of organizational and individual factors on employee's innovative behavior of Sri Lankan software companies, a conclusive research design based on the quantitative and qualitative approach should be used. This study should also help to identify the barriers in improving innovative behavior of employees. To do this, information should be gathered from different groups of employees who are engaging in activities related to software development in companies. Information should be collected from the management and both senior and non-senior software developers of the company to understand their motivation, obstacles, dissatisfactions, expectations, opinions, experiences regarding their innovative behavior and activities inside the company. In these kinds of situations, it is better to use concurrent mixed methods research design which allows researchers to collect quantitative and qualitative data concurrently. This approach to research is used when integration of qualitative and quantitative data provides a better understanding of the research problem than either of each alone and it also helps to collect information over different perspectives.

The quantitative survey method was chosen since it allows the collection of a large amount of data from a large population with a cost-effective manner. Therefore, to collect information, a questionnaire is used with a proper scale and scope. Then the responses of employees can be statistically analyzed to mine useful patterns. But, in the questionnaire the respondent provides the choice of replies which could be restricted within the scope, because it is limited only to what is in the questionnaire. Therefore, it is important to use qualitative methods such as face-to-face semi structured interview which provide a better way to obtain the true feeling, insight and to understand the interviewee responses. Therefore, by mixing both quantitative and qualitative data, we can gain in breadth and depth of understanding and verification, while offsetting the weaknesses inherent to using each approach by itself.

Research Design

Before making the questionnaire, nine hypotheses have been formulated to cover the scope of the study and to measure the innovative behavior of employees in software companies. They were formulated by considering previous done researches as stated below.

Simply organizational commitment can be stated as the bond employees experience with their organization. Changes in psychological contracts may also have implications for employee attitudes and behavior, especially organizational commitment (Agarwala, 2003). Past studies say that an employee's commitment increases when he takes responsibilities and when he is empowered because he has the feeling that his work belongs to him (Zannad, 2003). Therefore, it clearly emphasizes that psychological capital of an employee influences on organizational commitment. Organizational commitment is different from job satisfaction, as job satisfaction results from an individual relation to work, organizational commitment controls and guides the person in the organization. Emotional commitment generated by the internal motivation of the individual will be beneficial for employees to improve the efficiency of learning and working and to make fuller use of their own creativity (Tschang, 2001). Considering above facts stated in past research papers, following hypothesis is proposed.

- **H1:** Organizational commitment influences on employee innovative behavior.
- **H2:** Psychological capital influences on employee innovative behavior.
- **H3:** Organizational strategy influences on employee innovative behavior.
- **H4:** Organizational support influences on employee innovative behavior.
- **H5:** Personal rewards influences on employee innovative behavior.
- **H6:** Resource availability influences on employee innovative behavior.
- **H7:** Leadership influences on employee innovative behavior.
- **H8:** Social capital influences on employee innovative behavior.
- **H9:** Work characteristics influences on employee innovative behavior.

Questionnaire Design

Questionnaire was designed under two main factors and nine sub factors based on previous done researches. Figure 1 shows the research model developed in order to get clear idea about the relationship between those factors (Chatchawan et al., 2017; Dörner, 2012; Monteiro et al., 2016). Here innovative behavior (IB) acts as the dependent variable and all others are independent variables. Table 1 shows main factors, sub factors, number of items and their references used to design the questions during the preliminary questionnaire design. In the questionnaire, first respondent has to fill their name, age, designation, working years and their experience in their position. Then the rest of questions are provided with several options. Five-point Likert-type scale is used to capture responses from the employees which allows them to make their level of agreement such as strongly agree, agree, no idea, disagree, and strongly disagree. Respectively scores of 5, 4, 3, 2, and 1 were assigned for the above-mentioned categories. Therefore, considering Likert-type scale, all items can be divided in to three main categories as values over 3, and values below 3 and values equal to exactly 3. They can represent positive negative and neither positive or negative respectively. Value 3 is the mean value and it would be the decision criteria for this survey.

The preliminary designed questionnaire should be given to an expert in software engineering filed to ensure the content validity. All the questions should be examined and checked that the survey items were clear, meaningful, and understandable. After the confirmation of the questionnaire, a pilot test should be done by software engineers in Sri Lankan software companies. They should be invited to complete the survey, to comment on whether the questionnaire is legible, understandable and any other comments to improve the design of the questionnaire survey. Reliability of the questionnaire is checked using SPSS software. After the final confirmation, the

Figure 1. Research model

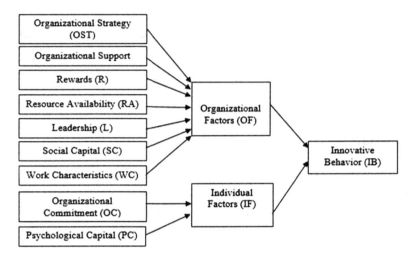

Table 1. Structure of the Questionnaire

Factors	Sub Factors	# of Items	References
Individual	Organizational Commitment	4	(Celliah, 2015) (Seba, Rowley, & Lambert, 2012) (Li & Zheng, 2014) (Lukes & Stephan, 2017) (Allen & Meyer, 1990)
	Psychological Capital	6	(Çavuş & Gökçen, 2015) (Seba et al., 2012) (Li & Zheng, 2014)
Organizational	Organizational Strategy	6	(Smith et al., 2008) (Abdel Aziz & Rizkallah, 2015) (Seba et al., 2012) (Li & Zheng, 2014)
	Organizational Support	6	(Chatchawan et al., 2017) (Lukes & Stephan, 2017) (Shahzad et al., 2017) (Monteiro et al., 2016)
	Rewards	2	(Patterson & Kerrin, 2014) (Thornberry, 2003) (Abdel Aziz & Rizkallah, 2015) (Smith et al., 2008) (Monteiro et al., 2016)
	Resource Availability	4	(Monteiro et al., 2016) (Smith et al., 2008) (Baragde & Baporikar, 2017) (Abdel Aziz & Rizkallah, 2015)
	Leadership	4	(Smith et al., 2008) (Seba et al., 2012) (Li & Zheng, 2014) (Lukes & Stephan, 2017)
	Social Capital	6	(Pratoom & Savatsomboon, 2012) (Shahzad et al., 2017) (Seba et al., 2012) (Li & Zheng, 2014)
	Work Characteristics	4	(Toner, 2011) (Li & Zheng, 2014) (Chatchawan et al., 2017) (Seba et al., 2012)

questionnaire was developed in google forms and link was provided to employees in companies to answer them easily through internet. Questionnaire was distributed to cover major growth dimensions; organic growth, acquisition growth and network growth.

RESULTS

Overall Analysis

This analysis is done using the whole dataset not dividing it according to the growth types. Demographic, descriptive, correlation and regression analysis are done in this section. Hypothesis are proved using linear regression analysis, based on the results with which research model was reconstructed.

Demographic Analysis

The dataset was analyzed by SPSS version 20 using various statistical tools. Demographic analysis was done while considering the frequencies of demographic variables to identify and recognize the patterns of respondents and their effect over the acquired results. A dataset consisted of 100 valid responses was used to carry out the analysis part. Out of 100 responses, 62% and 38% represented male and female respondents respectively. Therefore, we can see males engaging in IT related activities are somewhat higher in number than female. Most of the respondents were young individuals below 25 and between 25-35 years of age which was about 80% of total responses. This is important because young employees have big potential to carry out innovative activities. Rest of 30% was below 35 years of age. Therefore, results have covered all age ranges. Table 2 and Figure 2 shows the results of demographic analysis.

Measurement Model Assessment

Before doing descriptive, correlation and regression analysis, it is important to assess the measurement model. For that, reliability and validity of the questionnaire was checked. Validity of the questionnaire was tested using Kaiser–Meyer–Olkin (KMO) coefficient and Bartlett's test of sphericity (BTS). Sampling adequacy is measured by using KMO value. BTS is a statistical test used to test overall significance of correlation. Criteria: 0.90s-marvellous, 0.80s-meritorious, 0.70s-middling, 0.60-medicore, 0.5s-miserable and below 0.5 is unacceptable. Table 3 shows that KMO value is above 0.79 which is an acceptable value and BTS is also a strong

Table 2. Demographic analysis

Variable	Value	Count	Percentage %
Gender	Male	62	62.0%
	Female	38	38.0%
Age	Less than 25	22	22.0%
	25-35	70	70.0%
	36-45	7	7.0%
	Above 46	1	1.0%
Current Position	Software Engineer	61	61.0%
	Software Architect	1	1.0%
	System Analyst	2	2.0%
	Software Designer	6	6.0%
	Business Analyst	7	7.0%
	Quality Assurance Engineer	16	16.0%
	Project Manager	4	4.0%
	Technical Lead	2	2.0%
	High Level Management (CEO)	1	1.0%
Years of work experience in IT and software development industries	6 months or less	49	49.0%
	1-2 years	28	28.0%
	2-3 years	8	8.0%
	3-5 years	10	10.0%
	Above 5 years	5	5.0%

value. Reliability was checked using Cronbach's alpha technique. The value 0.50 was used as the threshold value to indicate adequate reliability for this study. The values of Cronbach's alpha were; OC= 0.71, PC= 0.62, OST= 0.87, OSU= 0.74, R= 0.52, RA= 0.60, L= 0.50, SC= 0.59, WC= 0.74 and IB= 0.54 as in the Table 4. As all the values were above 0.5, it was confirmed that reliability of the questionnaire was in a good state.

Descriptive Analysis

According to the Table 4, work characteristics and psychological capital has the highest mean values and rewards and innovative behavior has the lowest mean values. Table 4 shows mean, standard deviation and Cronbach's alpha for each variable.

Figure 2. Distribution of years of experience in IT and software industries

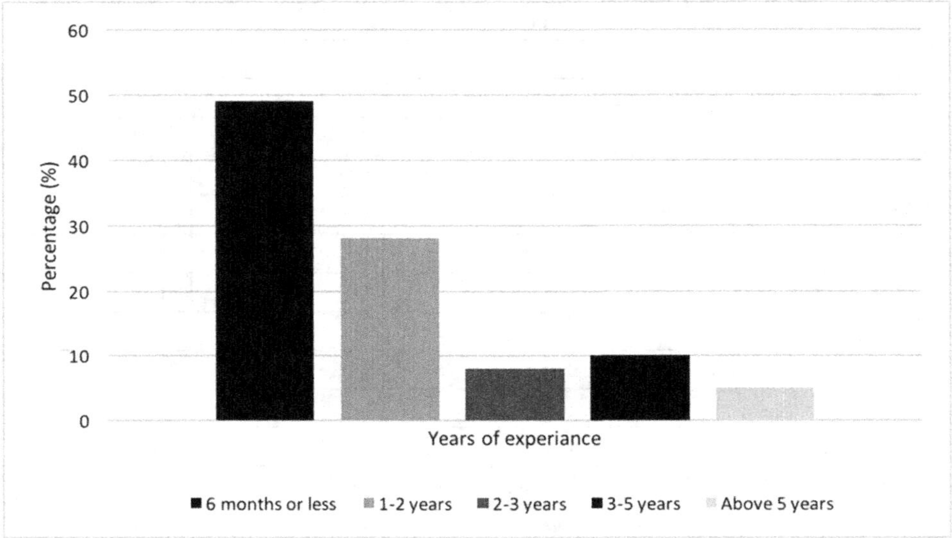

Table 3. KMO and Bartlett's test

Kaiser-Meyer-Olkin Measure of Sampling Adequacy.		.798
Bartlett's Test of Sphericity	Approx. Chi-Square	3310.348
	df	780
	Sig.	.000

Correlation Analysis

Pearson correlation analysis is used to test the linear relationships between data. Correlations are useful because relationship between variables can be found out using this. This is done by measuring the sample correlation coefficient. The correlation coefficient is denoted by r which ranged between -1 and +1 and quantifies the direction and strength of the linear association between the two variables. Therefore, correlation between two variables can be positive (i.e., higher levels of one variable are associated with higher levels of the other) or negative (i.e., higher levels of one variable are associated with lower levels of the other). The sign of the correlation coefficient shows the direction of the association and the magnitude of the correlation coefficient represents the strength of the association.

Table 4. Descriptive statistics and reliability

Factors	No of Items	Mean	Std. Deviation	Cronbach's Alpha
OC	4	3.73	0.61	0.71
PC	6	3.96	0.48	0.62
OST	6	3.88	0.63	0.87
OSU	4	3.71	0.74	0.74
R	2	3.66	0.85	0.52
RA	4	3.76	0.63	0.60
L	4	3.80	0.62	0.50
SC	6	3.75	0.55	0.59
WC	4	4.06	0.64	0.74
IB	3	3.68	0.72	0.54

Therefore, to analyze the relationship between organizational factors, individual factors and Innovative Behavior (IB) Pearson Correlation matrix was used as shown in Table 5. Many indicators were used to determine influence of factors over innovative behavior of employees. From the data it was found that all the variables have got positive correlation between each other with $\rho < 0.05$ significant value. The correlation of organizational support (OST) and innovative behavior (IB) was found as the highest correlation ($r = 0.88$, $\rho < 0.01$). Significant positive correlation was found between leadership (L) and innovative behavior (IB) ($r = 0.79$, $\rho < 0.01$). Next highest was between innovative behavior (IB) and psychological capital (PC) ($r = 0.66$, $\rho < 0.01$). Least correlation coefficient was found between organizational support (OST) and rewards (R) ($r = 0.27$, $\rho < 0.01$).

Regression Analysis

Regression analysis can be considered as a powerful statistical method that is used to examine the relationship between two or more variables of interest. Linear regression is a basic and commonly used type of predictive analysis. The Linear regression model has been developed in order to test hypothesis (Edison et al., 2013; Shahzad et al., 2017). Multiple correlation coefficient $R = 0.94$ indicates that there is a strong correlation between the innovative behavior (IB) with other variables. The most significant independent variables were in order: organizational support (OSU) ($\rho = 0.000$), leadership (L) ($\rho = 0.003$), psychological capital (PC) ($\rho = 0.007$), resource availability (RA) ($\rho = 0.033$), social capital (SC) ($\rho = 0.039$), and rewards (R) ($\rho = 0.040$). Other three variables, organizational commitment (OC), organizational

Table 5. Correlation

	OC	PC	OST	OSU	R	RA	L	SC	WC	IB
OC	1									
PC	0.57**	1								
OST	0.41**	0.48**	1							
OSU	0.33**	0.53**	0.27**	1						
R	0.44**	0.53**	0.66**	0.32**	1					
RA	0.35**	0.47**	0.39**	0.34**	0.58**	1				
L	0.38**	0.61**	0.41**	0.69**	0.53**	0.45**	1			
SC	0.39**	0.41**	0.40**	0.43**	0.55**	0.46**	0.56**	1		
WC	0.40**	0.49**	0.46**	0.48**	0.38**	0.28**	0.44**	0.33**	1	
IB	0.41**	0.66**	0.36**	0.88**	0.52**	0.52**	0.79**	0.58**	0.47**	1
**. Correlation is significant at the 0.01 level (2-tailed).										

strategy (OS), work characteristics (WC) were not significant in the regression model as their ρ values were over '0.05'. Therefore, according to the data H1, H3 and H9 were removed because they haven't got any relationship with innovative behavior (IB). And H2, H4, H5, H6, H7 and H8 were identified as supported hypothesis. They showed a positive influence as their regression coefficient and t values were positive ($\beta > 0$, $t > 0$). Results of regression analysis are shown in Table 6 and Table 7. Model was reconstructed according to proven results as shown in Figure 3.

Proved Hypothesis

Relationship Between Innovative Behavior and Psychological Capital

Psychological capital has a mean value of 3.96 and standard deviation of 0.48 which indicated that most of the values are scattered around the mean. This low standard

Table 6. Model Summary

Model	R	R Square	Adjusted R Square	Std. Error of the Estimate
1	.944[a]	.892	.881	.2489041
a. Predictors: (Constant), WC, RA, OC, SC, OSU, OST, PC, R, L				

Table 7. Coefficients[a]

Model		Unstandardized Coefficients		Standardized Coefficients	t	Sig.
		B	Std. Error	Beta		
1	(Constant)	-.842	.255		-3.299	.001
	OC	.006	.049	.005	.118	.906
	PC	.207	.076	.140	2.742	.007
	OST	-.092	.055	-.081	-1.656	.101
	OSU	.591	.050	.611	11.827	.000
	R	.100	.048	.118	2.082	.040
	RA	.111	.051	.098	2.163	.033
	L	.198	.066	.171	3.002	.003
	SC	.124	.059	.096	2.091	.039
	WC	-.040	.050	-.036	-.808	.421

[a]. Dependent Variable: Avg_Innovative behavior

Figure 3. Reconstructed research model

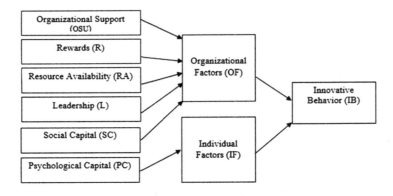

deviation value also confirms the stable results throughout the data sample. Results are shown in Table 8. Correlation between innovative behavior and psychological capital shows high positive value of 0.66, which is at 0.01 level (2-tailed) significant value. Therefore, proposes hypothesis has been proved and it can be modified as bellow.

H2: Psychological capital positively influences on employee innovative behavior

Table 8. Association between innovative behavior and psychological capital

Innovative behavior	Mean N=100	SD	Correlation
Psychological capital	3.96	0.48	0.66**
**. Correlation is significant at the 0.01 level (2-tailed).			

Relationship Between Innovative Behavior and Organizational Support

Organizational support has a 3.71 of high mean value and standard deviation of 0.74 which indicated that most of the values are scattered around the mean and less standard deviation confirms the stable results throughout the data sample. Results are shown in Table 9. Organizational support has the highest correlation with innovative behavior, which shows that organizational support has more influence on innovative behavior than other factors. The value is 0.88 at 0.01 level (2 - tailed) significant value. This positive value proves that organizational support has a positive relationship with innovative behavior. Therefore, hypothesis have been reformulated as shown below.

H4: Organizational support positively influences on employee innovative behavior.

Relationship Between Innovative Behavior and Reward

Reward has mean value of 3.66 which shows that most of the companies are providing reward for employees for their innovative ideas. 0.85 standard deviation value also confirms the stable results throughout the data sample. Results are shown in Table 10. High positive correlation of 0.55 which is significant at the 0.01 level (2-tailed) shows that rewards positively effects on innovative behavior. Therefore, the hypothesis has been reformulated.

Table 9. Association between innovative behavior and organizational support

Innovative behavior	Mean N=100	SD	Correlation
Organizational support	3.71	0.74	0.88**
**. Correlation is significant at the 0.01 level (2-tailed).			

H5: Personal rewards positively influences on employee innovative behavior.

Relationship Between Innovative Behavior and Resource Availability

Resource availability has a mean value of 3.76 and low standard deviation of 0.63 which indicates that most of the values are scattered around the mean. This low value also confirms the stable results throughout the data sample. Results are shown in Table 11. Resource availability and innovative behavior has 0.52 positive correlation value, which proves that the hypothesis is in positive manner. Reformulated hypothesis is as follows.

H6: Resource availability positively influences on employee innovative behavior.

Relationship Between Innovative Behavior and Leadership

Leadership has a 3.80 of high mean value and 0.62 of low standard deviation. Low standard deviation shows that all values are scattered around the mean and it confirms the stable results throughout the data sample. Results are shown in Table 12. Leadership has the second highest correlation with innovative behavior of 0.79, which is significant at the 0.01 level (2-tailed). It shows that leadership positively influences on innovative behavior. Reformulated hypothesis is as follows

H7: Leadership positively influences on employee innovative behavior.

Table 10. Association Between Innovative Behavior and Reward

Innovative behavior	Mean N=100	SD	Correlation
Reward	3.66	0.85	0.52**
**. Correlation is significant at the 0.01 level (2-tailed).			

Table 11. Association Between Innovative Behavior and Resource Availability

Innovative behavior	Mean N=100	SD	Correlation
Resource availability	3.76	0.63	0.52**
**. Correlation is significant at the 0.01 level (2-tailed).			

Table 12. Association Between Innovative Behavior and Leadership

Innovative behavior	Mean N=100	SD	Correlation
Leadership	3.80	0.62	0.79**
**. Correlation is significant at the 0.01 level (2-tailed).			

Relationship Between Innovative Behavior and Social Capital

Social capital also has 3.75 of high mean value and 0.55 of low standard deviation. Low standard deviation shows that all values are scattered around the mean and it also confirms the stable results throughout the data sample. Results are shown in Table 13. Correlation between social capital and innovative behavior is 0.58 of positive value, which proves that social capital positively influences on innovative behavior. Therefore, hypothesis have been reformulated as shown below.

H8: Social capital positively influences on employee innovative behavior.

Growth Type-Based Analysis

As stated in the methodology part responses were collected from different types of software companies to cover the three growth dimensions as organic growth, acquisitioned growth and networked growth. Literature review section stated that organic growth type companies are startup companies, acquisitioned growth type companies are medium size companies who are outsourcing services from others and networked growth type companies are large companies having strategic alliances with other companies. The number of responses were as 30, 35 and 35 respectively according to the above-mentioned growth types and for easy identification they were named as O, A and N respectively. In this section, these three types of companies are compared using their correlation, mean and standard deviation corresponding

Table 13. Association between innovative behavior and social capital

Innovative behavior	Mean N=100	SD	Correlation
Social capital	3.75	0.55	0.58**
**. Correlation is significant at the 0.01 level (2-tailed).			

with six factors that affect employee innovative behavior which have been proved in the previous section.

Table 14 shows that highest mean of innovative behavior is in network growth type companies and respectively acquisition and organic growth type companies are having less mean.

Table 15, Table 16 and Table 17 show the correlation between the factors affecting on employee innovative behavior in three growth type companies. When we consider organic growth type companies, most significant relationship is between innovative behavior and organizational support and equal significant relationship is between resource availability and rewards. Also, leadership, social capital and psychological capital show significant relationship with innovative behavior. Reward and resource availability doesn't show any relationship with organizational support. When we consider acquisitioned growth type companies, most significant relationship is between innovative behavior and organizational support same as in organic growth type companies.

Questionnaire Analysis (Growth Type Based)

In the Results section, six dimensions have been proved as the factors that affect employee innovative behavior in Sri Lankan software companies. Therefore, they can be act as barriers or enablers in enhancing employee innovative behavior too. In this section the most influential factors (enablers) and barriers in three growth type companies are compared in detail. Three growth types are organic, acquisitioned and networked growth type.

Table 14. Descriptive analysis according to three growth types

Factors	O (30)		A (35)		N (35)	
	Mean	SD	Mean	SD	Mean	SD
IB	3.57	0.74	3.69	0.74	3.76	0.68
PC	3.83	0.51	4.03	0.49	4.00	0.45
OSU	3.62	0.73	3.70	0.81	3.79	0.68
R	3.56	0.91	3.67	0.87	3.74	0.79
RA	3.63	0.80	3.77	0.57	3.86	0.50
L	3.81	0.57	3.80	0.61	3.79	0.68
SC	3.85	0.48	3.43	0.55	3.97	0.47

Table 15. Correlation of organic growth type companies

	PC	OSU	R	RA	L	SC	IB
PC	1						
OSU7	0.54**	1					
R	0.41**	0.19	1				
RA	0.43**	0.19	0.83**	1			
L	0.57**	0.67**	0.41**	0.41**	1		
SC	0.63**	0.47**	0.67**	0.65**	0.72**	1	
IB	0.72**	0.83**	0.53**	0.49**	0.73**	0.76**	1

Table 16. Correlation of acquisition growth type companies

	PC	OSU	R	RA	L	SC	IB
PC	1						
OSU	0.46**	1					
R	0.55**	0.39**	1				
RA	0.50**	0.44**	0.67**	1			
L	0.72**	0.61**	0.77**	0.59**	1		
SC	0.17	0.30	0.61**	0.33*	0.48**	1	
IB	0.59**	0.91**	0.58**	0.59**	0.76**	0.46**	1

Table 17. Correlation of network growth type companies

	PC	OSU	R	RA	L	SC	IB
PC	1						
OSU	0.62**	1					
R	0.63**	0.36*	1				
RA	0.47**	0.41*	0.12**	1			
L	0.57**	0.81**	0.43**	0.43**	1		
SC	0.75**	0.69**	0.51**	0.61*	0.70**	1	
IB	0.68**	0.88**	0.44**	0.49**	0.89**	0.76**	1

Most influential factors were identified and listed in Table 19. Mean value four was selected as the selection criteria for that. Confidence has been an influential factor in all three types of companies. There is also a significant point that, organic growth type companies are providing more time to express and develop new ideas. Most of the questions were having high mean values. Therefore, from them mean values less than 3.5 were listed as barriers as shown in Table 19.

Table 18. Most influential factors or enablers in innovative behavior

Category	Influential sub factors	Type of growth		
		O	A	N
Individual	Good confidence	✓	✓	✓
	Not giving up work easily			✓
	Ability to recover mistakes		✓	✓
	Sharing ideas		✓	✓
Organizational	Enough time	✓		
	Adequate training			✓
	Organizing work shops	✓		✓
	Company uses new technologies		✓	
	Sources to learn new things		✓	
	Good management support		✓	
	Good trust	✓		✓
	Good interaction with customers	✓		

Table 19. Barriers in innovative behavior

Barriers in innovative behavior	Type of growth		
	O	A	N
Lack of opportunities to learn about processes outside my department	✓	✓	✓
Lack of rewarding systems	✓	✓	
Lack of communication with members within and outside my department		✓	
Lack of interaction with senior management		✓	✓

DISCUSSIONS AND CONCLUSION

In this study, innovative behavior was measured via nine possible dimensions which were briefly discussed in the literature. Past researches have considered only limited factors, and most of the studies have followed a qualitative methodology. But in this study quantitative research methodology was used. Analysis of the results showed that almost 75% of respondents have engaged in innovative activities in software companies. From them about 20% of respondents have frequently engaged in innovative activities. In this study both individual and organizational factors that affect innovative behavior have been considered and also hypothesis related them have been proven. Monterio in his research has mentioned that both these factors affect employee innovative behavior. In this section six proven hypothesis are discussed and compared with results of this study and previously done research works. And suggested solutions to improve innovative behavior are discussed with the help of results. Furthermore, limitations of this study are discussed.

Discussion of Findings

Psychological Capital Positively Influence Employee Innovative Behavior (H2)

Psychological capital comprises of confidence, attitude, hope and recovery (tolerance) which are crucial factors that affect innovative behavior of an employee. Overall analysis results have proven that it has a significant relationship with innovative behavior. Correlation between psychological capital and innovative behavior is relatively high comparing with other values. Therefore, importance of this factor can be proven using the above results. These results are also consistent with Dorner's results. When we consider results from the growth type-based analysis, it shows that psychological capital is higher in acquisitioned growth type companies which are usually medium size companies. Employees in this type of companies are more psychological stronger than employees in other types of companies. This is because, working in such companies make employees more motive due to many reasons. For example: employees are engaging in lots of extracurricular activities, training session and workshops. Result also shows that psychological capital is lower in small or startup companies (low mean). It was not the expected results. But we can assume that motivation provided by smaller companies are less than large companies. This result in reducing their psychological strength. As psychological capital has shown positive significant correlation with innovative behavior in all three types of growth, it must be definitely considered. Therefore, this result suggests that small or startup companies should pay more attention toward psychological strength of employees than other two types of companies. Therefore, this study's and past studies' results have proven that psychological capital positively influences on innovative behavior of employees.

Organizational Support Positively Affect Employee Innovative Behavior (H4)

Organizational support has the most significant positive relationship with innovative behavior according to overall analysis results. It has the highest correlation with innovative behavior. Mean value of this factor shows that organizational support is also in considerable level in Sri Lankan software companies. Chatchawan has mentioned this factor as an important one in his proposed model (Chatchawan et al., 2017). Results from the growth type based-analysis show that networked type growth has highest mean, which proves that organizational support is higher in large companies. It is lowest in smaller companies. Therefore, these results suggest that smaller companies have to focus more on their support over innovative activities of employees. Companies in all growth types have significant higher positive correlation between innovative behavior and psychological capital. Results from the questionnaire analysis of this study show that more time is available in small or startup companies of organic type than other companies. There, employees have enough time to experiment new things in the company. There, result suggests that large companies have to provide more time to employees to engage in innovative activities. Results also show that training sessions and workshops are mostly available in large companies having networked growth type.

Personal Rewards Positively Influence on Employee Innovative Behavior (H5)

The results of overall analysis of this research indicated that reward also has a positive relationship with innovative behavior. The correlation between reward systems and innovative behavior is significant. These results are consistent with Hamdy's and Shahzad's studies. In the Sri Lankan context it is very important to motivate employees. Hamdy also have highlighted that higher rewards will lead to more innovative behaviors demonstrated by employees. Reward is a factor that directly affects employee's idea generation. Rewards should not be given to successful implementation and commercialization of ideas. When we consider the results of the growth-based analysis, networked type growth companies have highest mean in rewards. That means large companies are most successful in giving rewards to employees in the Sri Lankan context. Lowest mean is in small or startup organic growth type companies. Therefore, results suggest that smaller or startup companies have to give more rewards to employees in boosting their innovative behavior. Companies belong to all three growth-type have got significant correlation between rewards and innovative behavior. This shows that reward is an important factor to consider. But results from the questionnaire analysis show that, reward is not the most influential factor in improving innovative behavior with less mean values in rewards. It has also pointed out that rewards are less in small and medium size companies. Therefore, these companies have focus on employee satisfaction if this is not done they will switch to start their own business.

Resource Availability Positively Influences on Employee Innovative Behavior (H6)

Correlation between innovative behavior and resource availability has significant positive value. Therefore, resource availability is an important factor that affect innovative behavior of employees. Results from the overall analysis also prove that resources are limited in Sri Lankan software companies as it has the medium mean value compared to other factors. Results from growth type-based analysis show that resource availability is high in networked growth type companies. It is lowest in organic growth type companies. Therefore, small or startup companies should pay more attention in providing necessary resources to employees in order to boost their innovative behavior. Results from questionnaire analysis show that sources for learning and new technologies are mostly prominent in acquisitioned growth type companies. That means, medium size companies are mostly using new technologies and providing sources of learning for employees. And also, according to the results funding has not been much important factor that affect innovative behavior of employees. With regard to the organizational level, previous research has focused this under organizational support. Lukes has stated that organizational support includes the organization making resources available for the implementation of new ideas (Lukes & Stephan, 2017). These resources can be time, fund, technologies, tools etc. Therefore, Lukes results are also consistent with this study's results. Also, according to the results from questionnaire analysis, it can be identified that managing innovative idea is not the most influential factor in improving innovative behavior under the Sri Lankan context.

Leadership Positively Influences on Employee Innovative Behavior (H7)

Results of this research indicated that leadership is positively influencing the innovative behavior of employees in the regression analysis. Hamdy in his research has proven this relationship. In this study leadership is similar to management support. Usually employees get motivated if manager is evaluating their ideas (Li & Zheng, 2014). Monteiro in his research has discussed this. Results from growth-based analysis show that leadership have high mean value in organic growth type companies than other two. Among those two acquisitioned growth type company has highest mean value of leadership. This shows that small companies are having more support from management in improving innovative activities in software companies. The middle management layer has also a critical role in this, because they are more interacting with employees (Abdel Aziz & Rizkallah, 2015).

Social Capital Positively Influences on Employee Innovative Behavior (H8)

Overall analysis results have highlighted that social capital which can be described as interaction and trust between employees and customers has a significant positive influence on innovative behavior. Shahzad in his research has proven that team work has a positive relationship with innovation performance. This study's results also show that social capital has a significant relationship with innovative behavior. Results of the questionnaire analysis show that trust between employees in high in organic and acquisitioned growth type companies. That means, smaller and large companies are keeping good trust among employees. Actually, when we consider a small company, the number of employees are low. Therefore, everyone interacts with one another every day. So that helps them to build trust among them. But when we consider a large company, it is something different. They are maintaining strategic alliances with other companies. That means between those companies they need to create good trust. Before that, employees in the company have to trust themselves. So, in that way higher trust in large companies having network growth can be described. Another point is interaction with customers. It is higher in small companies. In large and medium sized companies, usually business analyst or HR managers are involving with customers. That is also a disadvantage to improve innovative behavior of employees.

LIMITATIONS OF THE RESEARCH

Several limitations were identified after completing this study. First it was identified that sample size in this survey is not very high as it was not easy to collect data from large number of respondents in a limited period of time. This sample was divided further into three data sets according to growth type of companies. Therefore, deviations may exist in the research findings when comparing the results. Second, the number of companies considered in this study were relatively less due to the time limitation of the research work because this study was done in a short period of time. Therefore, sample might not have covered the whole population. In future, it is expected to do this study by increasing number of companies and respondents. Third, data were collected from small, medium and large software companies in Sri Lanka. This study is only covering the Sri Lankan context. Therefore, findings of this research cannot be generalized to other countries. Fourth, responses from different levels of software engineering job hierarchy should be gathered to improve the results and to provide overall solutions. Fifth, only quantitative data has been collected to do this study. Therefore, the responses are limited only to the answers in the questionnaire. Therefore, in order to improve the data sample, qualitative methods such as face-to-face and semi-structured interviews are planned to be used in future studies. Qualitative studies provide ways to the interviewer to obtain the true feelings, gain insight, and understanding of the interviewee. Overcoming above limitations, future research works are meant to be done.

SUMMARY OF THE RESEARCH

Innovative behavior of employees is a crucial factor which leads to drive towards innovation. Therefore, lots of studies have been done on the topic innovation. The aim of this study is to find the factors that affect innovative behavior and check the effect of those factors on employee innovative behavior covering both individual and organizational perspectives in Sri Lankan software companies. In conclusion of results of this study, psychological capital, organizational support, rewards, resource availability, leadership and social capital were proved as the most significant factors influencing employee innovative behavior in Sri Lankan software companies. This research has provided strong evidence to prove their relationship. The research model has been reconstructed according to the findings. The results also emphasize that both individual and organizational factors effect on employee innovative behavior. According to the results, individual's psychological characteristics have a significant effect on employee innovative behavior. From the organizational view point, it is important to have good support from the company and adequate resources must be there for employees. Strong management support should be provided in order to evaluate employee ideas and to motivate them.

It was found that innovative behavior is higher in large networked type companies than other two types. Another important finding was that leadership was relatively high in small organic growth type companies. In all three growth types of company's significant relationship has been identified between all proved factors and innovative behavior. According to the result most of those factors were in a favorable level. Lack of opportunities to learn processes outside the department, lack of rewarding systems and lack of communication with members within and outside my department were identified as critical barriers in this study. Most influential factors were identified as psychological capital, organizational support and resource availability. Therefore, psychological strength of an individual is very important when going for an innovation. Confidence, hope, attitude and recovery of individual should be of high level to improve their innovative behavior. Organizational should provide necessary resources like time, technologies, tools and labor when going for innovations. Lack of time was identified as a barrier in large companies having networked type growth. Therefore, results of this study can be useful for software companies in Sri Lanka to motivate employees towards innovations.

IMPLICATIONS FOR FUTURE RESEARCHES

This research study was done considering the employees in Sri Lankan software companies and limited number of companies were considered. Therefore, future studies should be done to broaden the scope of the study to cover more software companies and also, we can do this research in other countries. In this study only a quantitative approach was followed to extract data from employees. There the responses were limited to the questionnaire and accurate true information were not found. Therefore, it is important to use a mixed method approach with both quantitative and qualitative methodology to collect data.

From this study, only few barriers have been identified in improving innovative behavior of employees. That result was having some ambiguity when considering it practically. Therefore, there is a need of future research to find barriers in improving innovative behavior.

REFERENCES

Abdel Aziz, H. H., & Rizkallah, A. (2015). Effect of organizational factors on employees' generation of innovative ideas: Empirical study on the Egyptian software development industry. *EuroMed Journal of Business*, *10*(2), 134–146. doi:10.1108/EMJB-12-2014-0044

Agarwala, T. (2003). Innovative human resource practices and organizational commitment: An empirical investigation. *International Journal of Human Resource Management*, *14*(2), 175–197. doi:10.1080/0958519021000029072

Allen, N. J., & Meyer, J. P. (1990). The measurement and antecedents of affective, continuance and normative commitment to the organization. *Journal of Occupational Psychology, 63*(1), 1–18. doi:10.1111/j.2044-8325.1990.tb00506.x

Balasooriya, B. (2014). *Analysis of barriers for innovations in Sri Lankan software organizations*. Academic Press.

Baragde, D., & Baporikar, N. (2017). Business innovation in Indian software industries. *Journal of Science and Technology Policy Management, 8*(1), 62–75. doi:10.1108/JSTPM-12-2015-0039

Çavuş, M. F., & Gökçen, A. (2015). Psychological capital: Definition, components and effects. *British Journal of Education. Society and Behavioural Science, 5*(3), 244–255.

Celliah, S. (2015). A Research on Employees Organizational Commitment in Organizations: A Case of Smes in Malaysia. *International Journal of Manajerial Studies and Research, 3*(7), 10–18.

Chatchawan, R., Trichandhara, K., & Rinthaisong, I. (2017). Factors Affecting Innovative Work Behavior of Employees in Local Administrative Organizations in the South of Thailand. *International Journal of Social Sciences and Management, 4*(3), 154–157. doi:10.3126/ijssm.v4i3.17755

de Souza Bermejo, P. H., Tonelli, A. O., Galliers, R. D., & et al, . (2016). Conceptualizing organizational innovation: The case of the Brazilian software industry. *Information & Management, 53*(4), 493–503. doi:10.1016/j.im.2015.11.004

Dörner, N. (2012). *Innovative work behavior: The roles of employee expectations and effects on job performance*. Verlag nicht ermittelbar.

Edison, H., Bin Ali, N., & Torkar, R. (2013). Towards innovation measurement in the software industry. *Journal of Systems and Software, 86*(5), 1390–1407. doi:10.1016/j.jss.2013.01.013

Gamal, D., Salah, E., & Elrayyes, E. (2011). How to measure organization innovativeness? An overview of innovation measurement frameworks and innovation audit/management tools. Giza Governorate, Egypt: Technology Innovation and Entrepreneurship Center.

Gourova, E., & Toteva, K. (2012). *Enhancing knowledge creation and innovation in SMEs*. Paper presented at the Embedded Computing (MECO), 2012 Mediterranean Conference on.

Hakimian, F., Farid, H., Ismail, M. N., & Nair, P. K. (2016). Importance of commitment in encouraging employees' innovative behaviour. *Asia-Pacific Journal of Business Administration*, *8*(1), 70–83. doi:10.1108/APJBA-06-2015-0054

Ikeda, K., & Marshall, A. (2016). How successful organizations drive innovation. *Strategy and Leadership*, *44*(3), 9–19. doi:10.1108/SL-04-2016-0029

Kukko, M. (2013). Knowledge sharing barriers in organic growth: A case study from a software company. *The Journal of High Technology Management Research*, *24*(1), 18–29. doi:10.1016/j.hitech.2013.02.006

Li, X., & Zheng, Y. (2014). The influential factors of employees' innovative behavior and the management advices. *Journal of Service Science and Management*, *7*(06), 446–450. doi:10.4236/jssm.2014.76042

Linder, J. C., Jarvenpaa, S., & Davenport, T. H. (2003). Toward an innovation sourcing strategy. *MIT Sloan Management Review*, *44*(4), 43.

Lukes, M., & Stephan, U. (2017). Measuring employee innovation: A review of existing scales and the development of the innovative behavior and innovation support inventories across cultures. *International Journal of Entrepreneurial Behaviour & Research*, *23*(1), 136–158. doi:10.1108/IJEBR-11-2015-0262

Monteiro, C. V., da Silva, F. Q., & Capretz, L. F. (2016). The innovative behaviour of software engineers: Findings from a pilot case study. *Proceedings of the 10th ACM/IEEE International Symposium on Empirical Software Engineering and Measurement.* 10.1145/2961111.2962589

Muller, A., Välikangas, L., & Merlyn, P. (2005). Metrics for innovation: Guidelines for developing a customized suite of innovation metrics. *Strategy and Leadership*, *33*(1), 37–45. doi:10.1108/10878570510572590

Patterson, F., & Kerrin, M. (2014). 11. Characteristics and behaviours associated with innovative people in small-and medium-sized enterprises. Handbook of Research on Small Business and Entrepreneurship, 187.

Pratoom, K., & Savatsomboon, G. (2012). Explaining factors affecting individual innovation: The case of producer group members in Thailand. *Asia Pacific Journal of Management*, *29*(4), 1063–1087. doi:10.100710490-010-9246-0

Rose, J., & Furneaux, B. (2016). Innovation drivers and outputs for software firms: Literature review and concept development. *Advances in Software Engineering*, 2016.

Seba, I., Rowley, J., & Lambert, S. (2012). Factors affecting attitudes and intentions towards knowledge sharing in the Dubai Police Force. *International Journal of Information Management, 32*(4), 372–380. doi:10.1016/j.ijinfomgt.2011.12.003

Shahzad, F., Xiu, G., & Shahbaz, M. (2017). Organizational culture and innovation performance in Pakistan's software industry. *Technology in Society, 51*, 66–73. doi:10.1016/j.techsoc.2017.08.002

Smith, M., Busi, M., Ball, P., & Van der Meer, R. (2008). Factors influencing an organisation's ability to manage innovation: A structured literature review and conceptual model. *International Journal of Innovation Management, 12*(04), 655–676. doi:10.1142/S1363919608002138

Thornberry, N. E. (2003). Corporate entrepreneurship: Teaching managers to be entrepreneurs. *Journal of Management Development, 22*(4), 329–344. doi:10.1108/02621710310467613

Toner, P. (2011). *Workforce skills and innovation.* Academic Press.

Tschang, T. (2001). *The basic characteristics of skills and organizational capabilities in the Indian software industry.* Academic Press.

Westerski, A., Iglesias, C. A., & Nagle, T. (2011). *The road from community ideas to organisational innovation: a life cycle survey of idea management systems.* Academic Press.

Zannad, H. (2003). Organizational commitment in innovative companies. Academic Press.

Chapter 9

Techniques and Trends Towards Various Dimensions of Robust Security Testing in Global Software Engineering

Muhammad Sulleman Memon
QUEST, Pakistan

ABSTRACT

With the growth of software vulnerabilities, the demand for security integration is increasingly necessary to more effectively achieve the goal of secure software development globally. Different practices are used to keep the software intact. These practices should also be examined to obtain better results depending on the level of security. The security of a software program device is a characteristic that permeates the whole system. To resolve safety issues in a software program security solutions have to be implemented continually throughout each web page. The motive of this study is to offer a complete analysis of safety, wherein protection testing strategies and equipment can be categorized into: technical evaluation strategies and non-technical assessment strategies. This study presents high-level ideas in an easy form that would help professionals and researchers solve software security testing problems around the world. One way to achieve these goals is to separate security issues from other enforcement issues so that they can be resolved independently and applied globally.

DOI: 10.4018/978-1-5225-9448-2.ch009

INTRODUCTION

The internet revolutionized our society, affected the software program industry, and the change of statistics and expertise became a principal part of software development, promoting the globalization of the software program industry (Banerjee & Pandey, 2009). this variation in information flow removes the constraints of conventional initiatives and promotes the free go with the flow of statistics, sources, and information between tasks. Software industry globalization includes several aspects, such as part of the external and collective externalization development process, extensive use of a collaborative environment to facilitate the introduction of an entire new software development model, such as resource exchange and open source (Sodiya, Onashoga, & Ajayī, 2006) Resources for sharing knowledge are more than just promoting reuse and teamwork. They also bring new challenges to the software engineering community (SE) knowledge and resources are no longer managed by a single project or organization, but are now distributed across multiple projects, organizations and even in the global software ecosystem (Porru, Pinna, Marchesi, & Tonelli, 2017). One of the challenges arising from this exchange of knowledge is Information Security (IS). This is becoming a major threat to the software development community. In essence, it promotes the notion that IS should take into account different security concepts (safe coding practices, knowledge of software security vulnerabilities in the development process and the importance of IS to the analytical software community are reflected in the fact that it is an integral part of the current SE best practices (Papadakis et al., 2019). Software checking out is a very useful manner to run an application looking for errors. It is identified that 40% to 50% of total growth spending is consumed on software testing. Some of the significant software testing techniques classified by purpose are precision tests, performance tests, safety tests and reliability tests. The software test can be called the software quality measurement process that is being developed and the detection of errors in a program. In addition, it is also a system to determine the consistency of the security characteristics of the software application with the design (Dhir & Kumar, 2019). the security requirements of the blanketed software program are: confidentiality, authentication, availability, authorization, integrity and non-repudiation. other requirements are the protection of private access control, protection management, auditing, and so on. software protection is the protection of software towards attacks. the priority for safety tests increases day by day (Villani, Pontes, Coracini, & Ambrósio, 2019). Software security testing is also categorized as revision techniques, objective identity and evaluation, and goal analysis of vulnerability. security checking out equipment have additionally been evolved for supply code analysis, code evaluate, packet analysis, binary code penetration takes a look at, wireless detector, static analysis tool, check gear, source code protection evaluation, static code evaluation, vulnerability analysis tools and vulnerability assessment. evaluation software program (Villani et al., 2019). The tools are important for collaboration amongst team participants as they facilitate, automate and manage the complete improvement system. Adequate software program assist is especially needed in global software engineering because distance exacerbates coordination and manipulate issues, at once or not directly, because of its poor results on conversation .

The unit test is carried out by the developers and the software is divided into smaller and more convenient units, which has the advantage of detecting functional and software warranty problems at the beginning of the life cycle. The regression test is essential if the code has changed. this could be used to calculate the relative assault surface from one model to any other and use it to see if the security status of the software program is enhancing or deteriorating. The distinction among software program safety and software program security is the existence of intelligent attackers who attempt to damage the system. software program excellent, reliability and safety belong to this family. Intruders can make the most this software to open protection holes. With the development of the internet, software safety issues are getting less applicable. Many critical software applications and offerings require complete security features in opposition to malicious attacks. The desires of protection testing on those systems encompass the identification and removal of software program flaws that could cause security breaches and security protection validation. Vulnerability tools are packages that perform the stages of vulnerability analysis and assessment evaluation. Vulnerability analysis defines, identifies, and categorizes security holes. Weaknesses in computer systems include networks, servers, or communication channels. similarly, vulnerability evaluation can predict the effectiveness of the proposed measures and examine how well they work after the use of them. These tools are based on a database containing system and port service security holes, package compilation anomalies, and all the information needed to validate potential routes to exploitable programs. Security controls used to determine whether these security controls work properly and security assessments that validate the presence of penetration tests are common security testing techniques (Braz & Robert, 2006).

GLOBAL SOFTWARE SECURITY TESTING

Global security software quality checking is the key factor of software engineering. The software is completely secure when it behaves certified in the existence of malicious attacks (Dhir & Kumar, 2019). To ensure the security of the software, the security check manner is implemented. software protection assessments are a chain of procedures designed to ensure that the computer code fulfills its function. The principle of the software check is to confirm the best, estimation the consistency of the software or confirm and validate it (Villani et al., 2019). Security tests are achieved to affirm statistics loss in the strict feel by encrypting the application or by the usage of an extensive variety of software and hardware, firewalls, and so on. After implementation, this will create troubles for quit users. the correct framework for developing protection during the design section is related to the quality and security of the software program (Arkin, Stender, & McGraw, 2005).

SOFTWARE SECURITY RULES

Banerjee and Pandey actually have 21 security rules that guarantee that there is space to create a safe and reliable software development when applied from the beginning of SDLC, that is, from the rules of the requirements analysis phase avoid the introduction of vulnerabilities in the software system (Banerjee & Pandey, 2009). The rules are the following:

1. Knowledge rules: These rules continually learn new information about security aspects and update existing knowledge for software development teams including software developers, software evaluators and software architecture (Sodiya et al., 2006).
2. Rules of prevention: You should avoid all types of threats from within but not from outside and synchronize the security of the software to solve it later.
3. Rules of responsibility: The rules of responsibility monitor all tasks / activities / acts performed during operations / events and achieve the prevention of violations of the security policy and compliance with the specific responsibility for those acts. Suggest that you need to maintain (Porru et al., 2017).
4. Confidentiality rule: This rule implies that confidentiality should be maintained by preventing unauthorized persons from accessing information (Papadakis et al., 2019).
5. Integrity rules: Integrity wishes to be maintained by ensuring that the data is not modified by unauthorized people and no longer detected with the aid of authorized users.
6. Availability rules: These rules define the need to maintain a balanced approach between security and availability. This always provides a highly secure and highly available system (Dhir & Kumar, 2019).
7. Rules of non-repudiation: The cause of non-repudiation is to ensure that the transaction by means of any of the parties that can be used by a relied on third birthday celebration is not desired (Dhir & Kumar, 2019).

8. Access control rules: This rule requires that get entry to to resources and services must be primarily based on permissions, and if allowed, users must be allowed and denied access to the resources and services. indicates get admission to to services accessed by those eligible users (Papadakis et al., 2019).

9. Identification and authentication rules: This rule mean that an identification and authentication process need to be implemented to determine which users can log in to the system and its legal context.

10. Precision rules: these rules propose that software development teams must carry out diverse moves, activities, techniques, approaches and tasks with accuracy and precision every time (Sodiya et al., 2006).

11. Integrity rules: these policies imply that the diverse necessities, protocols, requirements or guidelines designed to certify a software program system should anyhow be consistent.

12. Authorization rules: The guidelines suggest that an approval method wishes to be implemented to decide what an entity can do within the system.

13. Privacy regulations: guarantee that a person has the right to manipulate how, how it's far used, what it's miles used for and what it intends to apply personal data about personal information (Dhir & Kumar, 2019).

14. Evaluation rules: This rule evaluates all processes regardless of size and recommends that software developers be evaluated after they have been created (Sodiya et al., 2006).

15. Better rules: This rule implies that safety is a subset of quality and that control and variability of safety functions depend on quality (Sodiya et al., 2006).

16. Flexibility rules: these rules should not be strict security requirements, but should be viable and flexible (Sodiya et al., 2006).

17. Reinforcement rules (protection): This rule means that the various processes used in the security engineering process must be protected by their individuality and integrity (Sodiya et al., 2006).

18. Ambiguity rules: This rule means that the relevant details should be clear and concise in order to easily implement software security (Sodiya et al., 2006).

19. Error classification rules: These rules require that errors be classified according to a scheme that includes a series of security rules to better understand issues that may affect software security (Arkin et al., 2005; Braz & Robert, 2006).

20. Auditing rules: These rules should be implemented to determine responsibility for software security and to help redesign complete testing security policies and procedures for implementing secure software systems.

21. Interoperability rules: This rule means that if there is extra software program that interacts or communicates with each other, all software program involved in that interaction or communication desires to be protected.

LITERATURE REVIEW

Complete background details of software security appeared. In the black box, test tools were introduced. Information systems have been protected by a modeling language, where security is an essential measure of software engineering (Banerjee & Pandey, 2009). The ease of use and approval of user security systems have developed a main problem in efficiency research (Sodiya et al., 2006). The definition was discussed, as well as the category of software security tests and the methods and tools for software security testing were examined(Braz & Robert, 2006). Safety measures are developed with the arrival of security tools and techniques (Dias Neto, Subramanyan, Vieira, & Travassos, 2007). The main problem was the protection of data against unauthorized access and corruption of data resulting from malicious acts (Mistrík, Grundy, Van der Hoek, & Whitehead, 2010). The different security test methods proposed so far have been discussed here. Safety tests are considered a continuous process throughout the SDLC to involve security tests in the software development life cycle. The secure software development life cycle (SSDL) and SDLC security contact points are proposed for the same purpose. Software security tests can be updated using security attributes, tools, templates and, most importantly, the test cases used in the tests(Kumar, Khan, & Khan, 2014) . The security test consists of identifying the behavior of its attributes in front of an attack that can damage all the software. During each security test, it is verified that all security factors work correctly or not. If the factors work correctly, the software is safe. This is a set of activities that includes the preparation of the test plan and related activities. The safety assessments are part of the evaluation of the safety properties and their factors; the ones are as compared to the useful specification document and the pinnacle design of the development system (M. E. Khan, 2010). Security testing with a dependent technique throughout the lifecycle helps to understand the quality of the software and its protection against known threats and risks. To maintain the quality of the software, it's far needed to test the security of the software in a possible way. The final goals of the safety checks are to validate the robustness and to save you any security breach from stepping into the software (Kumar et al., 2014). Each software program is integrated into many modules, which has several protection attributes. Consequently, to gain the specific ways wherein a system needs to be modified, in which the safety attributes are within the center. From this system, we will decide, before the software program tests, what number of assessments have to be achieved. Safety tests can be supplemented in different ways and safety tests have different meanings or methods (Tian-yang, Yin-Sheng, & You-yuan, 2010). Research on human factors in software security is lacking and that developers are often considered the "weakest link". Developers have more technical experience than typical end-users, but should not be confused as security experts (Bayuk, 2013). Handling security tasks with developer-friendly security tools or programming languages to avoid security errors (Gupta, Verma, & Sangal, 2013) needs help. For this understand security concepts and developer knowledge, explore the utility of available security development tools, and propose tools and methodologies to help developers create secure applications.

RESEARCH BACKGROUND

How security is linked to software tests identify the quality of the software under development and find errors. The determination of the software program check may be shown with the following Figure 1 and Table 1.

Figure 1. Detail of software testing

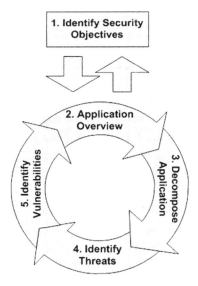

Table 1. Detail of software testing

Software Testing	Detail
Quality assurance	Observe the software engineering methods and techniques used to ensure quality
Verification/validation	Take a look at if the software program meets the specs and fulfills its feature
Correctness	It determines whether the software thus developed meets the requirements of the user or not
Reliability Estimation	This is the estimation of the reliability of our software, that is, it is free of defects

However, the software test refers to a process for looking for errors when running the program. Software tests could be divided into proofs of reliability, security tests and performance tests. The correction test could be divided into white zone, black area and gray zone. The black box is then divided with the participation of the user and without user participation and other methods. Robustness tests are subject to reliability tests. The security tests can be subdivided into techniques of objective analysis, identification, analysis and vulnerability. The following diagram shows some of the most important software testing techniques, classified according to their purpose (Bayuk, 2013). The correction test determines whether the software meets the requirement or not. The tests of white boxes, black boxes or gray boxes are not limited to precision tests. The goal of performance testing is to support low latency, high performance, and low performance on a web site. "Reliability tests" identify all faults in a system and eliminate them before system implementation. "Security tests" guarantee authorized access. The security tests have to do with the identification of the weaknesses and weaknesses of a system(Takanen, Demott, Miller, & Kettunen, 2018).

SECURITY REQUIREMENT ELICITATION

Requirements engineering is a key component of any software. The SDLC requirements collection phase is considered the most important and serious phase. This phase is for managing clients directly. The security requirements depend on the purpose of the construction of the system. Traditionally, security requirements have been viewed as "non-functional" or "quality" needs such as reliability, scalability and robustness. Security requirements are generally created once the product and sales are complete, which causes vulnerabilities in the software. The acquisition of requirements involves interactions with customers to find, verify, detail and analyze the requirements. This level is the key source for the remaining phases of SDLC, and when it becomes the most solid base, other phases can be firmly built to produce high quality products (Gupta et al., 2013). The software security requirements are:

- Verifiable (practical safety requirements are verifiable, however non-practical protection necessities are not verifiable)
- Clear, concise and clear.
- Software engineers can implement them without knowledge of security.
- Proper use for development can prevent recent software vulnerabilities(Bayuk, 2013) .

Categories of Security Requirements

Functional safety requirements are safety precautions that are incorporated into each functional requirement. It is often said that this will never happen again. This requirement artifact can, as an instance, be derived from misuse instances. Non-practical safety necessities list properties which can be architectural requirements associated with security, such as robustness and minimal overall performance and scalability. those forms of requirements are usually derived from architectural concepts and good exercise standards. Derived security requirements are derived from functional and non-functional protection requirements (M. E. Khan, 2010).

- Functional safety requirements
- Non-useful security requirements
- Derived protection requirements
- Software used in software development in case of abuse

Steps for Security Requirement Elicitation

It provides a requirement engineering process that includes the following activities took eight steps to get the following security requirements (Tian-yang et al., 2010).

1. Identify the asset
2. Functional Requirements
3. Security Requirements
4. Threat and Attack Tree
5. Assess Risk
6. In vivo and in vitro determination
7. Nonfunctional Requirements

Iteration: Claims that 1 to 7 may be repeated until it's far identified that each one security requirements have been met.

Kinds of Security Requirements

Security audit requirements, privacy requirements survival requirements, security system maintenance requirements and physical protection requirements (Bayuk, 2013).

Threat Modeling for Security Requirement Elicitation

threat modeling may be used as a basis to identify safety requirements. chance modeling entails knowledge and identifying diverse threats to the system. for the duration of the editing and evaluation of protection necessities, those threats were analyzed and it turned into decided to mitigate or accept the risks related to the threats (Gupta et al., 2013). The modeling of threats and the identity of safety necessities can provide the premise for the final levels of a security system. threat modeling system that begins with the identity of system belongings and capacity threats to those assets. If entry factors result in access to assets, there is a threat attacks to achieve that threat may be described using a variety of diagrams For instance, the system can save passwords which might be an asset to the adversary, and the risk is that the adversary steals those passwords (Takanen et al., 2018).

Modeling Security Requirements With Abuse Cases

In the case of misuse or abuse, it may be used to quickly obtain safety requirements. Business analysts need to research the business, discover important assets and safety services, become aware of vulnerabilities, analyze make the most instances, and endorse mechanisms for protection requirements (Devanbu & Stubblebine, 2000). An example of abuse is a use case in which the result of the interaction is detrimental to the system, one of the actors or one of the interested parties in the system. Interactions can be harmful if the system is compromised (sensitivity, integrity or availability). A method to achieve the objectives of a Distributed Aircraft Maintenance Environment (DAME) system by effectively combining the functional requirements with the safety requirements and the required iterations and interactions between the functional requirements processes and the requirements processes. The requirements process should focus on:

- Considering the system as a "black box"
- Consider the concerns of the assets
- That they are not system functions

Difficulties in Security Requirements Gathering

- Security is constantly changing.
- Software security requirements tone positive.
- Software security requirements should be language and platform independent.
- The security requirements of the software are verifiable and the development process can be verified to work.

- All you need for your project is security software requirements.

SOFTWARE TESTING TOOLS AND TECHNIQUES

in recent times, we will gain many software checking out tools within the market. the choice of equipment is primarily based totally on the requirements of the mission and the economic tools (Proprietary / commercial) or the unfastened gear (Open supply equipment) that interest free trial tools may additionally have some obstacles within the listing of product functions, consequently, it is far based totally entirely on what you are searching out and your necessities are met in the loose version or you pick a fee software with take a look at tools. The tools are divided into unique classes as follows: check control equipment is useful check equipment, load the test tools, Open source equipment and Proprietary / commercial tools (Tian-yang et al., 2010). In this study, many articles on safety testing techniques were reviewed. Software Engineering Basics.

- Code review
- Automatic static analysis
- Binary code analysis
- Fuzz test
- Fault injection risk analysis of source code and binary code
- Vulnerability scan
- Penetration test

1. **Risk Analysis:** Hazard analysis is accomplished in the course of the design segment of the improvement to identify security necessities and identify protection risks. danger modeling is a systematic system used to identify software threats and vulnerabilities. It enables you examine and bear in mind the safety threats that device designers may also face. consequently, risk modeling is executed as a risk evaluation of software improvement. In fact, designers can mitigate ability vulnerabilities and attention on restrained resources to awareness at the maximum vital parts of the gadget. it is advocated to create and file threat models for all programs. risk models must be created in SDLC as quickly as possible. moreover, as programs evolve and evolve, they must be reviewed. To create a threat model, comply with a simple technique according to NIST 800-30 [7] for threat evaluation. This technique means the following:

   a. Decomposition of the application: Over the manual inspection procedure, understand how the function, its assets, features and connectivity.

b. Asset definition and classification: Classify assets into tangible assets and intangible assets and classify them rendering to commercial status.

c. Investigate possible vulnerabilities (technical, operational or management).

d. Investigate possible risks: Use threat scenarios or attack trees to create realistic views of possible attack methods from an attacker's point of view.

e. Create mitigation strategies: develop mitigations for each threat that you consider realistic.

2. **Code Review:** Source code changes are made by fixed study. Procedure of manual verification of source code to detect security vulnerabilities. Many critical security flaws cannot be detected by other test and analysis procedures. according to the safety community, there's no substitute for certainly inspecting the code to hit upon subtle vulnerabilities. not like private third-party software testing, along with running systems, while trying out a software, you need to make the source code available for testing. Source code analysis is the best method for technical testing, as many unintended but important security issues are very difficult to find in other forms of analysis penetration testing. The advantages of code review are integrity, efficiency and accuracy. In large code bases, this shortcoming is not realistic. To detect run-time errors, you need a highly qualified, cumbersome and non-workable reviewer. Using source code, testers can determine exactly what is happening and eliminate black-box testing guessing. Source code reviews include concurrency issues, cryptographic weaknesses and even backdoors, trojans and other malicious code. These problems are often considered as the most damaging vulnerabilities of websites. The analysis of the source code is very effective in finding implementation problems, such as sections of code that have not been validated for entry procedures or open failure control. The source code that is being implemented may not be the same as the one being analyzed, so operational procedures must also be reviewed. Code review is a time-consuming task, but when a reviewer with the right level of experience runs the review, the most complete and accurate results are obtained at the beginning of the analysis procedure, before the reviewer becomes tired. It is common for reviewers to first check each line of code very carefully and then, gradually, skip most of the code. Determine the actual software landscape. It is important to note that it is not possible to perform a complete manual review as the base code size grows. Code revisions can also help detect signs of the presence of malicious code.

3. **Automatic Static Analysis:** Computerized static evaluation is an evaluation that performs inspections without running software program and makes use of static evaluation equipment. In maximum cases this indicates analyzing the supply code of this system, but there are several tools for statically analyzing

binary executables. because static evaluation does not require a fully integrated or installed model of the software program, it can be performed iteratively at some stage in the software implementation. automatic static analysis does not require test instances, and the code does not know what to do(Kumar et al., 2014). The primary purpose of static evaluation is to find security flaws and discover answers. The results of the static analysis tool provide sufficient detail about potential software failure points so that software vulnerabilities can be classified and prioritized according to the level of risk presented to the system by the developer. it's far viable in the existence cycle. The simplest tests are executed in small code devices (individual modules or functional processing units) that can be corrected tremendously without problems and quickly before being introduced to a big code base. by repeating the evaluate and checking out before the complete device code is fixed, you may ensure that the smallest flaws are addressed. Static evaluation tools are effective in detecting violations of language policies, including buffer overflows, library misuse, type checking, and other flaws. Static analysis equipment can scan very big code bases in a quite short time compared to other techniques. The reviewer's work is restrained to the execution of the tool and the interpretation of its results. Static analysis tools aren't efficient sufficient to come across anomalies that human reviewers can judge. This device can provide additional benefits by permitting developers to perform scans as they increase and cope with capacity safety vulnerabilities at the beginning of the method. in addition, the extent of revel in required for automatic critiques is lower than that required for manual evaluations. in many instances, this device gives certain statistics about the observed vulnerabilities, inclusive of recommended mitigations.

4. **Error Injection of Binary Code and Source Code:** Error injection of source code is a testing method designed by the software security community. Binary fault injection is intended to support security penetration testing. The injection of faults in the source code causes stress in the software, causes problems of interoperability between components, simulates a failure in the execution environment and, therefore, a security threat that is not revealed by traditional testing techniques. To reveal. Injection of safety failures extends the injection of standard faults by adding error injection. This allows the evaluator to analyze the security of the movement and the state changes that occur when the software is exposed to any change in the environmental data. The software program interacts with the execution environment through calls to the operating system, calls to remote processes, software application interfaces, man-machine interfaces and the like. Binary fault injection approach monitoring the execution of the fault injection software at runtime. as an instance, while monitoring a device name hint, the tester identifies the machine name call and the decision

code / return value (offers access strive success or failure. In case of binary failure is injected into environment resources) Environmental faults around the program are particularly useful due to the fact they are probably to reflect real assault eventualities. A tester that fully understands the safety of the software system's safe operation, conditions and properties under all possible operating conditions as completely as possible.

5. Fuzz Testing: Fuzzing is a generation that reveals extreme safety flaws in any software at a fraction of the cost and time. Fuzz testing randomly selects invalid information in the software under test, through its surroundings or different software additives. Fuzzing refers to a random character generator to test an software by inserting random data into the interface. In other words, it means injecting noise into the program's interface. Fuzzy assessments are applied via a application or script that sends a combination of inputs to the software to reveal the software program response. The concept is to look for exciting application behavior due to noise injection. this may indicate the presence of vulnerabilities consisting of HTTP entries and different software program failures. Their cost is their specificity because they often display protection vulnerabilities that cannot be recognized via commonplace testing tools such as vulnerability scanners and fault injectors. Fuzzing may be considered as the venture of blind fishing with the intention of discovering completely surprising problems in the software. as an instance, a tester intercepts data examines from a file by a software and replaces that data with random bytes. As a result, if the application fails, the application may not have performed the necessary checks on the data in the file, and the file can be considered to be in the correct format. The missing control can be exploited by an attacker who replaces the read file and replaces the file to exploit the race condition, or an attacker who has already destroyed the application that created the file. the principle purpose of fuzzing is to evaluate the protection of the capabilities. because fuzzing is basically a functional check, it can be accomplished in numerous steps throughout the development and testing manner.

6. **Binary Code Analyses:** Binary code analysis uses reverse engineering techniques and binary analysis. It is implemented as a decompiler, disassembly of binary code, and a scanner. This reflects the degree of reverse engineering that can be done in the binary. The most annoying way is the binary scan. Analyze the machine code to model independent representations of the binary scanner language, program behavior, data flow and control, call trees and external function calls. Such models can be traversed by automatic vulnerability scanners to find common coding errors and vulnerabilities caused by simple backdoors. Source code editors can use this model to generate a readable program behavior for the user. This allows you to manually review security

weaknesses at the design level and subtle backdoors that automatic scanners cannot find. The most annoying reverse engineering method is decompilation. The binary code is designed in reverse of the source code in all modes and they can acquire the equal security code assessment strategies as the original source code and other white box tests. However, be aware that decompilation is technologically problematic. The best of the supply code generated by the decompilation is frequently very poor. This code is not as easy to navigate and understand as the original supply code and might not appropriately reflect the original source code. this is especially true if the binary is obfuscated or if an optimization compiler is used to generate the binary. In fact, it isn't realistic to generate essential supply code in this manner. anyways, analyzing the decompiled source code is a great deal more difficult and slower than reviewing the original source code. due to this, decompilation for protection analysis makes feel only for the most crucial and highly effective components. The second exit is disassembly. In this assembly, binary code is designed for the language of intermediate assemblers (Porru et al., 2017). The disadvantage of disassembling is that the resulting assembler code only makes sense by experts who are familiar with its particular assembler language and are good at detecting safety-related components in the assembler code. It is something that can be analyzed in a certain way.

7. **Vulnerability Scanning:** Application vulnerability scanners are a totally critical software program safety testing technology. those tools scan the software's going for walks software to detect I / O styles related to recognized vulnerabilities. application-level software uses computerized vulnerability scanning. it is also used for web servers, database management systems, and some operating systems. These vulnerability patterns, or "signatures", are essentially an automatic comparison of tool patterns, as they match the signatures required by antivirus and the "dangerous code configuration" required by automatic source code scanners. Automated vulnerability scanners can find simple patterns related to vulnerabilities, but identify the risks associated with aggregating vulnerabilities, or identify vulnerabilities that result from unpredictable combos of enter and output patterns it can't be identified. similarly, to signature-based totally scanning, a few web software vulnerability scanners run "automatically assessing state applications" using vulnerability attack patterns based on simulated attack patterns and fuzz testing techniques and are based on vulnerability signatures Similar to analysis, full-state assessment analysis can only detect known types of attacks and vulnerabilities (Mistrík et al., 2010). Most vulnerability scanners attempt to offer a mechanism to feature vulnerability styles. The current technology of scanners can carry out unsophisticated evaluation of the risks related to vulnerability aggregation. in

many cases, particularly for industrial vulnerability scanners (COTS), this tool additionally affords information and steering on the way to mitigate detected vulnerabilities. common application vulnerability scanners can most effective recognize a number of the kinds of vulnerabilities found in large applications. In fact, it solves what patches can alleviate. recognition on the vulnerabilities that need to be done. As with different signature-based scanning tools, application vulnerability scanners can report fake positives except the tester recalibrates them. The evaluator interprets the scanner's results significantly to avoid identifying what is really a benign problem as a vulnerability and not to ignore the real vulnerability in question Detect detection It was ignored by the tool. For this reason, it is important to combine different test methods to verify the vulnerabilities of the software in different ways. While none of these methods alone is appropriate, they can be combined to greatly increase the likelihood of finding a vulnerability (Braz & Robert, 2006). Because automatic vulnerability scanners are based on signatures, such as antivirus, they must be updated frequently with new vendor signatures.

8. **Penetration Testing:** An alternative name for penetration testing is ethical piracy. Testing network security is a very common practice. even as penetration testing has established to be effective for network protection, this approach does no longer certainly translate into applications. Penetration analysis is the "art" of testing applications that work with your "live" execution environment to find security vulnerabilities for the purpose of this guide. Penetration testing examines whether the system resists an attack well, and what to do if it cannot withstand it. Penetration evaluators also try to exploit the vulnerabilities they have detected and those found in previous reviews (Sodiya et al., 2006). Penetration test types include black box, white box and gray box. The penetration tests of the black box do not give knowledge to the application of the testers (Dias Neto et al., 2007). The intrusion of the white box is the opposite of the black box, since it provides the tester with complete information about the application. The most commonly used gray box penetration test is a test that gives the examiner the same authority as a regular user to simulate a malicious prisoner. It became found via other tests achieved out of doors of the actual manufacturing environment. Intrusion assessors need to expose the device to sophisticated multi-pattern attacks designed to trigger a complex series of actions on all components of the machine, along with nonadjacent components. Those are kinds of conduct that cannot be imposed or discovered by another check technique. Because penetration tests are this type of vulnerability that is often overlooked in other test methods, it is used to find security issues that can be attributed to software architecture and design.

SECURITY TESTING

Software security might be expressed in capacity. The software security tests have been configured as a compliance verification process. The security tests are divided into functional tests and vulnerability tests. The security test software validates the functional safety requirements. To preserve the property of that software, it is vital to check the safety of the software in manageable manner. The viable objectives of the safety tests are to authorize the robustness and avoid the penetration of security flaws inside the software program. A tribulation procedure is vital to ensure that the entire system can be included against diverse malicious assaults and vulnerabilities due to the situation. To reap it, here is a projected in Figure 2 framework that complements in that of the security assessments. here are the steps on this existence cycle of safety assessments (Gupta et al., 2013).

Finalize the Security Test Plan

An adequate test strategy ought to be ready for a higher implementation of the protection tests that encompass those phases.

Finalize Security Test Types

The security tests embody one or more tests primarily based mostly on the preliminary targets of the security software program, defined at a few degrees in the interview with the mission. The reason for this project is to pick the safety assessments of the software program to be performed and no longer to put affect them. Ultimately, software program safety tests that may be automatic with security trying out tools ought to be completed (Mead & Stehney, 2005).

Finalize Security Test Schedule

The software protection test application ought cloud be finalized. It includes the test phases, the beginning of the intention, the cease dates of the aim and many obligations. It also describes how it is going to be studied, followed and tested.

Organize Security Test Team

With all kinds of safety tests, the software check has to be prepared. The software program finding out the crew is chargeable for the design and execution of the assessments and the assessment of the results. While the improvement corrects the

Figure 2. Security testing finalized life cycle
source: Gupta et al., 2013

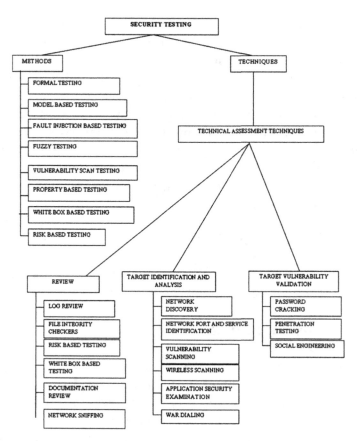

defects, the software program finding out institution retests the defects to affirm the correction.

Establish Software Security Test Environment

On this requirement, software protection test environments are finalized. The goal of the security check environment is to offer a physical framework for protection test actions. Key additives of security environments consist of the capability to carry out physical assessments, gear, and technology. software technology has to be configured. This consists of putting in test software and dealing with carriers.

Install Security Test Tool

Security techniques and tools should guide users through the test task. The fact that security tests are used to prevent smart opponents from reaching their goal is probably a useful tool to help human evaluators instead of trying to replace them. The test tools should be tested to see if they are ready for the test.

Software Security Design Test Case

The security strategy for designing software program security take a look at scenarios is to focus on the subsequent four protection additives: control, illegal activities are immaterial and material resources of an entity. The evaluation method to enumerate what needs to be included, which include the amount of software, is the fee, use and traits. Threats are the occasion which could cause damage to software loss or feasible damage to software program safety. security controls are measures of protection against loss or damage. it is crucial to evaluate the performance of the software's protection mechanisms, in addition to the capabilities themselves. beneath you may find a few questions and issues related to the security performance of the software program.

Availability

How long is the software program or manage available to perform vital safety responsibilities. Software security assessments generally require greater availability than different parts of the software program software.

Survival

How could be the software recognize the failures principle and assaults or normal failures? This consists of guide for emergency operations within the occasion of a failure, backup operations and then returning to the regular function.

Accuracy

How correct is the safety check of the software program? The accuracy of the measurement covers the quantity, regularity and implication of errors.

Response Time

Desirable reaction time or not? A sluggish response time can cause customers to pass software program protection controls. The reaction time can also be critical for manipulate management.

Through-Put

The safety verification of the software is like minded with the required usability. The potential consists of the average package and the user load of software program security and service requests.

Review \ Approve Software Security Tests

On this phase of the cycle, the test instances and gear are prepared and the security situations are authorized for execution inside the subsequent section. Includes the following steps.

Schedule \ Conduct Security Review

The software protection check plan have to be planned and reviewed in advance. The evaluators have to attain the ultimate copy of the examination. The proper motive of this project is for the improvement and development organization or the sponsor to accept and be given the revised plan. as with any revision or revision, the insured objects must be present. the primary is the definition of what is going to be mentioned approximately protection trying out (Gupta et al., 2013). the second one deals with important info related to this. The third is the synthesis of assessments and protection equipment. The last detail is precision.

Obtain Validation

Validation is essential in a test attempt as it improves test and development resource. The excellent technique is to set up a proper approval procedure for a software program application safety check plan. In this situation, use the control approval paperwork. in the connected record, the today's software protection check plan and suggests that everyone feedback to your remarks were blanketed. The software program protection check plan will evolve with each new release, but it will be protected within the change.

Execute Software Security Tests

This section executes all organized and accepted check instances the use of the tools and strategies defined within the ultimate section. This section consists of the following steps.

Regression Test the Software Security Fixes

The cause of this project is to retry protection checks that have detected screw ups throughout the preceding protection test cycle for that segment. The regression takes a look at method is used for this mission. The regression check is a software protection approach that detects errors that others purpose. specific check situations are prepared for this challenge in comparison to a checklist organized to hit upon mistakes. A reassessment matrix hyperlinks the test instances to the functions.

Execute New Software Security Test

The purpose of this mission is to carry out the brand-new software program application protection tests organized sooner or later of the preceding existence cycle of the safety exams. Inside the previous section, the check team had up to date the features, the software fragment and the popularity tests for the current phase.

Document Software Security Defects of Overall Result

At the same time as acting the software program safety take a look at, the outcomes ought to be recorded and recorded within the malicious program monitoring database. These software program protection flaws are classically associated with individual tests. A file is ready for this mistake record. The motive of this venture is to file the ones security flaws correctly with their lifestyles and the practice of a whole report of failures (Păsăreanu & Visser, 2009)

DESIGN LEVEL SECURITY

Here, designers, developers and designers conduct in-depth research on the specification of requirements and model the elements of secure design, software architecture, safe design revisions and threats according to specific requirements. The design phase is generally for functionality and is performed in accordance with the specifications provided by the client. Designers create very technical design specifications that focus on the way to implement the machine. purposeful and non-functional necessities are required to describe the security capabilities of the system.

Security Design Principles

There are numerous protection design principles that provide recommendations on the way to design a secure machine. safety layout suggestions want to be acknowledged earlier and may be integrated into SDLC in advance. Principles of security layout(Agrawal, Khan, & Chandra, 2008).

1. The principle of minimum privilege: the subject must have the necessary privileges to complete his task, and his rights must be destroyed after use.
2. Fail-safe default value principle: This principle way that the default value is the lack of access permission. A safety scheme identifies the conditions below which access can be granted. If a movement fails, the device is as secure as when the action became initiated.
3. The economic principles of the mechanism: keep the design mechanism called the KISS principle as simple as possible.
4. Complete Intermediary Principle: If access to privileges is authorized, all access must be verified and protected.
5. Principles of open design: Design must not be a secret, safety mechanisms should be unrelated to the lack of knowledge of capacity attackers, but should be unrelated to the presence of specific attackers which are more easily protected using passwords and other protection implementations.
6. Principle of privilege separation: It requires multiple conditions and presents privileges that do not depend on single situations.
7. Principle of the less common multiple mechanism: insist that the mechanisms should not be shared. When sharing, all exchange mechanisms represent the possibility of information routes between users, so they must be designed with great care so that security is not involuntarily compromised.
8. The principle of psychological acceptability: The addition of security mechanisms, especially in human interfaces, should not introduce further complexity to the system, and the proper protection mechanisms should be carried out automatically (Agrawal et al., 2008) .

Threat Modeling for Design Level Security

threat modeling is an iterative technique for modeling security threats, identifies design flaws that may be exploited by these threats, designs systems safely, and mitigates them You can take measures for add threat modeling at all stages of SDLC, but is basically considered at the design stage. At the time of design, the system allows the designer to verify and discover if the design meets the acceptable level of risk. Design flaws can be exposed, and information collected in this approach is used to enhance the satisfactory of design protection before imposing the system. Designers, software managers and designers can participate in threat modeling. The main benefits of risk modeling at design level security include identification of security issues, investigation of threats and potential vulnerabilities, planning of security tests in response to identified threats, and vulnerability in design and development. There is a design, identify and reduce software support costs. As when the product goes into production, protection flaws can be reduced extensively (M. E. Khan, 2010).

Systematic Approach to Create a Threat Model

The five main steps to modeling a threat are: It is an iterative approach that can be used to discover more about design throughout the development life cycle. Figure 3 Figure 3 illustrates the iterative threat modeling process.

The five steps in threat modeling are:

Figure 3. The iterative threat modeling process
source: S. A. Khan & Khan, 2013

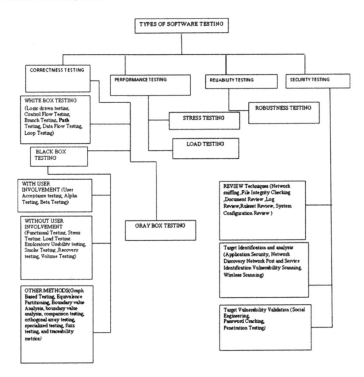

Step 1: Clarification of security objectives by clearly identifying security objectives and focusing on threat modeling activities, you can analyze the amount of work required in the next step.

Step 2: Create a general description of the application. This step helps to list the key features of the application that help identify the relevant threat used in step 4.

Step 3: Disassembly of applications A detailed investigation of the application and an understanding of the mechanism of the application facilitate the search of detailed threats.

Step 4: Threat Identification Use the details in steps 2 and 3 to identify the application context and the threats associated with that context.

Step 5: Identify vulnerabilities and identify application layers that identify vulnerabilities associated with threats. Use the vulnerability categories to focus on areas where errors occur most frequently.

Security Patterns for Design Phase

The first to adapt design patterns to information security. It is easy to document what the system should do, and difficult to identify to list what the system should not do. They proposed a safety design pattern for information security (M. E. Khan, 2010). The security pattern is as follows:

1. Single access point: provides a security module and a way to log in to the system. This pattern suggests that there is only one way to enter the system.
2. Management point: Security management organizations and their certification and impact approval are two basic elements of this pattern.
3. Role: Organize users with similar security privileges.
4. Session: The location of global information in a multi-user environment.
5. Full view with errors: Shows exceptions as necessary, show full view to the user
6. Restricted view: Users can only see what they have access to.
7. Secure access layer: application security integration and low-level security
8. Privilege Summary: Added support by other privileged users.
9. Journaling: keep a complete record of the use of resources.
10. Get out with grace: Design systems to fail safely.

at the end of the design, the attack surface is analyzed. If the place of the attack surface is large, the above method is repeated until the attack surface reaches the minimum degree. At each stage of software development, we proposed safety patterns from the point of view of the concept of security. In addition, the results of the research on the use of the proposed security standards are presented, such as the requirements phase, the design phase and the pattern of the implementation phase and the methodology to develop the software system (Vemulapati, Mehrotra, & Dangwal, 2011).

Design Review

The project manager oversees regular revisions of system features system performance, performance requirements, security requirements, and platform characteristics. At the end of the design phase, a system / subsystem design review is conducted to resolve any open issues related to one or more architectural designs and design decisions for the entire system or subsystem.

CATEGORY OF SECURITY TESTING

Protection exams may be classified as safety test techniques and protection test techniques Figure 4 indicates its classification.

Methods Security Testing

Formal Security Tests

The formal approach of safety testing is to build a mathematical model of the software program. It additionally presents a form specification that is compatible with some formal specification languages. The formal security test methods are essentially methods of model verification and verification of theorems. There are

Figure 4. Classification of Security Testing

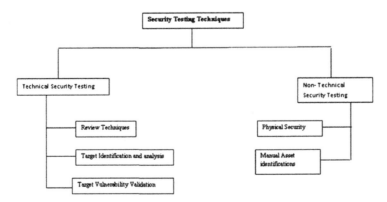

some limitations of the formal security test method. With regard to the proof of theorems, it is difficult to realize automatically, it is necessary that the members of good quality analyze it. Therefore, check the design instead of the current code. When, as in the verification method of the model, states of practical implementation are needed, they are less useful (Kumar et al., 2014).

Model Based Security Testing

This type of test creates a software behavior version and a structure model that analyzes its behavior and dimensions by using exploring situations from some UML models, which includes activity diagrams, software program structures (Kumar et al., 2014).

Safety Tests Based on Fault Injection

This method makes a specialty of the interaction points of the software and the surroundings, consisting of the user enter, the record system, the environment variable, and the network interface. This technique facilitates the software to reach this state, which is not possible with other strategies(Kumar et al., 2014).

Fuzzy Testing

Diffuse tests focus on detecting vulnerabilities related to security objectives. The purpose of the blur test is to test the program by injecting it with random data to see if it can function normally with unclear inputs. Fuzzy tests simply create coded data and detect flaws in the tested software that are very difficult to implement with other logical test techniques (Kumar et al., 2014).

Vulnerability Scanning Testing

The susceptibility analysis recognizes the risks and security vulnerabilities of the software during the analysis (Kumar et al., 2014).

Property Based Testing

Transfer the security property of the software to the specification. It is focus on specific safety properties that can meet the classification and priority requirements(Kumar et al., 2014).

White Box Based Security Testing

It is a static test technique that aims to directly view the information directly from the source code. You may encounter security errors, such as a buffer overflow. Advanced technologies for the integrated investigation of data flow analysis, limit analysis and assumption (Kumar et al., 2014).

Risk Based Security Testing

Gary McGraw investigated on safety tests and risk analysis of risks. Security tests combined with the life cycle of software development are combined, before, with risky security vulnerabilities (Kumar et al., 2014).

Classification of Security Testing Techniques

protection checking out strategies may be classified into technical protection assessments and non-technical protection exams. Technical security tests are divided into strategies to review, identify and analyze goals and validate vulnerabilities. Non-technical safety checking out may be divided into bodily safety and guide asset identification. there are numerous securities trying out strategies to assess the level of security of systems and software, grouped together in the review techniques, identification techniques and objective analysis and validation of vulnerabilities.

Review Techniques

those strategies are used to evaluate systems and software to locate vulnerabilities. these strategies are generally executed manually. View documentation, records, rule sets, system configuration, network and files.

Analysis Techniques and Target Identification

The technical procedures to find and analyze the objectives are to find active devices and their ports and associated facilities, and analyze them to detect possible vulnerabilities. These techniques are: network detection, vulnerability scan, wireless scan, passive wireless scan, active wireless scan, wireless device detection and Bluetooth scanning.

Validation Techniques and Target Vulnerability

The test techniques identify the presence of vulnerabilities according to the specific technique used. These techniques are: decryption of passwords, intrusion tests and social engineering.

ANALYSIS OF CURRENT TRENDS

RQ.1: What is the link between security testing and software testing? but, software program checking out is a technique of identifying capacity errors within the device so that it can be debugged quickly. Software tests are separated into several subcategories, such as test tests, performance tests, reliability tests and safety tests. The corrective evidence is divided into a black area, a white area and a gray area, while the black zone is divided with the user's participation and without user participation or other methods. Performance tests could be separated into stress tests and load tests. Robustness tests are subject to reliability tests. Security tests can be subdivided into techniques to review, identify and analyze objectives and validate the vulnerability of the destination. Figure 5 illustrates the software testing techniques.

RQ.2 How security tests can be labeled in distinct strategies. safety trying out strategies may be labeled as technical safety exams and non-technical protection assessments. The technical protection takes a look at is divided into strategies to study, discover and analyze goals and validate their vulnerabilities. Non-technical protection checks may be divided into physical security and manual identification of assets. This can be seen in Figure 6.

There are many protection testing techniques (shown in Figure 6) for evaluating the security measures of any system or community. The different software security testing techniques are as follows:

RQ.3: How to classify protection checks in exclusive methods? security trying out methods can be categorized into: property checks, vulnerability tests, blur exams, version-based totally safety tests, security checks, formal protection assessments, security testing based on test failures (monolithic functional) with white box test (based on functional synthesis).

RQ.4: How to classify the different security requirements? The requirements for protection checking out may be labeled into three classes: safety and safety characteristic. The useful protection necessities can be labeled in Figure 8 .

Figure 5. Types of Software Testing

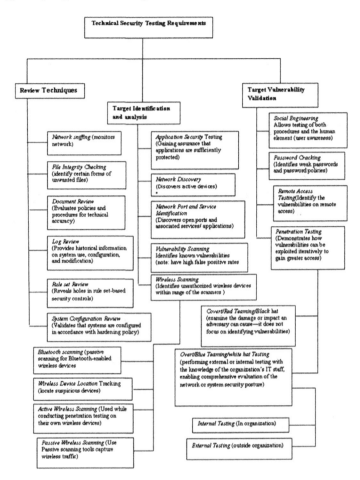

CONCLUSION AND FUTURE WORK

It analyzes the definition, type, principal methods, tools and techniques of software security and also introduces a software program protection life cycle. the principle strategies used in the protection checks are in brief defined. This record will help evaluators and beginners plan a security development lifecycle. This work is done to enhance the reliability and safety of the software. in-depth research into safety checking out strategies and techniques. Conclude that an objective vulnerability evaluation can assist the developer to find out vulnerabilities and solve them greater efficaciously. techniques and strategies of security tests. further, these strategies can be carried out in internet vulnerability detection tools to affirm the respective

Figure 6. Represents specific software testing techniques

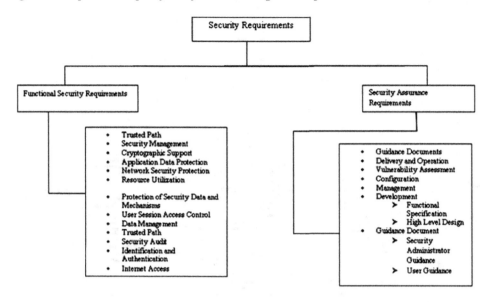

Figure 7. Represent different technical security testing techniques

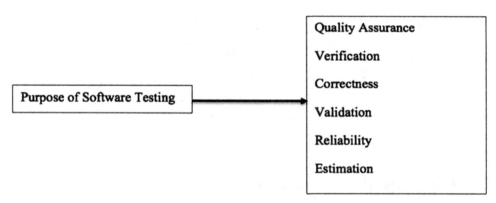

vulnerability so one can produce a better scanner in the destiny. We have completed our pleasant to symbolize the challenge very well and successfully. The future goal of this work will be to identify the factors and develop a security framework using security features to improve security and make the software more reliable.

Figure 8. Different security requirements

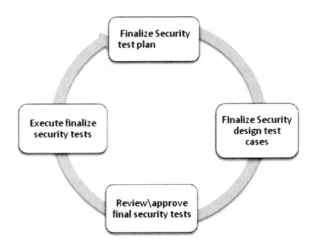

REFERENCES

Agrawal, A., Khan, R., & Chandra, S. (2008). Software Security Process–Development Life Cycle Perspective. *CSI Communications*, *32*(5), 39–42.

Arkin, B., Stender, S., & McGraw, G. (2005). Software penetration testing. *IEEE Security and Privacy*, *3*(1), 84–87. doi:10.1109/MSP.2005.23

Banerjee, C., & Pandey, S. (2009). *Software security rules, SDLC perspective.* arXiv preprint arXiv:0911.0494

Bayuk, J. L. (2013). Security as a theoretical attribute construct. *Computers & Security*, *37*, 155–175. doi:10.1016/j.cose.2013.03.006

Braz, C., & Robert, J.-M. (2006). *Security and usability: the case of the user authentication methods.* Paper presented at the IHM. 10.1145/1132736.1132768

Devanbu, P. T., & Stubblebine, S. (2000). Software engineering for security: a roadmap. *Proceedings of the Conference on the Future of Software Engineering.*

Dhir, S., & Kumar, D. (2019). Automation Software Testing on Web-Based Application. In Software Engineering (pp. 691–698). Singapore: Springer. doi:10.1007/978-981-10-8848-3_67

Dias Neto, A. C., Subramanyan, R., Vieira, M., & Travassos, G. H. (2007). A survey on model-based testing approaches: a systematic review. *Proceedings of the 1st ACM international workshop on Empirical assessment of software engineering languages and technologies: held in conjunction with the 22nd IEEE/ACM International Conference on Automated Software Engineering (ASE) 2007.* 10.1145/1353673.1353681

Gupta, S., Verma, H. K., & Sangal, A. L. (2013). Security attacks & prerequisite for wireless sensor networks. *Intl Journal of Engineering and Advanced Technology, 2*(5), 558-566.

Khan, M. E. (2010). Different forms of software testing techniques for finding errors. *International Journal of Computer Science Issues, 7*(3), 24.

Khan, S. A., & Khan, R. A. (2013). *Software security testing process: phased approach.* Paper presented at the International Conference on Intelligent Interactive Technologies and Multimedia. 10.1007/978-3-642-37463-0_19

Kumar, R., Khan, S. A., & Khan, R. A. (2014). Software Security Testing A Pertinent Framework. *Journal of Global Research in Computer Science, 4*(3).

Mead, N. R., & Stehney, T. (2005). Security quality requirements engineering (SQUARE) methodology (Vol. 30). New York, NY: ACM. doi:10.21236/ADA443493

Mistrík, I., Grundy, J., Van der Hoek, A., & Whitehead, J. (2010). Collaborative software engineering: challenges and prospects. In Collaborative Software Engineering (pp. 389–403). Berlin, Germany: Springer. doi:10.1007/978-3-642-10294-3_19

Papadakis, M., Kintis, M., Zhang, J., & et al, . (2019). Mutation testing advances: An analysis and survey. *Advances in Computers, 112*, 275–378. doi:10.1016/bs.adcom.2018.03.015

Păsăreanu, C. S., & Visser, W. (2009). A survey of new trends in symbolic execution for software testing and analysis. *International Journal of Software Tools for Technology Transfer, 11*(4), 339–353. doi:10.100710009-009-0118-1

Porru, S., Pinna, A., Marchesi, M., & Tonelli, R. (2017). *Blockchain-oriented software engineering: challenges and new directions.* Paper presented at the 2017 IEEE/ACM 39th International Conference on Software Engineering Companion (ICSE-C). 10.1109/ICSE-C.2017.142

Sodiya, A. S., Onashoga, S. A., & Ajayī, O. (2006). Towards Building Secure Software Systems. *Issues in Informing Science & Information Technology, 3.*

Takanen, A., Demott, J. D., Miller, C., & Kettunen, A. (2018). *Fuzzing for software security testing and quality assurance*. Artech House.

Tian-yang, G., Yin-Sheng, S., & You-yuan, F. (2010). Research on software security testing. *World Academy of Science, Engineering and Technology*, *69*, 647–651.

Vemulapati, J., Mehrotra, N., & Dangwal, N. (2011). *SaaS security testing: Guidelines and evaluation framework*. Paper presented at the 11th Annual International Software Testing Conference.

Villani, E., Pontes, R. P., Coracini, G. K., & Ambrósio, A. M. (2019). Integrating model checking and model-based testing for industrial software development. *Computers in Industry*, *104*, 88–102. doi:10.1016/j.compind.2018.08.003

Chapter 10
Dimensions of Robust Security Testing in Global Software Engineering:
A Systematic Review

Ali Akber
*Institute of Business Management,
Pakistan*

Syed Sajjad Hussain Rizvi
Hamdard University, Pakistan

Muhammad Waqar Khan
*Institute of Business Management,
Pakistan*

Vali Uddin
Hamdard University, Pakistan

Manzoor Ahmed Hashmani
*University Technology PETRONAS,
Malaysia*

Jawwad Ahmad
*Usman Institute of Technology,
Pakistan*

ABSTRACT

Over the last few decades, software security has become significant in parallel to general software testing. Previously, the scope of software security was relatively limited as compared to the software functionality. But now, in global software engineering, the scope and budget of software security are far more than its basic functionality. This has created a pressing need to devise the separate set of working boundaries between software quality testing, and software security testing in global software engineering. In the past literature, a massive number of software security testing methods has been devised. In this paper, a comprehensive literature review is presented on the recent global software security testing methods. In addition, the strength and limitation of each framework are discussed and analyzed. Finally, this work submits the open areas in the domain of global software security testing methods as one of the deliverables of this research work.

DOI: 10.4018/978-1-5225-9448-2.ch010

INTRODUCTION

It is an open evident that the world of Information and Communication Technology (ICT) is improving more broadly, deeply and rapidly than ever before. Specifically, in global software engineering industry is becoming agiler and market dynamics are getting changed. Systems on modern concepts like networking, IoT, cloud computing, e-commerce etc. are integrating to compete in industry & achieve innovation (Vu et. al. 2011). Apparently, the scenario looks benefiting; however, due to the massive usage in all financial and economic sectors, it is now more prone to the security attacks. In addition, the massive number of data and system security incidents have been reported in the archives. These attacks not only results in the financial loss of an organization but also damages the credibility of their system. Moreover, these security attacks can lead to severe damage to systems, information or its environment (Petrenko et. al. 2012). This has created a pressing need to devise the security methods to make the systems more secure, robust and intrusion free. Although the security framework has already revised for the classical system, the exercise for integrating the security measures into the global software engineering is still not very explored into the recent literature. In order to prevent the attacks in the software of global scope, security testing is indeed very essential to identify vulnerabilities and secure software functionality.

During the past decades due to the intensive development of information and communication engineering has evolved the concept of global software engineering. The framework of global software engineering is far distinguished from classical software engineering in terms of its scope, practices, and model. Classical software testing is mainly related to the functionality of the software, its scope and the requirements whereas, global security testing, on the other hand, ensures the secure software functionality, identification of weakness or loopholes to the system and maintains information confidentiality, integrity, and availability. The software quality standard ISO/IEC 9126 ensures the quality of the software (Coallier et. al. 2001).

Common security issues like SQL injection and cross-site scripting can easily handle through security testing techniques. (Bau et. al. 2010). Various models and application level tools have been devised to handle these basic security issues in classical software engineering. However, the basic security methods are found to be deficient to handle the security attacks at the global level. Given that the scope of global software engineering is far wider than classical software engineering. According to the National Institute of Standards and Technology (NIST), inadequate security testing of software results in a high cost of exposure (Planning, S et. al. 2002). Moreover, it eventually results in a massive catastrophic or non-catastrophic loss for the organization. Especially, the designing and development of e-commerce and mobile commerce based application in global software engineering may have massive vulnerability into the system and the information. Therefore, there is an increasing need to devise a more robust software security testing methods in global software engineering. In recent literature, the exhaustive study on the modern dimensions of software security testing mainly in the direction of global software engineering is not fully discussed. In this paper, a comprehensive review of the global testing method is discussed. Moreover, the performance and efficiency of each method are compared to the common benchmarks parameters. In the recent literature, the researchers have proposed to classify the global software security testing methods into four distinct classes namely, (1) model-based security testing, (2) code based testing and static analysis, (3) penetration testing and dynamic analysis, and (4) security regression testing. This employment of these security testing methods is not on their maturity stage. Rather, they are still open for further investigation by the research community.

In software testing, the programs that provide expected behavior on the finite set of cases called Test-Suite (TS), selected from the infinite execution domain (Bourque et. al. 1999). In addition, the system on which test is performed is termed as System-Under-Test (SUT). The software testing approach can be of either type static, and dynamic. Unlike dynamic testing, the static approach uses definite test cases, the most common type of static testing are manual reviews and automated static analysis (Bourque et. al. 1999). Generally, the security testing life-cycle consists of both static and dynamic approach. After running test cases on a system-under-test, multiple results are observed, which are compared with each other and provides a verdict as a result. The verdicts can be a pass, fail or inconclusive (ISO, G. (1991).

Primarily, the software security methods are designed to validate the system requirements related to security assets which include, but not limited to, confidentiality, integrity, availability, authentication, and non-repudiation. The software security requirements are generally classified into two classes (1) positive security requirement and (2) negative security requirement. Positive security requirement specifies the expected functionality of the system whereas negative security requirement specifies what the application should be limit at (Wichers, et. al. 2013). These requirements must be aligned with software quality standard International Standard Organization (ISO)/IEC 9216 (Coallier, et. al. (2001) .

The evolution of classical software engineering was established from the inception of the Software Development Life Cycle. The Software development life-cycle is a logical series of steps for development and managing life-cycle of software, generally, it comprises of different phases namely, (1) analysis (2) development (3) deployment, and (4) maintenance (Kurniawan et. al. 2017). However, these blocks are further extended to the various set of process and step inside each phase. Each of these phases has different artifacts like analysis phase specifies requirements of the system, development phase provides the code-level presentation of the system, deployment phase provides the running application to the real environment and in the end, all artifacts are maintained. The later models of software system development are actually the extended version of the basic software development life cycle. In classical SDLC, security testing starts shortly after the software is deployed. This practice is very ineffective and inefficient, so in order to make software development more efficient, effective, and secure the security must testing is applied to each phase of SDLC which makes its SDLC (Security SDLC) (Kurniawan et. al. 2017). The rationale of Security SDLC is very logical that the scope of data, system, and environmental security is indeed essential at each level of software engineering.

A global secure development life-cycle includes the security aspect in each phase of SDLC. The pictorial view of Security SDLC is shown in Figure 1. This figure illustrates like SDLC Security SDLC too have basic four phases, namely Design, Construction, Test, and Vulnerability response. In addition, the scope of each phase is also each phase cover various sub-activities. These sub-activities are depicted in Figure 1. In addition, it is to be explicitly noticed that another crucial factor in secure SDLC is the risk. By literature, the risk is any unwanted event that could occur and extend impact on the information asset or the system (Lund, et. al. 2010). Considering the obstructive nature of the security requirement, the concept of risk can be applied in selecting security countermeasures(Den et. al. 2007) (Potter et. al. 2004). In each phase of the development lifecycle, but specifically in the design phase, security testing and thus fault detection and vulnerabilities are identified and prevented more effectively and efficiently (Verdon et. al. 2004). Taking in an

Figure 1. Global secure software development lifecycle

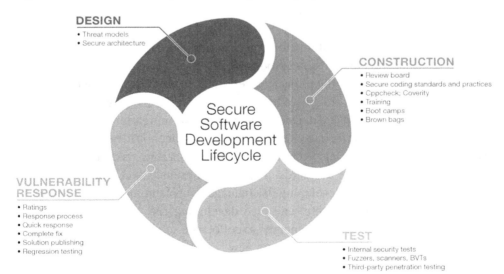

account in global SDLC security testing is applied in all phases, but keeping in view the research and experience the major focus of security testing should be on starting phases which includes analysis, designing, and development (Holik et. al. 2014).

Interest in Global Software Engineering is briskly growing in the software industry. The associate project members from different national, organizational cultures and time zones are involved in developing software and implemented at different locations with the help of information and communication technologies.

Recently, Software developing organizations transform global software Engineering with distributed development sites. GSE or also known as Global Software Development (GSD) or Distributed Software Development (DSD) It can be described as developing software with different development teams distributed in different geographical places1. (Vu et. al. 2011) . The distributed teams can be within the same organization or different organizations.

Aside from being geographically dispersed, globally dispersed teams face the probability of experiencing different time zones and having social, cultural and regularizing differences(Bau et. al. 2010) . These differences in time zones and cultural background may add challenges to GSE, particularly with respect to communication, coordination, and control. These problem gets a failure as result to complete the project on routine and went over the budget.

Different research studies have reported and suggested different mitigation approaches to some of the risks and challenges that may delay the success of a GSD project (Petrenko et. al. 2012). Given six centripetal forces are the solutions that can associate with global software teams together which make them more efficient. Those forces consist of telecommunication infrastructure, project architecture, team building, development technique, managerial approach collaborative technique. They can be used as bases determine strategies that can diminished issues come across in distributed projects.

Risk Management is a systematic approach to reduce impairment due to risks, making the project less sensitive and product heftier. Risk management is essential in every business and to make the project successful. The target of risk management is to identify uncertainties in order to reduce loss and decrease objective achievements. The implication of each risk determines by convenient mitigation actions.

The importance of risk management has made its application to be more structured over time. There are various approaches to implementing risk management as addressed in literature and standards. There is a consensus that risk management mainly entails processes in developing risk management planning, risk identification, risk evaluation, risk monitoring, and also developing risk mitigation strategies. GSD has additional challenges compared to collocated software development. GSD exacerbates existing risks and introduces new risks that are unique to this setting.

In the subsequent part of this paper, a comprehensive review of the modern software security testing methods is discussed. Afterward, the strength and limitation of each method are compared over the benchmark test parameters. Finally, the open area in the software security methods is highlighted as one of the deliverables of this research work. This research could facilitate the new domain researchers to devise a new method of security testing in global software engineering. Moreover, this comprehensive study also benefited to understand the direction of growth for the development of a new model, framework, or tools for security testing in global software engineering.

GLOBAL SECURITY TESTING TECHNIQUES

In the recent literature, the researchers have proposed to classify the global software security testing methods into four distinct classes namely, (1) model-based security testing, (2) code based testing and static analysis, (3) penetration testing and dynamic analysis, and (4) security regression testing. Moreover, the further extensions and variants of these approached is also reported in the literature. In the subsequent part of this manuscript, a comprehensive review of the framework, strengths, applications, and limitations of each approach is discussed.

Model-Based Global Security Testing

In Model-Based Global Security (MB) testing algorithms are selected manually, and then these selected algorithms generate test cases automatically that are applied to the system (Zander et. al. 2011). Model-Based provides an opportunity to make the test process efficient (Utting et. al. 2010) (Grieskamp et. al. 2011). A major benefit of Model-Based includes lower cost, better documentation of test case, and generality of the test process (Utting et. al. 2010). The fundamental principle of model-based testing is the instead creates the test cases in a customized fashion, rather selects algorithms in generating them automatically from a (set of) model(s) of the system under consideration or of its environment of the software system. Moreover, the test automation reinstates the manual test execution by automated test scripts, model-based testing replaces manual test designs by automated test generation. This approach is further consisting of three intermediate steps process:

- **Designing:** In designing phase model of SUT is created through informal requirements, existing specifications or a SUT, this results in a system that is used for test generation which is often called as the test model.

- **Execution:** If test cases are executable, then it runs through SUT, this single complete execution on a model is called test case, expected output through SUT. Since there can be a large set of test cases, therefore, selection criteria are defined for the test case.
- **Evaluation:** Once a criterion is defined for the test model and test selection, test generation is performed automatically. Test cases are further refined to support and adapted to the SUT.

A Model-Based Global Security Testing Approach for Web Applications

This creates a semi-automated model for testing and maintains a secure web application. Let's assume there is a secure model' that does not violate any security measure like confidentiality, availability etc. Thus, the model checker will report all the security property defining the security measure of the model. Modeler defines all the abstract messages that are being used by the end user to tell the system what to do. Modeler does not know the what to do on receiving these abstract message, the purpose of these messages is to tell the system what to do, like view profiles, delete or update profile etc.

In order to use such secure model, a semantic mutation is defined that represents some common vulnerability at the code level. This semantics is in abstract form so that they injected into the system. After applying semantic mutation operators to the model trace is detected if it leads to violating any security measure of the model. A trace attack is a series of steps consisting of abstract messages that lead to the condition where the system security is compromised; this is done through the model checker. After detecting any violation, the first step is to translate the actions performed on the browser; next step is linking of these browser actions to execute API calls to execute them on system, finally on third step specific test case is applied to SUT, if the execution leads to the same vulnerability it confirms leak in the system (Büchler et. al. 2012).

A Model-Based Framework for Global Security Policy Specification, Deployment and Testing

This approach is based on architectural, functional and fault models and the policies related to the security of the system (Mouelhi et. al. 2008). Through this approach, policies are specified, deployed and tested in applications. It begins with the generic security model of the application. Subsequently, it collects the higher-level access control policy implemented by the system and is expressed in a dedicated language. Before the model is used model, soundness and adequacy are tested with the requirements of the system. Afterward, policy decisions points are generated based on existing frameworks, the output of the transformation is XACML (Extended Access Control Markup Language). Model-based testing, the transformational process is necessary because it does not imply automatically in the implementation phase. Existing test cases are applied to the implementation generated from the mutated security model. If security vulnerabilities are detected it is adapted to the mutated model. Finally, the objective is to synchronize the security mode with security policy.

A Model-Based Framework for Risk Handling

It generally includes the risk factors to solve decisions in all phases of secure SDLC (Garvin et. al. 2011) (Felderer et. al. 2014) (Schneider et. al. 2013) It focuses on the most critical situation of the software system (Wendland et. al. 2012). Determining the critical risk has become the milestone within complex software development of testing techniques. According to the international standard ISO/IEC/IEEE (Felderer et. al. 2016), risk has become an integral part of the software testing process.

CODE-BASED TESTING AND STATIC ANALYSIS

In the past when there was no concept of software security testing, the static analysis was performed through which vulnerabilities are identified. Since this technique is practiced by looking at the code so vulnerabilities are identified at the early stage of SDLC where vulnerabilities fixing is comparatively cheap (Howard et. al. 2006). SAST is part of the implementation technique that highlights the activity of start testing as soon as the coding is started. In this section, we will discuss only static approaches which don't require an executable test system.

Static code analysis is a method for detecting the bugs in the system by examining the entire source code of the program/module before the execution of the program. This process is mainly done by analyzing a block of code for the corresponding set (or multiple sets) of coding rules. Static code analysis and static analysis are often used interchangeably in the literature, in parallel with source code analysis of the system.

This type of analysis addresses weaknesses in the source code that might lead to vulnerabilities. Of course, this may also be achieved through manual code reviews. But using automated tools is much more effective. Code analysis can either be done manually or automated. The manual approach is called static code analysis or Static Application Security Testing (SAST). We can also analyze the code that is coded by the coder or the compiled source code in byte-codes or binaries. From the vendor point of view, it is better to review code that is written by the developer because it is more precise and detailed instructions can be given to developer in order to fix vulnerability on the source code level.

Manual Code Review

Manual code review requires the expert with three main expertise, which includes application area, software architecture (i.e. programming language, frameworks used to develop software) and security. In this approach expert read code line by line to identified vulnerabilities. Firstly, a short interview is schedule between developer and testing expert in order to give him the overview of the program and architecture used for development, the expert review the code and as result prepare a report and list all the vulnerabilities in the code. These vulnerabilities are then explained to the developer and how to fix them. Knowledge of similar threats is also given to the developer in order to prevent vulnerabilities. Overall manual code review is a tedious process which requires skill, time, experience, patience, and persistence.

Static Application Security Testing

Automated static program analysis is also called SAST (Chess et. al. 2007). SAST tool is used to run the automated review of the code and reports the vulnerabilities in the application. This approach limits the time constraint and increases the scalability so more code can be within a specific time. On the other hand, the SAST tool only reports vulnerabilities that they are looking for (Bessey et. al. 2010) (Brucker et. al. 2014).

SAST tool employs two different types of analysis. *(1) Syntactic*: It checks to call an Insecure API within the program. For example, calling Java random function which returns an encrypted secure random number generator. *(2) Semantics:* It validates the program semantics such data flow or control flow of the program. For example, SQL integration to the program which can lead to SQL injection.

A SAST tool review program on the estimation of actual code and heuristic checks. It specifies potential vulnerabilities if exists. Thus, the human expert is required to access whether the detect vulnerability is (true positive) that can exploit system or its (false positive) that the vulnerability exists but it cannot exploit the system and does not need any effort to fix it. Similarly, if no issues are reported by the SAST tool, then it means

1. The software is secure and there is no vulnerability. (True negative)
2. Due to the limitation of the tool, it does report the security issue (False negative).

In the early stage of software development, life-cycle SAST tool can be applied as well as it provides detailed recommendations to fixed vulnerabilities. SAST tool has one advantage over dynamic approaches, that it can analyze all program flows. Therefore, the SAST tool covers a wider area of the program under test and because of this; it has a low rate of the false negative. Therefore, in detecting software vulnerability at early stage SAST tool is very effective (Scandariato et. al. 2013; Scarfone et. al. 2008; Tian et. al. 2009).

GLOBAL PENETRATION TESTING AND DYNAMIC ANALYSIS

This model primarily covers the two distinct domain of software security testing namely Penetration testing, and Dynamic Analysis. In the subsequent part, the scope, strength, and limitation of each domain are discussed and analyzed.

Global Penetration Testing

Global Penetration testing is well known black box testing. In this approach system is tested from the outside environment, the setup is comparable to the actual attack from the third party Malicious software. It means that the attacking entity has minimal information about the system under test and it's only able to interact with the system public interfaces. Prerequisites for global penetration testing is that should be filled with data so that all the workflows can be tested. This approach is commonly used for those systems which are open to network communication. According to the NIST Technical Guide to Information Security Testing and Assessment [32], penetration testing is partitioned into four distinct phases.

- **Planning:** In the planning phase document is prepared to define the boundaries and limitations of the test. Components of the system on which test is to be performed are defined, the scope of the test to be conducted and their significance level.
- **Discovery:** Discovery phase is divided into steps. Initially, the external interface of the system under test are symmetrically discovered and enumerated. This surface is the first layer where system attacks. In the next step, all test cases that are matched to identify with the external interface (e.g. SQL injection on applications containing database or cross-site scripting in HTTP services). In commercial penetration testing components that are discovered are tested to vulnerabilities which are publicly documented.
- **Attack:** In the attack phase, all the identified interface is tested by sending continuous payloads by the tester. If any leak is determined in the system

user privilege is widen to gather further information to which extent the vulnerability is exposed. After complete knowledge, the information is sent back to the discovery phase.

- **Reporting:** This phase is in continuation with all above three phases and all findings are documented with its sereneness.

Global Vulnerability Scanning

Global Vulnerability scanning is the combination of both manual testing and black box vulnerability scanners. It means the expert is required for carrying out testing with the help of black box scanner tool which helps to identify vulnerabilities in the SUT through predefined security test. In result system response to predefined test are analyzed if the attack is successful and if attack if false, subsequent tries are made to alter the attack. Overview of recent commercial and academic black box vulnerability scanners is provided by (Bau et. al. 2010). and (Doupé et. al. 2010).

Global Dynamic Taint Analysis

Taint analysis is another variant of black box testing. String-based code injection vulnerability is the most common technique used for security injection (Johns, M. (2011). Through this technique, the syntactic code is injected in to automatically execute programming statements which compromise the vulnerable execution context, SQL.(Halfond et. al. 2006). and Cross-Site Scripting (Grossman et. al. 2007) are the examples of this technique. In this technique, un-sensitized data from the un-trusted resource is sink into the system, in order to achieve it (dynamic) data tainting is used. Un-trusted data is cleared out the trusted information if the data reach to dedicated sanitized function.

In taint analysis, tester main objective is to notify the insecure data flows, unlike static testing technique which identifies the problematic data analysis, taint analysis is conducted transparently when SUT is in the execution state. In the taint analysis system should be aware of taint information from the un-trusted source and this data is maintained through execution, so it can be easily detected when the secure information sinks.

Fuzz Testing (Fuzzing)

Fuzzing testing is another form of dynamic testing pioneered by Barton Miller in 1980s at the University of Wisconsin. (Miller et. al. 990). In fuzzing testing, random data is fed to the system until the SUT crashes. Fuzzing testing has been approved effective technique for security testing.

It was started by feeding random data to the system but with the advancement of the symbolic computation and model-based testing further type of fuzzing testing has been introduced like mutation based fuzzing, generation based fuzzing and grey box fuzzing.

- **Random Fuzzing**: It is the oldest technique used for fuzzing. In random fuzzing, series data is inputted into the system randomly until the system under test is the crash. It is used to detect how the system responds to the large set of invalid data.
- **Mutation Fuzzing:** In mutation based fuzzing input format is known to fuzzed through past input data samples. Using this and with the help of heuristic mutant data is created for testing, for further information refers to this survey (Duchene et. al. 2014; Rawat et. al. 2011).
- **Generation Fuzzing:** In generation based fuzzing model of vulnerabilities or input data is used. Unlike the original fuzzing technique, generation based fuzzing covers the broader area of the system under test, for further information refer to these articles (Yang et. al. 2012; Zhao et. al. 2011).
- **Advanced Fuzzing:** Advance fuzzing testing is basically a combination of previously discussed fuzzing techniques like mutation and generation based testing as well as creative input data model by observing program under test, this turn fuzzing into a grey box testing technique.

GLOBAL SECURITY REGRESSION TESTING

Based on regression and security testing, this testing make sure changes to the system does not compromise its security, because of its importance demand for such approaches has increased (Yang et. al. 2012). It also makes sure that the intended behavior of the system is not affected by the changes (Zhao et. al. 2011). The ingenuousness of modern IT systems and their enduring transforms make it demanding to keep these systems secure. In this connection, the combination of statically modeled regression and the security testing are called 'security regression testing', in the literature. This approach makes certain that modifications employ to a system will not harm its level of security.

According to Yoo and Harman (Felderer et. al. 2015), security regression testing can be classified into three categories, namely Test Suite Minimization, Test Case Prioritization. and Test Case Selection.

Test Suite Minimization

Test case minimization techniques are used to reduce the cost as a function of execution time, resources etc. The prime motive of test case minimization is to create the representative set from the test suite. This test suite will satisfy all the essential needs of the original test suite with less number of test cease. Fundamentally, the test case minimization techniques are to eliminate the test cases that become repeated and obsolete over the span of the time.

An approach used to minimize the size of cases by certain criteria. An approach giving by (Leung et. al. 1989) apply automated testing to determine vulnerabilities by applying the test to the system that can lead to malware functions. If the malware is detected then the same test is applied to the new system to check if it's still vulnerable after fixing the fault. (Tian et. al. 2009) propose the approach in which vulnerabilities are detected in minor releases of the web application. The only strong bond relationship among pages from previous releases is optimized with iterations and are selected for investing vulnerabilities in these web pages. (Garvin et. al. 2011) propose testing of SUT by applying only those tests which have resulted in vulnerabilities in previous system release.

Test Case Prioritization

Test case prioritization is a technique which is used for ordering test case to achieve early fault detection. Current approaches that are being used for test case prioritization are discussed in referred articles (Huang et. al. 2012; Yu et. al. 2012; Viennot et. al. 2013). Different authors proposed techniques for test case prioritization which are described below.

(Khalilian et. al. 2012) proposed a regression security testing. In this technique, historical data is gathered and then determine the effectiveness of each test case implementation by some generic algorithm. (Yu et. al. 2012) proposed technique in which test case are prioritized according to their fault detection capability.

(Viennot et. al. 2013) proposed a system that allows replaying the execution by recording it first, this system is called a mutable record based system. In this technique test cases are prioritized with some cost function between the original and mutable execution.

Test Case Selection

Test case selection approach selects entire test cases or subset. This approach tests both security mechanism and vulnerability. Several subset approaches (Felderer et. al. 2011; Kassab et. al. 2011; Kassab et. al. 2011; Anisetti et. al. 2012; Hwang et. al.

2012; Huang et. al. 2009) and reset-all-approaches (Bruno et. al. 2005; Vetterling et. al. 2002; Kongsli et. al. 2006; Roychoudhury et. al. 2012) have been proposed (Felderer et. al. 2011) an approach based on UML model design for security regression testing on the requirement of authenticity, availability, integrity, authorization, and availability. Based on the requirements, the test represents a series of diagrams.

(Kassab et. al. 2011), To improved regression security testing, he proposed an approach based on non-functional requirements like security, safety, performance, and reliability. The test case is selected based on a changed or modified requirement. (Anisetti et. al. 2012), the proposed approach that is used to provide certification evidence for the security requirement of services. In this approach test cases are generated or existing ones are used based on the change detection in the service model. (Huang et. al. 2009), proposed an approach that focuses on access change policy, test cases are selected based on the elements that are covered in the changed policy.

(Huang et. al. 2009), proposed an approach for testing security policies evolution in the system under test. There are 3 coverage base techniques for its implementation. Each of this technique contains a series of steps which described that which subjects have access to which resource at what condition. Each technique is based on policy changed rules and evolution in policy or change in original policy through program decision.

DEDUCTIONS AND ANALYSIS

Hence we have discussed different techniques of security testing and how to implement it in different types of applications based on their structure, requirements, and model. Each technique has its own advantages and limitations. Security testing has become very important in the software development lifecycle as market dynamics are changing and business is shifting towards e-business security has become an important factor it is considered to be optional now. Since the secure software development life-cycle consists of different phases, so these security techniques are applied to each phase. As per the understanding through discussing the above methods it is better to detect vulnerability at the early stage which results in saving cost and required less amount of time to fix the fault. Each method of security technique has different approaches including static approach (required expert tester to conduct test) and dynamic approach that automatically execute test on SUT.

CONCLUSION

In this paper, we have discussed different techniques that are currently being used for security testing in SDLC and detecting vulnerabilities within the application. In order to understand this and give the general idea of SDLC, we have summarized software engineering and different type of testing techniques which include static and dynamic approaches. With the evaluation of ICT industry and the boom in the e-commerce industry, it has become essential for companies to integrate security in the phase of software development to save information asset in terms of accessibility, integrity, accountability, and authorization. This also improves the efficiency and effectiveness of the application which results in better Information Technology products.

REFERENCES

Anisetti, M., Ardagna, C. A., & Damiani, E. (2012, June). A low-cost security certification scheme for evolving services. In *2012 IEEE 19th International Conference on Web Services* (pp. 122-129). Piscataway, NJ: IEEE. 10.1109/ICWS.2012.53

Anisetti, M., Ardagna, C. A., & Damiani, E. (2012, June). A low-cost security certification scheme for evolving services. In *2012 IEEE 19th International Conference on Web Services* (pp. 122-129). Piscataway, NJ: IEEE. 10.1109/ICWS.2012.53

Bau, J., Bursztein, E., Gupta, D., & Mitchell, J. (2010, May). State of the art: Automated black-box web application vulnerability testing. In *2010 IEEE Symposium on Security and Privacy* (pp. 332-345). Piscataway, NJ: IEEE. 10.1109/SP.2010.27

Bau, J., Bursztein, E., Gupta, D., & Mitchell, J. (2010, May). State of the art: Automated black-box web application vulnerability testing. In *2010 IEEE Symposium on Security and Privacy* (pp. 332-345). Piscataway, NJ: IEEE. 10.1109/SP.2010.27

Bessey, A., Block, K., Chelf, B., & et al, . (2010). A few billion lines of code later: Using static analysis to find bugs in the real world. *Communications of the ACM*, *53*(2), 66–75. doi:10.1145/1646353.1646374

Bourque, P., Dupuis, R., Abran, A., & et al, . (1999). The guide to the software engineering body of knowledge. *IEEE Software*, *16*(6), 35–44. doi:10.1109/52.805471

Brucker, A., & Sodan, U. (2014). *Deploying static application security testing on a large scale. Sicherheit 2014–Sicherheit*. Schutz und Zuverlässigkeit.

Bruno, M., Canfora, G., Di Penta, M., et al. (2005, December). Using test cases as contract to ensure service compliance across releases. In *International conference on service-oriented computing* (pp. 87-100). Berlin, Germany: Springer. 10.1007/11596141_8

Büchler, M., Oudinet, J., & Pretschner, A. (2012, June). Semi-automatic security testing of web applications from a secure model. In *2012 IEEE Sixth International Conference on Software Security and Reliability* (pp. 253-262). Piscataway, NJ: IEEE. 10.1109/SERE.2012.38

Chess, B., & West, J. (2007). Secure programming with static analysis. London, UK: Pearson Education.

Coallier, F. (2001). *Software engineering–Product quality–Part 1: Quality model.* Geneva, Switzerland: International Organization for Standardization.

Coallier, F. (2001). *Software engineering–Product quality–Part 1: Quality model.* Geneva, Switzerland: International Organization for Standardization.

Den Braber, F., Hogganvik, I., Lund, M. S., & et al, . (2007). Model-based security analysis in seven steps—A guided tour to the CORAS method. *BT Technology Journal, 25*(1), 101–117. doi:10.100710550-007-0013-9

Doupé, A., Cova, M., & Vigna, G. (2010, July). Why Johnny can't pentest: An analysis of black-box web vulnerability scanners. In *International Conference on Detection of Intrusions and Malware, and Vulnerability Assessment* (pp. 111-131). Berlin, Germany: Springer. 10.1007/978-3-642-14215-4_7

Duchene, F., Rawat, S., Richier, J. L., & Groz, R. (2014, March). KameleonFuzz: evolutionary fuzzing for black-box XSS detection. In *Proceedings of the 4th ACM conference on Data and application security and privacy* (pp. 37-48). New York, NY: ACM. 10.1145/2557547.2557550

Felderer, M., Agreiter, B., & Breu, R. (2011, February). Evolution of security requirements tests for service–centric systems. In *International Symposium on Engineering Secure Software and Systems* (pp. 181-194). Berlin, Germany: Springer. 10.1007/978-3-642-19125-1_14

Felderer, M., Agreiter, B., & Breu, R. (2011, February). Evolution of security requirements tests for service–centric systems. In *International Symposium on Engineering Secure Software and Systems* (pp. 181-194). Berlin, Germany: Springer. 10.1007/978-3-642-19125-1_14

Felderer, M., Büchler, M., Johns, M., & et al, . (2016). Security testing: A survey. *Advances in Computers*, *101*, 1–51. doi:10.1016/bs.adcom.2015.11.003

Felderer, M., & Fourneret, E. (2015). A systematic classification of security regression testing approaches. *International Journal of Software Tools for Technology Transfer*, *17*(3), 305–319. doi:10.100710009-015-0365-2

Felderer, M., & Schieferdecker, I. (2014). *A taxonomy of risk-based testing*. Academic Press.

Garvin, B. J., Cohen, M. B., & Dwyer, M. B. (2011, September). Using feature locality: can we leverage history to avoid failures during reconfiguration? In *Proceedings of the 8th workshop on Assurances for self-adaptive systems* (pp. 24-33). New York, NY: ACM. 10.1145/2024436.2024443

Garvin, B. J., Cohen, M. B., & Dwyer, M. B. (2011, September). Using feature locality: can we leverage history to avoid failures during reconfiguration? In *Proceedings of the 8th workshop on Assurances for self-adaptive systems* (pp. 24-33). New York, NY: ACM. 10.1145/2024436.2024443

Grieskamp, W., Kicillof, N., Stobie, K., & Braberman, V. (2011). Model-based quality assurance of protocol documentation: Tools and methodology. *Software Testing, Verification & Reliability*, *21*(1), 55–71. doi:10.1002tvr.427

Grossman, J., Hansen, R., Petkov, P., et al. (2007). Cross site scripting attacks: XSS Exploits and defense. Burlington, MA: Syngress Publishing.

Halfond, W. G., Viegas, J., & Orso, A. (2006, March). A classification of SQL-injection attacks and countermeasures. In *Proceedings of the IEEE International Symposium on Secure Software Engineering* (Vol. 1, pp. 13-15). Piscataway, NJ: IEEE.

Holik, F., Horalek, J., & Marik, O. (2014, November). Effective penetration testing with Metasploit framework and methodologies. In *2014 IEEE 15th International Symposium on Computational Intelligence and Informatics (CINTI)* (pp. 237-242). IEEE. 10.1109/CINTI.2014.7028682

Howard, M., & Lipner, S. (2006). *The security development lifecycle* (Vol. 8). Redmond, WA: Microsoft Press.

Huang, C., Sun, J., Wang, X., & Si, Y. (2009, June). Selective regression test for access control system employing rbac. In *International Conference on Information Security and Assurance* (pp. 70-79). Berlin, Germany: Springer. 10.1007/978-3-642-02617-1_8

Huang, C., Sun, J., Wang, X., & Si, Y. (2009, June). Selective regression test for access control system employing rbac. In *International Conference on Information Security and Assurance* (pp. 70-79). Berlin, Germany: Springer. 10.1007/978-3-642-02617-1_8

Huang, Y. C., Peng, K. L., & Huang, C. Y. (2012). A history-based cost-cognizant test case prioritization technique in regression testing. *Journal of Systems and Software*, 85(3), 626–637. doi:10.1016/j.jss.2011.09.063

Hwang, J., Xie, T., El Kateb, D., et al. (2012, September). Selection of regression system tests for security policy evolution. In *Proceedings of the 27th IEEE/ACM international conference on automated software engineering* (pp. 266-269). New York, NY: ACM. 10.1145/2351676.2351719

ISO, G. (1991). Information Technology, Open Systems Interconnection, Conformance Testing Methodology and Framework. *International Standard IS, 9646*.

Johns, M. (2011). Code-injection Vulnerabilities in Web Applications—Exemplified at Cross-site Scripting. *It-Information Technology Methoden und innovative Anwendungen der Informatik und Informationstechnik, 53*(5), 256-260.

Kassab, M., Ormandjieva, O., & Daneva, M. (2011, May). Relational-model based change management for non-functional requirements: Approach and experiment. In *2011 FIFTH International Conference On Research Challenges In Information Science* (pp. 1-9). Piscataway, NJ: IEEE. 10.1109/RCIS.2011.6006830

Kassab, M., Ormandjieva, O., & Daneva, M. (2011, May). Relational-model based change management for non-functional requirements: Approach and experiment. In *2011 Fifth International Conference On Research Challenges In Information Science* (pp. 1-9). Piscataway, NJ: IEEE. 10.1109/RCIS.2011.6006830

Khalilian, A., Azgomi, M. A., & Fazlalizadeh, Y. (2012). An improved method for test case prioritization by incorporating historical test case data. *Science of Computer Programming, 78*(1), 93–116. doi:10.1016/j.scico.2012.01.006

Kongsli, V. (2006, October). Towards agile security in web applications. In *Companion to the 21st ACM SIGPLAN symposium on Object-oriented programming systems, languages, and applications* (pp. 805-808). New York, NY: ACM. 10.1145/1176617.1176727

Kurniawan, A., Riadi, I., & Luthfi, A. (2017). Forensic analysis and prevent of cross site scripting in single victim attack using open web application security project (OWASP) framework. *Journal of Theoretical & Applied Information Technology, 95*(6).

Leung, H. K., & White, L. (1989, October). Insights into regression testing (software testing). In *Proceedings. Conference on Software Maintenance-1989* (pp. 60-69). Piscataway, NJ: IEEE.

Lund, M. S., Solhaug, B., & Stølen, K. (2010). Model-driven risk analysis: the CORAS approach. New York, NY: Springer Science & Business Media.

Miller, B. P., Fredriksen, L., & So, B. (1990). An empirical study of the reliability of UNIX utilities. *Communications of the ACM, 33*(12), 32–44. doi:10.1145/96267.96279

Mouelhi, T., Fleurey, F., Baudry, B., & Le Traon, Y. (2008, September). A model-based framework for security policy specification, deployment and testing. In *International Conference on Model Driven Engineering Languages and Systems* (pp. 537-552). Berlin, Germany: Springer. 10.1007/978-3-540-87875-9_38

Petrenko, A. K., & Schlingloff, H. (2012). *Proceedings 7th Workshop on Model-Based Testing.* arXiv preprint arXiv:1202.5826

Planning, S. (2002). *The economic impacts of inadequate infrastructure for software testing.* National Institute of Standards and Technology.

Potter, B., & McGraw, G. (2004). Software security testing. *IEEE Security and Privacy, 2*(5), 81–85. doi:10.1109/MSP.2004.84

Qi, D., Roychoudhury, A., Liang, Z., & Vaswani, K. (2012). Darwin: An approach to debugging evolving programs. *ACM Transactions on Software Engineering and Methodology, 21*(3), 19. doi:10.1145/2211616.2211622

Rawat, S., & Mounier, L. (2011, March). Offset-aware mutation based fuzzing for buffer overflow vulnerabilities: Few preliminary results. In *2011 IEEE Fourth International Conference on Software Testing, Verification and Validation Workshops* (pp. 531-533). Piscataway, NJ: IEEE. 10.1109/ICSTW.2011.9

Scandariato, R., Walden, J., & Joosen, W. (2013, November). Static analysis versus penetration testing: A controlled experiment. In *2013 IEEE 24th international symposium on software reliability engineering (ISSRE)* (pp. 451-460). Piscataway, NJ: IEEE. 10.1109/ISSRE.2013.6698898

Scarfone, K., Souppaya, M., Cody, A., & Orebaugh, A. (2008). Technical guide to information security testing and assessment. *NIST Special Publication, 800*(115), 2–25.

Schneider, M., Großmann, J., Schieferdecker, I., & Pietschker, A. (2013, March). Online model-based behavioral fuzzing. In *2013 IEEE Sixth International Conference on Software Testing, Verification and Validation Workshops* (pp. 469-475). Piscataway, NJ: IEEE. 10.1109/ICSTW.2013.61

Tian, H., Xu, J., Lian, K., & Zhang, Y. (2009, August). Research on strong-association rule based web application vulnerability detection. In *2009 2nd IEEE International Conference on Computer Science and Information Technology* (pp. 237-241). IEEE. 10.1109/ICCSIT.2009.5234394

Utting, M., & Legeard, B. (2010). Practical model-based testing: a tools approach. Amsterdam, The Netherlands: Elsevier.

Verdon, D., & McGraw, G. (2004). Risk analysis in software design. *IEEE Security and Privacy*, *2*(4), 79–84. doi:10.1109/MSP.2004.55

Vetterling, M., Wimmel, G., & Wisspeintner, A. (2002, November). Secure systems development based on the common criteria: the PalME project. In *Proceedings of the 10th ACM SIGSOFT symposium on Foundations of software engineering* (pp. 129-138). New York, NY: ACM. 10.1145/587051.587071

Viennot, N., Nair, S., & Nieh, J. (2013, March). Transparent mutable replay for multicore debugging and patch validation. In ACM SIGARCH computer architecture news 41(1) (pp. 127-138). New York, NY: ACM. doi:10.1145/2451116.2451130

Viennot, N., Nair, S., & Nieh, J. (2013, March). Transparent mutable replay for multicore debugging and patch validation. ACM SIGARCH Computer Architecture News, *41*(1), 127-138. doi:10.1145/2451116.2451130

Vu, K. M. (2011). ICT as a source of economic growth in the information age: Empirical evidence from the 1996–2005 period. *Telecommunications Policy*, *35*(4), 357–372. doi:10.1016/j.telpol.2011.02.008

Wendland, M. F., Kranz, M., & Schieferdecker, I. (2012). A systematic approach to risk-based testing using risk-annotated requirements models. In *Proceeding of the Seventh International Conference on Software Engineering Advances (ICSEA'12)* (pp. 636-642). Academic Press.

Wichers, D. (2013). *Owasp top-10 2013*. OWASP Foundation.

Yang, D., Zhang, Y., & Liu, Q. (2012, June). Blendfuzz: A model-based framework for fuzz testing programs with grammatical inputs. In *2012 IEEE 11th International Conference on Trust, Security and Privacy in Computing and Communications* (pp. 1070-1076). Piscataway, NJ: IEEE. 10.1109/TrustCom.2012.99

Yu, Y. T., & Lau, M. F. (2012). Fault-based test suite prioritization for specification-based testing. *Information and Software Technology, 54*(2), 179–202. doi:10.1016/j. infsof.2011.09.005

Yu, Y. T., & Lau, M. F. (2012). Fault-based test suite prioritization for specification-based testing. *Information and Software Technology, 54*(2), 179–202. doi:10.1016/j. infsof.2011.09.005

Zander, J., Schieferdecker, I., & Mosterman, P. J. (Eds.). (2011). Model-based testing for embedded systems. Boca Raton, FL: CRC Press.

Zhao, J., Wen, Y., & Zhao, G. (2011, October). H-fuzzing: a new heuristic method for fuzzing data generation. In *IFIP International Conference on Network and Parallel Computing* (pp. 32-43). Berlin, Germany: Springer. 10.1007/978-3-642-24403-2_3

Chapter 11

Software Cost Estimation and Capability Maturity Model in Context of Global Software Engineering

Ayub Muhammad Latif
PAF Karachi Institute of Economics and Technology, Pakistan

Khalid Muhammad Khan
PAF Karachi Institute of Economics and Technology, Pakistan

Anh Nguyen Duc
University of South-Eastern Norway, Norway

ABSTRACT

Software cost estimation is the process of forecasting the effort needed to develop the software system. Global software engineering (GSE) highlights that software development knows no boundaries and majority of the software products and services are developed today by globally-distributed teams, projects, and companies. The problem of cost estimation gets more complex if the discussion is carried out in the context of GSE, which has its own issues. Temporal, cultural, and geographical distance creates communication and software process implementation issues. Traditional software process models such as capability maturity model (CMM) lacks the dynamism to accommodate the recent trends in GSE. The chapter introduces GSE and discusses various cost estimation techniques and different levels of CMM. A couple of GSE-based case studies having CMM-level projects from multiple organizations are studied to analyze the impacts of highly mature processes on effort, quality, and cycle time.

DOI: 10.4018/978-1-5225-9448-2.ch011

GLOBAL SOFTWARE ENGINEERING

The world has become a global village and software engineering industry has kept pace with the changing circumstances by establishing a new dimension known as Global Software Engineering (GSE) in which geographical location, culture and distance is no more a barrier and software engineers across the globe must collaborate and play their part in achieving the desired goal (Carmel, 1999; Prikladnicki et al, 2003). There are many technological factors that have made it possible but the most important is the advent of low cost international telecommunication infrastructure that facilitated the outreach of internet and email (O'Brien, 2002). Further, the political circumstances across the globe has also played its part as getting visa for the work force is no more simple and getting the people to fly to one location and providing them all the necessities is expensive as well. Letting the highly skilled software engineers work from low cost locations such as Eastern Europe, Latin America and Far East (Crow et al, 2003) is a better proposition. Another benefit of GSE is that the operations are established near emerging markets which has its own advantages. A variation of this model is just to shift the application development and maintenance by using out sourcing model to remote third party organizations. These remote organizations can even be subsidiaries of big companies established in low cost economies (Carmel et al, 2005; Toaff, 2005).

There can be several challenges in a typical GSE environment but the top most is team building and project management. The success of any GSE project depends upon the operations of virtual teams which forms the core building block of the virtual organization (Davidow et al, 1992; Jarvenpaa et al, 1994; Mohrman, 1999). Virtual teams are bit different from traditional teams hence they needed to be managed differently as well. A traditional team is a group of individuals who are gather to achieve a common objective. They undertake interdependent tasks, coordinate among each other and share responsibility of the outcomes (Powell et al, 2004).Though virtual teams also behave like traditional teams but with certain challenges involving different time zones and geographical location. There are no organizational boundaries as the environment is multicultural and multilingual. The most complex area of handling virtual teams is of communication as it is mostly dependent on electronic communication infrastructure. It is asynchronous with very few possibilities for synchronous contact. The virtual team may assemble / disassemble as per requirements which is true for traditional teams as well.

Project management become complex with virtual teams due to co-ordination, communication and cooperation (Nidiffer et al, 2005) challenges. The electronic and asynchronous means can never be equivalent to a good face to face discussion. Even the video calls cannot capture the emotions of all the participants or the positive / negative energy in the room. The distance is not just geographical; it's the temporal and cultural distance that creates new barriers and complexities in the project management activities (Herbsleb et al, 2003).

Temporal distance is a measure of the distance of time people participating in communication are experiencing (Agerfalk et al, 2005). It can be caused by time zone difference or different work timings. The difference in temporal distance effects communication (Sarker et al, 2004) and the response time increases when working hours at remote locations do not overlap. While developing virtual teams, one must take a note of the temporal overlap of the team members to facilitate better communication. The temporal overlap can be achieved by understanding time zone difference and by adjusting the time shifting work patterns.

The cultural distance of team members is the understanding of each other's values and cultural practices (Herbsleb et al, 2003). In (Kotlarsky et al, 2005), it is identified that culture can have a huge effect on how people would behave in certain situation. Cultural distance is dependent on many factors such as national culture, language, political understanding, individual motivations and work ethics. If there is a large cultural distance between team members in terms of national culture or language, it is difficult for them to adopt to same organizational culture. Cultural distance is not entirely based on geographical distance, low geographical distance does not automatically mean low cultural difference.

In the next section we discuss the process modeling and capability maturity model and introduce the reader with all the five levels of CMM.

Process Modeling and Capability Maturity Model

Software process can be defined as "a set of activities, methods, practices and transformations that people use to develop and maintain software and the associated products" (Curtiz et al, 1992). Software industry has come a long way which is depicted by huge number of improves software products available in the market. To develop better software products, software processes are required to be improved and many software process models have been proposed and utilized by the software practitioners. The most widely used process modelling technique is Capability Maturity Model Integration (CMMI).

The Capability Maturity Model (CMM) is a development model and the term "maturity" refers to formality and optimization (Paulk et al, 1993). The CMM deployment will take the organization from the ad hoc practices to formally defined steps that result into continuous improvement. The early adopter organizations have found it difficult to implement CMM due to integration issues with multiple models. To solve these issues, Capability Maturity Model Integration (CMMI) model was developed that defines five levels of maturity (Team, 2006). It is believed that organization's software processes would improve as the organization moves up the level. These levels are shown in Table 1.

Each maturity levels have Key Process Areas and for each such area there are five factors: goals, commitment, ability, measurement, and verification. The CMMI model provides a range of theoretical boundaries so that the process maturity can be developed incrementally. Skipping levels is neither recommended nor allowed/feasible.

Level 1: Initial

Processes at this level are (typically) undocumented and prone to changes. They are driven in an *ad hoc* and uncontrolled manner. They are handled reactively in light of user suggestions or other events. Such chaotic or unstable environment results in no or low process improvement.

Level 2: Repeatable

Having repeatable processes in an environment is a sign of maturity and if the results are also consistent then it is even better. Ability to keep the processes in place in stressful circumstances depicts deep rooted process discipline. The key process areas of this level are:

- **CM**: Configuration Management
- **MA:** Measurement and Analysis
- **PMC:** Project Monitoring and Control
- **PP:** Project Planning
- **PPQA:** Process and Product Quality Assurance
- **REQMP:** Requirements Management

Table 1. CMMI level description

CMMI Level No	CMMI Level Name	CMMI Level Description
1	Initial	Starting point for use of a new or undocumented repeat process
2	Repeatable	Process is documented sufficiently enough to attempt repeat
3	Defined	Process is defined/confirmed as a standard business process
4	Capable	Process is quantitatively managed in accordance with agreed-upon metrics
5	Efficient	Process management having deliberate process optimization/improvement

- **SAM:** Supplier Agreement Management

Level 3: Defined

At this level, processes are well defined and documented. Standard processes are established and get improved with the passage of time. The processes may not be used repeatedly but they are validated in multiple situations and are sufficient enough for the users to become competent. Implementation in wider range of conditions can take the process to next level of maturity. The key process areas of this level are:

- **DAR:** Decision Analysis and Resolution
- **IPM**: Integrated Project Management
- **OPD:** Organizational Process Definition
- **OPF:** Organizational Process Focus
- **OT:** Organizational Training
- **PI:** Product Integration
- **RD:** Requirements Development
- **RSKM:** Risk Management
- **TS:** Technical Solution
- **VAL -** Validation
- **VER**: Verification

Level 4: Capable

Process objectives can be achieved effectively in a range of operation conditions at this level by using process metrics. The processes are tested, refined and adapted in multiple environments. Process users also have developed competence on the processes in different conditions. Process maturity improves capability and enables adaptions to particular projects without much deviation from specifications. The key process areas of this level are:

- **OPP**: Organizational Process Performance
- **QPM:** Quantitative Project Management

Level 5: Optimizing (Efficient)

Processes at this level are continually improved through incremental and innovative technological changes. Statistical common causes of process variation are addressed to improve process performance. This would be done at the same time as maintaining the likelihood of achieving the established quantitative process-improvement objectives. The key process areas of this level are:

- **CAR:** Causal Analysis and Resolution
- **OPM:** Organizational Performance Management

Please refer (Chrissis et al, 2003), to clear the understanding on the key process areas of CMMI levels. The next section discusses the different costing and estimation techniques which can be used for making an estimate of effort and time of software that is undergoing development.

Software Costing and Estimation Techniques

The software development process comprises of numerous activities which needs to be performed separately. Cost estimation of software development project helps us in calculating the effort and time required for the development for a particular software system (Boehm et al, 2000). It can further help in even calculating the overall cost of the software that is being developed. The software costing and estimation helps in answering the following questions:

1. How much effort is required for a particular activity of the software process?
2. How much calendar time is needed to complete each activity?
3. What is the total cost of each activity?

Project cost estimation and project scheduling are two different activities which are usually carried out together and work breakdown structure which is a part of project scheduling also helps in estimating the different activities of the software. The costs of development are primarily the costs of the effort involved, so the effort computation is used in both the cost and the schedule estimate. The initial cost estimates may be used to establish a budget for the project and to set a price for the software for a customer. The total cost of a software development project is the sum of following costs:

1. Effort costs of paying software developers.
2. Ratio of the fixed expenditure for development house.
3. Hardware and software costs including maintenance.
4. Travel and training costs.

For most of the projects, the most significant cost is the effort cost. Effort costs are not just the salaries of the software engineers who are involved in the project. The following overhead costs can also be included in the effort cost:

1. Costs of support staff (accountants, administrators, system managers, cleaners, technicians etc.).
2. Capital Expenditure of networking and communications.
3. Capital Expenditure of the facilities for employees.
4. Costs spent on Employees' benefits.

Software Estimation Metrics

The software estimation metrics can be broadly divided in one of the two metrics which are given under (Trendowicz, 2013).

1. **Size-related software Metrics:** These metrics are related to the size of software. The most frequently used size-related metric is lines of delivered source code and it is also known as direct metric.
2. **Function-Related Software Metrics:** These are related to the overall functionality of the software. For example, function points and object points are metrics of this type and it falls under the category of indirect metric.

The reason to classify them as direct and indirect metric is that direct metric can be measured directly by using a single metric. A non software example of direct metric could be the weight of an individual which can be known in Kilograms. On the other hand indirect metrics initially use some direct measures and then give the result through some regression based formula. A non software example of indirect metric could be "that how a particular person is". This is more difficult to analyze as we need to look into many parameters of an individual to claim whether he/she is a good person, a bad person etc. Same goes for the indirect metrics of software.

The Productivity Metric and Lines of Code

Other then the stated metrics a metric known as the productivity metric is known by the source lines of code written by each developer in a month. It tells the general productivity of a developer in a given month (Trendowicz, 2013). Very important to note here is that if a software practitioner has a productivity of 1500 LOC per month, this simple doesn't mean that he/she will be writing 1500 Lines of code in any specific language. It will mean that the work he/she performs in his/her organization during a month is equivalent to writing 1500 lines of code. The case may be that the individual only writes 200 lines of code during the whole month is any development environment. It is also a known fact now that maximum effort in coding for particular software can never exceed 25% of the overall software development effort. This fact also helps in understanding that the total lines of code for the development of software does not mean the physical lines of code in the development environment.

The Function Point and Object Point Metric

In the function point metric the total number of function points in a program measures or estimates the following program features (Naik, 2018).

1. Number of external inputs
2. Number of external outputs
3. Number of user interactions/inquiries
4. Number of external interfaces,
5. Number of files used by the system.

These program features are also regarded as the information domain. To differentiate the complex feature with simple features the function point metric applies some weight to the listed information domains. The unadjusted function point count (UFC) is computed by multiplying the number of a given feature by its estimated weight for all features and finally summing products:

UFC=$\sum$(number of a given feature) $\times$ (weight for the given feature)

Object points are used as an alternate to function points. The number of object points is computed by the estimated weights of objects:

1. Separate screens that are displayed are counted as object points and a value of 1, 2 or 3 is assigned to them with respect to their complexity with 1 object point assigned as a value for a simple screen.
2. Reports that are produced are also counted as object points and value of 2, 5 or 8 are assigned to them with respect to their complexity with 2 object points as a value for a simple report.
3. All modules are also counted in object points that are developed to supplement the database programming code. Each of these modules are assigned a value of 10 object points.

The final code size is calculated by multiplying the number of function points and the estimated average number of lines of code (AVC) required for deploying a function point. Obviously organizations depends either on some historical data for assuming the LOC for each function point or by using the productivity metric of how many function points can be delivered by a staff member each month. The estimated code size is computed as follows:

CODE SIZE=AVC×UFC

Software Cost Estimation Techniques

Estimation is never an easy task; therefore few techniques are listed in the table 2 below that can be used for the estimation of the project (Keim et al, 2014). The management is interested in getting an early estimate of the software that is under development.

Each listed technique has its own merits and demerits and it is a known principle that if the estimate is within the range of plus/minus 25% of the actual outcome and an estimator can predict such efficiency in 75% of his all estimations then that estimator and estimate is considered good. This definition of good estimate is discussed in (Jarvenpaa, 1994). Please note that there can be different classification of software costing techniques then compared to the table which is stated above. We have kept things simple for basic understanding of the famous techniques, for more detailed classification and the reader can refer to the software cost estimation book by Steve McConell (Jarvenpaa, 1994).

Table 2. Software cost estimation techniques

Technique	Description
Algorithmic cost models	Relating some software metrics a mathematical model is developed to estimate the project cost
Expert judgment	Several experts on the proposed software development techniques and application domains are asked to estimate the project cost. The estimation process iterates until an agreed estimate is reached.
Estimation by previous projects	The cost of a new project is estimated by a completed project in the same application domain
Application of Parkinson's Law	Parkinson's Law states that work expands to fill the time available and the cost is determined by the resources used.
Pricing to win	The software cost is estimated by the price what the customer has available to spend on the project

Some Details of Algorithmic Cost Models

Algorithmic cost modeling uses a mathematical expression to predict project costs based on estimates of the project size, the number of software engineers, and other process and product factors (Naik, 2018). An algorithmic cost model can be developed by analyzing the costs and attributes of completed projects and finding the closest fit mathematical expression to actual project. In general, an algorithmic cost estimate for software cost can be expressed as:

$$EFFORT= A * SIZE^B * M$$

In this equation A is a constant factor that depends on local organizational practices and the type of software that is developed. Variable SIZE may be either the code size or the functionality of software expressed in function or object points. M is a multiplier made by combining process, product and development attributes, such as the dependability requirements for the software and the experience of the development team. The value of M is also known as the effort/environment adjustment factor (EAF). The EAF either increases the effort of decreases it. The exponential component B associated with the size estimate expresses the non-linearity of costs with project size. As the size of the software increases, extra costs are emerged. The value of exponent B usually lies between 1 and 1.5.

Now we have a basic understating of the software costing and estimation techniques, please note here the main purpose of this chapter is not to discuss the software costing and estimation techniques but to see how costing and estimation is applied along with the effects of CMM and Global software engineering. The next section discussed the CMMI perspective of the software costing and estimation.

CMMI PERSPECTIVE OF SOFTWARE COSTING AND ESTIMATION

The main purpose of this section is to analyze the connection between CMMI and the techniques that are used for the estimation of software. In this section we have tried to classify the costing and estimation techniques with respect to process areas of CMMI for the different levels.

Estimation Techniques for Level 1 of CMMI

At maturity level 1, processes are usually ad hoc and chaotic because the organizations don't have a stable environment for development. We know that success for such organization depends on the individual effort of individuals who are the star performers of an organization. The process itself is not defined so the success is not because of the define processes. These organizations end up creating products but the problem is they mostly exceed the time and allocated budget.

The best way to estimate software on Initial Level is to use LOC method as basic LOC method is simple and it is direct metric and therefore also easier to use. We have already discussed that at the initial level the companies do often exceed their budget due to the absence of proper process. Therefore it is best to use the LOC metric at this level of CMMI.

Estimation Techniques for Level 2 of CMMI

At maturity level 2, an organization has achieved all the key process areas of CMM level 2. It will not be wrong to state that at this level the organization have ensured that requirements are managed and that processes are planned performed, measured, and controlled. The process discipline reflected by maturity level 2 helps to ensure that existing practices are retained during times of stress. When these practices are in place, projects are performed and managed according to their documented plans (Wagner et al, 2018).

The best way to estimate software at the level 2 which is the managed Level is to use FP method because it decomposes the software in well defined functions and estimates accordingly.

Estimation Techniques for Level 3 of CMMI

At maturity level 3, an organization has achieved all the specific and generic goals of the key process areas which are assigned to maturity levels 2 and 3. At maturity level 3, processes are well characterized and understood, and are described in standards, procedures, tools, and methods (Vyas et al, 2018). A critical distinction between maturity level 2 and maturity level 3 is the scope of standards, process descriptions, and procedures, as at level three their scope is much wider than compared to the scope at level 2. At maturity level 2, the standards, process descriptions, and procedures may be quite different in each specific instance of the process (for example, on a particular project). At maturity level 3, the standards, process descriptions, and procedures for a project are tailored from the organization's set of standard processes to suit a particular project or organizational unit. A level three organization is much matured and generally specializes in the development of similar software systems that helps in much similar standardized procedures. COCOMO model with Function Point estimation is a good criterion to estimate cost at level 3 as at this stage companies can manage their input, output transaction and their transactions through proper documented procedures.

Estimation Techniques for Level 4 and 5 of CMMI

At maturity level 4 and 5, organizations collect project data for future use and it becomes historical data for upcoming projects that is why analogy based estimation is good for level 4 and level 5 as analogy based estimation is extensively used for very large projects. Estimation requires data and most accurate results can be acquired if project data that is the data of the current project is used for the estimation purpose. One limitation for using project data is that it can only be used in iterative development where the data of a previous iteration can be used for the estimation of later iterations. When the process models are less iterative then historical data can be used for the estimation of future projects. Historical data is the data of the previous projects. It is believed that estimation becomes easier at these maturity level as generally software development organizations specialize in similar type of software system development and generally because of similar types they are involved in similar sized software development which keeps away the problem of diseconomies of scale which comes into action when the project size increases then compared to previous estimations as simple ratio cannot work in such situations. This phenomenon is discussed in later sections of this chapter.

Table 3 summarizes the concepts learned in this section and shows the recommended estimation techniques that can be used at the different maturity levels of an organization. The next section talks more about GSE and identifies the limitations of CMMI in context of GSE.

Table 3. Recommended estimation techniques with respect to different maturity levels

CMMI Level	Recommended Software Estimation Techniques
Level 1: Initial	Basic Lines of Code technique because of its simplicity
Level 2: Repeatable	Function Points techniques as some form of decomposition is applied in CMMI level 2
Level 3: Defined	The very famous Constructive Cost Model (COCOMO), can be used with functions points or even LOC
Level 4: Capable	Analogy based techniques, based of previous data of the software. Proxy based techniques can also be used here.
Level 5: Efficient	Improved and better analogy based techniques that rely on project data along with historical data.

Global Software Engineering and Limitation of CMMI

As stated earlier, GSE is bit different from the traditional software engineering because the software is developed by different team members who are disbursed in different parts of the world. They have geographical, temporal and cultural distance; hence the traditional software process modelling techniques may not work. If we look at the software project management failures, the most common causes of the failure are identified as under (Dhir et al, 2019).

1. Insufficient end-user involvement
2. Poor communication among customers, developers, users and project managers
3. Poor Team Building Approaches
4. Unrealistic project goals
5. Inaccurate estimates of needed resources
6. Badly defined or incomplete system requirements and specifications
7. Poor reporting of the project's status
8. Poorly managed risks
9. Team competency
10. Inability to handle the project's complexity
11. Sloppy development practices
12. Stakeholder politics (e.g. absence of executive support, or politics between the customer and end-users)

A close look at the above mentioned points depicts that more than half of the causes are related to team building and management which is more complex in GSE hence it is logical to evaluate CMMI (the most widely used software modelling technique) in context of team handling in GSE. The use of planned processes to improve efficiency and productivity in software engineering has been appreciated for long (Leemans et al, 2018) but there have been arguments in favour of not implementing planned processes as well, suggesting that it decreases the efficiency of the software development process (Lacerda et al, 2018). We studied existing software process models to understand whether they can be helpful for GSE or not. We tried to analyse whether CMM in general and CMMI in particular would be able to accommodate the dynamism of GSE in the context of virtual teams.

CMM defines level of maturity along with key process areas and practices for process improvement but it does not provide any information regarding the effective implementation strategies and deployment of key practices. The CMM model does not discuss issues related to human nature, such as employee motivation etc. On the other hand, the structure of CMMI is based on the core components of CMM and talks about the integration of various process models. However, the CMMI model also does not provide detailed information about the implementation of key practices and team handling. It is observed that the support for the implementation of virtual teams is missing and therefore authors have proposed various ways to handle teams. By analyzing various team handling processes proposed for GSE, we describe here few general artefacts of team handling process for GSE with the assumption that team is comprised of members dispersed across the globe having geographical, temporal and cultural distances. Team management issues at individual locations can be handled with traditional process management techniques. The general artefacts for the team handling process in GSE are:

1.   Organisational and team structure
2.   Geographical distance allowed
3.   Cultural distance allowed
4.   Temporal distance allowed
5.   Team members competencies
6.   Communication strategy
7.   Task allocation approach
8.   Cooperation and coordination procedure
9.   Reporting procedure
10.   Risk management strategy

In the next section we have incorporated the CMMI levels and GSE to software costing and estimation case studies. We find some very interesting results about costing and estimation applied with GSE and CMMI.

APPLYING SOFTWARE COSTING AND ESTIMATION IN GLOBAL SOFTWARE ENGINEERING WITH CMMI PERSPECTIVE

There are certain known concepts which we have understood in this chapter. The core concepts are bulleted below so that you can refresh yourself:

• Global Software Engineering has numerous challenges and we have already discussed those challenges with respect to software project management, process modeling, team building and software costing and estimation.
• CMMI implements in improving the software development process and the greater maturity level we achieve the better predictability we have in our software process.

- Software costing and estimation is also a challenge for global software engineering and therefore we go through a case study for software costing and estimation using multiple techniques and see which technique helps us under which situation.

It is assumed that a software which is 10 times larger than some other software will require 10 times more effort than the smaller software or less than 10 times effort of the smaller software. In software development this is not the case as if the effort of the larger software would have been in proportion or lesser than the smaller software, this would have been the case of economies of scale which unfortunately does not apply to the software development. Here we have diseconomies of scale which means the effort of 10 tens larger software will be greater than 10 times effort of the smaller software. The reason we have diseconomies of scale in software development is because the communication path increases as squared functions with the increase in the number of team members for software. For example for a two member team there will only be one communication path but for a three member's team the communication paths will be three and for a four member team we will have six communication paths assuming that all team members will need to communicate with everyone else.

This phenomenon is also explained by Steve McConnell in his book (1999). The negativity of diseconomy of scale has also been discussed by (Mohrman et al, 1999) when the documentation of software increases.

Table 4 depicts the phenomenon of the diseconomies of scale.

It is evident from the table 4 above that productivity of staff member decreases when the

project size increases. There is good news about economies of scale and that is the mature organizations generally develop software which is of equal size and therefore the impact of diseconomies of scale is not evident on them. Unfortunately our study of two organizations reveled that irrespective of equal size of software the productivity decrease when the development organizations are geographically disbursed.

Table 4. Relation in between project size and productivity of staff members per month

Project Size (in Lines of Code)	Productivity of staff members(staff-month)
1000	400-500
10000	250-300
100000	150-200

CASE STUDIES AND RESULTS

We studied two organizations that have a fairly matured software development organization and it is between CMM level 3 and 4 and is involved in the process of global software engineering and gets software made through its development offices at multiple locations. We present the case studies for two different organizations which we have studied. One of the two organizations operates at three locations which are in Asia and the countries are Pakistan, Bangladesh and Sri Lanka. The other organization is spread in multiple continents and has development offices in Pakistan, USA and UK.

A very interesting factor here to analyze is the diseconomies of scale which is applicable to software costing and estimation. However after analyzing the two organizations we believe that the diseconomies of scale work differently for global software engineering and also when the organizations is more disbursed with respect to more geographical distance and more number of location offices.

We demonstrate the usage of the discussed principle about the diseconomy of scale applied to the global software engineering methodology identified few interesting results. The results proved that GSE in different locations with more cultural differences has more impact of the diseconomies of scale. Both the organizations we studied were involved in global software engineering and local software engineering. In this section of the chapter first we discuss the productivity of similar sized projects which were developed locally and did not involve the factors of global software engineering. As they are near the CMM level 4, their preferred costing technique was analogy based techniques; this was also discussed in section 6 of this chapter.

In analogy based technique, the organization A depends on historical data of previous projects for the development of new projects. We went through a payroll system that was made for local industry and was to be deployed in a company in Pakistan.

Table 5. The main use cases and actors of the payroll system

Use Case	Actors
Time Management	Hourly/Salaried Employee
Purchase Order Management	Commissioned Employee
Maintain Employee Information	Payroll Administrator
Run Payroll	Payroll Administrator

Problem Statement of the Payroll System

The table 5 shows that the company employs three types of employee, monthly salaried employees, hourly based employees and employees that work on commission. The hourly and monthly salaried employees enter information in the time management module,

whereas the commissioned employees enter information in the purchase management system so that the sales made by them could be recorded. The payroll administrator performs two major tasks, first is to maintain the employee information and the other is to run the payroll. After the payroll is run a message is sent to the respective employee that their salary is dispatched. It's a web based system and is developed in ASP .Net technology.

Case of Applying Historical Data to the Payroll System Developed Locally

In the case study for the purpose of effort calculation the organization has used the standard components technique. The main category of standard components is proxy based techniques. The proxy technique is used when you use something as a dummy for the actual effort calculation of software (Jarvenpaa et al, 1994). The core idea behind standard components is that you develop many programs that are architecturally similar to each other; you can use the standard components approach to estimate size. For estimation purpose, we have chart of historical data as depicted in table 6 to apply estimation using the standard components technique

The estimated components and total LOC for the payroll system are given in table 7

There was no historical data available for the business rule, that's why a value of 3000 LOC per component of business rules is used which can be seen in table 7. The estimate of the project was 32 KLOC, and the actual completion of the project was approximately 30 KLOC.

Table 6. Historical data for LOC per component

Standard Component	LOC per Component
Dynamic Web Pages	460
Static Web Pages	60
Database Tables	1350
Reports	450

Table 7. Estimate of the Payroll system developed locally

Type of Component	No. of Components in Payroll System	LOC/component	Total LOC for specific component
Dynamic Web Pages	12	460	5520
Static Web Pages	5	60	300
Database Tables	10	1350	13500
Reports	9	450	4050
Business Rules	3	3000	9000
Total LOC for the payroll system			**32370**

When we discussed the productivity metric used for this particular we were informed that productivity on such projects which had size of about 30 KLOC and were mainly information systems were about 1500 LOC persons-months. This means that an individual if deployed on such type of a project will be able to deliver 1500 Lines of code in a calendar month. When we used this productivity on the given case study the effort turned out to be:

Effort=*32370/1500 = 21.28 staff-months*

The effort of 21.28 staff months means that if a single developer works on this project then the project will be completed in 21 months approximately. Obviously the organization might have a team of 5 people working on this project wish would help to finish this sized software in 21/5 which will help in completing the software in approximately 4 calendar months. Obviously depending upon the supported concurrent activity we will never reach a stage where deploying 21 staff members will help in finishing the software in a single month because not all activities can be performed concurrently.

Productivity Metric for Global Software Engineering Organization A

When inquired about the productivity metric in case of GSE based development for organization A which only operated in three countries of Asia, we were informed that the productivity for 30 KLOC information systems decline from 1500 LOC to 1100 LOC. This actually increases the effort by 38 percent because the productivity for a similar sized software system developed through GSE by a company operating three offices in three different countries in the same continent the effort for 30 KLOC is:

Effort=32370/1100 = 29.42 staff-months

Percentage of Increased Effort When Similar Sized Software Was Developed Globally

The change in effort can be calculated by using the formula given below:

Percentage change in Effort=Change in Effort/Initial Effort * 100

Change in Effort=New Effort-Old Effort

Change in Effort= 29.42-21.28= 8.14

Percentage change in Effort=8.14/21.28*100 = 38.25%

Productivity Metric for Global Software Engineering Organization B

Initially we have already discussed that organization B operates in three countries of three different continents which were Asia, America and Europe and the countries were Pakistan, USA and UK.

When inquired about local development confined to a single country the productivity was about 1500 LOC per staff-month. The interesting thing to notice here is that when GSE based development was studied for organization B which operates in three countries of three different continents we identified that productivity metric for 30 KLOC information system was about 850 LOC. Putting the case of our studied payroll system we find that:

Effort= 32370/850 = 38.08 staff-months

The effort increased further from 29 staff-months to 38 staff-months when GSE comprised of multiple continents. The percentage from the local development case of organization A for the payroll system is given as under:

Percentage change in Effort=Change in Effort/Initial Effort * 100

Change in Effort=New Effort-Old Effort

Change in Effort= 38.08-21.28= 16.8

Percentage change in Effort=16.8/21.28*100 = 78.94%

For the multiple continents case the effort increased by 78.94%. This was tremendous increase in effort from the local development case. We also calculated the percentage change in effort for the two global development cases.

Percentage change in Effort=Change in Effort/Initial Effort * 100

Change in Effort=New Effort-Old Effort

Change in Effort= 38.08-29.42= 8.66

Percentage change in Effort=8.66/29.42*100 = 29.43%

SUMMARIZING THE CASE STUDIES

We summarize the case studies discussed in this section in the table 8.

The table 8 says it all; it creates an interesting relation between efforts of GSE based development and productivity of the team members. There is an inverse relation among the two factors. The more factors of GSE is applied to the development process with respect to cultural and geographical differences the effort of the software under development will increase and the productivity of people will decrease. Another interesting thing to notice here is that increase in effort does not always mean more development cost as monthly wages of staff members and operational cost of software development organizations varies in two to three times among developed and under developed countries.

CONCLUSION

We conclude the learning outcomes of this chapter in the points given below:

- When the development methodology changes from local development (which is within a single country) to global software engineering the effort of the software increases.

Table 8. Summary of the case studies

Software Development Methodology	Developed Software	Software Size	Software Effort	Productivity	Percentage change in Effort from local development
Local development	Payroll System Developed Locally (Information System)	30 KLOC	21.28 staff-months	1500 LOC per person-month	Not Applicable
GSE based development in single continent comprising three countries	Information Systems developed in multiple countries of same continent	30 KLOC	29.42 staff-months	1100 LOC per person-month	38.25%
GSE based development comprising three countries of three different continents	Information Systems developed in multiple countries of different continents	30 KLOC	38.08 staff-months	850 LOC per person-month	78.94%

- The increase in effort for GSE is similar to the concept of diseconomies of scale, but in the case of GSE diseconomies of scale is applied when number of development countries for single software (under development) increases.
- The more global you get in terms of number of countries or same number of countries but different cultures that is different continents the effort will always increase with respect to changing cultures.
- Increase in effort does not always mean more development cost as monthly wages fluctuates even three to four times between under developed countries and developed countries for people belonging to almost similar skill sets. The other reason is operational cost also vary two to three times among different countries.
- The more mature an organization is the better data they have at their disposal for achieving predictability in software process.
- Mature organizations use better practices for software costing and estimation and better techniques than compared to less matured organizations.

REFERENCES

Agerfalk, P. J., Fitzgerald, B., & Holmstrom Olsson, H. (2005). *A framework for considering opportunities and threats in distributed software development*. Academic Press.

Boehm, B. W., Madachy, R., & Steece, B. (2000). Software cost estimation with Cocomo II with Cdrom. Upper Saddle River, NJ: Prentice Hall PTR.

Carmel, E. (1999). *Global Software Teams: Collaboration Across Borders and Time Zones*. Saddle River, NJ: Prentice Hall.

Carmel, E., & Tjia, P. (2005). *Offshoring Information Technology: Sourcing and Outsourcing to a Global Workforce*. Cambridge, UK: Cambridge University Press. doi:10.1017/CBO9780511541193

Chrissis, M. B., Konrad, M., & Shrum, S. (2003). CMMI guidlines for process integration and product improvement. Boston, MA: Addison-Wesley Longman Publishing.

Crow, G., & Muthuswamy, B. (2003). International outsourcing in the information technology industry: Trends and implications. *Communications of the International Information Management Association*, *3*(1), 25–34.

Curtis, B., Kellner, M. I., & Over, J. (1992). Process modeling. *Communications of the ACM*, *35*(9), 75–90. doi:10.1145/130994.130998

Davidow, W. H., & Malone, M. S. (1992). *The Virtual Corporation*. New York, NY: Edward Brulingame Books/Harper Business.

Dhir, S., Kumar, D., & Singh, V. B. (2019). Success and Failure Factors that Impact on Project Implementation using Agile Software Development Methodology. In *Software Engineering* (pp. 647–654). Singapore: Springer. doi:10.1007/978-981-10-8848-3_62

Herbsleb, J. D., & Mockus, A. (2003). An empirical study of speed and communication in globally distributed software development. *IEEE Transactions on Software Engineering*, *29*(6), 481–494. doi:10.1109/TSE.2003.1205177

Jarvenpaa, S. L., & Ives, B. (1994). The global network organization of the future: Information management opportunities and challenges. *Journal of Management Science and Information Systems*, *10*(4), 25–57. doi:10.1080/07421222.1994.11518019

Keim, Y., Bhardwaj, M., Saroop, S., & Tandon, A. (2014). Software cost estimation models and techniques: A survey. *International Journal of Engineering*, *3*(2).

Kotlarsky, J., & Oshri, I. (2005). Social ties, knowledge sharing and successful collaboration in globally distributed system development projects. *European Journal of Information Systems*, *14*(1), 37–48. doi:10.1057/palgrave.ejis.3000520

Lacerda, T. C., & von Wangenheim, C. G. (2018). Systematic literature review of usability capability/maturity models. *Computer Standards & Interfaces*, *55*, 95–105. doi:10.1016/j.csi.2017.06.001

Leemans, M., Van Der Aalst, W. M., Van Den Brand, M. G., & et al, . (2018, September). Software Process Analysis Methodology–A Methodology Based on Lessons Learned in Embracing Legacy Software. In *2018 IEEE International Conference on Software Maintenance and Evolution (ICSME)* (pp. 665-674). Piscataway, NJ: IEEE. 10.1109/ICSME.2018.00076

Mohrman, S. A. (1999). The context for geographically dispersed teams and networks. In C. L. Cooper & D. M. Rousseau (Eds.), *The Virtual Organization (Trends in Organizational Behaviour)* 6, (pp. 63–80). Chichester, UK: John Wiley & Sons.

Naik, P. (2018). *Insights on Algorithmic and Non-algorithmic Cost Estimation Approaches Used by Current Software Industries across India*. Academic Press.

Nidiffer, K. E., & Dolan, D. (2005). Evolving distributed project management. *IEEE Software*, *22*(5), 63–72. doi:10.1109/MS.2005.120

O'Brien, J. A. (2002). *Management Information Systems – Managing Information Technology in the Business Enterprise* (6th ed.). New York, NY: McGraw Hill Irwin.

Paulk, M. C., Curtis, B., Chrissis, M. B., & Weber, C. V. (1993). Capability maturity model, version 1.1. *IEEE Software*, *10*(4), 18–27. doi:10.1109/52.219617

Powell, A., Piccoli, G., & Ives, B. (2004). Virtual teams: A review of current literature and direction for future research. *The Data Base for Advances in Information Systems*, *35*(1), 6–36. doi:10.1145/968464.968467

Prikladnicki, R., Audy, J. L. N., & Evaristo, R. (2003). Global software development in practice, lessons learned. *Software Process Improvement and Practice*, *8*(4), 267–279. doi:10.1002pip.188

Sarker, S., & Sahay, S. (2004). Implications of space and time for distributed work: An interpretive study of US–Norwegian systems development teams. *European Journal of Information Systems*, *13*(1), 3–20. doi:10.1057/palgrave.ejis.3000485

Team, C. P. (2006). *CMMI for Development, version 1.2*. Academic Press.

Toaff, S. S. (2005). Don't play with "mouths of fire" and other lessons of global software development. *Cutter IT Journal, 15*(11), 23–28.

Trendowicz, A. (2013). Software Cost Estimation, Benchmarking, and Risk Assessment: The Software Decision-Makers' Guide to Predictable Software Development. Berlin, Germany: Springer Science & Business Media. doi:10.1007/978-3-642-30764-5

Vyas, M., Bohra, A., Lamba, C. S., & Vyas, A. (2018). *A Review on Software Cost and Effort Estimation Techniques for Agile Development Process*. Academic Press.

Wagner, S., & Ruhe, M. (2018). *A systematic review of productivity factors in software development*. Academic Press.

Chapter 12
Scenario Based Test Case Generation Using Activity Diagram and Action Semantics

Manzoor Ahmed Hashmani
University Technology PETRONAS, Malaysia

Maryam Zaffar
University Technology PETRONAS, Malaysia

Reham Ejaz
NUST College of Electrical and Mechanical Engineering, Pakistan

ABSTRACT

Scenario is an account of description of user interaction with the system, presented in a sequence. They can be represented using unified modeling language (UML) diagrams such as use case diagram, state charts, activity diagrams etc. Scenario-based testing can be performed at higher abstraction level using the design diagrams. In this work activity diagrams are used which are annotated with action semantics to test scenario dependencies. The action semantics make activity diagram executable and the dependencies between multiple scenarios can be seen at execution level. The authors intend to propose an approach for scenario dependency testing. Dependency graphs will be then generated against all the dependencies present on activity diagram under test. The test paths extracted from these dependency graphs help in testing.

DOI: 10.4018/978-1-5225-9448-2.ch012

INTRODUCTION

Scenarios are used to elicit document and validate requirements. Scenario is a narrative description of the system use, basically, they capture the functionality of the system. A system is typically represented by a number of scenarios that cover the system functionality in detail. One of the ways is to use natural language scenarios to capture, document and validate requirements. These scenarios improve communication between different groups involved in system development, and also help the software developers in the understanding of the application domain (Ryser and Glinz, 2000).

For the generation of test cases through Scenarios different UML artifacts are used to represent system specification like use cases (Ryser and Glinz.,1999), (Barnett et al., 2004), (Briand et al.,2002), (Sarma and Mall, 2007), (Nebut et al., 2006), sequence diagram (Sarma and Mall, 2007), Interaction diagram (Najala et al., 2007) and UML activity diagram (Chandler et al., 2007), (Xu et al., 2005) and (Xiaqing et al., 2004). Presenting Scenarios in UML diagram makes the derivation of test cases in an easy way.

The executable UML helps in executing the UML model directly into code; it removes the gap between the implementation and the design models. In the executable model, some set of rules are defined to gather the UML elements for a particular purpose. Action semantics define the action and working of the action (Jiang et al., 2007). The action language is basically used to make the UML models executable. Many languages like small, Tall, Bridge point, +cal (Perseil et al., 2008), pal (jiang et al., 2007), and OCL (Motogna et al., 2008) are used to describe the actions.OCL defines constraint and requirements in the form of invariants, pre-post conditions (Montogana et al., 2008).

In this work, we intend to use the UML activity diagram decorated with action semantics for scenario-based testing. Our proposed work describes in detail the dependency analysis for scenario and on the basis of dependencies test cases are generated. A comprehensive survey on scenario-based testing approaches are mentioned in the work.

LITERATURE REVIEW

Scenario-based testing using functional regression testing is proposed by Sai *et al* (2002). The technique defines the scenario based functional regression testing approach, in which test scenario which is the semi-formal representation of system are represented through a template model using end-to-end(E2E) integration testing.

The E2E testing life cycle consists of test planning, test design, and test execution procedures. E2E test includes thin threads and condition trees as the basis for a test scenario, these trees help to produce the complex scenario. And inputs for tests are also generated by these test scenarios by applying random, partition and stress testing criteria's. Test scenario model is basically represented by three perspectives, Test scenario specification, dependencies between test scenarios and traceability to other software artifacts by test dependency information. Effected test scenarios are generated through test slicing algorithm and traceability information gives all associated test scenarios. After the generation of test cases for regression testing, further traceability information is also used for Ripple effect analysis (REA), direct and in -direct scenarios are obtained after a change and from there a set of test cases are obtained. Here test scenarios are detailed test requirements and describe all normal and abnormal inputs. A template for describing test scenarios is presented by the technique, which contains the sections of general, policy Input/output, execution, condition linkage and other. All these sections have attributes as well as representation. These test scenarios could be represented through a tree where commonalities can be easily detected. After the test scenario representation dependency analysis is performed. The analysis lists the functional in/output, persistent data, execution, and condition. Dependence traceability analysis is done through test scenarios. Template linkage section has the requirements attributes and test scripts, which stores all test scenarios. Template linkage affect the mapping of requirement test scenarios and generation of test cases. The approach uses Ripple Effect Analysis (REA), used to remove all side effects caused by the changes. It detects direct and indirectly affected scenarios, to receive the set of test cases from regression testing. The REA process initially checks the change request and identifies all test scenarios through traceability analysis, all effected components are identified and test scenarios are revalidated to get all the affected test scenarios by the change. Slicing algorithm is applied and a selected slicing criterion is used, to get the entire set of attributes. The subset attributes and hybrid approach for dependent test scenarios are applied. After getting test scenarios traceability analysis is done which gives a set of software components affected test scenarios and test cases corresponding to that affected test scenarios (Sai et al., 2002).

Activity Based Testing Approaches

A lot of work is done on Scenario-based testing using an activity diagram. Researchers have adopted different techniques to derive test cases from an activity diagram. Following is a brief discussion of different activity based testing technique proposed by different researchers.

Briand et al. (2002) have proposed a TOTEM system, test methodology. The approach is applied to the artifacts used in the analysis development stage. The scenarios are represented by use cases and their description. The sequential dependencies of use cases are represented by the UML activity diagram. The vertices, edges, join and fork describes use case, sequential dependencies in use cases and independent use cases simultaneously. The dependencies are determined by using actual parameters on an activity diagram. The activity diagram is traversed by depth-first search, to generate use case sequence in order to retrieve test requirements. In the second part of the proposed approach use case scenarios are represented by Interaction diagrams, like sequence diagram. Sequence diagrams are expressed in the form of regular expressions and labeled with operations in order to automate it. The guard conditions are expressed in OCL. Then operation sequence, realization condition, and test oracles are generated. For every use case, a transition table is constructed in order to get data for test cases.

Linzhang et al. (2004) approach use a gray box method for test case generation through UML model. In this approach, gray box method is used that is the combination of white box and black box testing. It covers the defects covered by the other two testing methodologies. At first, the activity diagram is defined with all constructs, and then it is annotated with all information of system under test. All the executing paths in an activity diagram are testing scenarios in which from the initial to final activity state transition including the guard condition and sequence of control is present but only a subset of execution paths are retrieved through the traversal of AD, by depth-first search method. To avoid exhaustive testing basic path coverage criteria is being used. generator algorithm is used to generate test scenarios from the activity diagram, through that current state set and transition of AD are retrieved for every test scenarios. So that algorithm results in all the test scenarios from AD. Then by category portioning all input, output parameter values are retrieved, and for every test scenario, a test case is generated to support the approach a tool UMLTGF is also used, which is used to parse the activity diagram, takes the specification of AD then generate test cases. That generator consists of a test case generator and test case manager. The approach easily helps to describe the defects in the design model during the design phase.

To prioritize test cases for scenarios-based testing using activity diagram Li et al. (2005) proposes a technique. Anti Ant like agents is used for the generation of thin threads. ACO algorithm is being used to generate three trees, thin thread, conditioned, and data object tree through the traversal of activity directed graph dependencies. Thin threads are extracted from system level activity diagram. These thin threads are suitable for risk, dependency, traceability, coverage, and competence analysis. Whereas data object tree captures the important content dependent relationship between the thin threads. The conditions in the condition tree are associated with sub-scenarios of this thread in the approach.

Lam et al. (2005) propose an approach to automatically derive usage scenarios from the activity diagram. An AD2US process is proposed which is divided into three steps. Firstly modeling and exporting, in which Poseidon 2.4.1 used to model UML activity diagram, that is suitable for XMI format exporting so that in that step all the data is exported. Secondly, data capturing and storing is done, in that exported diagram is created to DOM (Document Object Model) parser. In the start of the document, activity diagram identifier, name and graphical metadata model is placed. The graphical section contains all identifier, nodes and edges details, whereas OCL is present at the end. The DOM parser moves around the document when some activity diagram is located, a suitable activity graph is allocated to it and all elements of the activity graph are stored in a vector. All information for the activity diagram is captured and every activity diagram is captured and stored and also all associations are captured. A modified depth-first search algorithm is proposed in which all elements of the activity diagram are encountered. All elements are tagged as undiscovered, discovered and finished. All elements are initialized with undiscovered and when moved towards the vector tagged as discovered then its type is tested then for edges target-id is tested. When the AD traverses completed and finished is tagged, the output is a scenario. For activity diagram, there is an XML format scenarios output. The technique is explained through making its activity diagram, Sequence of scenario are also identified by tagging elements.

Mingsong *et al.* (2006) propose an approach to derive the test cases from UML activity diagram. Firstly the random test cases are generated from an under test java program. Then test cases are generated from the activity diagram of the same program by using basic path coverage criteria, and irrelevant test cases are ignored by comparing these test cases with Java program generated random test cases. So that approach is used to check the consistency between specifications and corresponding programs.

Hyungchoul et al. (2007) propose an approach by using an activity diagram to present the system specification. Then an Input/Output explicit activity diagram (IOAD) is generated. Two types of actions Send Signal and Accept Event Action are presented on the activity diagram. That IOAD is converted into a directed graph by using Single Stimulus Principle. The test cases are generated through that graph by using All Path Coverage Criteria.

Chandler et al. (2007) propose an approach that uses the usage scenarios from activity diagrams for testing. The focus of the approach is on the concurrent region, having looping and skipping constraints. A status variable is defined on vertices and edges in order to avoid the unlimited traversal by using Depth-first search and Breadth First Search. Each looping guard condition is traversed twice, whereas, in nested looping constructs, each internal looping constructs are traversed at least twice. An algorithm is also defined in the approach, which uses the method getNextAD (AD), to get possible usage scenarios. The concurrent region description is extended in order to get the usage scenario from looping and skipping constructs. The number of scenarios derived from the concurrent regions is calculated as the product of the number of outgoing edges and branches. The approach is supported by the case study of Trouble-Ticket system.

Use case sequencing constructs are used by Some (2007). The proposed approach handles the use case sequential, execution, alternative execution, and concurrent execution. Two constructs of the use case are defined which specifies which use case need to proceed a use case and how these use cases are synchronized. Whereas the second construct specifies that which use cases are enabled by a use case and how they are concurrently executed. These use cases sequencing constructs are mapped on a UML activity diagram to check the consistency; it is helpful in depicting sequencing relations from use case improved with sequencing constructs.

Kundu et al. (2009) used an activity diagram to generate the test cases. The approach consists of three steps. Firstly the scenario is represented in the form of an activity diagram and presented with a higher level of abstraction. The activity diagram is presented with information in order to generate necessary test information. Secondly, the activity diagram is converted into an activity graph which is a directed graph, having ten different types of nodes. The nodes of the activity graph represent constructs and edges show the flow in the activity diagram. The mapping rules are defined in the approach in order to generate the nodes from the nodes of the activity diagram, whereas edges of the activity graph are derived from one-to-one mapping from the edges between two nodes. Every node in the activity graph store data in Node Description Table (NDT). Thirdly the test cases are generated from the activity graph. To generate test cases fault in the decision, loop and synchronization are considered, and activity path coverage criteria are used to cover the appropriate elements for test case design. The concurrent and non-concurrent activity paths are considered, using the definition of persistence relation path selection done. The minimal loop testing avoids path explosion. Depth-first search and Breath first search is used to traverse the activity graph. Generate Activity Paths algorithm is used to generate the activity paths. At the end test cases are generated, these test cases consist of four components, Sequence of branch conditions for test inputs, and Activity sequence, Object state changes, and object created used to provide the expected behaviors(output)for test cases Kundu et al. (2009).

Test case generation through activity diagram applying Conditioned Slicing technique proposed by Ray et al. (2009) minimizes the test cases generated while deriving all use full test cases. Flow dependency graph (FDG) is derived through an activity diagram. Then on each predicate node of FDG Conditioned Slicing is applied. Test cases are generated corresponding to each slice. ConSUS slicing tool is used, to test the dependent paths in FDG. According to the approach input domain and slicing, FDG is continuously portioned until simple paths are extracted. These simple paths automatically generate test data, to test the program by ConSUS tool.

Dependencies among activities at run time are discussed by Samuel et al. (2009). FDG is generated through the Activity Diagram. Slices are extracted through FDG using edge marking method. Test data is automatically generated through slices by using the minimization method. For reducing both validation and specification effort Chen et al. (2008) propose a methodology of generating test cases using activity diagram. Coverage data is extracted from an activity diagram. Three fault models Activity, Transition, and Key path fault model are generated. These fault models then check the properties on formal model NUSMV and help in generating test cases.

Test scenarios are automatically derived using an activity diagram. Xu et al. (2005) propose an approach through which an activity diagram is firstly converted into a scenario tree, where every node of a tree presents elements of an activity diagram. An algorithm using anti-ant like agent is proposed to derive test cases from scenario tree. Ant works like bacteria and explores the activity diagram from the initial node to the final node. The approach is automated through TSGAD.

Activity Based Testing Approaches

In this section, we discuss the evaluation parameters for the approaches discussed so far. Following is the discussion on the evaluation parameters. Activity hypergraph, activity graph, flow dependency graph are the intermediate model used by various approaches.

Intermediate Form

This criterion gives information about the model which is derived from the activity diagram. The intermediate model provides a way to easily extract the test cases. Activity Graph (Kundu et al., 2009), Activity HyperGraph (Bai et al., 2004) and Flow Dependency graph are the intermediates used in the proposed techniques.

Traversal Criteria

This criterion tells that which type of searching algorithm is used to traverse the paths to get all possible test paths. DFS (Lizhang et al., 2004) and BFS (Kundu et al., 2009) is used to traverse the model in activity based testing.

Action Language

This criterion shows that whether the action language is used on the activity diagram or not to make the diagram executable. Writing actions in a defined syntax makes the action easily readable. The parser of action languages actually helps in reading the actions from a model under discussion. Little work is done on the models having actions. OCL (Lam et al 2005), (Briand et al 2002), and (Chandler et al 2005) is used an action language on an activity diagram.

Presentation of Dependencies on an Activity Diagram

The criterion gives information that whether the testing is done by keeping the paths dependencies on focus. Sequential Dependency (Bai et al., 2004) Control Dependency (Ray et al., 2009) and Content dependency (Briand et al., 2002) are presented in the existing techniques.

Resolving Issue

This criterion describes the main issues resolved by the techniques. Likewise to avoid path explosion (Kundu et al., 2009) and testing cluster level behavior (Philip et al., 2009) are one of the issues resolved by the existing techniques. Each proposed technique tries to overcome the issues remain unsolved by the previous work.

Data for Test Cases

This criterion explains what type of test data is used to derive all possible test cases. Node Description scenario test table (D.Kundu et al., 2009), Decision Table (L.Briand et al., 2002) are used to get test data for the test cases. This storage helps to make efficient test cases.

Coverage Criteria

Coverage criteria show the extent to which a model is being covered by the testing technique. This criterion gives information about the coverage criteria used within the given technique. Basic Path Coverage Criteria (W.Lizhang et al., 2004) and Activity Path Coverage Criteria (D.Kundu et al ., 2009) are the examples of the coverage criteria used to traverse for activity based testing.

Case Study

This criterion tells that the technique is provided with the help of a case study or not. Library System (Chandler et al., 2007), Trouble Ticket System (Chandler et al., 2009), ATM (Ray et al., 2009), and Invoice system (Kim et al., 2007) are the case studies taken by existing techniques.

Tool Support

The criterion tells that the tool is developed for the technique or not. Like (Briand et al., 2002) has tool support, it is automated.

Limitations in Existing Work

Many limitations are identified in the existing work on the basis of the knowledge gained from literature review. No work is done on adding actions on an activity diagram. When activity diagram is used as an input artifact for scenario-based testing then dependencies between different nodes are not identified; only traversal methods are used to generate the all possible test paths. All the details are added on the model in only one step, there is no approach to which actions are added on each step, to make it executable. No work is done to add actions to the activity diagram, by using some specific action language. The proposed technique covers all the limitations identified form the literature and propose a solution for them.

METHOD

Scenario-based testing using an activity diagram and action semantics is presented in this chapter. An activity diagram is used as an input artifact in the proposed technique, as it is good at describing the flow of control. In existing work, actions are not mentioned in the activity diagram to make it executable, so the proposed technique uses actions to make the activity diagram executable. The dependencies between the activity nodes are clear according to the proposed approach. In the proposed approach, the action makes the dependencies very clear. These dependencies are not described in the existing works. These dependencies reduce the redundant derivation of test cases and also generate all dependent paths. The proposed technique covers all the limitations identified form the literature and propose a solution for them.

Table 1.

Parameters / Techniques	Traversal criteria for activity diagram	Intermediate Representation	Actions on activity diagram	Action Language	Presentation of dependencies on AD	Resolving issue	Data for Test Cases	Coverage criteria	Tool Support	Case Study
Stephane et al 2007	NO	Use Case Sequencing Constraints	NO	NO	NO	NO	NO	NO	NO	NO
Lizhang et al 2004	DFS	Test scenarios from the execution paths of AD	NO	NO	NO	Finite set of test scenarios	Action Sequence, Guard conditions	Basic Path Coverage Criteria	UMLTG	NO
Kundu et al 2009	BFS(For sub tree) and DFS	Activity Graph	NO	NO	NO	Path Explosion	Node Description scenario testable(	Activity Path Coverage criteria	NO	NO
R.Chandler et al 2007	DFS	Usage scenario	YES	NO	NO	Skipping and Looping constructs	-	Path, condition & data coverage	NO	Trouble-Ticket System
Chen et al 2006	DFS	Activity diagram and corresponding Java program	NO	NO	NO	Checking Consistency among specification and corresponding program	NO	Activity Coverage, Transition Coverage, Simple Path Coverage	AGTCG	NO
Lam et al. 2005	Modified DFS	Activity Graph	YES	OCL	NO	To include control and data flow coverage for the test suite	Vector	No	NO	NO
Briand et al 2002	DFS	Use Case Sequences	YES	OCL	Sequential Dependencies on Edges (By adding actual parameters on use cases)	Use case Sequences	Decision Table		NO	TOTEM/ Library System
Ray et al. 2009	Conditioned Slicing	Flow dependency graph	NO	NO	Control Dependency	Analyzing run time behavior of the system	Slice Domain	High Path Coverage Criterion	ConSUS Slicing Tool	ATM
Philip et al 2009	Edge Marking Method	FDG	NO	NO	YES	Testing Cluster level behavior	Predicate Function	Path Coverage	UTG	ATM
B.N.Biswal et al 2008	Modified DFS	Test scenarios	NO	NO	NO	Complicacy of the nested fork and join	Objects of a sequence diagram for each	Path coverage criteria	TC-ASEC	ATM

Proposed Approach

In the proposed approach the system specification is presented through the UML activity diagram. The activity diagram is annotated with actions. The activity diagram is decorated with Link action, Call action, Broad cast action, Send signal action. The activity diagram with actions helps in analyzing scenario dependencies. Actions make the activity diagram executable. After traversing the activity diagram the dependency graphs are generated. Test paths are generated through these dependency graphs. To avoid the exhaustive testing redundant test paths are ignored. So these test paths give the test cases that need to be tested. The flow chart of the proposed approach is given in Figure 1.

Scenario Specification

Scenarios are used to depict the specifications. The informal method is mostly used to describe the scenarios. A scenario depicts the specifications of the system. A scenario describes the system with one perspective.

Figure 1. The flow of the proposed approach

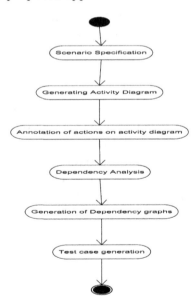

Generating Activity Diagram

The proposed technique uses an activity diagram as an input artifact for scenario-based testing. In the proposed approach two components vertex and edges are in focus. The activity diagram clearly describes the flow of control.

Representing Actions on Activity Diagram

Actions are applied to an activity diagram to develop an executable model. Actions defined in UML action semantics are of various types. In the proposed approach call action, send signal action, broadcast signal action, accept event action, and link action is used to make the executable activity diagram. The activity diagram is analyzed first, and then all the actions according to the suitable conditions are added on it. The edge between each node is decorated with some action.

Dependency Analysis

The proposed approach work on the analysis of dependencies between different paths of input artifact activity diagram. On the basis of actions, the dependencies are derived. Link dependency, call dependency, signal dependency, operational dependency. The proposed technique also describes the definitions of the dependencies shown on the activity diagram due to the decoration of actions. The above-mentioned dependencies on an activity diagram are explained as follows.

Call Dependency

In an activity diagram AD, when siblings {ni1,……..} of a node nj does not start their execution until the node nj performs the call action. Such type of dependency between two nodes is called call dependency. The node nj may have one or more siblings. Call action calls an operation without specifying the object on which it is called. Call dependency have a subtype Call Operation Dependency. When two nodes are connected with an edge having call operation action, then such type of dependency between the two nodes is called call operation dependency. The call operation action is a subtype of call action. So that the actions on the edges of the activity diagram make the dependency analysis easy.

Create Link Dependency

In an activity diagram AD, when the execution of two nodes say ni and nj depends on the create link action on the edge between these nodes. Such type of dependency between the nodes is called create link dependency. Create link action creates a link by writing a link object. Create link dependency has a subtype to destroying link dependency. In Destroy link dependency the execution of two nodes ni and nj are dependent on the destroy link action on the edge between the nodes ni and nj.

Send Signal Dependency

When two nodes in an activity diagram AD, are connected in such a way that edge between the two nodes say ni and nj contains send signal action, then such type of dependency between the nodes is called send signal dependency. Send signal action sends a signal to the target object, which may in turn trigger some event.

Broadcast Signal Dependency

Let ni and nj be the two nodes in an activity diagram AD and ek is an edge between ni and nj, if the execution of ni and nj depends on the broadcast signal action present on ek, then such type of dependency between the nodes ni and nj is called broadcast signal dependency. The broadcast signal action transmits a signal object to the target objects, and on receiving a signal object the target may cause triggering some activity.

Accept Event Dependency

Let ni and nj are the two nodes in an activity diagram AD, and ek be the edge between ni and nj if the execution of ni and nj depends on the accept event action annotated on edge ek, then such type of dependency between the nodes ni and nj is called accept event dependency. Accept event action is a basic action that waits for an event to occur. The event occurring is specified by the trigger.

Generation of Dependency Graphs

Definitions of dependencies on the basis of actions help in analyzing the dependent paths. All the dependent paths on an activity diagram are separated. The dependent paths graphs are then generated. Keeping the track of each dependent path the graphs are generated.

Generating Test Cases

The proposed approach uses transition coverage criteria to traverse the dependency graphs. All dependent paths help in giving the all possible test cases. To avoid the redundancy in test cases the repetitive dependent paths are eliminated. Like if the path of two dependencies is the same, then it is considered only once.

Algorithm for Storing in a Queue

Following is a step by step algorithm for storing actions in a queue.

```
Create_Action_Queues(G)
lstatus   ←  cstatus ←  sstatus ←  costatus ← ulstatus ←
bcstatus ← aestatus ← false
1. For each edge e € edge[G]
2. do
3.          If (e.name = = "link")
4.                  Enqueue (Qlink, e.source)
5.                  Enqueue (Qlink,e.target)
6.              If lstatus = =false
7.                      Enqueue(QtempActions, "Link")
8.                      lstatus ← true
 9.          Else if (e.name = = "call")
10.             Enqueue (Qcall, e.source)
11.             Enqueue (Qcall,e.target)
12.             If cstatus = = false
13.                     Enqueue(QtempActions, "call")
14.                     cstatus ← true
 15.          Else if (e.name = ="signal")
16.             Enqueue (Qsignal, e.source)
17.             Enqueue (Qsignal,e.target)
18.             If sstatus = = false
 19.                    Enqueue(QtempActions, "signal")
20.                     sstatus ← true
21.         Else if (e.name = = "call operation")
22.             Enqueue (Qcoperation, e.source)
23.             Enqueue (Qcoperation,e.target)
24.             if costatus = = false
25.                     Enqueue(QtempActions,
"calloperation")
26.                     costatus ← true
 27.         Else if (e.name = = "unlink")
28.             Enqueue (Qunlink, e.source)
29.             Enqueue (Qunlink, e.target)
```

```
30.                     if ulstatus = = false
31.                             Enqueue(QtempActions, "unlink")
32.                         ulstatus ← true
33.          else if (e.name = = "Broadcast signal")
34.              Enqueue (Qbcast, e.source)
35.              Enqueue (Qbcast, e.target)
36.              if bcstatus = = false
37.                          Enqueue(QtempActions, "Broadcast
signal")
38.                     bcstatus ← true
39.            else if (e.name = = "Accept Event action")
40.                Enqueue (Qaevent, e.source)
41.              Enqueue (Qaevent, e.target)
42.              if aestatus = = false
43.                          Enqueue(QtempActions, "accept
event")
44.                     aestatus ← true
```

Algorithm for Creating Paths for Actions Stored in Queue

Following are the steps to create paths for actions.

```
Create_Paths(QActions)
1        while QActions ≠ ɸ
2        do
3                u ← Dequeue(QActions)
4                if (u = = "Link")
5                        C_Paths(QLink, "Link")
6                else if (u = = "Call")
7                        C_Paths(QCall, "Call")
8                else if (u = = "Signal")
9                        C_Paths(QSignal, "Signal")
10              else if (u = = "Call Operation")
11                      C_Paths(QCoperation, "Call
Operation")
12              else if (u = = "Unlink")
13                      C_Paths(Qunlink, "Unlink")
14              else if (u = = "Broadcast signal")
15                      C_Paths(Qbcast, "Broadcast signal")
```

311

```
16                      else if (u = = "Accept event")
17                            C_Paths(Qaevent, "Accept event")
```

The above algorithm creates paths for all the actions present in the temporary queue of actions i.e. QActions. It passes on the name of the desired queue to another function C_Paths where actually paths are created against the queue passed onto it.

Algorithm for Tracing Action Paths

```
C_Paths(Q, str)
1          if Q ≠ Φ
2      Enqueue(CopyQ, Dequeue(Q))      ▶copying starting edge as it
is.
3                      Enqueue(CopyQ, Dequeue(Q))
4          if Q.size > 2
5          While Q ≠ Φ
6          do
7                      s ← Q[front]
8                  if s = = CopyQ[tail] && s != TargetNode.id
9                          Dequeue(Q)
10                          Enqueue(CopyQ, Dequeue(Q))
11              Else
12                          eid ← edge.id where CopyQ[tail] = =
edge.source
13                      if   eid.target != TargetNode.id
14                              Enqueue(CopyQ, eid.target)
15                      else
16                                  Enqueue(CopyQ, eid.
target)
17                              Status ← true
18                              While status = = true
19                              do      if   edge.name !=
str   where CopyQ[tail] = = edge.target
        20
Dequeue(CopyQ)
21                                          else
22                                          Status ←
false
```

```
23                                                              Print_
Path(CopyQ)
24                                  C_Paths(Q)
25        else
26                    Print_Paths(Q)
```

The above algorithm reads a queue and traces out possible action paths from it. In line 2-3 the first two elements of the queue are copied into a new queue CopyQ. If the size of the queue is equal to 2 then the elements are printed out. If the size is greater than 2 then following is done:

An element of the queue is inspected if it is equal to the last element present in the CopyQ then the next element present in the queue is inserted into the CopyQ as in line 12 the id of the edge whose source is equal to the last element of CopyQ id placed in eid. If eid is not equal to the target node then the target of eid is placed in the CopyQ as in 14. else if the target node is reached we have to place it in the CopyQ and check all the last entries if any of those do not contain the corresponding action then they are removed from the CopyQ (shown in $18 - 22$). Then the elements of CopyQ are printed and the remaining Q is passed to the same function C_paths to go through the same process.

Above algorithm of figure 2 prints the elements of queue passed in other words the paths

RESULTS AND DISCUSSION

ATM Case Study

The proposed approach is explained with the help of an example. The functionality of withdrawing money from ATM is taken as an example. The user needs to enter the access code first and in case of failure; he can input the access code again. The operation will abort if the access code is wrong in both cases. If the input access

Figure 2. Algorithm for printing test paths

```
Print_Path(Q)
1        While    Q ≠ φ
2        do
3                    Print Dequeue(Q)
```

code is right, the user will enter the amount of the money he wants to withdraw. At the same time, in order to print the receipt, the printer will be warmed. Once the ATM decides whether there is enough money the user can withdraw, it provides cash and generates the information of this withdraw operation. Finally, the printer will print a receipt.

The activity diagram is created with the help of the specifications. UML action semantics are applied using the help of action language ASL. Link action, Send signal Action, Broadcast signal Action, Call operation Action, call the action, and destroy action is applied on an activity diagram. Each transition is decorated with possible action. The executable model thus represents all the dependencies. Link action is present on the transition between verifying access code (node) and decision node. The decision node is dependent on the Link action. Until the link action is not executed the control does not come towards the decision node. The actions on the activity diagram with the help of an action semantic language are presented on Figure 3.

Figure 3. Activity diagram of cash withdrawal from ATM with actions

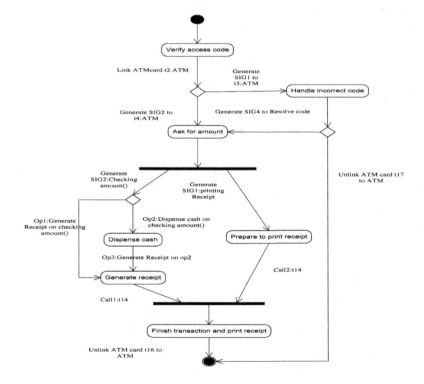

Table 2. Action on ATM activity diagram

Action Name	Source Node	Target Node
Link Action	Verify access Code	Decision Node
Send Signal Action	Decision Node	Handle incorrect Code
Send Signal Action	Decision Node	Ask for Amount
Broadcast signal action	Ask for Amount	Prepare to print a receipt
Broadcast signal action	Ask for Amount	Decision Node
Call operation Action	Decision Node	Dispense Cash
Call operation Action	Dispense Cash	Generate Receipt
Call Action	Generate Receipt	Finish transaction and generate Receipt
Call Operation Action	Decision Node	Generate Receipt
Call Action	Prepare to print a receipt	Finish transaction and generate Receipt
Send Signal Action	Handle Incorrect Code	Decision Node
Destroy Link Action	Finish transaction and print receipt	Final Node
Destroy Link Action	Resolving incorrect code(Decision Node)	Final Node

By analyzing Table 2 all the dependent paths are retrieved. When the same path having different actions is repeated twice then it is considered at once only, to avoid the redundancy in test paths. Test cases in the proposed approach are hence accurate and not redundant.

Dependency Graph of Annotated Activity Diagram

Shown in Figure 4.

Test Paths for ATM Activity Diagram

The test paths are derived through the dependency graph of ATM activity diagram. The test path for each action is shown in table 3.

EMPIRICAL STUDY

An Empirical study conducted on ATM case study. Comparing the proposed approach with other 10 existing approaches. The proposed algorithm is analyzed by the type

Figure 4. Dependency graph of ATM activity diagram

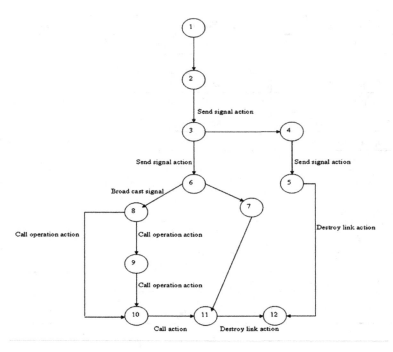

Table 3. Test paths from ATM dependency graph

Action	Test Path Name	Test Path
link action	TP1	2,3
send signal	TP2	3,4,5
Broad cast signal	TP3	3,6
Destroy Link	TP4	6,8
Call operation	TP5	6,7

of tests paths, No of test paths, action on transition and dependencies between the nodes of activity diagram.

Research Questions

The empirical study address the research question.

Research Question 1

The proposed algorithm is compared with other existing approaches and it is analyzed that test paths are exhaustive or not and how many paths are generated through the graphs.

Research Question 2

Whether the existing approaches are decorated with action or not.
Table 4 will give an analysis of the existing approaches.

Table 4. Test paths from ATM dependency graph

Approach	Test Paths	Dependency Analysis
Linzhang et al(2004)	TP1→(1,2,3) TP2→(3,4,5,12) TP3→(3,6) TP4→(8,9,10) TP5→(8,10) TP6→(8,9,10,11) TP7→(7,11,12)	NO
Xu et al (2005)	TP1→(1,2,4,5,12) TP2→(1,2,3,6,7,11,12) TP3→(1,2,3,6,9,10,11,12)	NO
Kundu et al(2009)	TP1→(1,2,6,7,11,12) TP2→(1,2,3,8,9,10,11,12) TP3→(1,2,3,6,8,10,11,12) TP4→(1,2,3,4,5,12) TP5→(1,2,3,4,5,6,7,11,12) TP6→(1,2,3,4,5,6,7,8,9,10)	NO
Kim et al (2007)	TP1→(1,2,3,6,11) TP2→(1,2,3,4,5,6,7,8,9,10,11,12) TP3→(1,2,3,6,8,9,10,7,11,12) TP4→(1,2,3,6,8,9,10,11,4,5,12)	NO
Mitrabinda Ray et (2009)	No Test Path Generation	NO
Robert Chandler(2007)	No Of Paths 2+ 2+1=5 (Test path generation steps are not mentioned)The formula for counting the number of paths is given	NO
Briand et al(2002)	No test path generation	NO
Mingsong et al(2008)	TP1→(1,2,3,4,5,12) TP2→(1,2,3,6,7,11) TP3→(1,2,3,6,8,9,10,11,12) TP4→(1,2,3,6,8,10,11,12)	NO

CONCLUSION

Scenario-based testing is a way of testing the UML models in such a way that possible test cases are retrieved easily. UML activity diagram demonstrates the flow of control. When actions are added on the Activity diagram, each transition of the model becomes executable. By applying actions on the transitions of the activity diagram the relationship between each node of the model become strong. On the basis of proposed dependencies definitions, all the dependent paths are separated.

Actions make the activity model executable. The test paths generated through the executable models are very accurate. As the redundancy of test paths is removed in the proposed approach so it avoids exhaustive testing. In the existing approaches, no work is done on the scenario-based testing using action. So the proposed approach gives the new dimension in scenario-based testing. Our thesis includes the surveys on scenario-based testing and Activity Based testing are included. The comprehensive analysis of existing techniques helps us in deciding the new dimensions.

In the proposed approach, we give a way of testing avoiding Exhaustive testing. We present an example to demonstrate our proposed work practically. Even due to the selection of activity diagram as an input artifact flow of activities are represented in the best manner.

In future, we will try to automate the process of generating an activity diagram from a scenario written in formal language. As well as we will try to write the action language specific for activity diagram.

REFERENCES

Alspaugh, T. A., Richardson, D. J., & Standish, T. A. (2005). Scenarios, State Machines and Purpose-Driven Testing. New York, NY: ACM SIGSOFT. doi:10.1145/1083183.1083185

Bai, X., Lam, C. P., & Li, H. (2004). An Approach to Generate the Thin-threads from the UML Diagrams. In *Proceedings of the 28th Annual International Computer Software and Application Conference(COMPSAC'04)*. Piscataway, NJ: IEEE.

Barnett, M., Grieskamp, W., Gurevich, Y., & et al, . (2003). Scenario-Oriented Modeling in AsmL and its Instrumentation for Testing. In *Proceedings of second International Workshop on Scenarios and State Machines (SCESM'03). Piscataway, NJ: IEEE.*

Briand, L., & Labiche, Y. (2002). A UML-Based Approach to System Testing. *Software and System Modeling, 1*(1).

Canevet, C. (2004). Analysing UML 2.0 activity diagrams in the software performance engineering process. *Proceedings of the 4th International Workshop on Software and Performance Engineering Process (WOSP 2004)*. 10.1145/974044.974055

Chandler, C., Lam, C. P., & Li, H. (2005). AD2US: An Automated Approach to Generating Usage Scenarios from UML Activity Diagrams. In *Proceedings of the 12th Asia-Pacific Software Engineering Conference (APSEC'05)*. Piscataway, NJ: IEEE. 10.1109/APSEC.2005.25

Chandler, R., Lam, C. P., & Li, H. (2007). Dealing with Concurrent Regions During Scenario Generation from Activity Diagrams. In Innovations and Advanced Techniques in Computer and Information Sciences and Engineering (pp. 415–420). Springer.

Chen, M., Mishra, P., & Kalita, D. (2008). Coverage-driven Automatic Test Generation for UML Activity Diagrams. *GLSVLSI*.

Jiang, K., Zhang, L., & Miyake, S. (2007). An Executable UML with OCL-based Action Semantics Language. In *Proceedings of the 14th Asia-Pacific Software Engineering*. Washington, DC: IEEE Computer Society.

Jorgensen, J. B. (2007). Executable Use Cases: a Supplement to Model Driven Development? In *Fourth International workshop on Model-Based Methodologies for Pervasive and Embedded Software*. Braga, Portugal. IEEE Computer Society. 10.1109/MOMPES.2007.6

Kim, H., Kang, S., Baik, J., & Ko, I. (2007). Test Cases Generations from UML Activity Diagrams. In *Eighth International Conference on Software Engineering, Artificial Intelligence, Networking and Parallel/Distributed Computing*. Qingdao, China: IEEE. 10.1109/SNPD.2007.189

Kundu, D., & Samanta, D. (2009). A Novel Approach to Generate Test Cases from UML Activity Diagrams. *Journal of Object Technology*, 8(3), 65–83. doi:10.5381/jot.2009.8.3.a1

Li, H., & Lam, C. P. (2005, May). Using Anti-Ant-Like Agents to Generate Test Threads from the UML Diagrams. In *IFIP International Conference on Testing of Communicating Systems* (pp. 69-80). Berlin, Germany: Springer.

Linzhang, W., Jiesong, Y., Xiafeng, Y. et al. (2004). Generating Test Cases from UML Activity Diagram Based on Gray-box Method. In *11th Asia-Pacific Software Engineering Conference (APSEC'04)*, (pp. 284–291). Busan, Korea: Academic Press. 10.1109/APSEC.2004.55

Mingsong, C., Xiaokang, Q., & Xuandong, L. (2006). Automatic Test Case Generation For UML Activity Diagrams. *National Natural Science Foundation Of China, AST'06.*

Motogna, S., Parv, B., & Lazar, I. (2008). *Extensions of an OCL-Based Executable UML Components Action Language.* Academic Press.

Nayak, A., & Samanta, D. (2009). Synthesis of test scenarios using UML activity diagrams. Software System Model. Berlin, Germany: Springer-Verlag.

Nebut, C., Fleurey, F., Troan, Y. L., & JzeQuell, J. M. (2006). *Automatic Test Generation: A Use Case Driven Approach.* Washington, DC: IEEE Computer Society.

Perseil, I., & Pautent, L. (2008). A Concrete syntax for UML 2.1 Action Semantic Using +CAL. In *Proceedings of the 13th IEEE International Conference on Engineering of Complex Computer System*, (pp. 217-221). IEEE Computer Society. 10.1109/ICECCS.2008.34

Ray, M., Barpanda, S.S., & Mohapatra, D.P. (2009). Test case Design Using Conditioned Slicing of Activity Diagram. *International Journal of Recent Trends in Engineering, 1*(2).

Raza, N., Nadeem, A., Zohib, M., & Iqbal, Z. (2007). An automated approach to system testing based on Scenarios and operations Contracts. In *Seventh international conference on quality software.* Piscataway, NJ: IEEE. 10.1109/QSIC.2007.4385504

Ryser, J., & Glinz, M. (1999). A Scenario-Based Approach to Validating and Testing Software Systems Using Statecharts. *12th International conference on Software and Systems Engineering and their Application. Proceedings.*

Ryser, J., & Glinz, M. (2000). Using Dependency Charts to improve Scenario-Based Testing. Presented at the *17th International Conference on Testing Computer Software TCS'2000, Washington*, DC.

Samuel, P., & Mall, R. (2009). Slicing-Based Test Case Generation from UML Activity Diagrams. *Software Engineering Notes, 34*(6), 1–14. doi:10.1145/1640162.1666579

Sarma, M., & Mall, R. (2007). Automatic Test Case Generation from UML Models. In *Proceedings of the 10th International Conference on Information Technology.* Orissa, India. IEEE. 10.1109/ICIT.2007.26

Sinha, A., Paradkar, A., & Williams, C. (2007). On Generating EFSM models from use Cases. In *Sixth International Workshop on Scenarios and State Machines.* IEEE. 10.1109/SCESM.2007.3

Some, S. S. (2007). Specifying Use Case Sequencing Constraints using Description Elements. In *Sixth International Workshop on Scenarios and State Machines (SCESM'07)*. IEEE. 10.1109/SCESM.2007.6

Sun, C. (2008, July). A Transformation-based Approach to Generating Scenario-oriented Test Cases from UML Activity Diagrams For Concurrent Applications. In *32nd Annual IEEE International Computer Software and Applications Conference* (pp. 160-167). IEEE. 10.1109/COMPSAC.2008.74

Sun, C., Zhang, Z. B., & Li, J. (2009). TSGen A UML Activity Diagram-based Test Scenario Generation Tool. In *International Conference on Computational Science and Engineering*. IEEE Computer Society. 10.1109/CSE.2009.99

Tsai, Bai, Paul, & Yu. (2001). *Scenario based Functional Regression Testing*. IEEE.

Tsai, W. T., Saimi, A., & Yu, L. (2003, November). Scenario-Based Object-Oriented Testing Framework. In *Proceedings of the third international conference on Quality Software*. IEEE Computer Society. 10.1109/QSIC.2003.1319129

Tsai, W. T., Yu, L., & Liu, X. X. (2003). *Scenario-Based test case Generation for state-based embedded systems*. Piscataway, NJ: IEEE. doi:10.1109/PCCC.2003.1203716

Whittle, J., & Jayaraman, P. K. (2006, September). Generating Hierarchical State Machines From Use Case Charts. In *Fourteenth International Requirements Engineering Conference*. IEEE Computer Society. 10.1109/RE.2006.25

Wittevrongel, J., & Maurer, F. (2001). Using UML to Partially Automate Generation of Scenario-Based Test Drivers. In *Proceedings of the seventh International Conference on Object Oriented Information Systems (OOIS'01), 2001,* (pp. 303-306). Academic Press.

Xu, D., Li, H., & Lam, C. P. (2005). Using Adaptive Agents to Automatically Generate Test Scenarios from the UML Activity Diagrams. In *Proceedings of the 12th Asia-Pacific Software Engineering Conference (APSEC'05)*. IEEE.

Chapter 13

The Effect of Team Work Quality on Team Performance in Global Software Engineering

Mazni Omar
(iD) https://orcid.org/0000-0003-1816-2940
Universiti Utara Malaysia, Malaysia

Mawarny Md Rejab
Universiti Utara Malaysia, Malaysia

Mazida Ahmad
Universiti Utara Malaysia, Malaysia

ABSTRACT

Global software engineering (SE) has increased in popularity and is now commonplace in most software organizations. This is due to the fact that business and technology have evolved, which has had an impact on the borderless world. As a consequence, software teams are often geographically dispersed, though they all have the same goal—to produce high-quality software. In order to achieve that goal, quality teamwork is important to build a high-performance team. This study aims to get an in-depth understanding of what quality teamwork is, as well as investigate how communication and socialization can have an impact on team performance. This study took a qualitative approach to the data collection process by carrying out interviews with three experts of agile distributed teams. The results of this study demonstrate that active communication stimulates socialization, and thus increases and maintains morale and motivation among team members. Future studies could focus on the impact of other quality teamwork, such as the influence of trust on team performance among global SE teams.

DOI: 10.4018/978-1-5225-9448-2.ch013

INTRODUCTION

Global software engineering (SE) is gaining prominence in today's software industry. As a consequence of a number of issues, such as tight budgets and shortages of resources and time, most companies build joint ventures and set up development sites in low-cost countries (Smite et al., 2010). Therefore, global software engineering involves software development across more than one single location, which requires rules and procedures to coordinate the geographically-dispersed teams.

Several factors can affect software failure in global SE. This includes the absence of project management skills, client commitment, teamwork and collaboration among team members (Porrawatpreyakorn, Quirchmayr, & Chutimaskul, 2009). Owing to the rapid development of the software industry; specifically, in global SE, human and social factors play a critical role in software development. However, research on the human factors in global SE is still scarce. During software development, communication among team members is compulsory in order to communicate the status of a project. When communication happens actively, socialization among team members can increase. This can promote informal communication and confidence among team members. Previous research has demonstrated that a lack of communication can impact the high risk of poor performance (De Farias, De Azevedo, De Moura, & Da Silva, 2012). In addition, the absence of communication may also affect low productivity among team members (Moe, Dingsøyr, & Dybå, 2010). Moreover, a lack of socialization may affect the communication, and thus, lower team performance (Steinke, 2011). These two components are crucial in a global SE teamwork. Thus, this paper focuses on two quality team factors; namely, communication and socialization on team performance.

RELATED WORKS

Software organization relies on teamwork in order to accomplish tasks and assignments effectively. Working in a team may increase team results efficiently rather than working in silo (Fung & Ali, 2011). This is specifically true in any software development activity that requires human extensive tasks that involve communication and socialization among team members. Thus, online collaboration tools have emerged in the market to encourage active communication with less cost among global SE teams (Sudhakar, Farooq & Patnaik, 2011; Lavallée & Robillard, 2018).

Many organizations strive to gain benefits offered by global software engineering (Lous et al., 2017; Smite et al., 2014). Global SE tends to produce a high return in investment; however, there are many challenges related to global SE. Most global software development companies find that the process of developing and launching new software applications is too complex to accomplish successfully (Ebert, 2016) because it is hard to integrate skills, people and processes when they are scattered across different sites.

Besides complexity, lacking direct communication hinders proper software development activities (Ebert, 2016). Communication across project sites is the most remarkable barrier for distributed software development; hence, poor communication also hinders coordination and management processes. Project delivery failures, insufficient quality of software product, distance and culture clashes, staff turnover and salary are other challenges and reasons for the failure of a global software development project.

Since global software development is a human-centred process, a number of human factors have an impact on software engineering that also tend to influence team performance. Team performance can be measured by the degree of quality met among team members when the objective set is wholly achieved (Wu, 2014). The performance of team depends on the integration of members' diverse skills, experiences, personality among team members. When the team members can understand their roles and responsibilities, shared common goals and values, software projects can be accomplished effectively. In addition, it can promote cohesiveness among the team members, and thus members may appreciate each others. Moreover, to provide better services, team members need to be good in technical advancement, adopting modern management approach, mainly in team work in global SE to cope with the changing environment demands.

The performance of a software development team can rely on several team quality criteria: cohesion, coordination of expertise, communication, value, diversity, trust, mutual support and socialization, all of which contribute to the higher team performance (Hoegl and Gemuenden, 2001; Ahuja and Galvin, 2003; Weimar, 2013). However, these factors have not been investigated extensively among global SE teams. It is vital to understand how these factors can impact team performance.

The most common risks identified in the global software engineering field are related to these quality team factors, with communication being especially important (Nicolas et al, 2018). Communication happens when team members share ideas by coordinating their efforts and providing feedback through any communication means (Kozak, 2013; Hoegl and Gemuenden, 2001). The communication problems commonly involved in global software engineering are generally due to the distribution of development teams. Different languages, cultures and time zones are factors that tend to influence the success of communication in distributed software development (Binder, 2016). The diversity in language and culture can be the source of conflicts and misunderstandings, whereas having teams located in different time zone can often make it difficult to organize meetings in common office hours. The failure of a project can typically be the result of poor and ineffective communication, which tends to affect team productivity (Kozak, 2013); therefore, it is prevalent for global organizations to apply standard communication rules, practices and templates across locations to reduce the possibility of communication problems arising (Binder, 2016).

Through effective communication, the dispersed team members can socialize in an effective way (Ahuja and Galvin, 2003). Socialization requires the individual behaviours, attitudes and knowledge necessary to participate in an organization. Several activities support socialization between members of a team; these include bonding exercises, training programs and mentoring schemes (Oshri et al., 2007). Besides activities, Oshri et al. (2007) have proposed a process of socialization in global software development in three phases: *Introduction*, *Build-Up* and *Renewal*. Research has consistently shown that socialization has a positive influence on team performance (Hinds and Weisband, 2003). Nevertheless, there is still a lack of empirical evidence on the impact of socialization between global SE teams. Thus, more research is required to explore and understand how the team members communicate and socialize towards achieving the same software project goals and delivering products within budget and time constraints.

METHODOLOGY

In this study, a qualitative study was used as an initial understanding of the effect of teamwork quality, with a specific focus on socialization and communication among agile distributed teams towards team performance. A qualitative approach was used in order to explore a phenomenon and investigate the varying perspectives of participants (Creswell, 2013). Although this phase only involved preliminary and basic work, the foundation of the study is essential to ensure that the researchers have defined the problem to be studied correctly and to make sure the researcher is heading in the right direction for building the conceptual model.

In qualitative research, the researchers intentionally select participants who have experience with the central phenomenon or key concept being explored (Creswell, 2013). Thus, the participants involved in this study were among those who have experienced working with agile distributed teams for more than 5 years. Regarding this study, three (3) experts agreed and showed a willingness to participate in the semi-structured interview.

In this study, several interview sessions were carried to collect data from the experts. The questions for this study focuses on how communication and socialization are practices among team members in global SE. Table 1 below listed the questions that exploited to extract the raw data from the experts through the interview session.

Table 1. Sample of interview questions

Interview Questions
1. How many times you communicate with team members per week?
2. How do you get feedback from your team members?
3. What kind of tools used by your team members to communicate?
4. Does your team members always give immediate and consistent feedback?
5. Does your team members helpful?
6. Any issues related to communication and socialization among team members?
7. How the team members collaborate on the online communication?
8. Are you satisfied with communication existed among team members?

The interview sessions with the experts were conducted face-to-face and lasted between 10-15 minutes. The interviews were audio recorded and transcribed. Online communication applications, such as email and WhatsApp, were used for follow-up questions and clarifications.

RESULT AND DISCUSSION

In this study, three experts were interviewed in order to gain an in-depth understanding of how team members in global SE teams, and distributed teams in particular, communicate and socialize. All of the experts were working in a software house in Malaysia and used agile practices during their software development activities. Table 2 depicts the experts' profiles.

Table 2. Experts' profile

Experts	Gender	Age	Role	Expert Experience	Team Location
Expert 1	Male	32 years old	Programmer, Project Leader	6-10 years	USA, Sweden
Expert 2	Female	40 years old	Requirement Analyst, Architect	More than 16 years	USA, United Kingdom
Expert 3	Male	32 years old	Requirement Analyst	6-10 years	Germany, Portugal

Most of the experts experienced more than 5 years as members of agile distributed teams. They are working on new system development and system maintenance. The role of the experts varied from programmer, project leader, requirement analyst, and software architecture. Their team members are geographically dispersed in various continents, such as The United States of America (USA), United Kingdom (UK), and European countries, which includes Sweden, Germany and Portugal.

During the interviews, all experts agreed that they communicated with the team members on a weekly basis, but that it also depended on the project deadline. This is especially true, when the deadline is near, more frequent discussion and meeting will be held. Expert 1 asserted that

We communicate with the project manager on a daily basis regarding the project progress or to clarify requirements. But, with other team members, the communication is less frequent. It is around 1 -2 times per week.

In addition, Expert 2 highlighted that,

It depends on the team. Sometimes daily or weekly. If 'hot cakes', very urgent...or near to the deadline of the 'go live' date, or after 'go live' issues... there would be frequent call.

Expert 3 also mentioned that the team would have a weekly meeting to report the project progress, issues and solutions. This demonstrates that the main agenda of the meeting is to report the project progress.

Nevertheless, Expert 1 highlighted that,

If there is a dependency on a particular task, we can ask about the progress...we need to learn how such a task is accomplished (share knowledge). In addition, there is a general channel we use if we find a bug or general issues in the system, which is visible to all team members. Also, we can hold a discussion about the system architecture with all team members. Finally, we have a weekly progress meeting where we can all share our progress and our current challenges. We can also share ideas and talk about whether we need to update the estimation.

Expert 2 sheds light on issues related to working in different time zones when stating that teams need to ensure that all team members can participate during the meeting. For example, between Malaysia and USA (San Francisco), they need to arrange the meeting between 6 am to 11 pm. Expert 2 also stated that,

If the team members involved are from the UK, we (team members from Malaysia) have to participate or join the meeting from home because the meeting can only be held at 4 pm or later.

This excerpt shows that cultural and time zone differences require team members to be committed to accomplishing tasks efficiently. Team members need to understand the constraint and manage time among team members appropriately.

Regarding the communication tools used, Expert 1 pointed out that,

We used Jira, to track and plan task, it is an Agile Board. In addition, we used Skype for voice communication and Group calls (e.g., weekly progress meetings). The WhatsApp tool should only be used if there is an urgent case outside working hours. Google drive to write some document collaboratively.

Expert 3 also mentioned that,

We used Skype to hold video and conference calls and sent emails to communicate outside of the weekly meetings.

This shows that any means of communication tools were used by the distributed teams in order for them to discuss the project status and risks. The software organization also allocated a part of their budget to spend on online communication tools. In addition, based on the interviews, team members also have a private channel (1 to1) communication and general communication between the team members. The findings show that in global software engineering teams, communication is vital to ensure that all members are 'in the loop' and the project is on track. However, the accuracy of information received from other team members can be questioned among the members.

Based on experts' views, all the team members actively engage and collaborate during the online communication. Knowledge sharing is always promoted to ensure team members have the same level of understanding. For example, one of the experts stated that they applied the Bitbucket tool for code quality management.

We can initiate some discussion regarding the written code, in term of quality, or if there is better we to solve such a problem. Whenever a task is done, also, team members will get a notification whenever the code is changed using the sourcetree application.

All the experts agreed that using online communication tools helps them to know the exact amount of work completed. These tools also allow tasks to be carried out efficiently and as quickly as possible. In addition, the experts added that active communication stimulates socialization among team members, and hence, helps to maintain high morale during the development process. This demonstrate that team members becoming more enthusiastic when socialization increases to lessen stress during software development.

CONCLUSION AND RECOMMENDATIONS

Software development comprises an extensive range of human activities and processes that involve human interaction in the context of a team. Thus, it is important to understand the teamwork factors that influence performance when planning strategic action to improve performance. This study demonstrated the importance of communication and socialization among global SE teams, with a specific focus on agile distributed teams. The technological advancement of communication tools encourages team members to communicate and socialize actively. Although the members appreciated the active feedback among the members, the accuracy of information relays and communication among team members still emerged as challenging issues during the development project. This may be due to the different cultures and levels of trust among team members. In addition, different expectations and goals may also affect the issue of accuracy.

Learning more about this issue helps the practitioners and researchers to investigate other team work quality factors, such as trust among global SE teams at a broader level. This study included three experts from Malaysia; therefore, the results cannot be generalized. Nevertheless, more data can be collected in different context and countries in order to generalize the findings. The knowledge gained from this study will be useful for software project managers to better understand how communication and socialization can impact team performance, especially in the context of global teamwork. Further, through this knowledge, managers can take strategic action to build and manage their teams effectively in global SE and thus improve the organization's performance.

REFERENCES

Ahuja, M. K., & Galvin, J. E. (2003). Socialization in virtual groups. *Journal of Management*, 29(2), 161–185. doi:10.1177/014920630302900203

Azmy, N. (2012). The role of team effectiveness in construction project teams and project performance. Ames, IA: Iowa State University. doi:10.31274/etd-180810-2950

Binder, J. (2016). *Global project management: communication, collaboration and management across borders*. Abingdon, UK: Routledge. doi:10.4324/9781315584997

Creswell, J. W. (2013). Research design: Qualitative, quantitative, and mixed methods approaches. Thousand Oaks, CA: Sage Publications.

De Farias, I. H., De Azevedo, R. R., De Moura, H. P., & Da Silva, D. S. M. (n.d.). Elicitation of communication inherent risks in distributed software development. In *IEEE 7th International Conference on Global Software Engineering Workshops, ICGSEW 2012*. Porto Alegre, Brazil: IEEE. doi:10.1109/ICGSEW.2012.18

Ebert, C., Kuhrmann, M., & Prikladnicki, R. (2016, August). Global software engineering: evolution and trends. In *Global Software Engineering (ICGSE), 2016 IEEE 11th International Conference on* (pp. 144-153), Irvine, CA. IEEE. 10.1109/ICGSE.2016.19

Hinds, P., & Weisband, S. (2003). Chapter. In C. Gibson & S. Cohen (Eds.), Creating Conditions for EVective Virtual Teams (pp. 21–36). San Francisco, CA: Jossey-Bass.

Hoegl, M., & Gemuenden, H. G. (2001). Teamwork quality and the success of innovative projects: A theoretical concept and empirical evidence. *Organization Science*, *12*(4), 435–449. doi:10.1287/orsc.12.4.435.10635

Kozak, Y. (2013). *Barriers against better team performance in agile software projects. Chalmers University of Technology.*

Lous, P., Kuhrmann, M., & Tell, P. (2017, May). Is Scrum fit for global software engineering? In *Proceedings of the 12th International Conference on Global Software Engineering* (pp. 1-10). Buenos Aires, Argentina. IEEE Press. 10.1109/ICGSE.2017.13

Moe, N. B., Dingsøyr, T., & Dybå, T. (2010). A teamwork model for understanding an agile team: A case study of a scrum project. *Information and Software Technology*, *52*(5), 480–491. doi:10.1016/j.infsof.2009.11.004

Nicolás, J., De Gea, J. M. C., & Nicolás, B. et al. (2018). On the risks and safeguards for requirements engineering in global software development: Systematic literature review and quantitative assessment. *IEEE Access: Practical Innovations, Open Solutions*, *6*, 59628–59656. doi:10.1109/ACCESS.2018.2874096

Oshri, I., Kotlarsky, J., & Willcocks, L. P. (2007). Global software development: Exploring socialization and face-to-face meetings in distributed strategic projects. *The Journal of Strategic Information Systems*, *16*(1), 25–49. doi:10.1016/j.jsis.2007.01.001

Porrawatpreyakorn, N., Quirchmayr, G., & Chutimaskul, W. (2009, December). Requirements for a knowledge transfer framework in the field of software development process management for executive information systems in the telecommunications industry. In International Conference on Advances in Information Technology (pp. 110-122). Berlin, Germany: Springer.

Qureshi, M. R. J., Alshamat, S. A., & Sabir, F. (2014). Significance of the teamwork in agile software engineering. *Sci. Int.(Lahore)*, *26*(1), 117–120.

Šmite, D., Wohlin, C., Galviņa, Z., & Prikladnicki, R. (2014). An empirically based terminology and taxonomy for global software engineering. *Empirical Software Engineering*, *19*(1), 105–153. doi:10.100710664-012-9217-9

Steinke, J. A. (2011). *Team conflict and effectiveness in competitive environments* (Master's thesis). Department of Psychology, Wright State University.

Sudhakar, G. P., Farooq, A., & Patnaik, S. (2011). Soft factors affecting the performance of software development teams. *Team Performance Management*, *17*(3/4), 187–205. doi:10.1108/13527591111143718

Wu, M., & Chen, Y. H. (2014). A factor Analysis on Teamwork Performance -an Empirical Study of Inter-instituted Collaboration : *Eurasian Journal of Educational Research*, (55), 37–54.

Compilation of References

Abdel Aziz, H. H., & Rizkallah, A. (2015). Effect of organizational factors on employees' generation of innovative ideas: Empirical study on the Egyptian software development industry. *EuroMed Journal of Business*, *10*(2), 134–146. doi:10.1108/EMJB-12-2014-0044

Abrahamsson, P., Salo, O., Ronkainen, J., & Warsta, J. (2017). *Agile software development methods: Review and analysis.* arXiv preprint arXiv:1709.08439

Acuña, S. T., Gómez, M., & Juristo, N. (2008). Towards understanding the relationship between team climate and software quality—A quasi-experimental study. *Empirical Software Engineering*, *13*(4), 401–434. doi:10.100710664-008-9074-8

Agarwala, T. (2003). Innovative human resource practices and organizational commitment: An empirical investigation. *International Journal of Human Resource Management*, *14*(2), 175–197. doi:10.1080/0958519021000029072

Agerfalk, P. J., Fitzgerald, B., & Holmstrom Olsson, H. (2005). *A framework for considering opportunities and threats in distributed software development.* Academic Press.

Ågerfalk, P. J., Fitzgerald, B., Olsson, H. H., & Conchúir, E. Ó. (2008, May). Benefits of global software development: the known and unknown. In *International Conference on Software Process* (pp. 1-9). Berlin, Germany: Springer. 10.1007/978-3-540-79588-9_1

Agovic, A., & Agovic, A. (2014). *U.S. Patent No. 8,719,781.* Washington, DC: U.S. Patent and Trademark Office.

Agrawal, A., Khan, R., & Chandra, S. (2008). Software Security Process–Development Life Cycle Perspective. *CSI Communications*, *32*(5), 39–42.

Ahmadvand, H., & Goudarzi, M. (2017). Using Data Variety for Efficient Progressive Big Data Processing in Warehouse-Scale Computers. *IEEE Computer Architecture Letters*, *16*(2), 166–169. doi:10.1109/LCA.2016.2636293

Ahuja, M. K., & Galvin, J. E. (2003). Socialization in virtual groups. *Journal of Management*, *29*(2), 161–185. doi:10.1177/014920630302900203

Alahyari, H., Svensson, R. B., & Gorschek, T. (2017). A study of value in agile software development organizations. *Journal of Systems and Software*, *125*, 271–288. doi:10.1016/j.jss.2016.12.007

Alavi, M., & Leidner, D. E. (2001). Review: Knowledge management and knowledge management systems: Conceptual foundations and research issues. *Management Information Systems Quarterly*, *25*(1), 107–136. doi:10.2307/3250961

Aldhahri, E., Shandilya, V., & Shiva, S. (2015). Towards an effective crowdsourcing recommendation system: A survey of the state-of-the-art. *Proceedings - 9th IEEE International Symposium on Service-Oriented System Engineering, IEEE SOSE 2015*. 10.1109/SOSE.2015.53

Allen, N. J., & Meyer, J. P. (1990). The measurement and antecedents of affective, continuance and normative commitment to the organization. *Journal of Occupational Psychology*, *63*(1), 1–18. doi:10.1111/j.2044-8325.1990.tb00506.x

Allport, G. W. (1961). *Pattern and growth in personality*. Academic Press.

AlMahmoud, A., Damiani, E., Otrok, H., & Al-Hammadi, Y. (2017). Spamdoop: A privacy-preserving Big Data platform for collaborative spam detection. *IEEE Transactions On Big Data*, 1-1. doi:10.1109/tbdata.2017.2716409

Almomani, M. A., Basri, S., & Gilal, A. R. (2018). Empirical study of software process improvement in Malaysian small and medium enterprises: The human aspects. *Journal of Software: Evolution and Process*. doi:10.1002mr.1953

Alspaugh, T. A., Richardson, D. J., & Standish, T. A. (2005). Scenarios, State Machines and Purpose-Driven Testing. New York, NY: ACM SIGSOFT. doi:10.1145/1083183.1083185

Altshuller, G. (1984). *Creativity as an exact science: the theory of the solution of inventive problems*. New York, NY: Gordon and Breach Science Publishers. Retrieved from http://cds.cern.ch/record/450367

Altshuller, G. (2002). *40 principles: TRIZ keys to innovation (3rd ed.)*. Worcester, MA: Technical Innovation Center. Retrieved from https://books.google.com.mx/books?id=mqlGEZgn5cwC&dq=triz&lr=&hl=es&source=gbs_navlinks_s

Amayah, T. A. (2013). Determinants of knowledge sharing in a public sector organization. *Journal of Knowledge Management*, *17*(3), 454–471. doi:10.1108/JKM-11-2012-0369

Ambati, V., Vogel, S., & Carbonell, J. (2011). Towards Task Recommendation in Micro-Task Markets. *Human Computation AAAI Workshop*.

Andreasian, G., & Andreasian, M. (2013). *Knowledge Sharing and Knowledge Transfer Barriers* (Dissertation).

Andreasian, G., & Andreasian, M. (2013). *Knowledge Sharing and Knowledge Transfer Barriers. A Case Study*. Academic Press.

Angelis, A., & Kanavos, P. (2013). A Multiple Criteria Decision Analysis Framework For Value-Based Assessment Of New Medical Technologies. *Value in Health*, *16*(3), A53. doi:10.1016/j.jval.2013.03.302

Anisetti, M., Ardagna, C. A., & Damiani, E. (2012, June). A low-cost security certification scheme for evolving services. In *2012 IEEE 19th International Conference on Web Services* (pp. 122-129). Piscataway, NJ: IEEE. 10.1109/ICWS.2012.53

Anthony, P., & Ezeh, A. (2013). Factors Influencing Knowledge Sharing in Software Development: A Case Study at Volvo Cars IT Torslanda. Gothenburg, Sweden: Gothenburg University Publications Electronic Archive.

Anwer, F., Aftab, S., Waheed, U., & Muhammad, S. S. (2017). Agile Software Development Models TDD, FDD, DSDM, and Crystal Methods: A Survey. *International Journal of Multidisciplinary Sciences and Engineering, 8*(2), 1-10.

Arbel, L. (2015). Data loss prevention: The business case. *Computer Fraud & Security, 2015*(5), 13–16. doi:10.1016/S1361-3723(15)30037-3

Arkin, B., Stender, S., & McGraw, G. (2005). Software penetration testing. *IEEE Security and Privacy, 3*(1), 84–87. doi:10.1109/MSP.2005.23

Askitas, N. (2016). Big Data is a big deal but how much data do we need?. *Asta Wirtschafts- Und Sozialstatistisches Archiv, 10*(2-3), 113-125. doi:10.100711943-016-0191-3

Azmy, N. (2012). The role of team effectiveness in construction project teams and project performance. Ames, IA: Iowa State University. doi:10.31274/etd-180810-2950

Bacardit, J., & Llorà, X. (2013). Large-scale data mining using genetics-based machine learning. *Wiley Interdisciplinary Reviews. Data Mining and Knowledge Discovery, 3*(1), 37–61. doi:10.1002/widm.1078

Bae, S., Lee, J. M., & Chu, C. N. (2002). Axiomatic Design of Automotive Suspension Systems. *CIRP Annals, 51*(1), 115–118. doi:10.1016/S0007-8506(07)61479-6

Bai, X., Lam, C. P., & Li, H. (2004). An Approach to Generate the Thin-threads from the UML Diagrams. In *Proceedings of the 28th Annual International Computer Software and Application Conference(COMPSAC'04)*. Piscataway, NJ: IEEE.

Balasooriya, B. (2014). *Analysis of barriers for innovations in Sri Lankan software organizations.* Academic Press.

Banerjee, C., & Pandey, S. (2009). *Software security rules, SDLC perspective.* arXiv preprint arXiv:0911.0494

Bang, I. C., & Heo, G. (2009). An axiomatic design approach in development of nanofluid coolants. *Applied Thermal Engineering, 29*(1), 75–90. doi:10.1016/j.applthermaleng.2008.02.004

Baragde, D., & Baporikar, N. (2017). Business innovation in Indian software industries. *Journal of Science and Technology Policy Management, 8*(1), 62–75. doi:10.1108/JSTPM-12-2015-0039

Bariani, P. F., Berti, G. A., & Lucchetta, G. (2004). A Combined DFMA and TRIZ approach to the simplification of product structure. *Proceedings of the Institution of Mechanical Engineers. Part B, Journal of Engineering Manufacture*, *218*(8), 1023–1027. doi:10.1243/0954405041486091

Barnett, M., Grieskamp, W., Gurevich, Y., & et al, . (2003). Scenario-Oriented Modeling in AsmL and its Instrumentation for Testing. In *Proceedings of second International Workshop on Scenarios and State Machines (SCESM'03). Piscataway, NJ: IEEE.*

Basri, S., Omar, M., Capretz, L. F., Aziz, I. A., Jaafar, J., & Gilal, A. R. (2017). Finding an effective classification technique to develop a software team composition model. *Journal of Software: Evolution and Process*. doi:10.1002mr.1920

Batarseh, F., Yang, R., & Deng, L. (2017). A comprehensive model for management and validation of federal big data analytical systems. *Big Data Analytics*, *2*(1), 2. doi:10.118641044-016-0017-x

Bau, J., Bursztein, E., Gupta, D., & Mitchell, J. (2010, May). State of the art: Automated black-box web application vulnerability testing. In *2010 IEEE Symposium on Security and Privacy* (pp. 332-345). Piscataway, NJ: IEEE. 10.1109/SP.2010.27

Bayuk, J. L. (2013). Security as a theoretical attribute construct. *Computers & Security*, *37*, 155–175. doi:10.1016/j.cose.2013.03.006

Begoña Lloria, M. (2008). A review of the main approaches to knowledge management. *Knowledge Management Research and Practice*, *6*(1), 77–89. doi:10.1057/palgrave.kmrp.8500164

Bessey, A., Block, K., Chelf, B., & et al, . (2010). A few billion lines of code later: Using static analysis to find bugs in the real world. *Communications of the ACM*, *53*(2), 66–75. doi:10.1145/1646353.1646374

Binder, J. (2016). *Global project management: communication, collaboration and management across borders.* Abingdon, UK: Routledge. doi:10.4324/9781315584997

Bjørnson, F. O., & Dingsøyr, T. (2008). Knowledge management in software engineering: A systematic review of studied concepts, findings and research methods used. *Information and Software Technology*, *50*(11), 1055–1068. doi:10.1016/j.infsof.2008.03.006

Block, M. (2012). Knowledge Sharing as the Key Driver for Sustainable Innovation of Large Organizations. In *Sustainable Manufacturing* (pp. 337-342). Berlin, Germany: Springer.

Block, J. (1995). A contrarian view of the five-factor approach to personality description. *Psychological Bulletin*, *117*(2), 187–215. doi:10.1037/0033-2909.117.2.187 PMID:7724687

Boden, A., & Avram, G. (2009). *Bridging knowledge distribution-The role of knowledge brokers in distributed software development teams.* Paper presented at the Cooperative and Human Aspects on Software Engineering, 2009. CHASE'09. ICSE Workshop on. 10.1109/CHASE.2009.5071402

Boehm, B. W., Madachy, R., & Steece, B. (2000). Software cost estimation with Cocomo II with Cdrom. Upper Saddle River, NJ: Prentice Hall PTR.

Borgianni, Y., & Matt, D. T. (2016). Applications of TRIZ and Axiomatic Design: A Comparison to Deduce Best Practices in Industry. In Procedia CIRP, 39. doi:10.1016/j.procir.2016.01.171

Bourque, P., Dupuis, R., Abran, A., & et al, . (1999). The guide to the software engineering body of knowledge. *IEEE Software, 16*(6), 35–44. doi:10.1109/52.805471

Braz, C., & Robert, J.-M. (2006). *Security and usability: the case of the user authentication methods.* Paper presented at the IHM. 10.1145/1132736.1132768

Brereton, P., Kitchenham, B. A., Budgen, D., & et al, . (2007). Lessons from applying the systematic literature review process within the software engineering domain. *Journal of Systems and Software, 80*(4), 571–583. doi:10.1016/j.jss.2006.07.009

Briand, L., & Labiche, Y. (2002). A UML-Based Approach to System Testing. *Software and System Modeling, 1*(1).

Brucker, A., & Sodan, U. (2014). *Deploying static application security testing on a large scale. Sicherheit 2014–Sicherheit.* Schutz und Zuverlässigkeit.

Bruno, M., Canfora, G., Di Penta, M., et al. (2005, December). Using test cases as contract to ensure service compliance across releases. In *International conference on service-oriented computing* (pp. 87-100). Berlin, Germany: Springer. 10.1007/11596141_8

Büchler, M., Oudinet, J., & Pretschner, A. (2012, June). Semi-automatic security testing of web applications from a secure model. In *2012 IEEE Sixth International Conference on Software Security and Reliability* (pp. 253-262). Piscataway, NJ: IEEE. 10.1109/SERE.2012.38

Calinescu, R., Ghezzi, C., Kwiatkowska, M., & Mirandola, R. (2012). Self-adaptive software needs quantitative verification at runtime. *Communications of the ACM, 55*(9), 69–77. doi:10.1145/2330667.2330686

Canevet, C. (2004). Analysing UML 2.0 activity diagrams in the software performance engineering process. *Proceedings of the 4th International Workshop on Software and Performance Engineering Process (WOSP 2004).* 10.1145/974044.974055

Capretz, L. F., Ahmed, F., & da Silva, F. Q. B. (2017). Soft sides of software. *Information and Software Technology, 92*, 92-94.

Capretz, L. F., & Ahmed, F. (2010a). Making sense of software development and personality types. *IT Professional, 12*(1), 6–13. doi:10.1109/MITP.2010.33

Capretz, L. F., & Ahmed, F. (2010b). Why do we need personality diversity in software engineering? *Software Engineering Notes, 35*(2), 1. doi:10.1145/1734103.1734111

Carayon, P., Hundt, A., Karsh, B. T., Gurses, A. P., Alvarado, C. J., Smith, M., & Flatley Brennan, P. (2006). Work system design for patient safety: The SEIPS model. *Quality & Safety in Health Care, 15*, i50–i58. doi:10.1136/qshc.2005.015842 PMID:17142610

Carmel, E., de Souza, C. R. B., Meneguzzi, F., Machado, L., & Prikladnicki, R. (2016). *Task allocation for crowdsourcing using AI planning.* doi:10.1145/2897659.2897666

Carmel, E. (1999). *Global software teams: Collaborating across borders and time zones.* Prentice Hall PTR.

Carmel, E. (1999). *Global Software Teams: Collaboration Across Borders and Time Zones.* Saddle River, NJ: Prentice Hall.

Carmel, E., & Agarwal, R. (2001). Tactical approaches for alleviating distance in global software development. *IEEE Software, 18*(2), 22–29. doi:10.1109/52.914734

Carmel, E., & Tjia, P. (2005). *Offshoring Information Technology: Sourcing and Outsourcing to a Global Workforce.* Cambridge, UK: Cambridge University Press. doi:10.1017/CBO9780511541193

Carpenter, B., & Huang, Z. (1998). *Multilevel bayesian models of categorical data annotation.* Unpublished Manuscript. doi:10.1023/A:1009769707641

Cascini, G., & Rissone, P. (2004). Plastics design: Integrating TRIZ creativity and semantic knowledge portals. *Journal of Engineering Design, 15*(4), 405–424. doi:10.1080/0954482041 0001697208

Casey, V. (2009, July). Leveraging or exploiting cultural difference? In *2009 Fourth IEEE International Conference on Global Software Engineering* (pp. 8-17). Piscataway, NJ: IEEE. 10.1109/ICGSE.2009.9

Cavallucci, D., Lutz, P., & Thiébaud, F. (2002). Methodology for bringing the intuitive design method's framework into design activities. *Proceedings of the Institution of Mechanical Engineers. Part B, Journal of Engineering Manufacture, 216*(9), 1303–1307. doi:10.1243/095440502760291853

Çavuş, M. F., & Gökçen, A. (2015). Psychological capital: Definition, components and effects. *British Journal of Education. Society and Behavioural Science, 5*(3), 244–255.

Cearley, D., Walker, M., & Burke, B. (2016). Top 10 Strategic Technology Trends for 2017. *Gartner.* Retrieved from https://www.gartner.com/doc/3471559?plc=ddp

Celik, M. (2009a). A hybrid design methodology for structuring an Integrated Environmental Management System (IEMS) for shipping business. *Journal of Environmental Management, 90*(3), 1469–1475. doi:10.1016/j.jenvman.2008.10.005 PMID:19038488

Celik, M. (2009b). Designing of integrated quality and safety management system (IQSMS) for shipping operations. *Safety Science, 47*(5), 569–577. doi:10.1016/j.ssci.2008.07.002

Celik, M. (2009c). Establishing an Integrated Process Management System (IPMS) in ship management companies. *Expert Systems with Applications, 36*(4), 8152–8171. doi:10.1016/j.eswa.2008.10.022

Celik, M., Cebi, S., Kahraman, C., & Er, I. D. (2009a). An integrated fuzzy QFD model proposal on routing of shipping investment decisions in crude oil tanker market. *Expert Systems with Applications, 36*(3), 6227–6235. doi:10.1016/j.eswa.2008.07.031

Celik, M., Cebi, S., Kahraman, C., & Er, I. D. (2009b). Application of axiomatic design and TOPSIS methodologies under fuzzy environment for proposing competitive strategies on Turkish container ports in maritime transportation network. *Expert Systems with Applications, 36*(3), 4541–4557. doi:10.1016/j.eswa.2008.05.033

Celik, M., Kahraman, C., Cebi, S., & Er, I. D. (2009). Fuzzy axiomatic design-based performance evaluation model for docking facilities in shipbuilding industry: The case of Turkish shipyards. *Expert Systems with Applications, 36*(1), 599–615. doi:10.1016/j.eswa.2007.09.055

Celliah, S. (2015). A Research on Employees Organizational Commitment in Organizations: A Case of Smes in Malaysia. *International Journal of Manajerial Studies and Research, 3*(7), 10–18.

Chandler, R., Lam, C. P., & Li, H. (2007). Dealing with Concurrent Regions During Scenario Generation from Activity Diagrams. In Innovations and Advanced Techniques in Computer and Information Sciences and Engineering (pp. 415–420). Springer.

Chandler, C., Lam, C. P., & Li, H. (2005). AD2US: An Automated Approach to Generating Usage Scenarios from UML Activity Diagrams. In *Proceedings of the 12th Asia-Pacific Software Engineering Conference (APSEC'05)*. Piscataway, NJ: IEEE. 10.1109/APSEC.2005.25

Chapram, S. B. (2018). An Appraisal of Agile DSDM Approach. *International Journal of Advanced Studies in Computers. Science and Engineering, 7*(5), 1–3.

Cha, S.-W., & Cho, K.-K. (1999). Development of DVD for the Next Generation by Axiomatic Approach. *CIRP Annals, 48*(1), 85–88. doi:10.1016/S0007-8506(07)63137-0

Chatchawan, R., Trichandhara, K., & Rinthaisong, I. (2017). Factors Affecting Innovative Work Behavior of Employees in Local Administrative Organizations in the South of Thailand. *International Journal of Social Sciences and Management, 4*(3), 154–157. doi:10.3126/ijssm.v4i3.17755

Chen, K.-Z., Feng, X.-A., & Zhang, B.-B. (2003). Development of computer-aided quotation system for manufacturing enterprises using axiomatic design. *International Journal of Production Research, 41*(1), 171–191. doi:10.1080/00207540210161687

Chen, M., Mishra, P., & Kalita, D. (2008). Coverage-driven Automatic Test Generation for UML Activity Diagrams. *GLSVLSI*.

Chen, S.-J., Chen, L.-C., & Lin, L. (2001). Knowledge-based support for simulation analysis of manufacturing cells. *Computers in Industry, 44*(1), 33–49. doi:10.1016/S0166-3615(00)00071-3

Chess, B., & West, J. (2007). Secure programming with static analysis. London, UK: Pearson Education.

Child, I. L. (1968). Personality in culture. Handbook of Personality Theory and Research, 82–145.

Chilton, L. B., Horton, J. J., & Miller, R. C. (2010). Task search in a human computation market. *Proceedings of the ACM SIGKDD Workshop on Human Computation*, 1–9. 10.1145/1837885.1837889

Chrissis, M. B., Konrad, M., & Shrum, S. (2003). CMMI guidlines for process integration and product improvement. Boston, MA: Addison-Wesley Longman Publishing.

Cimolini, P., & Cannell, K. (2012). Agile Software Development. In Agile Oracle Application Express (pp. 1–13). New York, NY: Apress. doi:10.1007/978-1-4302-3760-0_1

Coallier, F. (2001). *Software engineering–Product quality–Part 1: Quality model.* Geneva, Switzerland: International Organization for Standardization.

Cochran, D. S., Eversheim, W., Kubin, G., & Sesterhenn, M. L. (2000). The application of axiomatic design and lean management principles in the scope of production system segmentation. *International Journal of Production Research*, *38*(6), 1377–1396. doi:10.1080/002075400188906

Cockburn, A. (2002). *Agile software development.* Agile Software Development Series.

Conchúir, E. Ó., Ågerfalk, P. J., Olsson, H. H., & Fitzgerald, B. (2009). Global software development: Where are the benefits? *Communications of the ACM*, *52*(8), 127–131. doi:10.1145/1536616.1536648

Conchúir, E. Ó., Holmstrom, H., Agerfalk, J., & Fitzgerald, B. (2006, October). Exploring the assumed benefits of global software development. In *2006 IEEE International Conference on Global Software Engineering (ICGSE'06)* (pp. 159-168). Piscataway, NJ: IEEE. 10.1109/ICGSE.2006.261229

Cram, W. A., & Marabelli, M. (2018). Have your cake and eat it too? Simultaneously pursuing the knowledge-sharing benefits of agile and traditional development approaches. *Information & Management*, *55*(3), 322–339. doi:10.1016/j.im.2017.08.005

Creswell, J. W. (2013). Research design: Qualitative, quantitative, and mixed methods approaches. Thousand Oaks, CA: Sage Publications.

Crow, G., & Muthuswamy, B. (2003). International outsourcing in the information technology industry: Trends and implications. *Communications of the International Information Management Association*, *3*(1), 25–34.

Curtis, B., Kellner, M. I., & Over, J. (1992). Process modeling. *Communications of the ACM*, *35*(9), 75–90. doi:10.1145/130994.130998

Daellenbach, H., & McNickle, D. (2012). *Management Science - Decision-making through systems thinking* (2nd ed.). Palgrave Macmillan.

Dafferianto Trinugroho, Y. (2014). Information Integration Platform for Patient-Centric Healthcare Services: Design, Prototype, and Dependability Aspects. *Future Internet*, *6*(1), 126–154. doi:10.3390/fi6010126

Dang, D., Liu, Y., Zhang, X., & Huang, S. (2016). A Crowdsourcing Worker Quality Evaluation Algorithm on MapReduce for Big Data Applications. *IEEE Transactions on Parallel and Distributed Systems*, 27(7), 1879–1888. doi:10.1109/TPDS.2015.2457924

Davalos, S., & Merchant, A. (2015). Using Big Data to Study Psychological Constructs: Nostalgia on Facebook. *Journal of Psychology & Psychotherapy*, 05(06). doi:10.4172/2161-0487.1000221

Davenport, T., & Prusak, L. (2000). *Working knowledge: How organizations manage what they know*. Brighton, MA: Harvard Business Press.

Davidow, W. H., & Malone, M. S. (1992). *The Virtual Corporation*. New York, NY: Edward Brulingame Books/Harper Business.

Dawid, A. P., & Skene, A. M. (2006). Maximum Likelihood Estimation of Observer Error-Rates Using the EM Algorithm. *Applied Statistics*. doi:10.2307/2346806

De Farias, I. H., De Azevedo, R. R., De Moura, H. P., & Da Silva, D. S. M. (n.d.). Elicitation of communication inherent risks in distributed software development. In *IEEE 7th International Conference on Global Software Engineering Workshops, ICGSEW 2012*. Porto Alegre, Brazil: IEEE. doi:10.1109/ICGSEW.2012.18

de Souza Bermejo, P. H., Tonelli, A. O., Galliers, R. D., & et al, . (2016). Conceptualizing organizational innovation: The case of the Brazilian software industry. *Information & Management*, 53(4), 493–503. doi:10.1016/j.im.2015.11.004

Dempster, A. P., Laird, N. M., & Rubin, D. B. (2018). Maximum Likelihood from Incomplete Data Via the EM Algorithm. *Journal of the Royal Statistical Society. Series B. Methodological*. doi:10.1111/j.2517-6161.1977.tb01600.x

Den Braber, F., Hogganvik, I., Lund, M. S., & et al, . (2007). Model-based security analysis in seven steps—A guided tour to the CORAS method. *BT Technology Journal*, 25(1), 101–117. doi:10.100710550-007-0013-9

Deo, H. V., & Suh, N. P. (2004). Mathematical Transforms in Design: Case Study on Feedback Control of a Customizable Automotive Suspension. *CIRP Annals*, 53(1), 125–128. doi:10.1016/S0007-8506(07)60660-X

Design Patterns. (2015). Design Patterns for TDD and DDD. Retrieved from https://8408bcbcd6 613c300fa58123cb291b2defe56766.googledrive.com/host/0Bwf9odcK3Cu0bFAzS3kzTDI4Tms/

Devanbu, P. T., & Stubblebine, S. (2000). Software engineering for security: a roadmap. *Proceedings of the Conference on the Future of Software Engineering*.

Dhir, S., & Kumar, D. (2019). Automation Software Testing on Web-Based Application. In *Software Engineering* (pp. 691–698). Singapore: Springer. doi:10.1007/978-981-10-8848-3_67

Dhir, S., Kumar, D., & Singh, V. B. (2019). Success and Failure Factors that Impact on Project Implementation using Agile Software Development Methodology. In *Software Engineering* (pp. 647–654). Singapore: Springer. doi:10.1007/978-981-10-8848-3_62

Dias Neto, A. C., Subramanyan, R., Vieira, M., & Travassos, G. H. (2007). A survey on model-based testing approaches: a systematic review. *Proceedings of the 1st ACM international workshop on Empirical assessment of software engineering languages and technologies: held in conjunction with the 22nd IEEE/ACM International Conference on Automated Software Engineering (ASE) 2007.* 10.1145/1353673.1353681

Dickinson, A. L. (2006). Integrating Axiomatic Design Into a Design for Six Sigma Deployment (DFSS). *Design*, 2–7.

Diesner, J. (2015). Small decisions with big impact on data analytics. *Big Data & Society*, *2*(2). doi:10.1177/2053951715617185

Dingsoyr, T., & Smite, D. (2014). Managing knowledge in global software development projects. *IT Professional*, *16*(1), 22–29. doi:10.1109/MITP.2013.19

Ding, X., Erickson, T., Kellogg, W., & Patterson, D. (2011). Informing and performing: Investigating how mediated sociality becomes visible. *Personal and Ubiquitous Computing*, *16*(8), 1095–1117. doi:10.100700779-011-0443-8

Donnarumma, A., Pappalardo, M., & Pellegrino, A. (2002). Measure of independence in soft design. *Journal of Materials Processing Technology*, *124*(1–2), 32–35. doi:10.1016/S0924-0136(01)01135-9

Dorairaj, S., Noble, J., & Malik, P. (2012). *Knowledge management in distributed agile software development.* Paper presented at the Agile Conference (AGILE), 2012. 10.1109/Agile.2012.17

Dörner, N. (2012). *Innovative work behavior: The roles of employee expectations and effects on job performance.* Verlag nicht ermittelbar.

Do, S.-H., & Suh, N. P. (1999). Systematic OO programming with axiomatic design. *Computer*, *32*(10), 121–124. doi:10.1109/2.796146

Doupé, A., Cova, M., & Vigna, G. (2010, July). Why Johnny can't pentest: An analysis of black-box web vulnerability scanners. In *International Conference on Detection of Intrusions and Malware, and Vulnerability Assessment* (pp. 111-131). Berlin, Germany: Springer. 10.1007/978-3-642-14215-4_7

Drucker, P. F. (1999). Knowledge-worker productivity: The biggest challenge. *California Management Review*, *41*(2), 79–94. doi:10.2307/41165987

Duchene, F., Rawat, S., Richier, J. L., & Groz, R. (2014, March). KameleonFuzz: evolutionary fuzzing for black-box XSS detection. In *Proceedings of the 4th ACM conference on Data and application security and privacy* (pp. 37-48). New York, NY: ACM. 10.1145/2557547.2557550

Dullemond, K., Van Gameren, B., & Van Solingen, R. (2010, August). Virtual open conversation spaces: Towards improved awareness in a GSE setting. In *2010 5th IEEE International Conference on Global Software Engineering* (pp. 247-256). IEEE.

Dullemond, K., van Gameren, B., & van Solingen, R. (2009, July). How technological support can enable advantages of agile software development in a GSE setting. In *2009 Fourth IEEE International Conference on Global Software Engineering* (pp. 143-152). Piscataway, NJ: IEEE. 10.1109/ICGSE.2009.22

Duque Barrachina, A., & O'Driscoll, A. (2014). A big data methodology for categorizing technical support requests using Hadoop and Mahout. *Journal Of Big Data*, *1*(1), 1. doi:10.1186/2196-1115-1-1

Durmusoglu, M., & Kulak, O. (2008). A methodology for the design of office cells using axiomatic design principles. *Omega*, *36*(4), 633–652. doi:10.1016/j.omega.2005.10.007

Dybå, T., & Dingsøyr, T. (2008). Empirical studies of agile software development: A systematic review. *Information and Software Technology*, *50*(9), 833–859. doi:10.1016/j.infsof.2008.01.006

Ebert, C., Kuhrmann, M., & Prikladnicki, R. (2016, August). Global software engineering: evolution and trends. In *Global Software Engineering (ICGSE), 2016 IEEE 11th International Conference on* (pp. 144-153), Irvine, CA. IEEE. 10.1109/ICGSE.2016.19

Edison, H., Bin Ali, N., & Torkar, R. (2013). Towards innovation measurement in the software industry. *Journal of Systems and Software*, *86*(5), 1390–1407. doi:10.1016/j.jss.2013.01.013

Èmite, D., & Wohlin, C. (2011). A whisper of evidence in global software engineering. *IEEE Software*, *28*(4), 15–18. doi:10.1109/MS.2011.70

Endres, M., & Chowdhury, S. (2013). The Role of Expected Reciprocity in Knowledge Sharing. *International Journal of Knowledge Management*, *9*(3), 1–19. doi:10.4018/jkm.2013040101

Erica, F. D. S., Ricardo, D A F., & Nandamudi, L. V. (2014). Knowledge management initiatives in software testing: A mapping study. *Information and Software Technology*, *57*(1), 378–391.

Farid, A. M. (2016). An Engineering Systems Introduction to Axiomatic Design. In A. M. Farid & P. Suh Nam (Eds.), *Axiomatic Design in Large Systems* (pp. 3–47). Cham, Switzerland: Springer International Publishing. doi:10.1007/978-3-319-32388-6_1

Felderer, M., & Schieferdecker, I. (2014). *A taxonomy of risk-based testing*. Academic Press.

Felderer, M., Agreiter, B., & Breu, R. (2011, February). Evolution of security requirements tests for service–centric systems. In *International Symposium on Engineering Secure Software and Systems* (pp. 181-194). Berlin, Germany: Springer. 10.1007/978-3-642-19125-1_14

Felderer, M., Büchler, M., Johns, M., & et al, . (2016). Security testing: A survey. *Advances in Computers*, *101*, 1–51. doi:10.1016/bs.adcom.2015.11.003

Felderer, M., & Fourneret, E. (2015). A systematic classification of security regression testing approaches. *International Journal of Software Tools for Technology Transfer*, *17*(3), 305–319. doi:10.100710009-015-0365-2

Feljan, A. V., Karapantelakis, A., Mokrushin, L., Liang, H., Inam, R., Fersman, E., & Souza, R. S. (2017). *A Framework for Knowledge Management and Automated Reasoning Applied on Intelligent Transport Systems.* Academic Press.

Fernando Capretz, L. (2014). Bringing the human factor to software engineering. *IEEE Software*, *31*(2), 104. doi:10.1109/MS.2014.30

Ferrer, I., Rios, J., & Ciurana, J. (2009). An approach to integrate manufacturing process information in part design phases. *Journal of Materials Processing Technology*, *209*(4), 2085–2091. doi:10.1016/j.jmatprotec.2008.05.009

Fowler, M., & Highsmith, J. (2001). The agile manifesto. *Software Development*, *9*(8), 28–35.

Fu, Y., Chen, H., & Song, F. (2015). STWM: A solution to self-adaptive task-worker matching in software crowdsourcing. Lecture Notes in Computer Science. doi:10.1007/978-3-319-27119-4_27

Gamal, D., Salah, E., & Elrayyes, E. (2011). How to measure organization innovativeness? An overview of innovation measurement frameworks and innovation audit/management tools. Giza Governorate, Egypt: Technology Innovation and Entrepreneurship Center.

Gardner, H. (1999). *Intelligence Reframed: Multiple Intelligences for the 21st Century.* New York, NY: Basic Books.

Garvin, B. J., Cohen, M. B., & Dwyer, M. B. (2011, September). Using feature locality: can we leverage history to avoid failures during reconfiguration? In *Proceedings of the 8th workshop on Assurances for self-adaptive systems* (pp. 24-33). New York, NY: ACM. 10.1145/2024436.2024443

Gazdík, I. (1996). Zadeh's extension principle in design reliability. *Fuzzy Sets and Systems*, *83*(2), 169–178. doi:10.1016/0165-0114(95)00388-6

Geiger, D., & Schader, M. (2014). Personalized task recommendation in crowdsourcing information systems - Current state of the art. *Decision Support Systems*, *65*(C), 3–16. doi:10.1016/j.dss.2014.05.007

Gentle, J. E., McLachlan, G. J., & Krishnan, T. (2006). The EM Algorithm and Extensions. *Biometrics.* doi:10.2307/2534032

Gilal, A. R., Jaafar, J., Basri, S., Omar, M., & Abro, A. (2016). Impact of software team composition methodology on the personality preferences of Malaysian students. *2016 3rd International Conference on Computer and Information Sciences, ICCOINS 2016 - Proceedings.* 10.1109/ICCOINS.2016.7783258

Gilal, A. R., Omar, M., & Sharif, K. I. (2013). Discovering personality types and diversity based on software team roles. In *International Conference on Computing and Informatics, ICOCI 2013* (pp. 259–264). Academic Press.

Gilal, A. R., Omar, M., Jaafar, J., Sharif, K. I., Mahesar, A. W., & Basri, S. (2017). Software Development Team Composition: Personality Types of Programmer and Complex Networks. In *6th International Conference on Computing and Informatics (ICOCI-2017)* (pp. 153–159). Academic Press.

Gilal, A. R., Jaafar, J., Abro, A., Umrani, W. A., Basri, S., & Omar, M. (2017). Making programmer effective for software development teams: An extended study. *Journal of Information Science and Engineering*. doi:10.6688/JISE.2017.33.6.4

Gilal, A. R., Jaafar, J., Basri, S., Omar, M., & Tunio, M. Z. (2016). Making programmer suitable for team-leader: Software team composition based on personality types. *2015 International Symposium on Mathematical Sciences and Computing Research, iSMSC 2015 - Proceedings.* doi:10.1109/ISMSC.2015.7594031

Gilal, A. R., Jaafar, J., Omar, M., Basri, S., Aziz, I. A., Khand, Q. U., & Hasan, M. H. (2017). *Suitable Personality Traits for Learning Programming Subjects: A Rough-Fuzzy Model. International Journal of Advanced Computer Science and Applications.*

Gilal, A. R., Jaafar, J., Omar, M., Basri, S., & Din, I. (2016). Balancing the Personality of Programmer: Software Development Team Composition. *Malaysian Journal of Computer Science*, 29(2), 145–155. doi:10.22452/mjcs.vol29no2.5

Gilal, A. R., Jaafar, J., Omar, M., Basri, S., & Waqas, A. (2016). A Rule-Based Model for Software Development Team Composition: Team Leader Role with Personality Types and Gender Classification. *Information and Software Technology*, 74, 105–113. doi:10.1016/j.infsof.2016.02.007

Goel, P. S., & Singh, N. (1998). Creativity and Innovation in Durable Product Development. *Computers & Industrial Engineering*, 35(1–2), 5–8. doi:10.1016/S0360-8352(98)00006-0

Goldberg, L. R. (1990). An alternative" description of personality": The big-five factor structure. *Journal of Personality and Social Psychology*, 59(6), 1216–1229. doi:10.1037/0022-3514.59.6.1216 PMID:2283588

Gonçalves-Coelho, A. M., & Mourão, A. J. F. (2007). Axiomatic design as support for decision-making in a design for manufacturing context: A case study. *International Journal of Production Economics*, 109(1–2), 81–89. doi:10.1016/j.ijpe.2006.11.002

Gourova, E., & Toteva, K. (2012). *Enhancing knowledge creation and innovation in SMEs*. Paper presented at the Embedded Computing (MECO), 2012 Mediterranean Conference on.

Greefhorst, D. (2009). *Using the Open Group's Architecture Framework as a pragmatic approach to architecture*. Informatica.

Grieskamp, W., Kicillof, N., Stobie, K., & Braberman, V. (2011). Model-based quality assurance of protocol documentation: Tools and methodology. *Software Testing, Verification & Reliability*, 21(1), 55–71. doi:10.1002tvr.427

Grossman, J., Hansen, R., Petkov, P., et al. (2007). Cross site scripting attacks: XSS Exploits and defense. Burlington, MA: Syngress Publishing.

Gumus, B., Ertas, A., Tate, D., & Cicek, I. (2008). The Transdisciplinary Product Development Lifecycle model. *Journal of Engineering Design, 19*(3), 185–200. doi:10.1080/09544820701232436

Gunasekare, U. (2015). Mixed Research Method as the Third Research Paradigm: A Literature Review. *International Journal of Science and Research, 4*(8).

Gunasekera, J. S., & Ali, A. F. (1995). A three-step approach to designing a metal-forming process. *JOM, 47*(6), 22–25. doi:10.1007/BF03221198

Gupta, M. R. (2011). Theory and Use of the EM Algorithm. *Foundations and Trends® in Signal Processing*. doi:10.1561/2000000034

Gupta, S., Verma, H. K., & Sangal, A. L. (2013). Security attacks & prerequisite for wireless sensor networks. *Intl Journal of Engineering and Advanced Technology, 2*(5), 558-566.

Hakimian, F., Farid, H., Ismail, M. N., & Nair, P. K. (2016). Importance of commitment in encouraging employees' innovative behaviour. *Asia-Pacific Journal of Business Administration, 8*(1), 70–83. doi:10.1108/APJBA-06-2015-0054

Halfond, W. G., Viegas, J., & Orso, A. (2006, March). A classification of SQL-injection attacks and countermeasures. In *Proceedings of the IEEE International Symposium on Secure Software Engineering* (Vol. 1, pp. 13-15). Piscataway, NJ: IEEE.

Hamoud, A., & Obaid, T. (2013). *Building Data Warehouse for Diseases Registry: First Step for Clinical Data Warehouse*. SSRN Electronic Journal. doi:10.2139srn.3061599

Hanssen, G. K., Šmite, D., & Moe, N. B. (2011, August). Signs of agile trends in global software engineering research: A tertiary study. In *2011 IEEE Sixth International Conference on Global Software Engineering Workshop* (pp. 17-23). Piscataway, NJ: IEEE. 10.1109/ICGSE-W.2011.12

Harutunian, V., Nordlund, M., Tate, D., & Suh, N. P. (1996). Decision Making and Software Tools for Product Development Based on Axiomatic Design Theory. *CIRP Annals, 45*(1), 135–139. doi:10.1016/S0007-8506(07)63032-7

Hassani-Mahmooei, B., Berecki-Gisolf, J., & Collie, A. (2017). Using Bayesian Model Averaging to Analyse Hierarchical Health Data: Model implementation and application to linked health service use data. *International Journal For Population Data Science, 1*(1). doi:10.23889/ijpds.v1i1.89

Hau, Y. S., Kim, B., Lee, H., & Kim, Y. G. (2013). The effects of individual motivations and social capital on employees' tacit and explicit knowledge sharing intentions. *International Journal of Information Management, 33*(2), 356–366. doi:10.1016/j.ijinfomgt.2012.10.009

Hazzan, O., & Hadar, I. (2008). Why and how can human-related measures support software development processes? *Journal of Systems and Software, 81*(7), 1248–1252. doi:10.1016/j.jss.2008.01.037

Heeager, L., & Nielsen, P. A. (2013). Agile Software Development and the Barriers to Transfer of Knowledge: An Interpretive Case Study. In M. Aanestad, & T. Bratteteig (Eds.), *Proceedings of the Nordic Contributions in IS Research (SCIS), Lecture Notes in Business Information Processing* (pp. 18-39). Berlin, Germany: Springer Publications.

Helander, M. G. (2007). Using design equations to identify sources of complexity in human–machine interaction. *Theoretical Issues in Ergonomics Science, 8*(2), 123–146. doi:10.1080/14639220601092442

Heo, G., & Lee, S. K. (2007). Design evaluation of emergency core cooling systems using Axiomatic Design. *Nuclear Engineering and Design, 237*(1), 38–46. doi:10.1016/j.nucengdes.2006.06.001

Herbsleb, J. D., & Mockus, A. (2003). An empirical study of speed and communication in globally distributed software development. *IEEE Transactions on* Software Engineering, *29*(6), 481–494.

Herbsleb, J. D., & Mockus, A. (2003). An empirical study of speed and communication in globally distributed software development. *IEEE Transactions on Software Engineering, 29*(6), 481–494. doi:10.1109/TSE.2003.1205177

Herbsleb, J. D., & Moitra, D. (Eds.). (2001). Special Issue on Global Software Development. *IEEE Software, 18*(2).

Highsmith, J. R. (2013). Adaptive software development: a collaborative approach to managing complex systems. Boston, MA: Addison-Wesley.

Highsmith, J., & Cockburn, A. (2001). Agile software development: The business of innovation. *Computer, 34*(9), 20–127. doi:10.1109/2.947100

Hinds, P., & Weisband, S. (2003). Chapter. In C. Gibson & S. Cohen (Eds.), Creating Conditions for EVective Virtual Teams (pp. 21–36). San Francisco, CA: Jossey-Bass.

Hirani, H., & Suh, N. P. (2005). Journal bearing design using multiobjective genetic algorithm and axiomatic design approaches. *Tribology International, 38*(5), 481–491. doi:10.1016/j.triboint.2004.10.008

Hoda, R., Salleh, N., & Grundy, J. (2018). The rise and evolution of agile software development. *IEEE Software, 35*(5), 58–63. doi:10.1109/MS.2018.290111318

Hoda, R., Salleh, N., Grundy, J., & Tee, H. M. (2017). Systematic literature reviews in agile software development: A tertiary study. *Information and Software Technology, 85*, 60–70. doi:10.1016/j.infsof.2017.01.007

Hoegl, M., & Gemuenden, H. G. (2001). Teamwork quality and the success of innovative projects: A theoretical concept and empirical evidence. *Organization Science, 12*(4), 435–449. doi:10.1287/orsc.12.4.435.10635

Holik, F., Horalek, J., & Marik, O. (2014, November). Effective penetration testing with Metasploit framework and methodologies. In *2014 IEEE 15th International Symposium on Computational Intelligence and Informatics (CINTI)* (pp. 237-242). IEEE. 10.1109/CINTI.2014.7028682

Holmstrom, H., Conchúir, E. Ó., Agerfalk, J., & Fitzgerald, B. (2006, October). Global software development challenges: A case study on temporal, geographical and socio-cultural distance. In *2006 IEEE International Conference on Global Software Engineering (ICGSE'06)* (pp. 3-11). Piscataway, NJ: IEEE. 10.1109/ICGSE.2006.261210

Horton, J., & Tambe, P. (2015). Labor Economists Get Their Microscope: Big Data and Labor Market Analysis. *Big Data*, *3*(3), 130–137. doi:10.1089/big.2015.0017 PMID:27442956

Hossen, A., Moniruzzaman, A., & Hossain, S. (2015). Performance Evaluation of Hadoop and Oracle Platform for Distributed Parallel Processing in Big Data Environments. *International Journal Of Database Theory And Application*, *8*(5), 15–26. doi:10.14257/ijdta.2015.8.5.02

Houshmand, M., & Jamshidnezhad, B. (2006). An extended model of design process of lean production systems by means of process variables. *Robotics and Computer-integrated Manufacturing*, *22*(1), 1–16. doi:10.1016/j.rcim.2005.01.004

Howard, M., & Lipner, S. (2006). *The security development lifecycle* (Vol. 8). Redmond, WA: Microsoft Press.

Howe, J. (2006). *The Rise of Crowdsourcing. Wired Magazine.*

Huang, C., Sun, J., Wang, X., & Si, Y. (2009, June). Selective regression test for access control system employing rbac. In *International Conference on Information Security and Assurance* (pp. 70-79). Berlin, Germany: Springer. 10.1007/978-3-642-02617-1_8

Huang, G. Q. (2002). Web-based support for collaborative product design review. *Computers in Industry*, *48*(1), 71–88. doi:10.1016/S0166-3615(02)00011-8

Huang, G. Q., & Jiang, Z. (2002). Web-based design review of fuel pumps using fuzzy set theory. *Engineering Applications of Artificial Intelligence*, *15*(6), 529–539. doi:10.1016/S0952-1976(03)00010-1

Huang, Y. C., Peng, K. L., & Huang, C. Y. (2012). A history-based cost-cognizant test case prioritization technique in regression testing. *Journal of Systems and Software*, *85*(3), 626–637. doi:10.1016/j.jss.2011.09.063

Hussain, A., & Roy, A. (2016). The emerging era of Big Data Analytics. *Big Data Analytics*, *1*(1), 4. doi:10.118641044-016-0004-2

Hwang, J., Xie, T., El Kateb, D., et al. (2012, September). Selection of regression system tests for security policy evolution. In *Proceedings of the 27th IEEE/ACM international conference on automated software engineering* (pp. 266-269). New York, NY: ACM. 10.1145/2351676.2351719

Ikeda, K., & Marshall, A. (2016). How successful organizations drive innovation. *Strategy and Leadership*, *44*(3), 9–19. doi:10.1108/SL-04-2016-0029

Inayat, I., Salim, S. S., Marczak, S., & et al, . (2015). A systematic literature review on agile requirements engineering practices and challenges. *Computers in Human Behavior*, *51*, 915–929. doi:10.1016/j.chb.2014.10.046

ISO, G. (1991). Information Technology, Open Systems Interconnection, Conformance Testing Methodology and Framework. *International Standard IS, 9646.*

Jaafar, J., Gilal, A. R., Omar, M., Basri, S., Abdul Aziz, I., & Hasan, M. H. (2017). A Rough-Fuzzy Inference System for Selecting Team Leader for Software Development Teams. In *Advances in Intelligent Systems and Computing* (Vol. 661, pp. 304–314). Cham, Switzerland: Springer.

Jalali, S., & Wohlin, C. (2010, August). Agile practices in global software engineering-A systematic map. In *2010 5th IEEE International Conference on Global Software Engineering* (pp. 45-54). IEEE. 10.1109/ICGSE.2010.14

Jalali, S., & Wohlin, C. (2012). Global software engineering and agile practices: A systematic review. *Journal of Software. Ecological Processes, 24*(6), 643–659.

Jang, B.-S., Yang, Y.-S., Song, Y.-S., Yeun, Y.-S., & Do, S.-H. (2002). Axiomatic design approach for marine design problems. *Marine Structures, 15*(1), 35–56. doi:10.1016/S0951-8339(01)00015-6

Jarvenpaa, S. L., & Ives, B. (1994). The global network organization of the future: Information management opportunities and challenges. *Journal of Management Science and Information Systems, 10*(4), 25–57. doi:10.1080/07421222.1994.11518019

Ji, F., & Sedano, T. (2011, May). Comparing extreme programming and Waterfall project results. In *2011 24th IEEE-CS Conference on Software Engineering Education and Training (CSEE&T)* (pp. 482-486). Piscataway, NJ: IEEE. 10.1109/CSEET.2011.5876129

Jiang, K., Zhang, L., & Miyake, S. (2007). An Executable UML with OCL-based Action Semantics Language. In *Proceedings of the 14th Asia-Pacific Software Engineering.* Washington, DC: IEEE Computer Society.

Jin, C., Liu, N., & Qi, L. (2012). Research and Application of Data Archiving based on Oracle Dual Database Structure. *Journal of Software, 7*(4). doi:10.4304/jsw.7.4.844-848

Johns, M. (2011). Code-injection Vulnerabilities in Web Applications—Exemplified at Cross-site Scripting. *It-Information Technology Methoden und innovative Anwendungen der Informatik und Informationstechnik, 53*(5), 256-260.

Jorgensen, J. B. (2007). Executable Use Cases: a Supplement to Model Driven Development? In *Fourth International workshop on Model-Based Methodologies for Pervasive and Embedded Software.* Braga, Portugal. IEEE Computer Society. 10.1109/MOMPES.2007.6

Joseph, B., & Jacob, M. (2011). Knowledge sharing intentions among IT professionals in India. Information Intelligence, Systems. *Technology and Management, 141*(1), 23–31.

Kahraman, C., & Çebi, S. (2009). A new multi-attribute decision making method: Hierarchical fuzzy axiomatic design. *Expert Systems with Applications, 36*(3 PART 1), 4848–4861. doi:10.1016/j.eswa.2008.05.041

Karn, J. S., & Cowling, A J. (2006). Using ethnographic methods to carry out human factors research in software engineering. *Behavior Research Methods, 38*(3), 495–503. Retrieved from http://www.ncbi.nlm.nih.gov/pubmed/17186760

Kassab, M., Ormandjieva, O., & Daneva, M. (2011, May). Relational-model based change management for non-functional requirements: Approach and experiment. In *2011 FIFTH International Conference On Research Challenges In Information Science* (pp. 1-9). Piscataway, NJ: IEEE. 10.1109/RCIS.2011.6006830

Kaur, P., & Sharma, S. (2014). Agile software development in global software engineering. *International Journal of Computers and Applications, 97*(4).

Kavitha, R., & Ahmed, M. I. (2011). *A knowledge management framework for agile software development teams.* Paper presented at the Process Automation, Control and Computing (PACC), 2011 International Conference on. 10.1109/PACC.2011.5978877

Kazai, G., Kamps, J., & Milic-Frayling, N. (2011). *Worker types and personality traits in crowdsourcing relevance labels.* doi:10.1145/2063576.2063860

Keim, Y., Bhardwaj, M., Saroop, S., & Tandon, A. (2014). Software cost estimation models and techniques: A survey. *International Journal of Engineering, 3*(2).

Kekwaletswe, R., & Lesole, T. (2016). A Framework for Improving Business Intelligence through Master Data Management. *Journal of South African Business Research*, 1-12. doi:10.5171/2016.473749

Khalilian, A., Azgomi, M. A., & Fazlalizadeh, Y. (2012). An improved method for test case prioritization by incorporating historical test case data. *Science of Computer Programming, 78*(1), 93–116. doi:10.1016/j.scico.2012.01.006

Khan, S. A., & Khan, R. A. (2013). *Software security testing process: phased approach.* Paper presented at the International Conference on Intelligent Interactive Technologies and Multimedia. 10.1007/978-3-642-37463-0_19

Khan, M. E. (2010). Different forms of software testing techniques for finding errors. *International Journal of Computer Science Issues, 7*(3), 24.

Kharabsheh, R., Bittel, N., Elnsour, W., Bettoni, M., & Bernhard, W. (2016). A Comprehensive Model of Knowledge Sharing. In *Proceedings of the 17th European conference of KM*. Ulster University.

Kim, H., Kang, S., Baik, J., & Ko, I. (2007). Test Cases Generations from UML Activity Diagrams. In *Eighth International Conference on Software Engineering, Artificial Intelligence, Networking and Parallel/Distributed Computing*. Qingdao, China: IEEE. 10.1109/SNPD.2007.189

Kim, D.-E., Chung, K.-H., & Cha, K.-H. (2003). Tribological design methods for minimum surface damage of HDD slider. *Tribology International, 36*(4–6), 467–473. doi:10.1016/S0301-679X(02)00236-0

Kim, S.-J., Suh, N. P., & Kim, S.-G. (1991). Design of software systems based on axiomatic design. *Robotics and Computer-integrated Manufacturing*, *8*(4), 243–255. doi:10.1016/0736-5845(91)90036-R

Kim, Y.-S., & Cochran, D. S. (2000). Reviewing TRIZ from the perspective of Axiomatic Design. *Journal of Engineering Design*, *11*(1), 79–94. doi:10.1080/095448200261199

Kitchenham, B., & Charters, S. (2007). *Guidelines for performing Systematic Literature Reviews in Software Engineering*. Academic Press.

Kitchenham, B. A., Budgen, D., & Brereton, O. P. (2011). Using mapping studies as the basis for further research–a participant-observer case study. *Information and Software Technology*, *53*(6), 638–651. doi:10.1016/j.infsof.2010.12.011

Kongsli, V. (2006, October). Towards agile security in web applications. In *Companion to the 21st ACM SIGPLAN symposium on Object-oriented programming systems, languages, and applications* (pp. 805-808). New York, NY: ACM. 10.1145/1176617.1176727

Koskela, L. (2007). *Test driven: practical tdd and acceptance tdd for java developers*. Greenwich, CT: Manning Publications.

Kotlarsky, J., & Oshri, I. (2005). Social ties, knowledge sharing and successful collaboration in globally distributed system development projects. *European Journal of Information Systems*, *14*(1), 37–48. doi:10.1057/palgrave.ejis.3000520

Kozak, Y. (2013). *Barriers against better team performance in agile software projects*. Chalmers University of Technology.

Kremer, G., Chiu, M.-C., Lin, C.-Y., Gupta, S., Claudio, D., & Thevenot, H. (2012). Application of axiomatic design, TRIZ, and mixed integer programming to develop innovative designs: A locomotive ballast arrangement case study. *International Journal of Advanced Manufacturing Technology*, *61*(5-8), 827–842. doi:10.100700170-011-3752-1

Kruchten, P. (2013). Contextualizing agile software development. *Journal of Software: Evolution and Process*, *25*(4), 351–361.

Kuiler, E. (2014). From Big Data to Knowledge: An Ontological Approach to Big Data Analytics. *The Review of Policy Research*, *31*(4), 311–318. doi:10.1111/ropr.12077

Kukko, M. (2013). Knowledge sharing barriers in organic growth: A case study from a software company. *The Journal of High Technology Management Research*, *24*(1), 18–29. doi:10.1016/j.hitech.2013.02.006

Kukko, M., & Helander, N. (2012). Knowledge sharing barriers in growing software companies. In *Proceedings of the Hawaii International Conference on System Sciences*. IEEE Publications. 10.1109/HICSS.2012.407

Kulak, O. (2005). A decision support system for fuzzy multi-attribute selection of material handling equipments. *Expert Systems with Applications*, *29*(2), 310–319. doi:10.1016/j.eswa.2005.04.004

Kulak, O., Cebi, S., & Kahraman, C. (2010). Applications of axiomatic design principles : A literature review. *Expert Systems with Applications*, *37*(9), 6705–6717. doi:10.1016/j.eswa.2010.03.061

Kulak, O., Durmuşoğlu, M. B., & Kahraman, C. (2005). Fuzzy multi-attribute equipment selection based on information axiom. *Journal of Materials Processing Technology*, *169*(3), 337–345. doi:10.1016/j.jmatprotec.2005.03.030

Kulak, O., Durmusoglu, M. B., & Tufekci, S. (2005). A complete cellular manufacturing system design methodology based on axiomatic design principles. *Computers & Industrial Engineering*, *48*(4), 765–787. doi:10.1016/j.cie.2004.12.006

Kulak, O., & Kahraman, C. (2005a). Fuzzy multi-attribute selection among transportation companies using axiomatic design and analytic hierarchy process. *Information Sciences*, *170*(2–4), 191–210. doi:10.1016/j.ins.2004.02.021

Kulak, O., & Kahraman, C. (2005b). Multi-attribute comparison of advanced manufacturing systems using fuzzy vs. crisp axiomatic design approach. *International Journal of Production Economics*, *95*(3), 415–424. doi:10.1016/j.ijpe.2004.02.009

Kumar, R., Khan, S. A., & Khan, R. A. (2014). Software Security Testing A Pertinent Framework. *Journal of Global Research in Computer Science*, *4*(3).

Kundu, D., & Samanta, D. (2009). A Novel Approach to Generate Test Cases from UML Activity Diagrams. *Journal of Object Technology*, *8*(3), 65–83. doi:10.5381/jot.2009.8.3.a1

Kuner, C., Cate, F., Millard, C., & Svantesson, D. (2012). The challenge of 'big data' for data protection. *International Data Privacy Law*, *2*(2), 47–49. doi:10.1093/idpl/ips003

Kurniawan, A., Riadi, I., & Luthfi, A. (2017). Forensic analysis and prevent of cross site scripting in single victim attack using open web application security project (OWASP) framework. *Journal of Theoretical & Applied Information Technology*, *95*(6).

Lacerda, T. C., & von Wangenheim, C. G. (2018). Systematic literature review of usability capability/maturity models. *Computer Standards & Interfaces*, *55*, 95–105. doi:10.1016/j.csi.2017.06.001

Lanubile, F., Ebert, C., Prikladnicki, R., & Vizcaíno, A. (2010). Collaboration Tools for Global Software Engineering. *IEEE Journals & Magazines, 27*(2).

Lanubile, F., Damian, D., & Oppenheimer, H. L. (2003). Global software development: Technical, organizational, and social challenges. *Software Engineering Notes*, *28*(6), 2–2. doi:10.1145/966221.966224

Lanubile, F., Ebert, C., Prikladnicki, R., & Vizcaíno, A. (2010). Collaboration tools for global software engineering. *IEEE Software*, *27*(2), 52–55. doi:10.1109/MS.2010.39

Latoza, T. D., & Van Der Hoek, A. (2015). A Vision of Crowd Development. *Proceedings - International Conference on Software Engineering*. 10.1109/ICSE.2015.194

Lazar, I., Motogna, S., & Parv, B. (2010). Behaviour-Driven Development of Foundational UML Components. Department of Computer Science. Cluj-Napoca, Romania: Babes-Bolyai University. doi:10.1016/j.entcs.2010.07.007

Lee, H., Seo, H., & Park, G.-J. (2003). Design enhancements for stress relaxation in automotive multi-shell-structures. *International Journal of Solids and Structures, 40*(20), 5319–5334. doi:10.1016/S0020-7683(03)00291-9

Lee, J., & Shin, H. (2008). Parameter design of water jet nozzle utilizing independence axiom. *Proceedings of the Institution of Mechanical Engineers. Part E, Journal of Process Mechanical Engineering, 222*(3), 157–169. doi:10.1243/09544089JPME202

Leemans, M., Van Der Aalst, W. M., Van Den Brand, M. G., & et al, . (2018, September). Software Process Analysis Methodology–A Methodology Based on Lessons Learned in Embracing Legacy Software. In *2018 IEEE International Conference on Software Maintenance and Evolution (ICSME)* (pp. 665-674). Piscataway, NJ: IEEE. 10.1109/ICSME.2018.00076

Lenz, R. K., & Cochran, D. S. (2000). The application of axiomatic design to the design of the product development organization. Academic Press.

Leung, H. K., & White, L. (1989, October). Insights into regression testing (software testing). In *Proceedings. Conference on Software Maintenance-1989* (pp. 60-69). Piscataway, NJ: IEEE.

Liang, S. F. M. (2007). Applying axiomatic method to icon design for process control displays. In R. N. Pikaar, E. Koningsveld, & P. J. M. Settels (Eds.), *Meeting Diversity in Ergonomics* (pp. 155–172). Amsterdam, The Netherlands: Elsevier Science. doi:10.1016/B978-008045373-6/50011-8

Li, H., & Lam, C. P. (2005, May). Using Anti-Ant-Like Agents to Generate Test Threads from the UML Diagrams. In *IFIP International Conference on Testing of Communicating Systems* (pp. 69-80). Berlin, Germany: Springer.

Linder, J. C., Jarvenpaa, S., & Davenport, T. H. (2003). Toward an innovation sourcing strategy. *MIT Sloan Management Review, 44*(4), 43.

Lindkvist, L., & SÖDerberg, R. (2003). Computer-aided tolerance chain and stability analysis. *Journal of Engineering Design, 14*(1), 17–39. doi:10.1080/0954482031000078117

Lin, H. F. (2006). Impact of organizational support on organizational intention to facilitate knowledge sharing. *Knowledge Management Research and Practice, 4*(1), 26–35. doi:10.1057/palgrave.kmrp.8500083

Lin, H. F. (2007). Effects of extrinsic and intrinsic motivation on employee knowledge sharing intentions. *Journal of Information Science, 33*(2), 135–149. doi:10.1177/0165551506068174

Linzhang, W., Jiesong, Y., Xiafeng, Y. et al. (2004). Generating Test Cases from UML Activity Diagram Based on Gray-box Method. In *11th Asia-Pacific Software Engineering Conference (APSEC'04)*, (pp. 284–291). Busan, Korea: Academic Press. 10.1109/APSEC.2004.55

Liu, X., Lu, M., Ooi, B. C., Shen, Y., Wu, S., & Zhang, M. (2012). Cdas: A crowdsourcing data analytics system. *Proceedings of the VLDB Endowment International Conference on Very Large Data Bases, 5*(10), 1040–1051. doi:10.14778/2336664.2336676

Li, X., & Zheng, Y. (2014). The influential factors of employees' innovative behavior and the management advices. *Journal of Service Science and Management, 7*(06), 446–450. doi:10.4236/jssm.2014.76042

Lomotey, R., & Deters, R. (2015). Unstructured data mining: Use case for CouchDB. *International Journal of Big Data Intelligence, 2*(3), 168. doi:10.1504/IJBDI.2015.070597

Lo, S., & Helander, M. G. (2007). Use of axiomatic design principles for analysing the complexity of human–machine systems. *Theoretical Issues in Ergonomics Science, 8*(2), 147–169. doi:10.1080/14639220601092475

Lous, P., Kuhrmann, M., & Tell, P. (2017, May). Is Scrum fit for global software engineering? In *Proceedings of the 12th International Conference on Global Software Engineering* (pp. 1-10). Buenos Aires, Argentina. IEEE Press. 10.1109/ICGSE.2017.13

Lukes, M., & Stephan, U. (2017). Measuring employee innovation: A review of existing scales and the development of the innovative behavior and innovation support inventories across cultures. *International Journal of Entrepreneurial Behaviour & Research, 23*(1), 136–158. doi:10.1108/IJEBR-11-2015-0262

Lund, M. S., Solhaug, B., & Stølen, K. (2010). Model-driven risk analysis: the CORAS approach. New York, NY: Springer Science & Business Media.

Luo, H., Zhang, H., Zukerman, M., & Qiao, C. (2014). An incrementally deployable network architecture to support both data-centric and host-centric services. *IEEE Network, 28*(4), 58–65. doi:10.1109/MNET.2014.6863133

Maldonado-Macías, A., Guillén-Anaya, L., Barrón-Díaz, L., & García-Alcaraz, J. L. (2011). Evaluación Ergonómica para la Selección de Tecnología de Manufactura Avanzada: una Propuesta de Software. *Revista de La Ingeniería Industrial, 5*, 1–11. Retrieved from https://s3.amazonaws.com/academia.edu.documents/36650920/MandonadoIE2011_6029-89.pdf?AWSAccessKeyId=AKIAIWOWYYGZ2Y53UL3A&Expires=1516140763&Signature=7nYcphKAorNP1QNm%2F7jlwjcgKQo%3D&response-content-disposition=inline%3Bfilename%3DEvaluacion_Ergonomica

Maldonado-Macías, A. (2009). *Modelo de evaluación ergonómica para la planeación y selección de tecnología de manufactura avanzada.* Instituto Tecnológico de Ciudad Juárez.

Mao, K., Yang, Y., Wang, Q., Jia, Y., & Harman, M. (2015). Developer recommendation for crowdsourced software development tasks. *Proceedings - 9th IEEE International Symposium on Service-Oriented System Engineering, IEEE SOSE 2015.* 10.1109/SOSE.2015.46

Mao, K., Capra, L., Harman, M., & Jia, Y. (2017). A survey of the use of crowdsourcing in software engineering. *Journal of Systems and Software, 126*, 57–84. doi:10.1016/j.jss.2016.09.015

Martínez, L. G., Rodríguez-Díaz, A., Licea, G., & Castro, J. R. (2010). Big five patterns for software engineering roles using an ANFIS learning approach with RAMSET. In *Advances in Soft Computing* (pp. 428–439). Springer. doi:10.1007/978-3-642-16773-7_37

Mavridis, I., & Karatza, H. (2017). Performance evaluation of cloud-based log file analysis with Apache Hadoop and Apache Spark. *Journal of Systems and Software*, *125*, 133–151. doi:10.1016/j.jss.2016.11.037

Mead, N. R., & Stehney, T. (2005). Security quality requirements engineering (SQUARE) methodology (Vol. 30). New York, NY: ACM. doi:10.21236/ADA443493

Melvin, J. W., & Suh, N. P. (2002). Simulation Within the Axiomatic Design Framework. *CIRP Annals*, *51*(1), 107–110. doi:10.1016/S0007-8506(07)61477-2

MID. (2014). *Enterprise Architecture Modeling with ArchiMate*. MID GmbH.

Miller, B. P., Fredriksen, L., & So, B. (1990). An empirical study of the reliability of UNIX utilities. *Communications of the ACM*, *33*(12), 32–44. doi:10.1145/96267.96279

Mingsong, C., Xiaokang, Q., & Xuandong, L. (2006). Automatic Test Case Generation For UML Activity Diagrams. *National Natural Science Foundation Of China, AST'06*.

Mistrík, I., Grundy, J., Van der Hoek, A., & Whitehead, J. (2010). Collaborative software engineering: challenges and prospects. In Collaborative Software Engineering (pp. 389–403). Berlin, Germany: Springer. doi:10.1007/978-3-642-10294-3_19

Moe, N. B., Dingsøyr, T., & Dybå, T. (2010). A teamwork model for understanding an agile team: A case study of a scrum project. *Information and Software Technology*, *52*(5), 480–491. doi:10.1016/j.infsof.2009.11.004

Mohammad, A. H., & Alwada'n, T. (2013). Agile software methodologies: Strength and weakness. *International Journal of Engineering Science and Technology*, *5*(3), 455.

Mohrman, S. A. (1999). The context for geographically dispersed teams and networks. In C. L. Cooper & D. M. Rousseau (Eds.), *The Virtual Organization (Trends in Organizational Behaviour)* 6, (pp. 63–80). Chichester, UK: John Wiley & Sons.

Monplaisir, L., Jugulum, R., & Mian, M. (1998). Application of TRIZ and Taguchi methods: Two case examples. In *Proceedings of the Taguchi methods conference, 4th total product development symposium*. Retrieved from http://www.triz-journal.com

Monteiro, C. V., da Silva, F. Q., & Capretz, L. F. (2016). The innovative behaviour of software engineers: Findings from a pilot case study. *Proceedings of the 10th ACM/IEEE International Symposium on Empirical Software Engineering and Measurement*. 10.1145/2961111.2962589

Moore, J. (2014). *Java programming with lambda expressions-A mathematical example demonstrates the power of lambdas in Java 8*. Retrieved from http://www.javaworld.com/article/2092260/java-se/java-programming-with-lambda-expressions.html

Motogna, S., Parv, B., & Lazar, I. (2008). *Extensions of an OCL-Based Executable UML Components Action Language*. Academic Press.

Mouelhi, T., Fleurey, F., Baudry, B., & Le Traon, Y. (2008, September). A model-based framework for security policy specification, deployment and testing. In *International Conference on Model Driven Engineering Languages and Systems* (pp. 537-552). Berlin, Germany: Springer. 10.1007/978-3-540-87875-9_38

Muller, A., Välikangas, L., & Merlyn, P. (2005). Metrics for innovation: Guidelines for developing a customized suite of innovation metrics. *Strategy and Leadership*, *33*(1), 37–45. doi:10.1108/10878570510572590

Munassar, N. M. A., & Govardhan, A. (2010). A comparison between five models of software engineering. *International Journal of Computer Science Issues*, *7*(5), 94.

Murali, A., & Kumar, S. K. (2014). Knowledge Management and Human Resource Management (HRM): Importance of Integration. *FIIB Business Review*, *3*(1), 3–10.

Myers, I. B., McCaulley, M. H., Quenk, N. L., & Hammer, A. L. (1998). *MBTI manual: A guide to the development and use of the Myers-Briggs Type Indicator* (Vol. 3). Palo Alto, CA: Consulting Psychologists Press.

Mynarz, J. (2014). Integration of public procurement data using linked data. *Journal Of Systems Integration*, 19-31. doi:10.20470/jsi.v5i4.213

Naik, P. (2018). *Insights on Algorithmic and Non-algorithmic Cost Estimation Approaches Used by Current Software Industries across India*. Academic Press.

Nakamori, Y. (2013). Knowledge and systems science: enabling systemic knowledge synthesis. Boca Raton, FL: CRC Press. doi:10.1201/b15155

Nakao, M., Kobayashi, N., Hamada, K., Totsuka, T., & Yamada, S. (2007). Decoupling Executions in Navigating Manufacturing Processes for Shortening Lead Time and Its Implementation to an Unmanned Machine Shop. *CIRP Annals - Manufacturing Technology, 56*(1), 171–174. doi:10.1016/j.cirp.2007.05.041

Nawaz, N. A., Waqas, A., Yusof, Z. M., Mahesar, A. W., & Shah, A. (2017). WSN based sensing model for smart crowd movement with identification: An extended study. *Journal of Theoretical and Applied Information Technology*.

Nawaz, N. A., Waqas, A., Yusof, Z. M., & Shah, A. (2016). WSN based sensing model for smart crowd movement with identification: a conceptual model. *Multi Conference on Computer Science And Information Systems 2016*.

Nayak, A., & Samanta, D. (2009). Synthesis of test scenarios using UML activity diagrams. Software System Model. Berlin, Germany: Springer-Verlag.

Nebut, C., Fleurey, F., Troan, Y. L., & JzeQuell, J. M. (2006). *Automatic Test Generation: A Use Case Driven Approach*. Washington, DC: IEEE Computer Society.

Neumann, G. (2002). Programming Languages in Artificial Intelligence. In Bidgoli (Ed.), Encyclopedia of Information Systems (pp. 31-45). San Diego, CA: Academic Press.

Neves, F. T., Rosa, V. N., Correia, A. M. R., & de Castro Neto, M. (2011). *Knowledge creation and sharing in software development teams using Agile methodologies: Key insights affecting their adoption.* Paper presented at the Information Systems and Technologies (CISTI), 2011 6th Iberian Conference on.

Ng, N. K., & Jiao, J. (2004). A domain-based reference model for the conceptualization of factory loading allocation problems in multi-site manufacturing supply chains. *Technovation, 24*(8), 631–642. doi:10.1016/S0166-4972(02)00125-6

Nguyen-Duc, A., & Cruzes, D. S. (2013, August). Coordination of Software Development Teams across Organizational Boundary--An Exploratory Study. In *2013 IEEE 8th International Conference on Global Software Engineering* (pp. 216-225). IEEE.

Nguyen-Duc, A., Cruzes, D. S., & Conradi, R. (2015). The impact of global dispersion on coordination, team performance and software quality–A systematic literature review. *Information and Software Technology, 57*, 277–294. doi:10.1016/j.infsof.2014.06.002

Nicolás, J., De Gea, J. M. C., & Nicolás, B. et al. (2018). On the risks and safeguards for requirements engineering in global software development: Systematic literature review and quantitative assessment. *IEEE Access: Practical Innovations, Open Solutions, 6*, 59628–59656. doi:10.1109/ACCESS.2018.2874096

Nidiffer, K. E., & Dolan, D. (2005). Evolving distributed project management. *IEEE Software, 22*(5), 63–72. doi:10.1109/MS.2005.120

Nonaka, I., & Takeuchi, H. (1995). *The knowledge-creating company: How Japanese companies create the dynamics of innovation.* New York, NY: Oxford University Press.

Nonaka, I., Toyama, R., & Konno, N. (2000). SECI, Ba and leadership: A unified model of dynamic knowledge creation. *Long Range Planning, 33*(1), 5–34. doi:10.1016/S0024-6301(99)00115-6

North, K., & Kumta, G. (2018). *Knowledge management: Value creation through organizational learning.* Springer. doi:10.1007/978-3-319-59978-6

North, N. (2010). *Behaviour-Driven Development Writing software that matters.* DRW Publications.

Nurika, O., Hassan, M., & Zakaria, N. (2017). Implementation of Network Cards Optimizations in Hadoop Cluster Data Transmissions. *ICST Transactions On Ubiquitous Environments, 4*(12). doi:10.4108/eai.21-12-2017.153506

O'Brien, J. A. (2002). *Management Information Systems – Managing Information Technology in the Business Enterprise* (6th ed.). New York, NY: McGraw Hill Irwin.

Omidi, M., & Alipour, M. (2016). Why NoSQL And The Necessity of Movement Toward The NoSQL Data Base. *IOSR Journal Of Computer Engineering, 18*(05), 116–118. doi:10.9790/0661-180502116118

Omotayo, F. O. (2015). Knowledge Management as an important tool in Organisational Management: A Review of Literature. University of Nebraska-Lincoln.

Oshri, I., Kotlarsky, J., & Willcocks, L. P. (2007). Global software development: Exploring socialization and face-to-face meetings in distributed strategic projects. *The Journal of Strategic Information Systems*, *16*(1), 25–49. doi:10.1016/j.jsis.2007.01.001

Paasivaara, M., Blincoe, K., Lassenius, C., et al. (2015, May). Learning global agile software engineering using same-site and cross-site teams. In *2015 IEEE/ACM 37th IEEE International Conference on Software Engineering* (Vol. 2, pp. 285-294). Piscataway, NJ: IEEE. 10.1109/ICSE.2015.157

Palmer, S. R., & Felsing, M. (2001). A practical guide to feature-driven development. London, UK: Pearson Education.

Pan, E., Wang, D., & Han, Z. (2016). Analyzing Big Smart Metering Data Towards Differentiated User Services: A Sublinear Approach. *IEEE Transactions On Big Data*, *2*(3), 249–261. doi:10.1109/TBDATA.2016.2599924

Papadakis, M., Kintis, M., Zhang, J., & et al, . (2019). Mutation testing advances: An analysis and survey. *Advances in Computers*, *112*, 275–378. doi:10.1016/bs.adcom.2018.03.015

Pappalardo, M., & Naddeo, A. (2005). Failure mode analysis using axiomatic design and non-probabilistic information. *Journal of Materials Processing Technology*, *164–165*, 1423–1429. doi:10.1016/j.jmatprotec.2005.02.041

Park, J., & Lee, J. (2012). Knowledge sharing in information systems development projects: Explicating the role of dependence and trust. *International Journal of Project Management*, *32*(1), 153–165. doi:10.1016/j.ijproman.2013.02.004

Păsăreanu, C. S., & Visser, W. (2009). A survey of new trends in symbolic execution for software testing and analysis. *International Journal of Software Tools for Technology Transfer*, *11*(4), 339–353. doi:10.100710009-009-0118-1

Patterson, F., & Kerrin, M. (2014). 11. Characteristics and behaviours associated with innovative people in small-and medium-sized enterprises. Handbook of Research on Small Business and Entrepreneurship, 187.

Paulin, D., & Sunneson, K. (2012). Knowledge Transfer, Knowledge Sharing and Knowledge Barriers – Three Blurry Terms in KM. *Electronic Journal of Knowledge Management*, *10*(1), 81–91.

Paulk, M. C., Curtis, B., Chrissis, M. B., & Weber, C. V. (1993). Capability maturity model, version 1.1. *IEEE Software*, *10*(4), 18–27. doi:10.1109/52.219617

Perseil, I., & Pautent, L. (2008). A Concrete syntax for UML 2.1 Action Semantic Using +CAL. In *Proceedings of the 13th IEEE International Conference on Engineering of Complex Computer System*, (pp. 217-221). IEEE Computer Society. 10.1109/ICECCS.2008.34

Petersen, K., Feldt, R., Mujtaba, S., & Mattsson, M. (2008). Systematic mapping studies in software engineering. In *Proceedings of the 12th international conference on Evaluation and Assessment in Software Engineering.* BCS Learning & Development Ltd.

Petersen, K., Feldt, R., Mujtaba, S., & Mattsson, M. (2008). *Systematic Mapping Studies in Software Engineering.* Paper presented at the EASE.

Peterson, S. (2011). *Why it Worked: Critical Success Factors of a Financial Reform Project in Africa.* Faculty Research Working Paper Series. Cambridge, MA: Harvard Kennedy School.

Petrenko, A. K., & Schlingloff, H. (2012). *Proceedings 7th Workshop on Model-Based Testing.* arXiv preprint arXiv:1202.5826

Phil, M. (2015). Comparative analysis of different agile methodologies. *International Journal of Computer Science and Information Technology Research, 3*(1).

Phung, V. D., Hawryszkiewycz, I., & Binsawad, M. H. (2016). Classifying knowledge-sharing barriers by organizational structure in order to find ways to remove these barriers. In *Proceedings of the Eighth International Conference on Knowledge and Systems Engineering (KSE).* IEEE Publications. 10.1109/KSE.2016.7758032

Pirzadeh, L. (2010). *Human Factors in Software Development: A Systematic Literature Review* (Unpublished Master's thesis). Department of Computer Science and Engineering Division of Networks and Distributed Systems Chalmers University of Technology, Göteborg, Sweden.

Planning, S. (2002). *The economic impacts of inadequate infrastructure for software testing.* National Institute of Standards and Technology.

Ploskas, N., Stiakakis, E., & Fouliras, P. (2014). Assessing Computer Network Efficiency Using Data Envelopment Analysis and Multicriteria Decision Analysis Techniques. *Journal Of Multi-Criteria Decision Analysis, 22*(5-6), 260–278. doi:10.1002/mcda.1533

Porrawatpreyakorn, N., Quirchmayr, G., & Chutimaskul, W. (2009, December). Requirements for a knowledge transfer framework in the field of software development process management for executive information systems in the telecommunications industry. In International Conference on Advances in Information Technology (pp. 110-122). Berlin, Germany: Springer.

Porru, S., Pinna, A., Marchesi, M., & Tonelli, R. (2017). *Blockchain-oriented software engineering: challenges and new directions.* Paper presented at the 2017 IEEE/ACM 39th International Conference on Software Engineering Companion (ICSE-C). 10.1109/ICSE-C.2017.142

Portillo-Rodríguez, J., Vizcaíno, A., Piattini, M., & Beecham, S. (2012). Tools used in Global Software Engineering: A systematic mapping review. *Information and Software Technology, 54*(7), 663–685. doi:10.1016/j.infsof.2012.02.006

Potter, B., & McGraw, G. (2004). Software security testing. *IEEE Security and Privacy, 2*(5), 81–85. doi:10.1109/MSP.2004.84

Powell, A., Piccoli, G., & Ives, B. (2004). Virtual teams: A review of current literature and direction for future research. *The Data Base for Advances in Information Systems, 35*(1), 6–36. doi:10.1145/968464.968467

Pratoom, K., & Savatsomboon, G. (2012). Explaining factors affecting individual innovation: The case of producer group members in Thailand. *Asia Pacific Journal of Management, 29*(4), 1063–1087. doi:10.100710490-010-9246-0

Prikladnicki, R., Audy, J. L. N., & Evaristo, R. (2003). Global software development in practice, lessons learned. *Software Process Improvement and Practice, 8*(4), 267–279. doi:10.1002pip.188

Qi, D., Roychoudhury, A., Liang, Z., & Vaswani, K. (2012). Darwin: An approach to debugging evolving programs. *ACM Transactions on Software Engineering and Methodology, 21*(3), 19. doi:10.1145/2211616.2211622

Qureshi, M. R. J., Alshamat, S. A., & Sabir, F. (2014). Significance of the teamwork in agile software engineering. *Sci. Int.(Lahore), 26*(1), 117–120.

Ranasinghe, G., & Jayawardana, A. K. L. (2011). Impact of knowledge sharing on project success in the Sri Lankan software industry. *Sri Lankan Journal of Management, 16*(1).

Rao, K. N., Naidu, G. K., & Chakka, P. (2011). A study of the Agile software development methods, applicability and implications in industry. *International Journal of Software Engineering and Its Applications, 5*(2), 35–45.

Ravada, S. (2015). Big data spatial analytics for enterprise applications. *SIGSPATIAL Special, 6*(2), 34–41. doi:10.1145/2744700.2744705

Rawat, S., & Mounier, L. (2011, March). Offset-aware mutation based fuzzing for buffer overflow vulnerabilities: Few preliminary results. In *2011 IEEE Fourth International Conference on Software Testing, Verification and Validation Workshops* (pp. 531-533). Piscataway, NJ: IEEE. 10.1109/ICSTW.2011.9

Ray, M., Barpanda, S.S., & Mohapatra, D.P. (2009). Test case Design Using Conditioned Slicing of Activity Diagram. *International Journal of Recent Trends in Engineering, 1*(2).

Raykar, V. (2009). *Supervised Learning from Multiple Experts : Whom to trust when everyone lies a bit.* doi:10.1145/1553374.1553488

Raza, N., Nadeem, A., Zohib, M., & Iqbal, Z. (2007). An automated approach to system testing based on Scenarios and operations Contracts. In *Seventh international conference on quality software.* Piscataway, NJ: IEEE. 10.1109/QSIC.2007.4385504

Razzak, M. A. (2015). *Knowledge Management in Globally Distributed Agile Projects--Lesson Learned.* Paper presented at the Global Software Engineering (ICGSE), 2015 IEEE 10th International Conference on, Sri Lanka.

Razzak, M. A., & Ahmed, R. (2014). *Knowledge sharing in distributed agile projects: Techniques, strategies and challenges*. Paper presented at the Computer Science and Information Systems (FedCSIS), 2014 Federated Conference on. 10.15439/2014F280

Realyvásquez, A., Hernández-Escobedo, G., & Maldonado-Macías, A. A. (2018). Ergonomic Bench to Decrease Postural Risk Level on the Task of Changing Forklift's Brake Pads: A Design Approach. In J. L. Hernández-Arellano, A. A. Maldonado-Macías, J. A. Castillo-Martínez, & P. Peinado-Coronado (Eds.), Handbook of Research on Ergonomics and Product Design (pp. 28–47). Hershey, PA: IGI Global. doi:10.4018/978-1-5225-5234-5.ch002

Realyvásquez, A., Maldonado-Macías, A., García-Alcaraz, J. L., & Arana, A. (2018). Macroergonomic Compatibility Index for Manufacturing Systems. A Case Study. In S. Trzcielinski (Ed.), *Advances in Ergonomics of Manufacturing: Managing the Enterprise of the Future* (pp. 179–189). Los Ángeles, CA: Springer International Publishing; doi:10.1007/978-3-319-60474-9_17

Realyvásquez-Vargas, A., Maldonado-Macías, A., García-Alcaraz, J. L., & Alvarado-Iniesta, A. (2014). Expert System Development Using Fuzzy If–Then Rules for Ergonomic Compatibility of AMT for Lean Environments. In J. L. García-Alcaraz, A. A. Maldonado-Macías, & G. Cortés-Robles (Eds.), *Lean Manufacturing in the Developing World. Methodology, Case Studies and Trends from Latin America* (pp. 347–369). Cham, Switzerland: Springer International Publishing. doi:10.1007/978-3-319-04951-9_16

Rey-del-Castillo, P., & Cardeñosa, J. (2016). An Exercise in Exploring Big Data for Producing Reliable Statistical Information. *Big Data*, *4*(2), 120–128. doi:10.1089/big.2015.0045 PMID:27441716

Rho, S., & Vasilakos, A. (2017). Intelligent collaborative system and service in value network for enterprise computing. *Enterprise Information Systems*, *12*(1), 1–3. doi:10.1080/17517575.2016.1238962

Rose, J., & Furneaux, B. (2016). Innovation drivers and outputs for software firms: Literature review and concept development. *Advances in Software Engineering*, 2016.

Ryser, J., & Glinz, M. (1999). A Scenario-Based Approach to Validating and Testing Software Systems Using Statecharts. *12th International conference on Software and Systems Engineering and their Application. Proceedings.*

Ryser, J., & Glinz, M. (2000). Using Dependency Charts to improve Scenario-Based Testing. Presented at the *17th International Conference on Testing Computer Software TCS'2000, Washington*, DC.

Samuel, P., & Mall, R. (2009). Slicing-Based Test Case Generation from UML Activity Diagrams. *Software Engineering Notes*, *34*(6), 1–14. doi:10.1145/1640162.1666579

Sandhu, M., Jain, K., & Ahmad, I. (2011). Knowledge sharing among public sector employees: Evidence from Malaysia. *International Journal of Public Sector Management*, *24*(1), 206–226. doi:10.1108/09513551111121347

Sani, A., Firdaus, A., Jeong, S. R., & Ghani, I. (2013). A review on software development security engineering using dynamic system method (DSDM). *International Journal of Computers and Applications*, *69*(25).

Sarker, S., & Sahay, S. (2004). Implications of space and time for distributed work: An interpretive study of US–Norwegian systems development teams. *European Journal of Information Systems*, *13*(1), 3–20. doi:10.1057/palgrave.ejis.3000485

Sarma, M., & Mall, R. (2007). Automatic Test Case Generation from UML Models. In *Proceedings of the 10th International Conference on Information Technology*. Orissa, India. IEEE. 10.1109/ICIT.2007.26

Savransky, S. (2000). *Engineering of creativity : introduction to TRIZ methodology of inventive problem solving*. Boca Raton, FL: CRC Press. doi:10.1201/9781420038958

Scandariato, R., Walden, J., & Joosen, W. (2013, November). Static analysis versus penetration testing: A controlled experiment. In *2013 IEEE 24th international symposium on software reliability engineering (ISSRE)* (pp. 451-460). Piscataway, NJ: IEEE. 10.1109/ISSRE.2013.6698898

Scarfone, K., Souppaya, M., Cody, A., & Orebaugh, A. (2008). Technical guide to information security testing and assessment. *NIST Special Publication*, *800*(115), 2–25.

Schneider, M., Großmann, J., Schieferdecker, I., & Pietschker, A. (2013, March). Online model-based behavioral fuzzing. In *2013 IEEE Sixth International Conference on Software Testing, Verification and Validation Workshops* (pp. 469-475). Piscataway, NJ: IEEE. 10.1109/ICSTW.2013.61

Schnetzler, M. J., Sennheiser, A., & Schönsleben, P. (2007). A decomposition-based approach for the development of a supply chain strategy. *International Journal of Production Economics*, *105*(1), 21–42. doi:10.1016/j.ijpe.2006.02.004

Schwaber, K., & Beedle, M. (2002). Agile software development with Scrum (Vol. 1). Upper Saddle River, NJ: Prentice Hall.

Schwaber, K. (2004). *Agile project management with Scrum*. Microsoft Press.

Schwaber, K., & Beedle, M. (2002). *Agile software development with Scrum* (Vol. 1). Upper Saddle River, NJ: Prentice Hall.

Seba, I., Rowley, J., & Lambert, S. (2012). Factors affecting attitudes and intentions towards knowledge sharing in the Dubai Police Force. *International Journal of Information Management*, *32*(1), 372–380. doi:10.1016/j.ijinfomgt.2011.12.003

Selic, B. (2003). The pragmatics of model-driven development. *IEEE Software, 20*(5).

Seth, N., & Khare, R. (2015). ACI (Automated Continuous Integration) using Jenkins: Key for successful embedded software development. In *Recent Advances in Engineering & Computational Sciences (RAECS), 2015 2nd International Conference on* (pp. 1-6). IEEE.

Shafique, M., & Labiche, Y. (2010). *A systematic review of model based testing tool support.* Carleton University.

Shaheen, J. (2017). Apache Kafka: Real Time Implementation with Kafka Architecture Review. *International Journal Of Advanced Science And Technology, 109*, 35–42. doi:10.14257/ijast.2017.109.04

Shahzad, F., Xiu, G., & Shahbaz, M. (2017). Organizational culture and innovation performance in Pakistan's software industry. *Technology in Society, 51*, 66–73. doi:10.1016/j.techsoc.2017.08.002

Sheng, V. S., Provost, F., & Ipeirotis, P. G. (2008). *Get another label? improving data quality and data mining using multiple, noisy labelers.* doi:10.1145/1401890.1401965

Shin, M. K., Lee, H. A., Lee, J. J., Song, K. N., & Park, G. J. (2008). Optimization of a nuclear fuel spacer grid spring using homology constraints. *Nuclear Engineering and Design, 238*(10), 2624–2634. doi:10.1016/j.nucengdes.2008.04.003

Shirwaiker, R. A., & Okudan, G. E. (2008). Triz and axiomatic design: A review of case-studies and a proposed synergistic use. *Journal of Intelligent Manufacturing, 19*(1), 33–47. doi:10.100710845-007-0044-6

Shmueli, G. (2017). Research Dilemmas with Behavioral Big Data. *Big Data, 5*(2), 98–119. doi:10.1089/big.2016.0043 PMID:28632441

Singh, A., Singh, K., & Sharma, N. (2015). Agile in global software engineering: An exploratory experience. *International Journal of Agile Systems and Management, 8*(1), 23–38. doi:10.1504/IJASM.2015.068607

Sinha, A., Paradkar, A., & Williams, C. (2007). On Generating EFSM models from use Cases. In *Sixth International Workshop on Scenarios and State Machines.* IEEE. 10.1109/SCESM.2007.3

Šmite, D., Moe, N. B., & Ågerfalk, P. J. (Eds.). (2010). Agility across time and space: Implementing agile methods in global software projects. Berlin, Germany: Springer Science & Business Media. doi:10.1007/978-3-642-12442-6

Šmite, D., Wohlin, C., Galviņa, Z., & Prikladnicki, R. (2014). An empirically based terminology and taxonomy for global software engineering. *Empirical Software Engineering, 19*(1), 105–153. doi:10.100710664-012-9217-9

Šmite, D., Wohlin, C., Gorschek, T., & Feldt, R. (2010). Empirical evidence in global software engineering: A systematic review. *Empirical Software Engineering, 15*(1), 91–118. doi:10.100710664-009-9123-y

Smith, M., Busi, M., Ball, P., & Van der Meer, R. (2008). Factors influencing an organisation's ability to manage innovation: A structured literature review and conceptual model. *International Journal of Innovation Management, 12*(04), 655–676. doi:10.1142/S1363919608002138

Smith, N. (2015). Wearable Tech: Smart Watches. *Engineering & Technology, 10*(4), 20–21. doi:10.1049/et.2015.0451

Snow, R., Connor, B. O., Jurafsky, D., & Ng, A. Y. (2008). Cheap and Fast - But is it Good? Evaluating Non-Expert Annotations for Natural Language Tasks. *Proceedings of EMNLP.* 10.3115/1613715.1613751

Sodiya, A. S., Onashoga, S. A., & Ajayī, O. (2006). Towards Building Secure Software Systems. *Issues in Informing Science & Information Technology, 3.*

Soltani, Z., & Navimipour, N. (2016). Customer relationship management mechanisms: A systematic review of the state of the art literature and recommendations for future research. *Computers in Human Behavior, 61,* 667–688. doi:10.1016/j.chb.2016.03.008

Some, S. S. (2007). Specifying Use Case Sequencing Constraints using Description Elements. In *Sixth International Workshop on Scenarios and State Machines (SCESM'07).* IEEE. 10.1109/SCESM.2007.6

Steinke, J. A. (2011). *Team conflict and effectiveness in competitive environments* (Master's thesis). Department of Psychology, Wright State University.

Stoica, M., Mircea, M., & Ghilic-Micu, B. (2013). Software Development: Agile vs. Traditional. *Informatica Economica, 17*(4).

Stratton, R., & Mann, D. (2003). Systematic innovation and the underlying principles behind TRIZ and TOC. *Journal of Materials Processing Technology, 139*(1–3), 120–126. doi:10.1016/S0924-0136(03)00192-4

Stratton, R., & Warburton, R. D. (2003). The strategic integration of agile and lean supply. *International Journal of Production Economics, 85*(2), 183–198. doi:10.1016/S0925-5273(03)00109-9

Sudhakar, G. P., Farooq, A., & Patnaik, S. (2011). Soft factors affecting the performance of software development teams. *Team Performance Management, 17*(3/4), 187–205. doi:10.1108/13527591111143718

Suh, N. P. (1990). *The principles of design. Oxford series on advanced manufacturing: 6.* New York, NY: Oxford University Press.

Suh, N. P. (1995). Designing-in of quality through axiomatic design. *IEEE Transactions on Reliability, 44*(2), 256–264. doi:10.1109/24.387380

Suh, N. P. (1995a). Design and operation of large systems. *Journal of Manufacturing Systems, 14*(3), 203–213. doi:10.1016/0278-6125(95)98887-C

Suh, N. P. (1997). Design of Systems. *CIRP Annals, 46*(1), 75–80. doi:10.1016/S0007-8506(07)60779-3

Suh, N. P. (1998). Axiomatic Design Theory for Systems. *Research in Engineering Design, 10*(4), 189–209. doi:10.1007001639870001

Suh, N. P. (2001). *Axiomatic Design: Advances and Applications.* Oxford University Press.

Suh, N. P. (2005). Complexity in Engineering. *CIRP Annals, 54*(2), 46–63. doi:10.1016/S0007-8506(07)60019-5

Suh, N. P., Cochran, D. S., & Lima, P. C. (1998). Manufacturing System Design. *CIRP Annals, 47*(2), 627–639. doi:10.1016/S0007-8506(07)63245-4

Suh, N. P., & Do, S.-H. (2000). Axiomatic Design of Software Systems. *CIRP Annals, 49*(1), 95–100. doi:10.1016/S0007-8506(07)62904-7

Suh, N. P., & Sekimoto, S. (1990). Design of Thinking Design Machine. *CIRP Annals, 39*(1), 145–148. doi:10.1016/S0007-8506(07)61022-1

Su, J. C.-Y., Chen, S.-J., & Lin, L. (2003). A structured approach to measuring functional dependency and sequencing of coupled tasks in engineering design. *Computers & Industrial Engineering, 45*(1), 195–214. doi:10.1016/S0360-8352(03)00031-7

Sun, C. (2008, July). A Transformation-based Approach to Generating Scenario-oriented Test Cases from UML Activity Diagrams For Concurrent Applications. In *32nd Annual IEEE International Computer Software and Applications Conference* (pp. 160-167). IEEE. 10.1109/COMPSAC.2008.74

Sun, C., Zhang, Z. B., & Li, J. (2009). TSGen A UML Activity Diagram-based Test Scenario Generation Tool. In *International Conference on Computational Science and Engineering*. IEEE Computer Society. 10.1109/CSE.2009.99

Takanen, A., Demott, J. D., Miller, C., & Kettunen, A. (2018). *Fuzzing for software security testing and quality assurance*. Artech House.

Tang, D., Zhang, G., & Dai, S. (2009). Design as integration of axiomatic design and design structure matrix. *Robotics and Computer-integrated Manufacturing, 25*(3), 610–619. doi:10.1016/j.rcim.2008.04.005

Team, C. P. (2006). *CMMI for Development, version 1.2*. Academic Press.

Technical Innovation Center. (2013). *40 Principles*. Retrieved from http://triz.org/index.php/triz/principles

Teddlie, C., & Tashakkori, A. (2006). A general typology of research designs featuring mixed methods. *Research in the Schools, 13*(1), 12–28.

The Open Group. (2011a). *Architecture Development Method*. The Open Group. USA. Retrieved from http://pubs.opengroup.org/architecture/togaf9-doc/arch/chap05.html

Thielman, J., & Ge, P. (2006). Applying axiomatic design theory to the evaluation and optimization of large-scale engineering systems. *Journal of Engineering Design, 17*(1), 1–16. doi:10.1080/09544820500287722

Thielman, J., Ge, P., Wu, Q., & Parme, L. (2005). Evaluation and optimization of General Atomics' GT-MHR reactor cavity cooling system using an axiomatic design approach. *Nuclear Engineering and Design*, *235*(13), 1389–1402. doi:10.1016/j.nucengdes.2004.11.015

Thomas, A. (2015). *Gartner, Innovation Insight for Microservices*. Stamford, CT: Gartner.

Thompson, S., Varvel, S., Sasinowski, M., & Burke, J. (2016). From Value Assessment to Value Cocreation: Informing Clinical Decision-Making with Medical Claims Data. *Big Data*, *4*(3), 141–147. doi:10.1089/big.2015.0030 PMID:27642718

Thornberry, N. E. (2003). Corporate entrepreneurship: Teaching managers to be entrepreneurs. *Journal of Management Development*, *22*(4), 329–344. doi:10.1108/02621710310467613

Tian, H., Xu, J., Lian, K., & Zhang, Y. (2009, August). Research on strong-association rule based web application vulnerability detection. In *2009 2nd IEEE International Conference on Computer Science and Information Technology* (pp. 237-241). IEEE. 10.1109/ICCSIT.2009.5234394

Tian-yang, G., Yin-Sheng, S., & You-yuan, F. (2010). Research on software security testing. *World Academy of Science, Engineering and Technology*, *69*, 647–651.

Tidd, J. (2006). *From Knowledge Management to Strategic Competence* (2nd ed.). London, UK: Imperial College. doi:10.1142/p439

Tirumala, S., Ali, S., & Babu, A. (2016). A Hybrid Agile model using SCRUM and Feature Driven Development. *International Journal of Computers and Applications*, *156*(5), 1–5. doi:10.5120/ijca2016912443

Toaff, S. S. (2005). Don't play with "mouths of fire" and other lessons of global software development. *Cutter IT Journal*, *15*(11), 23–28.

Togay, C., Dogru, A. H., & Tanik, J. U. (2008). Systematic Component-Oriented development with Axiomatic Design. *Journal of Systems and Software*, *81*(11), 1803–1815. doi:10.1016/j.jss.2007.12.746

Tomiyama, T., Gu, P., Jin, Y., Lutters, D., Kind, C., & Kimura, F. (2009). Design methodologies: Industrial and educational applications. *CIRP Annals*, *58*(2), 543–565. doi:10.1016/j.cirp.2009.09.003

Toner, P. (2011). *Workforce skills and innovation*. Academic Press.

Trad, A. (2018c). The Transformation Framework's Resources Library. IBISTM.

Trad, A. (2018a). *The Business Transformation Framework's Resources Library. Internal project*. IBISTM.

Trad, A. (2018b). *The Transformation Framework Proof of Concept. Internal project and paper*. IBISTM.

Trad, A. (2018d). *The Transformation Framework Proof of Concept*. IBISTM.

Trad, A., & Kalpić, D. (2017a). *An Intelligent Neural Networks Micro Artefact Patterns' Based Enterprise Architecture Model*. Hershey, PA: IGI-Global.

Trad, A., & Kalpić, D. (2017b). *A Neural Networks Portable and Agnostic Implementation Environment for Business Transformation Projects. The Basic Structure*. Annecy, France: IEEE. doi:10.1109/CIVEMSA.2017.7995318

Trad, A., & Kalpić, D. (2017c). *A Neural Networks Portable and Agnostic Implementation Environment for Business Transformation Projects. The Framework*. Annecy, France: IEEE. doi:10.1109/CIVEMSA.2017.7995319

Trad, A., & Kalpić, D. (2018a). *An applied mathematical model for business transformation-The Holistic Critical Success Factors Management System (HCSFMS). In Encyclopaedia of E-Commerce Development, Implementation, and Management*. Hershey, PA: IGI-Global.

Trad, A., & Kalpić, D. (2018a). *The Business Transformation Framework and Enterprise Architecture Framework for Managers in Business Innovation-Knowledge and Intelligence Driven Development (KIDD). In Encyclopedia of E-Commerce Development, Implementation, and Management*. Hershey, PA: IGI-Global.

Tratz, S., Hovy, E., Nulty, P., Costello, F., Verhoeven, B., Daelemans, W., … Han, J. (2016). *Cheap and fast - but is it good? Evaluation non-expert annotiations for natural language tasks*. doi:10.3115/1119282.1119287

Trendowicz, A. (2013). Software Cost Estimation, Benchmarking, and Risk Assessment: The Software Decision-Makers' Guide to Predictable Software Development. Berlin, Germany: Springer Science & Business Media. doi:10.1007/978-3-642-30764-5

Tromp, E., Pechenizkiy, M., & Gaber, M. (2017). Expressive modeling for trusted big data analytics: Techniques and applications in sentiment analysis. *Big Data Analytics*, *2*(1), 5. doi:10.118641044-016-0018-9

Tsai, Bai, Paul, & Yu. (2001). *Scenario based Functional Regression Testing*. IEEE.

Tsai, C. C., Chang, C. Y., & Tseng, C. H. (2004). Optimal design of metal seated ball valve mechanism. *Structural and Multidisciplinary Optimization*, *26*(3–4), 249–255. doi:10.100700158-003-0342-3

Tsai, W. T., Saimi, A., & Yu, L. (2003, November). Scenario-Based Object-Oriented Testing Framework. In *Proceedings of the third international conference on Quality Software*. IEEE Computer Society. 10.1109/QSIC.2003.1319129

Tsai, W. T., Yu, L., & Liu, X. X. (2003). *Scenario-Based test case Generation for state-based embedded systems*. Piscataway, NJ: IEEE. doi:10.1109/PCCC.2003.1203716

Tschang, T. (2001). *The basic characteristics of skills and organizational capabilities in the Indian software industry*. Academic Press.

Tseng, M. M., & Jiao, J. (1997). A module identification approach to the electrical design of electronic products by clustering analysis of the design matrix. *Computers & Industrial Engineering, 33*(1–2), 229–233. doi:10.1016/S0360-8352(97)00081-8

Tunio, M. Z., Luo, H., Wang, C., Zhao, F., Gilal, A. R., & Shao, W. (2018). Task Assignment Model for crowdsourcing software development: TAM. *Journal of Information Processing Systems*. doi:10.3745/JIPS.04.0064

Tunio, M. Z., Luo, H., Cong, W., Fang, Z., Gilal, A. R., Abro, A., & Wenhua, S. (2017). Impact of Personality on Task Selection in Crowdsourcing Software Development: A Sorting Approach. *IEEE Access: Practical Innovations, Open Solutions, 5*, 18287–18294. doi:10.1109/ACCESS.2017.2747660

Utting, M., & Legeard, B. (2010). Practical model-based testing: a tools approach. Amsterdam, The Netherlands: Elsevier.

Vasanthapriyan, S., Tian, J., & Xiang, J. (2015). *A survey on knowledge management in software engineering.* Paper presented at the Software Quality, Reliability and Security-Companion (QRS-C), 2015 IEEE International Conference on, Vancouver, Canada. 10.1109/QRS-C.2015.48

Vasanthapriyan, S. (2017). Agile and scrum in a small software development project: a case study. In *Proceedings of 7th International Symposium.* South Eastern University of Sri Lanka.

Vasanthapriyan, S., Xiang, J., Tian, J., & Xiong, S. (2017). Knowledge synthesis in software industries: a survey in Sri Lanka. *Knowledge Management Research & Practice, 15(3), 413-430.*10.105741275-017-0057-7

Vemulapati, J., Mehrotra, N., & Dangwal, N. (2011). *SaaS security testing: Guidelines and evaluation framework.* Paper presented at the 11th Annual International Software Testing Conference.

Verdon, D., & McGraw, G. (2004). Risk analysis in software design. *IEEE Security and Privacy, 2*(4), 79–84. doi:10.1109/MSP.2004.55

Verner, J. M., Brereton, O. P., Kitchenham, B. A., Turner, M., & Niazi, M. (2012). Systematic Literature Reviews in Global Software Development: A Tertiary Study. *16th International Conference on Evaluation & Assessment in Software Engineering (EASE 2012)*, 2 – 11. 10.1049/ic.2012.0001

Vetterling, M., Wimmel, G., & Wisspeintner, A. (2002, November). Secure systems development based on the common criteria: the PalME project. In *Proceedings of the 10th ACM SIGSOFT symposium on Foundations of software engineering* (pp. 129-138). New York, NY: ACM. 10.1145/587051.587071

Viennot, N., Nair, S., & Nieh, J. (2013, March). Transparent mutable replay for multicore debugging and patch validation. In ACM SIGARCH computer architecture news 41(1) (pp. 127-138). New York, NY: ACM. doi:10.1145/2451116.2451130

Villani, E., Pontes, R. P., Coracini, G. K., & Ambrósio, A. M. (2019). Integrating model checking and model-based testing for industrial software development. *Computers in Industry, 104*, 88–102. doi:10.1016/j.compind.2018.08.003

Vu, K. M. (2011). ICT as a source of economic growth in the information age: Empirical evidence from the 1996–2005 period. *Telecommunications Policy, 35*(4), 357–372. doi:10.1016/j.telpol.2011.02.008

Vyas, M., Bohra, A., Lamba, C. S., & Vyas, A. (2018). *A Review on Software Cost and Effort Estimation Techniques for Agile Development Process*. Academic Press.

Wagner, S., & Ruhe, M. (2018). *A systematic review of productivity factors in software development*. Academic Press.

Waqas, A., Yusof, Z. M., Shah, A., & Khan, M. A. (2014). ReSA : Architecture for Resources Sharing Between Clouds. In *Conference on Information Assurance and Cyber Security (CIACS2014)* (pp. 23–28). Academic Press. 10.1109/CIACS.2014.6861326

Waqas, A., Yusof, Z. M., Shah, A., & Mahmood, N. (2014). Sharing of Attacks Information across Clouds for Improving Security: A Conceptual Framework. In *IEEE 2014 International Conference on Computer, Communication, and Control Technology* (pp. 255–260). IEEE. 10.1109/I4CT.2014.6914185

Waqas, A., Gilal, A. R., Rehman, M. A., Uddin, Q., Mahmood, N., & Yusof, Z. M. (2017). C3F: Cross-Cloud Communication Framework for Resource Sharing amongst Cloud Networks: An Extended Study. *International Journal of Computer Science and Network Security, 17*(8), 216–228.

Waqas, A., Rehman, M. A., Gilal, A. R., & Khan, M. A. (2016). CloudWeb: A Web-based Prototype for Simulation of Cross-Cloud Communication Framework (C3F). *Bahria University Journal of Information & Communication Technology, 9*(2), 65–71.

Waqas, A., Rehman, M. A., Gilal, A. R., Khan, M. A., Ahmed, J., & Yusof, Z. M. (2017). A Features-based Comparative Study of the State-of-the-Art Cloud Computing Simulators and Future Directions. *International Journal of Advanced Computer Science and Applications, 8*(8), 51–59. doi:10.14569/IJACSA.2017.080807

Waterman, K., & Hendler, J. (2013). Getting the Dirt on Big Data. *Big Data, 1*(3), 137–140. doi:10.1089/big.2013.0026 PMID:27442195

Weber, C., Königsberger, J., Kassner, L., & Mitschang, B. (2017). M2DDM – A Maturity Model for Data-Driven Manufacturing. *Procedia CIRP, 63*, 173–178. doi:10.1016/j.procir.2017.03.309

Wellman, J. (2009). *Organizational learning: How companies and institutions manage and apply knowledge*. Springer. doi:10.1057/9780230621541

Wendland, M. F., Kranz, M., & Schieferdecker, I. (2012). A systematic approach to risk-based testing using risk-annotated requirements models. In *Proceeding of the Seventh International Conference on Software Engineering Advances (ICSEA'12)* (pp. 636-642). Academic Press.

Westerski, A., Iglesias, C. A., & Nagle, T. (2011). *The road from community ideas to organisational innovation: a life cycle survey of idea management systems.* Academic Press.

Whitehill, J., Ruvolo, P., Wu, T., Bergsma, J., & Movellan, J. (2009). Whose Vote Should Count More: Optimal Integration of Labels from Labelers of Unknown Expertise. *Advances in Neural Information Processing Systems.*

Whittle, J., & Jayaraman, P. K. (2006, September). Generating Hierarchical State Machines From Use Case Charts. In *Fourteenth International Requirements Engineering Conference.* IEEE Computer Society. 10.1109/RE.2006.25

Wichers, D. (2013). *Owasp top-10 2013.* OWASP Foundation.

Wickramasinghe, V., & Widyaratne, R. (2012). Effects of interpersonal trust, team leader support, rewards, and knowledge sharing mechanisms on knowledge sharing in project teams. *The Journal of Information and Knowledge Management Systems, 42*(2), 214–236.

Wieringa, R., Maiden, N., Mead, N., & Rolland, C. (2006). Requirements engineering paper classification and evaluation criteria: A proposal and a discussion. *Requirements Engineering, 11*(1), 102–107. doi:10.100700766-005-0021-6

Williams, R. L., & Bukowitz, W. R. (1999). *The knowledge management field book.* London, UK: FT Management.

Wittevrongel, J., & Maurer, F. (2001). Using UML to Partially Automate Generation of Scenario-Based Test Drivers. In *Proceedings of the seventh International Conference on Object Oriented Information Systems (OOIS'01), 2001,* (pp. 303-306). Academic Press.

Wohlin, C. (2014, May). Guidelines for snowballing in systematic literature studies and a replication in software engineering. In *Proceedings of the 18th international conference on evaluation and assessment in software engineering* (p. 38). New York, NY: ACM. 10.1145/2601248.2601268

Won, K., & Joon, Y. (2005, November). Mutual Compensation of TRIZ and Axiomatic Design. *Design,* 1–12.

Wood, S., Michaelides, G., & Thomson, C. (2013). Successful extreme programming: Fidelity to the methodology or good teamworking? *Information and Software Technology, 55*(4), 660–672. doi:10.1016/j.infsof.2012.10.002

Wright, H. K., Kim, M., & Perry, D. E. (2010, November). Validity concerns in software engineering research. In *Proceedings of the FSE/SDP workshop on Future of software engineering research* (pp. 411-414). New York, NY: ACM. 10.1145/1882362.1882446

Wu, M., & Chen, Y. H. (2014). A factor Analysis on Teamwork Performance -an Empirical Study of Inter-instituted Collaboration : *Eurasian Journal of Educational Research,* (55), 37–54.

Xu, D., Li, H., & Lam, C. P. (2005). Using Adaptive Agents to Automatically Generate Test Scenarios from the UML Activity Diagrams. In *Proceedings of the 12th Asia-Pacific Software Engineering Conference (APSEC'05).* IEEE.

Yang, D., Zhang, Y., & Liu, Q. (2012, June). Blendfuzz: A model-based framework for fuzz testing programs with grammatical inputs. In *2012 IEEE 11th International Conference on Trust, Security and Privacy in Computing and Communications* (pp. 1070-1076). Piscataway, NJ: IEEE. 10.1109/TrustCom.2012.99

Yang, K., & Zhang, H. (2000a). A Comparison of TRIZ and Axiomatic Design. In *First International Conference on Axiomatic Design* (pp. 235–243), Cambridge, MA: Academic Press. Retrieved from http://moodle.stoa.usp.br/file.php/1359/TRIZ_AD.pdf

Yang, K., & Zhang, H. (2000b). *Compatibility analysis and case studies of axiomatic design and TRIZ.* Retrieved from https://triz-journal.com/compatiability-analysis-case-studies-axiomatic-design-triz/

Yang, J., & Yecies, B. (2016). Mining Chinese social media UGC: A big-data framework for analyzing Douban movie reviews. *Journal Of Big Data*, *3*(1), 3. doi:10.118640537-015-0037-9

Yang, Y., Karim, M. R., Saremi, R., & Ruhe, G. (2016). Who Should Take This Task?: Dynamic Decision Support for Crowd Workers. *Proceedings of the 10th ACM/IEEE International Symposium on Empirical Software Engineering and Measurement.* 10.1145/2961111.2962594

Yi, J. (2009). A measure of knowledge sharing behavior: Scale development and validation. *Knowledge Management Research and Practice*, *7*(1), 65–81. doi:10.1057/kmrp.2008.36

Yi, J.-W., & Park, G.-J. (2005). Development of a design system for EPS cushioning package of a monitor using axiomatic design. *Advances in Engineering Software*, *36*(4), 273–284. doi:10.1016/j.advengsoft.2004.06.016

Yu, C., Yurovsky, D., & Xu, T. (2011). Visual Data Mining: An Exploratory Approach to Analyzing Temporal Patterns of Eye Movements. *Infancy*, *17*(1), 33–60. doi:10.1111/j.1532-7078.2011.00095.x

Yuen, M. C., King, I., & Leung, K. S. (2011). Task matching in crowdsourcing. *Proceedings - 2011 IEEE International Conferences on Internet of Things and Cyber, Physical and Social Computing, iThings/CPSCom 2011.* 10.1109/iThings/CPSCom.2011.128

Yu, Y. T., & Lau, M. F. (2012). Fault-based test suite prioritization for specification-based testing. *Information and Software Technology*, *54*(2), 179–202. doi:10.1016/j.infsof.2011.09.005

Zammit, J. P., Gao, J., & Evans, R. (2016). A Framework to Capture and Share Knowledge Using Storytelling and Video Sharing in Global Product Development. In *Proceedings of the 12th IFIP International Conference on Product Lifecycle Management (PLM).* IFIP Advances in Information and Communication Technology. 10.1007/978-3-319-33111-9_24

Zammit, J., Gao, J., & Evans, R. (2016). Capturing and sharing product development knowledge using storytelling and video sharing. *Procedia CIRP*, *56*, 440–445. doi:10.1016/j.procir.2016.10.081

Zander, J., Schieferdecker, I., & Mosterman, P. J. (Eds.). (2011). Model-based testing for embedded systems. Boca Raton, FL: CRC Press.

Zannad, H. (2003). Organizational commitment in innovative companies. Academic Press.

Zhao, J., Wen, Y., & Zhao, G. (2011, October). H-fuzzing: a new heuristic method for fuzzing data generation. In *IFIP International Conference on Network and Parallel Computing* (pp. 32-43). Berlin, Germany: Springer. 10.1007/978-3-642-24403-2_3

About the Contributors

Mobashar Rehman is currently working as Assistant Professor in Faculty of Information and Communication Technology, Universiti Tunku Abdul Rahman, Perak, Malaysia. He has more than six years of teaching and research experience. His research expertise includes Software Engineering, cyberpsychology, human factors in Software Engineering, especially personality and organizational factors in the field of Software Engineering and Knowledge Management.

Manzoor Hashmani has more than 25 years of broad IT experience both in the fields of research and development. He has done both his M.E. and Ph.D. from Nara Institute of Science & Technology, Japan, in a very short duration of four years. He did B.E. (Computer Systems Engineering) in 1991 from Mehran University of Engineering & Technology, Jamshoro, Pakistan. After Ph.D., he worked in NS Solutions Corporation, Japan, for about three years. Here, he supervised parts of a large Japanese governmental project and worked as a lead researcher and developer. He then worked for BBR (Broadband Research) Japan for about two years. Here, he participated in a project which involved HDTV, VoIP and teleconferencing. As part of this project, Dr. Hashmani designed and developed a bandwidth broker to allocate and manage network bandwidth. Besides industry experience of five years, Dr. Hashmani has worked in academia for around 20 years. He has on his credit many funded research projects. He successfully supervised seven PhD projects and 50 MS/MPhil projects. He has more than 70 research papers (in journals and conferences of international repute) on his credit. His research areas of interest include: Data Analytics, Deep Learning, Artificial Intelligence, Soft Computing, Software Engineering, High Speed Communication Networks.

* * *

Jawwad Ahmad has done his bachelors in Electronic Engineering from Sir Syed University of Engineering and Technology Karachi in 2002. Soon after the graduation, he started his academic career as Lecturer at one of the leading engineering institutions of Karachi. In 2006, he completed his masters in Telecommunication Engineering from Hamdard University, Karachi. He supervised a number of students' groups in their final year projects at undergraduate level. He did his PhD in Telecommunication Engineering from Iqra University Karachi in 2014. In PhD, his area of research was adaptive filtering. Currently, Jawwad Ahmad is serving as Assistant Professor in Electrical Engineering department at an engineering institution affiliated with NED University of Engineering and Technology, Karachi. He has been given the title of 'Approved PhD supervisor' by the Higher Education Commission (HEC) of Pakistan. His research interests include adaptive filtering, artificial neural network, machine learning, wireless communications, and signal processing, etc.

Mazida Ahmad is an Associate Professor at the School of Computing, College of Arts and Sciences, Universiti Utara Malaysia. She received the BMIS degree from International Islamic University of Malaysia, in 2001, the MSc. degree in Software Engineering from Universiti Teknologi Malaysia, in 2003, and the Ph.D. degree in Knowledge Management from Universiti Sains Malaysia, in 2010. Her current research interests include knowledge management, information system development and software engineering education.

Malek Almomnai holds a Ph.D. in Computer Science from the Department of Computer and Information Sciences, Universiti Teknologi Petronas. His research interest is Software Process Improvement in Malaysian Small and Medium Software development industry. He is currently doing research under Software quality and Quality Assurance (SQ'E) Research cluster at Universiti Teknologi Petronas, in Malaysia.

Ruqaya Gilal is a PhD student in Universiti Utara Malaysia. Her areas of specialization are software engineering, data mining and human psychology.

Guadalupe Hernández-Escobedo Profile: PROMEP; PhD from the University of Leeds, UK; more than 22 years of experience in teaching, research and application of Industrial Engineering at Instituto Tecnológico de Tijuana.

Ramgopal Kashyap's areas of interest are image processing, pattern recognition, and machine learning. He has published many research papers in international journals and conferences like Springer, Inderscience, Elsevier, ACM, and IGI Global, indexed by Science Citation Index (SCI) and Scopus (Elsevier) and many book chapters. He has Reviewed Research Papers in the Science Citation Index Expanded, Springer Journals and was an Editorial Board Member and conferences programme committee member of the IEEE, Springer international conferences and journals held in: Czech Republic, Switzerland, UAE, Australia, Hungary, Poland, Taiwan, Denmark, India, USA, UK, Austria, and Turkey. He has written many book chapters published by IGI Global, Springer, Elsevier.

Muhammad Khalid Khan is a seasoned professional having more than 18 years of experience in Information System implementation, training, coaching and research. After spending the initial five years of his career in software development, he moved towards academia. He holds a PhD in Computer Science, and before that attended two Master programs, one in Computer Science and the other in Business Administration. Dr. Khalid has published and presented more than 30 research papers in peer-reviewed international journals and conferences. Currently, he is working as the Associate Professor and Director, College of Computing and Information Sciences, PAF-KIET, Karachi, Pakistan (www.pafkiet.edu.pk).

Muhammad Waqar Khan is an eminent scholar and a renowned academician. He has earned his Master's in the area of Telecommunication Engineering, Post Graduate Diploma in Computer and Information Sciences, Master in Computer Science and Bachelors in Electrical Engineering. Currently, he is a Ph.D. scholar in the area of Machine Learning. Khan has been associated with academics for over 22 years at University Level. Likewise, he has made a significant contribution to the industry as a Consultant. Mr. Khan has been an active and an eminent member of various academic, regulatory, and Professional bodies. Moreover, Khan has played a key role at both national and multinational industries like Pakistan Telecommunication Company Limited (PTCL), Wateen Telecom Pvt. Ltd., Pakistan Electronic Media Regulatory Authority (PEMRA), Comstar (ISA) Ltd. He is also a permanent member of Pakistan Engineering Council (PEC). He has executed and supervised various projects of Industrial Standards.

Sajid Khan was born in Sukkur, Pakistan, in 1988. He received the B. S. degree in Telecom Engineering from the FAST-NUCES University, Pakistan, in 2011, and M. S leading to Ph. D. degree in Electronics and Communication Engineering from Hanyang University, Ansan, South Korea, in 2017. From 2011 to 2012, he was a Software Engineer at Gameview Studios, Pakistan. Since 2017, he has been an Assistant Professor with the Computer Science Department, Sukkur IBA University, Sukkur, Pakistan. He is the author of two articles and co-author of two other articles. His research interests include image denoising, edge detection, interpolation, deinterlacing, fingerprint detection and biomedical image processing. Dr. Khan is a member of Pakistan Engineering Council. He was awarded scholarships for B. S and M. S. leading Ph.D. by ministry of ICT Pakistan and HEC, respectively.

Ayub Latif is a senior academician with more than 18 years of experience in teaching and research. He is currently pursuing PhD and holds two Master's degrees. He has served the software industry as well and provides consultancy services to leading organizations.

Aide Maldonado-Macías actually works as a professor-Investigator for the Autonomous University of Juarez Mexico. Dr. Maldonado has published several papers in various international journals and conference proceedings. She has been a member of the programme committee and scientific committee of several national and international conferences, in most cases also serving as referee. She is a certified professional in ergonomics in Mexico and she serves as Member of the Mexican Society on Ergonomics and the Society of Industrial Engineers. She also serves as Associate Editor of the AcademiaJournals.com journals and the Occupational Ergonomics Advances and Applications. She serves as referee for the International Journal of Advanced Manufacturing Technology and the World Conference of Industrial Engineering. She has also been evaluator and reviewer for research projects in Mexico. She has obtained the recognition with her research as the best investigator in Industrial Engineering in Mexico for the Technological Institute of Juarez México and has participated in the most prestigious International Conferences and Congresses on Ergonomics and Computers and Industrial Engineering. She has publications on indexed journals in her country and the International Journal of Advanced Manufacturing Technology and the International Journal of Industrial Engineering. She also has contributions in book chapters for prestigious editorials.

Moiz Mansoor is a professional banker looking at Banking IT systems. He is a Computer Engineering Graduate and completed his Master's in Business Administration. He has been in industry for over five years. He likes sports and spends his free time in research and development.

M. Sulleman Memon received his B.E. in Computer Engineering and M.E. in Software Engineering from Mehran University of Engineering & Technology, Jamshoro, Pakistan, in 1990 and 2004 respectively. He got Ph.D. in I. T. (Software Engineering) from Quaid e Awam University of Engineering, Science and Technology, Nawabshah, Pakistan. He is working as Professor at the Department of Computer Engineering. QUEST, Nawanshahr. He is author of many International and national papers. He has presented his work at many countries of the word in International Conferences. His fields of interests are Wireless communications and Ad hoc networks. He is Senior Member of IACSIT and member of Pakistan Engineering Council, ACM, and IEEE.

Anh Nguyen Duc is an Associate Professor at the Department of Business and IT, University of South-Eastern Norway. His research interests include Empirical Software Engineering, Data Mining, Software Startups Research and Cybersecurity.

Mazni Omar is a senior lecturer at the School of Computing, College of Arts and Sciences, Universiti Utara Malaysia. She received the BSc. degree (with honors) in information technology from Universiti Utara Malaysia, in 2000, the MSc. degree in software engineering from Universiti Teknologi Malaysia, in 2002, and the Ph.D. degree in information technology and quantitative sciences from Universiti Teknologi MARA, Malaysia, in 2012. Her current research interests include empirical software engineering, data mining, and knowledge management.

Arturo Realyvásquez has studied Ergonomics since 2008. At the beginning, he contributed to this science developing an expert system to measure ergonomic compatibility of advanced manufacturing technology. Most recently, he developed the Macroergonomic Compatibility Questionnaire (MCQ), he proved that macro-ergonomic compatibility has positive effects on work systems' performance, and he proposed the macroergonomic compatibility index (MCI). He has published and edited books in the most recognised publishers. Also, he has published several articles in JCR journals. Currently, he works as full-time professor in Instituto Tecnológico de Tijuana. He offers the classes of Ergonomics, Operations Research, and Research Fundamentals, and he is member of the National System of Researchers of the National Council of Science and Technology (CONACYT).

Mawarny Rejab is a senior lecturer at the School of Computing, College of Arts and Sciences, Universiti Utara Malaysia. She received the BSc. degree (with honors) in information technology from Universiti Utara Malaysia, in 2000, the MSc. degree in software engineering from Universiti Teknologi Malaysia, in 2003, and the Ph.D. degree in Computer Science from Victoria University of Wellington, New Zealand, in 2017. Her current research interests include agile software engineering, and knowledge management.

Syed Sajjad Hussain Rizvi is an eminent scholar and an active academician. He is a certified Professional Engineer (PE) of Computer System Engineering (CSE) with Master's Degrees in 'Telecommunication' (MS-TEL) and 'Business Administration' (MBA). Dr. Rizvi has earned his Ph.D. in the area of 'Image Processing and Information Retrieval'. In addition, he has also been awarded with the status of "Approved Ph.D. Supervisor" by Higher Education Commission, Pakistan. He poses rich teaching experience and used to teach the courses in the domain of 'Computer Sciences', 'Communication' and 'Management' both at Undergraduate and Postgraduate level. So far, Dr. Rizvi has supervised more than 20 Undergraduate and Master's level project/thesis. He is supervising five PhD students at Hamdard University, Karachi. Dr. Rizvi has a comprehensive expertise on modern-day tools used for research and development. Dr. Rizvi is well known in the research and academic community and an active member of various local and international academic bodies like IEEE, PEC, HEC, IEP, IAENG, etc. The research areas of Dr. Rizvi include, but are not limited to: EEG signal processing and classification, optimization, image de-noising, image retrieval, and adaptive filtering. He always takes an active leading role in various conferences, competitions, workshops etc. organized at local and international level. Dr. Rizvi has provided the consulting solutions to many of the local industries and provides active assistance in many of the industrial projects.

Antoine Trad is a holder of a PhD in computer sciences degree and a DBA in business administration. He is a professor and a researcher at IBISTM in France. His research field's title is: "The Selection, Architecture, Decision Making, Controlling and Training Framework (STF) for Managers in Business Innovation and Transformation Projects"; where he published more than 60 articles on the subject. In this research project, he worked on inspecting enterprise architecture solutions in business transformation projects; parallel to that he worked as a consultant in enterprise architecture projects.

Muhammad Zahid Tunio has done his PhD in Software Engineering from Beijing University of Posts and Telecomunications China. He is author of many research articles which are published in international impact journals. His areas of interest are software engineering, crowdsourcing software development, and human computer interaction.

Shanmuganathan Vasanthapriyan was born on Jan. 9, 1979. He received a B.Sc. (Hons) in Computer Science degree from University of Peradeniya, Sri Lanka, in 2004. He was awarded with Ashoka Amunugama Memorial award for the best performances in University of Peradeniya. He obtained his Master of Science in Computer Science and Engineering at Eindhoven University of Technology in The Netherlands in 2010. In 2017, he obtained his Doctor of Engineering Degree in Computer Science in Wuhan University of Technology in PR China. He received a number of prestigious international awards including Nuffic Fellowship Awards (in 2007) and Chinese Government Scholarship (in 2014). For More: http://www.sab.ac.lk/staff-directory/216.

Ahmad Waqas is working as an Associate Professor and Head of Department in the Department of Computer Science, Sukkur IBA University Pakistan. He has been involved in research and teaching at graduate and post-graduate levels in the field of computer science for the last 13 years. He has obtained his PhD from the Department of Computer Science, Faculty of Information and Communication Technology, International Islamic University Malaysia. Prior to that, he got his MS (Computer Communication and Networks) from Sukkur IBA Pakistan, and MCS (Master in Computer Science) from University of Karachi with second position in faculty. His areas of interest are Blockchain, Distributed Computing, Cloud Computing Security and Auditing, Computing architectures, theoretical computer science, Data structure and algorithms. He has published more than 60 research papers in renowned international journals and conference proceedings (ACM, IEEE, and Scopus) and has 10 h-index. Dr. Waqas is the Chief Editor of Sukkur IBA Journal of Computing and Mathematical Sciences and has organized many international conferences that were technically sponsored by IEEE. He is also working as the editorial board member of numerous journals and program committee member for various international conferences.

Maryam Zaffar is a PhD student in Department of Computer and Information Sciences University Teknologi Petronas, Malaysia. Her area of research is Educational data mining. She is currently working on students' performance prediction techniques. She has numerous publications in journals and conferences. She has nine years of teaching experience in a college.

Muhammad Zubair Ahmad did his B.E. (Electrical Engineering) in 1992. Soon after the graduation, he joined Siemens Pakistan Engineering Co., Ltd. as Commissioning Engineer. In the organization; he was selected to participate in a power automation training course offered by Siemens France. After the successful completion of the course; he worked on various power and automation projects locally and abroad. During his job at Siemens; Dr. Zubair completed his M.S. (Electrical Engineering) in 1998. He served Siemens for around six years and left the organization in the capacity of Senior Executive Engineer. After this industrial exposure, he joined the field of academia and decided to transfer the technical knowledge to the youth. In the meantime, Dr. Zubair continuously strived to further enhance his academic qualification both vertically and horizontally. He therefore completed PhD (in Antenna Optimization) to achieve terminal engineering degree in vertical direction. Horizontally, he earned an MBA (in Marketing) degree. Currently, he is serving at IQRA University as Associate Dean and Associate Professor in the Faculty of Engineering, Sciences & Technology. He has been selected as 'Approved PhD Supervisor' by Higher Education Commission, Pakistan. Moreover, he has been given 'Best University Teacher's Award' by Higher Education Commission, Pakistan, in 2016. In addition, Dr. Zubair is being selected as Co-Convener of Curriculum Development Committee for Electrical Engineering Programme by Higher Education Commission, Pakistan. Dr. Zubair also participates in various national and international technical, social and religious seminars and conferences as Speaker, Facilitator and Session Chair.

Index

A

a mapping study 84-85, 105
ADM 21, 27-28, 33-34, 41, 49
Advanced Manufacturing Technology 50-51, 76
agile software development 109-111, 113, 165-166, 170, 182
Agile Software Engineering 165
algorithm 1, 3, 7, 9-11, 264, 299-303, 310-313, 315, 317
and vulnerability 221, 226, 235, 241, 255, 264
assessment 5, 50-52, 76, 91, 145, 198, 219, 221, 235, 261
axiomatic design 50, 52, 66, 76

B

barriers 95, 97, 104-105, 122, 126, 166, 189, 194, 207, 209, 215, 275
Big Data Analytics 141, 156
Big data drivers 137
business transformation 20-21, 23, 29, 32, 45, 49

C

Capability Maturity Model 273, 275
classical software engineering 253-254
communication 25, 27, 30, 35, 95, 113-114, 165-169, 171, 177, 179-182, 215, 221, 253, 256, 261, 273-275, 287, 298, 322-329
companies 21, 31, 66, 76, 84-86, 88, 91-92, 95-97, 100-105, 112, 125, 127, 165, 167-169, 188-196, 198, 204, 206-207, 209-215, 266, 273-274, 283-284, 323
creation 53, 55, 110-113, 149
Critical Success Factors 22-23, 26, 28-29, 35, 42, 45, 49

D

Decision making systems 49
distributed software engineering 166
distributed team 180-181
DM 24, 163
DMS 21-22, 31, 33, 41-43, 49

E

EMS 49
enterprise architecture 20-21, 25, 32, 38, 41-42
environment 5, 10, 20-21, 24-25, 27, 29-31, 33, 38-43, 45, 49, 51, 113-114, 167, 169, 171, 175, 193, 220, 228, 236, 244, 253, 255, 257, 261, 274, 276, 280, 282-283, 324
ergonomic 50-52, 60, 62, 66, 76
ergonomic attributes 50-52, 66
Ergonomic Compatibility 50-51, 62, 76
Ergonomic Compatibility Assessment 50
ergonomic incompatibility content 60
Ergonomics 76

F

Flow dependency graph (FDG) 302

G

global software engineering 20-21, 24-25,

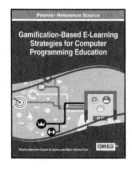
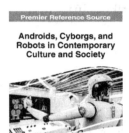

Ensure Quality Research is Introduced to the Academic Community

Become an IGI Global Reviewer for Authored Book Projects

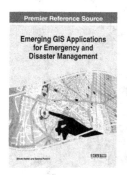

Premier Reference Source

Emerging GIS Applications for Emergency and Disaster Management

Premier Reference Source

Managerial Strategies and Green Solutions for Project Sustainability

Premier Reference Source

Comparative Approaches to Using R and Python for Statistical Data Analysis

Premier Reference Source

Solutions for High-Touch Communications in a High-Tech World

The overall success of an authored book project is dependent on quality and timely reviews.

In this competitive age of scholarly publishing, constructive and timely feedback significantly expedites the turnaround time of manuscripts from submission to acceptance, allowing the publication and discovery of forward-thinking research at a much more expeditious rate. Several IGI Global authored book projects are currently seeking highly qualified experts in the field to fill vacancies on their respective editorial review boards:

Applications may be sent to:
development@igi-global.com

Applicants must have a doctorate (or an equivalent degree) as well as publishing and reviewing experience. Reviewers are asked to write reviews in a timely, collegial, and constructive manner. All reviewers will begin their role on an ad-hoc basis for a period of one year, and upon successful completion of this term can be considered for full editorial review board status, with the potential for a subsequent promotion to Associate Editor.

If you have a colleague that may be interested in this opportunity, we encourage you to share this information with them.

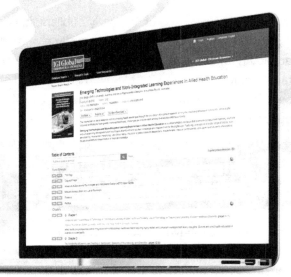

Printed in the United States
By Bookmasters